# COLUMNS III

## 2014 — 2015

## Murphy Givens

# COLUMNS III

## 2014 — 2015

# Murphy Givens

*www.nuecespress.com*

Corpus Christi, Texas

Library of Congress Control Number  2014936212

Givens, Murphy

COLUMNS III    2014 — 2015


Includes index.

  1.  South Texas — History.
  2.  Nueces County — History.
  3.  Corpus Christi — History.

ISBN    978-0-9832565-8-8

Published by Nueces Press, Corpus Christi, Texas.

Cover design by Jeff Chilcoat


*www.nuecespress.com*

# PUBLISHER'S NOTE

South Texas was the distant frontier after the Texas Revolution, claimed by the Republic of Texas based on the unratified Treaty of Velasco which led to Mexico's competing claim. The area was home to the Wild Horse Desert, the origin of the first cattle drives and the establishment of the Western ranching tradition. Murphy Givens has been writing and talking about the people and events of this historic land since 1998 in newspaper columns and on public radio.

This volume is our third collection of Givens' columns that were previously printed in the Corpus Christi Caller-Times. The weekly newspaper columns are eagerly awaited by many of Murphy Givens' fans. Some, like me, collect his articles for future reference, only to find that when time comes to research a topic, it is almost impossible to page through the many papers to find that particular column or certain reference. This book, Columns III, will negate the need to save the individual newspaper articles. A comprehensive index for each of the three books allows readers to easily find any topic. In my own case, this makes it possible to discard my old files of Murphy's articles.

Writing is difficult and writing to meet a deadline more so. I am amazed that Murphy Givens is able to write a weekly column on South Texas history, week after week and year after year, and in a way that makes history, which can be a dull subject, entertaining and enjoyable.

Givens covered many topics in the two years' worth of columns that are included in this volume. In some cases, several weeks of columns address the same subject, allowing more depth to the subject, while in others one column was sufficient.

Since 2009 Murphy and I have teamed up to publish nine books on the history of South Texas via the Nueces Press. I believe that each book offers new insights into the fascinating history of South Texas. I am pleased to bring you this latest volume.

Jim Moloney
Nueces Press

# Table of Contents

# Fandango Riot, 1854

After the end of the Mexican War, the U.S. War Department created the Eighth Military District, which was charged with manning new army forts. Supplies came in by ship to Indianola and were hauled by wagon trains to San Antonio and from there dispersed to the newly built forts on the Texas frontier.

It was in 1852 when Gen. Persifor Smith, the commander of the Eighth Military District, moved his headquarters and supply depot from San Antonio to Corpus Christi. Military provisions began to flow through Corpus Christi rather than Indianola and San Antonio. This was a major boon for the town, which had languished after Zachary Taylor's army decamped for the Rio Grande at the start of the Mexican War six years before.

In 1852, the army established storerooms, saddler's shops, wheelwright and blacksmith shops, a wagon yard, and quarters for soldiers. The army brought in officers and enlisted men and civilian contract workers, mainly teamsters and muleskinners, wheelwrights and clerks to a town of 700 people, based on the 1850 census. Of the town's population, based on that census, about a third, or 220 people, was Hispanic. Almost all of them lived just west of the bluff, an area called Little Mexico because of its concentration of Mexican-American jacals where the Spanish language prevailed.

Corpus Christi became a transit point not only for supplies for Texas forts but also for officers and soldiers being sent to man those garrisons.

After Phil Sheridan left West Point in 1853, he was ordered to report to Fort Duncan, opposite Piedras Negras, on the Rio Grande. From New Orleans he took a steamer to Indianola and then a small schooner to Corpus Christi. "Here I met some of my old friends from the Military Academy. A day or two after my arrival a train of government wagons, loaded with subsistence stores and

1

quartermaster's supplies, started for Laredo, below Fort Duncan. I proceeded to join it, sitting on boxes or bags of coffee and sugar, as I might choose. It took our lumbering train many days to reach Laredo, a distance of 160 miles from Corpus Christi."

Less than two years after the depot was moved to Corpus Christi, trouble erupted between army teamsters, soldiers and Hispanic residents on the bluff.

On New Year's Eve, the last day of the year of 1853, a Saturday night, a big dance, a fandango, was held outside the home of Blas Falcón. A fight started at midnight between teamsters and soldiers on one side and Mexican-American men on the other. What set it off is unknown, but two soldiers were stabbed and one of them died on Sunday morning.

On Monday morning Jan. 2, 1854, about 30 irate teamsters and soldiers stormed the fandango grounds and started shooting and setting fires to nearby jacals. At least four jacals were burned to the ground and a Mexican-American who had had no part in the affair was shot and killed. He had been out of town and had the misfortune to ride up at the wrong time.

The Nueces Valley, Corpus Christi's newspaper, reported that Henry Kinney, the town's founder, did what he could to suppress the riot and protect the Spanish-speaking inhabitants from the wrath of soldiers and teamsters. Kinney and army officers finally persuaded the rampaging soldiers and teamsters to withdraw.

One account of the fandango riot came from Maria Blucher in a letter to her parents, from "Maria von Blucher's Corpus Christi."

"On Jan. 2 we had a big revolution here in Little Mexico," she wrote. "On the bay there is the town and part way up the hill is Little Mexico. Parallel to the town on the hill are the Mexicans' huts, the last of which borders our fence. On New Year's Eve the Mexicans had a fandango. Government wagon drivers and soldiers were there and a quarrel began. Though the Americans took flight and had no weapons, the Mexicans stabbed one, thoroughly butchered him, and wounded four others. One died the following day. On Jan. 2, the affair was scheduled to be legally examined and the criminals called to account. But of course these murderers had at once stolen horses and made their escape.

"The soldiers were so angry about the crimes going unpunished that at noon of the same day, some 30 men took up arms and began searching the Mexican huts (jacals). I looked out and saw three

*A Corpus Christi scene in the 1850s, about the time of the 1854 fandango riot, shows the Ohler building on the Bayfront. It was located where the Nueces Hotel was later built at Water Street and Peoples. (From the Corpus Christi Central Library.)*

houses in flames already and the soldiers shooting right and left. They shot a Mexican down only 20 paces from our fence. As the fire was spreading, the officers rode up at a full gallop and intervened. The soldiers gradually retired, but swore to come back again. In the evening there were no more living beings in all the houses in Little Mexico."

The military guard was doubled in the town and the County Commissioners authorized a police patrol to prevent more disturbances, although most of the inhabitants of Little Mexico, as it was called, about 70 families, left their homes during the rampage and fled into the brush. Tensions remained high and it was two weeks before Hispanics returned to their homes on the bluff. A judicial investigation did not lead to any charges or indictments.

A year later, in 1855, the Eighth District Headquarters and supply depot were moved back to San Antonio. Indianola again became the port of entry for army supplies, which led to another spate of violence between Anglo teamsters and Mexican-Americans.

The army move created a huge business at Indianola. Goods came in by ship and were freighted out by wagon. The heavily traveled Cart Road ran from Indianola to Victoria, Goliad, Runge, Helena,

3

Floresville and San Antonio. Sometime after 1855, Mexican cartmen from Chihuahua were recruited to haul supplies at cheaper rates than Anglo teamsters. Some angry Anglo freighters, idled by the competition, slipped into the camps of Mexican cartmen and cut the spokes of wagon wheels, creating mayhem when wagons broke down on the trail.

As the feud intensified, Mexican cartmen were attacked and killed. The governor called out the Rangers to end the bloodshed and military escorts were assigned to guard supply trains. Two instigators of violence against Mexican cartmen were hanged in Goliad. Rocky times, rocky times, in days gone by.

*—Jan. 1, 2014*

# Gutzon Borglum's Plan

When I read about plans in London to build a new airport on fill material in the Thames estuary, I remembered Gutzon Borglum's proposal to build Corpus Christi's airport in the bay. The plan was introduced in January 1928.

Borglum, later famous as the sculptor of Mount Rushmore, was commissioned in 1927 to design a bayfront plan for Corpus Christi. The airport on a created landmass in the bay was part of his plan.

Borglum recommended building a bulkhead in the bay which would be filled with material dredged from deepening the ship channel to create an island for the airport. He also recommended erecting a 32-foot bronze statue of Christ standing just outside the breakwater with uplifted hand to calm the waters of the bay.

Borglum's plan for a seawall, statue of Christ and airport in the bay never made it past the design and talking stage. It was done in by controversy over the colossal statue of Christ and because some influential hotel-owners vehemently opposed the plan. Borglum had met Lorena Jones Spoonts, president of the Chamber of Commerce, in connection with a major sculpture for the Trail Drivers Association in San Antonio. Her father, W. W. Jones, owned the Nueces Hotel. Other hotel-owners argued that Borglum's plan would give the Nueces Hotel a competitive advantage.

Borglum was unlucky here. His statue of Christ was turned down. His seawall plan never came about. His idea for an airport in the bay was rejected. His plan for a grand thoroughfare from Corpus Christi to Brownsville, lined with 10,000 palm trees and colossal statues of legendary Texas heroes, was also rejected.

Borglum, bitter about the failure of his plans, said of Corpus Christi — "I don't think I have ever seen a town where the crooks and respectable people are so like scrambled eggs." He did much better with his colossal sculpture in the Black Hills of South Dakota.

5

Though Borglum's airport in the bay was dead, the city was still interested in building a municipal airport. In April 1928 voters passed a bond issue and the city spent $35,000 to buy a 186-acre pasture off Old Brownsville Road. The site was cleared and graded that June.

The history of aviation in Corpus Christi began 16 years before when pioneer aviator Oscar Brindley flew a Wright brothers' plane over North Beach on July 3 and July 4, 1911. This was eight years after Wilbur and Orville made history at Kitty Hawk and 63 years after a German immigrant in San Antonio, Jacob Brodbeck, designed and flew a spring-coiled-powered aircraft in 1865.

The North Beach flights in 1911 were part of a July 4th program. The plane was shipped in crates and assembled on North Beach. A big crowd gathered on Monday, July 3 and July 4, north of the Epworth League encampment. Admission cost 50 cents for adults and 25 cents for kids.

Another Wright plane was shipped to Corpus Christi in 1912 and assembled on North Beach. The Mills School of Aviation had been enticed by the Commercial Club to locate in Corpus Christi and give flying lessons. The instructor was former stunt pilot Lionel DeRemer. On Christmas Day 1912, DeRemer flew over the city and on the last day of the year took up members of the Commercial Club. After several months, DeRemer returned to Chicago.

In 1917, ten Army planes from Kelly Field landed on North Beach. The flats on North Beach served as the city's landing site until the municipal airport was built.

After Charles Lindbergh flew over Corpus Christi on his flight from Washington to Mexico in 1927, the city began building an airport. The runway was still unfinished when Cliff Maus, a barnstorming pilot from San Antonio, landed with his business partner Bob Maverick. Shortly afterwards, Maus and Maverick moved their Texas Air Company to Corpus Christi.

Maus, Maverick and Glover Johns operated a pilot training school, the Southern Academy of Aeronautics, with lessons priced at $5 a flight. The first to graduate were J. A. Knolle and J. Luther Petty. Knolle, who was in high school at the time, didn't tell his family he was taking flying lessons. They found out when his name was printed in the paper as a graduate of the flying school.

Passenger service to and from Corpus Christi began in 1929. Southern Air Transport, with a six-seat Fokker, flew between San

Antonio, Corpus Christi, and Brownsville. A round-trip flight cost $27.90.

Maus was named airport manager at a salary of $250 a month. By the end of 1930, the airport was logging some 250 planes a month landing or taking off. The airport was enlarged and three runways added.

In 1930 Jimmy Doolittle touched down for a few minutes during his attempt to set a speed record from Ottawa to Mexico City. On June 1, 1932, American Airways began passenger service to Corpus Christi. A 10-passenger Fairchild landed at Corpus Christi on an afternoon flight from Brownsville and when it took off for San Antonio the plane was carrying 360 pounds of mail, inaugurating air-mail service for Corpus Christi.

Maus quit as airport manager in 1934 to fly for Braniff. He was killed soon afterwards when his plane crashed in a fog. After his death, the name of the airport was changed to Cliff Maus Municipal Airport, shortened to Cliff Maus Field.

A year later, on March 31, 1935, a mid-air collision of two planes in a Sunday air show at the airport killed a stunt pilot, Jack Barstow, and a reporter for the Caller-Times, Jack Cowgill. The airport manager, Eddie Johnson, who was flying the second plane, was injured in the crash. Horrified spectators watched as the wings of the two planes got entangled before they crashed, one on a fence and the other on a runway. Both planes were demolished.

The city in 1947 took over Cuddihy Field and considered making it the city's major airport but, in the 1950s, the need for a larger airport became evident and the city decided to build a new airport in the Clarkwood area. When Corpus Christi International Airport opened in 1960, dignitaries were flown from the old Cliff Maus Field to the new airport for the opening. Corpus Christi had come a long way since 1928 when Gutzon Borglum proposed building an airport in the bay.

*—Jan. 8, 2014*

*Pilot Lionel de Remer (left) with Corpus Christi residents W.G. Blake, E.G. Crabbe and Eli Merriman. De Remer attempted to deliver mail from Corpus Christi to Port Aransas five years before national air-mail service began. Mechanical trouble forced him to return to North Beach.*

*Corpus Christi's first airport was built in 1928 and in 1935 named after Cliff Maus, the first airport manager. Cliff Maus Field served as the city's airport until the new Corpus Christi International Airport in the Clarkwood area opened in 1960.*

8

*Cliff Maus (left) was Corpus Christi's first airport manager. He was killed in a plane crash in 1934. Gutzon Borglum, (right) the sculptor of Mount Rushmore, proposed building an airport on a landmass in Corpus Christi Bay as part of his bayfront plan. Borglum's plan, which also included a colossal statue of Jesus in the bay, was shelved.*

# Mr. Giles and Mr. McCaughan

Almost 50 years ago, A. C. McCaughan died, on Feb. 10, 1964. He was one of the city's most progressive mayors, the last to hold office before the city manager form of government was adopted, and McCaughan ran in three of the hottest political contests in city history, from 1935 to 1939, when he and H. R. Giles were opposing candidates for mayor.

Allan Charles McCaughan was born in Winterset, Iowa in 1869. He graduated from Drake University with a degree in civil engineering and the University of Michigan Law School. When his father was appointed U.S. consul in Durango, Mexico, McCaughan was named vice-consul. In 1898, he married Jessie Holderby, a teacher in the Methodist mission in Durango.

A. C. McCaughan got to read his own obituary in Mexico when newspapers reported that he was killed during a revolutionary attack. A mistake had been made in a coded message to the embassy in Mexico City. With Mexico in turmoil, McCaughan moved his family to the U.S and they settled in Corpus Christi in 1914.

McCaughan went into real estate and developed the subdivisions of Hillcrest and Oak Park. In 1933, he was elected to the City Council. Under the commission form of government, he served as finance commissioner in the administration of Mayor William Shaffer.

When Shaffer opted not to seek re-election in 1935, McCaughan, Dr. H. R. Giles, and G. O. Garrett filed for mayor. Each candidate headed his own ticket or slate. It was a fierce contest. Giles and McCaughan swapped scurrilities, calling each other names like they meant it. Texas Rangers were dispatched to keep order after telegrams were sent warning that the April 2 election might lead to bloodshed. No violence erupted. It was close. Giles was the winner, receiving 2,914 votes, McCaughan 2,659, and Garrett 775.

11

Dr. Giles had practiced medicine in Corpus Christi since 1911. His son, Elbert Jackson Giles, once remembered making house calls with his father when he was a boy. He would hold a flashlight during births and would run home to get forceps or some other medical tool. He also recalled that no one worked harder than his father. "He attended council meetings and would then made four or five house calls every night. I don't guess he saw a football game or a picture show. It was always back to the office every night."

During Giles' tenure, in 1935, Corpus Christi annexed North Beach and some high-spirited North Beach honkytonks became a hot issue. Mayor Giles pushed to close the worst joints but not all of them. "We don't want an air-tight city," he said. "There are certain pleasures the citizens and visitors demand."

In 1937, Giles ran for re-election and was faced with McCaughan again. Each man led his forces like generals with opposing armies. City Council candidates running with Giles and his Peoples Party ticket were Joe Simon, Hicks Nieman, Dr. William Rhodes, and Walter Nolte. McCaughan and his Progressive Party slate included Dr. C. O. Watson, Dave Segrest, Thomas McGee and Joe Mireur.

A week before the election, newspapers reported that it was a foregone conclusion Giles would be re-elected. People liked him and were pleased with the achievements of his administration, which included a new sewage disposal plant that ended dumping raw sewage in the bay. A new water reservoir was built, North Beach streets were paved, and lighting was installed at the city airport financed with money from oil discovered on city property.

On election day there were fist fights at polling places between Giles and McCaughan supporters. Much to the town's surprise, McCaughan won, receiving 3,506 votes with Giles getting 2,317.

In office, McCaughan cracked down on brothels on Sam Rankin Street in the town's red-light district. Sam Rankin had become a busy street and some objected to seeing sporting girls sitting in lighted windows. They were forced to move to an area called the Flats. "We can't exterminate them," Police Commissioner C. O. Watson said, "but we can move them to a location that is the least objectionable in the public eye."

Giles ran for mayor again in 1939. It was another fierce contest. Giles and McCaughan charged each other with poll-tax buying, intimidating voters, and promising city jobs for votes. The Giles camp charged that city employees were fired if they refused to put

*Dr. H. R. Giles stands in front of his home (later known as the Giles-Farenthold house) in 1940. He was mayor for one term and ran three hotly contested races against A. C. McCaughan (right, in 1956). McCaughan served four terms before the city switched to the city manager form of government.*

McCaughan stickers on their cars and that men seeking work building the seawall had to pledge to vote for McCaughan to get hired.

McCaughan won by a two-to-one margin. Dr. Giles never ran again. He died on Jan. 19, 1948. McCaughan was unopposed for a third term in 1941 and handily won a fourth term in 1943. It was his last. When voters approved switching to a city manager form of government, McCaughan chose not to seek a fifth term. The switchover in 1946 did not go smoothly, prompting the recall of the mayor and four council members, but that's another story.

McCaughan's tenure, from 1937 to 1945, marked a time of great progress for Corpus Christi, much of it coming despite the hardships imposed by World War II. To find a period of comparable civic progress, you have to go back to Roy Miller's administration from 1913 to 1919 when downtown streets were paved and the bluff balustrade was built.

During McCaughan's eight years, water and sewer lines were extended to new subdivisions, 12 miles of streets were paved, the city's park system was expanded, the city and the county built Memorial Hospital, the city adopted a civil service system, and the foundations for a larger city were laid.

However, the most tangible accomplishment during McCaughan's tenure was the bayfront project that added the seawall, two T-heads and an L-head, and an attractive yacht basin. When work on the seawall was completed in 1941, the city had been extended two blocks into the bay and the shoreline behind and above the stepped seawall, in effect a levee, had been elevated to 14 feet above sea level. The seawall's clean lines along two miles of what had been a ragged shoreline dramatically improved the city's appearance, giving it a bayfront second to none in point of beauty.

A. C. McCaughan, the last of the city's strong mayors, should be remembered for leading Corpus Christi during a period of unprecedented progress.

*—Jan. 15, 2014*

# Caller's First Edition, 1883

The first edition of Caller was printed on Jan. 21, 1883. It was a night so cold that a bucket of oyster stew brought from John Superach's to feed the pressmen froze solid. Scuttles of hot coals were used to thaw out the press and the ink, frozen hard, had to be cut with a knife and mixed with coal oil to soften it.

News in that first edition included the birth of triplets, two boys and a girl, in the Mark Downey family. "Twins were getting plentiful," the paper said, "but triplets! well, we refrain." The newspaper reported an attempted burglary at Lichtenstein's and that Uriah Lott was back from a trip to the North. The Caller quoted the Lagarto Echo and Pleasanton Monitor about prospects for a railroad being built from San Antonio to Corpus Christi.

The newspaper noted that a bill in Congress would cut the cost of mailing a letter to one cent and reported that the national debt had been pared down to $13 million, which scared bankers, afraid the debt would be paid off and undermine the banking system.

The streets in 1883 were dirt and when it rained heavy delivery wagons bogged down in deep mud. There were no electric lights; stores, homes and streets were lit by kerosene lanterns. A municipal water system was 10 years away; people relied on cisterns filled with rainwater captured from rooftops. In a drought, when cisterns ran low, water carriers called barrileros sold water on the streets.

Signs of progress included Western Union, the Tex-Mex Railroad to Laredo, and a city transit system which consisted of mule-drawn Herdic Coaches, named after the inventor Peter Herdic.

Most stores advertised in that first edition, which provides a good commercial picture of Corpus Christi in 1883. The stores were concentrated within a few blocks of Chaparral and Mesquite.

On the east side of Chaparral at the corner of William was the Berry boarding home. Mrs. Berry would send a boy out with a dinner bell fixed to a pole to let boarders know it was meal time. Down the street were David Hirsch's wool warehouse and the Crescent Hotel. The Caller ad said the Crescent was under the new management of Nick Constantine and had reduced its prices to $1.50 and $2 a day. Next door was George Roberts' Favorite Saloon, which advertised "choice liquors, fine cigars, and polite bartenders." On the corner was E. Frank's, which sold farm and ranch supplies, including wool sacks and sheep dip tobacco, used to treat scabies. Frank's later became Frank & Weil.

Between Lawrence and Schatzel, east side, was the Doddridge and Davis Bank, dating back to 1869. In this building was E. H. Wheeler's shoe store, which promised that buttons would be re-fastened on shoes for free. Wheeler came to Corpus Christi as part of the Union occupation forces at the end of the Civil War. Next was Julius Henry's store and down the street were Gradwhol's drygoods store, Blumenthal and Jordt's furniture store, and George Westervelt's grocery and ship chandlery. Westervelt's sold liquor, tobacco and bought and sold country produce.

From Schatzel to Peoples, east side, was Keller's Saddlery, decorated with a big white horse on the building. It was followed by E. Morris' drygoods. The store's slogan was "C.T.T.C. — Cheaper Than The Cheapest." Next door was Norwick Gussett's bank, store and wool warehouse, topped with a rooster weathervane. A youngster in town, not yet of school age, wanted to show off his ability to spell. He said, "g-u-s-s-e-t-t — rooster." To Mexican traders, Gussett's place was known as "la tienda del gallo."

Between Peoples and Starr, east side, was Lichtenstein's first store, followed by McKenzie's paint store and J. B. Mitchell's hardware and furniture store. Mitchell sold Glidden's barbed-wire and Moen's Galvanized Smooth Wire, Studebaker wagons and Buckeye mowers. Mitchell's was followed by John Woessner's warehouse, bank and general merchandise store. Above Woessner's warehouse was a big hall used for dances, with a floor said to be "springy and fine." Past Woessner's was George French's grocery and drygoods, which later became Evans & Hickey.

On the west side of Chaparral, corner of Lawrence, was the St. James Hotel, built in 1869 by rancher J. T. "Tom" James. Soon after the hotel was finished, Billy Rogers sold his Palo Alto Ranch and used the money to buy the St. James and hired William Biggio, a veteran of the Confederate Navy, to run it.

*Chaparral Street scenes about 1883. John Woessner's wool warehouse (top) was on the east side of Chaparral in the 600 block. Down the street was George French's wholesale and retail grocery store. In the bottom photo, on the east side of the 500 block, was Keller's Saddlery with a white horse on the side of the building. The rooster weathervane decorated Norwick Gussett's store and bank.*

Between Schatzel and Peoples on the west side was Max and Otto Dreyer's toy store, which sold candy, toys, and soft drinks. At Peoples and Chaparral, west side, was the DeRyee and Westervelt Drug Store. DeRyee framed the windows with mahogany driftwood he collected on Padre Island. Down the block was John Hall's tin shop, which sold Filley's, Texas Girl, Iron King, and Buck's Brilliant iron cook stoves.

On Mesquite Street at William, east side, was Thayer's store, which sold Yankee notions, guns, sewing machines, Montgolfier balloons (from three to 30 feet inflated), and 8-Day Clocks, wound every eighth day. Near Thayer's was John Fogg's Livery, including wagon sheds and a hay storage area. Fogg's rented hacks and stabled horses.

In the next block, on the opposite side of Mesquite, was Uehlinger's Bakery. Bread carts left here every morning and evening to make deliveries at restaurants and homes. From Schatzel to Peoples, west side, was Market Hall, which housed city offices, a fire station, and several business stalls, including Dreyer's and Gutierrez's meat markets.

Next to Market Hall was Heath's Emporium, which sold iron stoves, groceries, crockery and glassware. The advertisement in the Caller said the store's philosophy was "Quick Sales, Small Profits."Across the street was Conrad Uehlinger's Saloon and W. S. Rankin's grocery store on the ground floor of the McCampbell Building. In the next block was Blossman's Groceries, with a wagon yard for its customers.

The Caller's first edition carried an editorial criticism of its name. "We don't like the name," said the San Antonio Evening Light, which added that " 'Call Me to Dinner' would have been better." The Caller in its reply said "We regret that we did not consult the shining light of San Antonio before selecting a name. 'Call me to Dinner' is probably the sweetest sound to his ear."

*—Jan. 22, 2014*

# When the Century Was Young

In the summer of 1950, Theodore Fuller and wife went punting on the Thames with an Oxford don and his wife. When Fuller asked to try his hand with the pole, the Oxford don was reluctant. "It's a tricky sport, this punting, old boy. No rudder, you know, nothing like pulling an oar."

They put the wives ashore as a precaution and Fuller took the pole. But he knew very well how to pole a boat, having become something of an expert as a boy on Corpus Christi Bay. Gliding along on the Thames, Fuller thought of a boyhood friend on North Beach. "In our youthful days neither one of us would have passed up a chance like this. With a feigned awkward movement we would have upset that punt and fished out a dripping don."

Theodore "Ted" Fuller tells this story in "When the Century and I Were Young," his memoirs that were privately printed in 1970.

When Ted was five years old in 1913 his family moved to Corpus Christi from West Texas. Corpus Christi was a resort town then, with beach cottages, bath houses and fishing piers. It was a boy's paradise. There were water slides made wet with a hand pump and duck-hunting within a mile of the courthouse. Fuller learned to shoot when he was eight and had his own shotgun when he was 10.

During recess at the David Hirsch school Fuller and friends played marbles, mumble-peg and one-eyed cat. After school, they went fishing, crabbing or sailing. They ran barefoot along the shore, with supervision casual or nonexistent. "Boys were given more freedom and more responsibility," Fuller writes. "They were subjected to things now deemed dangerous to children of a like age. Why? I'm not so sure, but Corpus Christi was a wonderful place for boisterous boys and adventurous adolescents."

On shopping trips with his mother, he was fascinated by the mechanical wire baskets at Lichtenstein's. On a trip with his father, he peeked inside the Ben Grande. The air was pungent with the smell of whisky and beer. "As I was striving for a closer look, my foot felt an uneven place in the concrete. It was the imprint of a six-shooter."

On Saturday afternoons were the theaters, the Amusu, Liberty and Queen. Later there was the Rex, operated by old Billy Gray, and the Aldine. Serials were shown at the Queen, with Pearl White in "Perils of Pauline," Elmo Lincoln as "Tarzan" and the Farnum brothers in Westerns. "I was terrified the first time a serial left off with a girl tied to the railroad track while a train thundered toward her. A serial or two later, when we had become film sophisticates, we would nod knowingly when a beauty was tied to the track."

The fanciest barber shop in town, Fuller recalled, was in the Nueces Hotel, where haircuts cost 50 cents. The Dixie Barber Shop in the St. James displayed shaving mugs of its customers.

"In the early part of my decade," Fuller wrote, "Corpus boomed. Some 25 miles of streets were paved. Streetcars connected residential districts with downtown. Everyone rode the streetcars, some leaving automobiles at home in doing so." They would stop for passengers at any corner and they followed in rapid succession. Girls, a joke said, were like streetcars. "If you fail to catch one, another will be along in a few minutes."

When Fuller and his older brother visited the old Alta Vista Hotel at Three-Mile Point, it was ankle-deep in fleas. "Lord knows what they fed on."

The army established Camp Scurry south of town (in the vicinity of Spohn Hospital today) where men were trained for trench warfare in France. Boys were allowed to wander around the camp. "So long as soldiers were not training in an area, we roamed through it, trotting through hundreds of trenches and around barbed wire."

In the second week of September 1919 Fuller was vaguely aware something was different. Flounder moved in to the water's edge and were speared with cooking forks. On Sunday morning, Sept. 14, a hurricane was threatening. The Fuller family on North Beach rolled up carpets and carried them upstairs in case the house flooded. The parents and older brother went ahead while Theodore, his sister Esther, and his Aunt Doshie waded through rising water to a nearby house, a place of refuge.

They watched as adjacent houses floated away. When their house of refuge collapsed, they escaped into a raging vortex of wind and

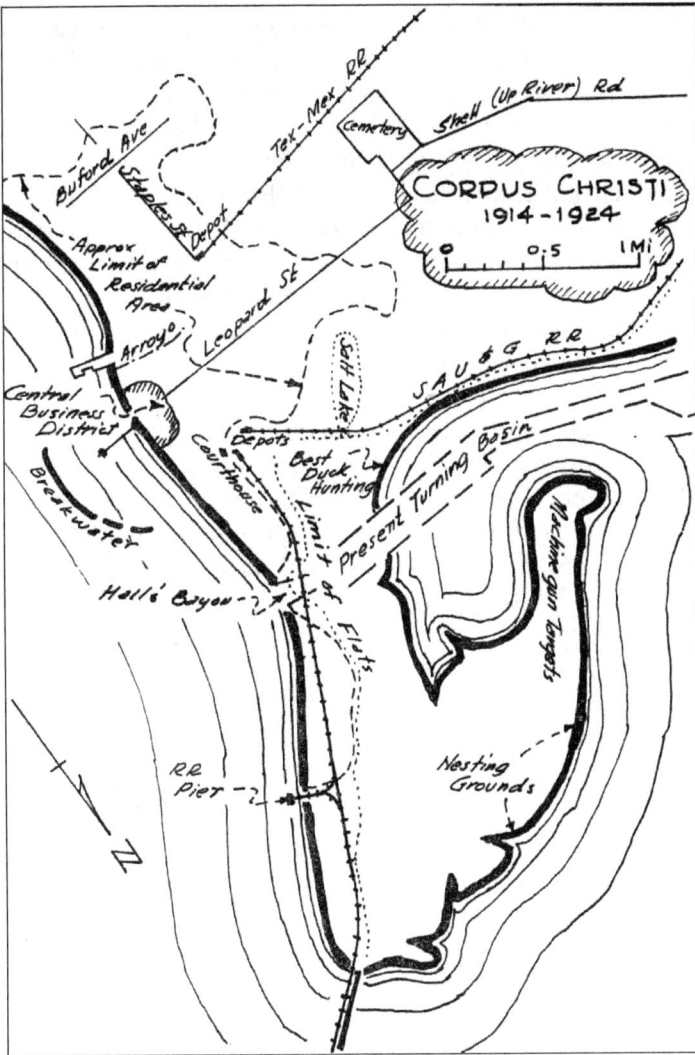

*Theodore Fuller's map of Corpus Christi, dated 1914-1924, shows Hall's Bayou, the Salt Lake, the arroyo, and the best place to go duck-hunting. From his memoirs, "When the Century and I Were Young."*

water. The roof they chose for a raft overturned and their Aunt Doshie, heavy with water-soaked petticoats, drowned. "For only a second, we watched in horror as Aunt Doshie struggled, threw both arms in the air, and screamed. Her voice was piercing, even over the sound of the storm. Then Esther said in a tone calm by resignation, 'There goes Aunt Doshie.' "

They clung to the raft as the wind shrieked and waves hurled debris at them. "The drifting boards, poles, planks and furniture were merciless. They hit our faces and pounded our bodies." Finally, after 18 hours of battering and terror, they washed up at the back of Nueces Bay. They were taken to Sinton.

When their father arrived, he said, " 'Brother is waiting for us in Corpus. He will be eager to see you two.' Esther got the message but I, having just seen one miracle and heard another, was ready for a third. 'And Mama?' He looked me over, with his eyes on the horizon. Papa had a clear, deep voice, which was soothing. 'No, son, she is with Aunt Doshie and we won't see them for a long, long time. They are in heaven.' "

For Theodore Fuller, the town was never the same. It was never again the calm, languid, carefree town it was before the storm. He went on to become an engineer and a lieutenant colonel in the U.S. Army. He served on the staff of Gen. Omar Bradley in World War II and after the war he was stationed in London as a military attache with the U.S. Embassy. He retired in 1961 and died in 1990 in Sylva, N.C. He was buried in Arlington National Cemetery.

Theodore Fuller's book is a good one, not because of who he was, but because of what he remembered about Corpus Christi when the century and he were young.

*—Jan. 29, 2014*

# Remember Pick's?

Every town went through a drive-in craze. The term "drive-in" covered a multitude of services, including a funeral home in Mississippi where you could pull up in front of a big window, take a look at the recently departed, his casket propped up for a good view, pay your respects and drive on.

But I'm talking about drive-in restaurants with car hops — curb hops, we called them — bringing out hamburgers, fries and frosted shakes on metal trays. As a teenager, I hopped curbs at the Globe Drive-In in Cullman, Ala. We knew the customers by name and knew who would tip. I don't remember making much money at it.

The drive-in craze began in the 1930s and lasted, mainly, through the 1960s. Old articles credit Royce Hailey with opening the first, the Pig Stand, in Dallas in 1921. His popular offering was a Pig Sandwich made of roast pork slathered with barbecue sauce and pickle relish. The Pig Stand slogan said, "A delightful meal served at your wheel."

There were three Pig Stands in Corpus Christi in the 1930s, two on Leopard and one on Chaparral near the bascule bridge. Pig Stand No. 1 was at its busiest when the bridge was raised for a ship.

After the Pig Stands came other drive-ins. In the early 1930s a man named Kyle Dowdy ran an A&W drive-in at Taylor and Water. One of the most popular drive-ins in Corpus Christi was Pick's. The first one opened in 1938 on Ayers, owned by J. B. Pickens, which gave it its name. By the mid-1940s it was sold to Vito "Pop" Salvo and the Salvo family eventually owned four Pick's. The first one on Ayers was famous for its enchiladas.

George Zackie owned two drive-ins on Water Street, which were book-ends on either side of Gillespie Buick: Zackie's Playhouse, which opened in 1939, and Zackie's No. 2. The second Zackie's later became the Purple Cow Drive-In and still later Pick's

Downtown, where the U&I Restaurant is today. The late Bill Walraven in a column remembered Pick's on Water Street where, "You could nearly always see someone there you knew in the postwar years. It was sort of a scene from the TV show, 'Happy Days.' "

Another popular drive-in was the High Hat on Staples at Marguerite. The curb-hops were young women who sometimes wore top hats. It was gone by the mid-1950s. On South Staples at Louisiana was the Tri-Drive, a drive-in restaurant and grocery store combined, with car hops wearing uniforms that looked like those of Greyhound bus drivers.

For a time, there were two Mac's drive-ins, one on Staples at Ohio and another on Shoreline. There were two drive-ins on North Beach, at different times. The first was La Palma, owned by John Mosser, near the amusement park, and for a year or so in the early 1960s there was the Frisby Drive-In.

Alvin Neff owned Neff's Drive-Ins, one at Morgan and 15th and another at Morgan and Port, with car hops dressed like drum majorettes. Neff's closed after he died in 1962. There were several short-lived drive-ins, including Pete's Inn on Chaparral, the Jitter Bug and the Eight Ball on Antelope, and I'm sure there were many others with less claim to fame that escaped my search of the records.

The heyday of the drive-ins came in the 1950s, which was my era, a time when teenagers got their own cars and with them a newfound freedom. In my case, it was a 1957 Chevy, pale yellow with a black interior, a real beauty. The drive-ins were gathering places, with juke boxes and easy laughter and good food, a refuge for the restless, a sanctuary from school and home and parents. At popular drive-ins like Pick's, it was said that youngsters went there to see who else would show up, and most everybody did.

Then the culture changed. When the last of four Pick's closed in 1978, Gregory Salvo, whose father "Pop" Salvo started the business in 1945, said their customers changed. In the old days, he said, they would come in from the high schools and Del Mar.

"Remember the Vikings football team? They used to go out on Rabbit Run Road (now Greenwood Drive) and catch rabbits," Gregory Salvo said. "I would butcher them and they would go out to the island to barbecue them, with blanket parties and beer. They had a ball. We never had any knifings, shootings, no ambulances running all night. Oh, we may have had a fist fight now and then, but it was over in a few minutes. I can't talk to the young ones any more. I can't reach them. It's all changed. That's why we had to close the drive-in on Staples (near King High School). The kids got destructive and annoyed the paying customers."

Most of the drive-ins were gone by the 1970s. The Pick's on Staples was torn down in 1971 to become an automobile dealership. The last Pick's at Ayers and Padre Island Drive (where the A&W was before that) was torn down in 1978 to make way for a Whataburger. The original Pick's on Ayers became the Magic Curb Service, which closed in 1984. Tri-Drive at Staples and Louisiana was torn down; McDonald's occupies that site today. Zackie's Play House became an insurance agency and the High Hat was torn down to build Suniland Furniture.

Zackie's, Mac's, Pick's, the High Hat, all gone. After the McDonaldization of America, they were no longer what people wanted. Snapka's, founded in 1948 by Method and Rudolph Snapka, is an anachronism that has survived, and Sonic's is flourishing.

As I remember it, the old drive-ins made the best hamburgers in the world. The chains, with their standardized banality, have all the business now, but they will never make a burger as good as the ones made at the Globe where I worked or, I'm sure, as good as the ones made at Pick's. In my own memories, it always seems to be a summer evening at the drive-in, with the jukebox playing, the air scented with the inviting sizzle of fried burgers, while overhead silver clouds race across a pale yellow moon, just about the color of my 1957 Chevy. Happy days, they were, happy days.

*—Feb. 5, 2014*

*Pick's on Ayers, founded in 1938 by J. B. Pickens, was later owned by Pop Salvo and family. The original Pick's was one of the most popular of Corpus Christi drive-ins. This photo was taken on April 7, 1941, from the John Fred'k "Doc" McGregor photographic collection of the Corpus Christi Museum of Science and History.*

*Kyle Dowdy's A&W Drive-In at the corner of Water and Taylor Streets. This Doc McGregor photo was taken sometime in the early 1930s from the John Fred'k "Doc" McGregor photographic collection of the Corpus Christi Museum of Science and History.*

On a September day in 1939 a band performs in front of George Zackie's Playhouse Drive-In on Water Street. The special that week was a fried chicken basket for 35 cents.

Car hops at the High Hat Drive-In on Staples. The menu listed a barbecue beef sandwich for 15 cents, a cheeseburger, 15 cents, a fried-chicken dinner, 35 cents, and an oyster loaf with a half dozen oysters for 30 cents. Songs on the music selection board were 1940 hits, including "Honeysuckle Rose," "Woud Ja Mind," "My Baby Smiles at Me," and "Tuxedo Junction."

# Donigan's Castle

It was in 1882 when Khatchadour Donigian immigrated to the United States from the village of Geyve near Constantinople in Asia Minor (today's Turkey). With him were his wife and five children, his brother and his family. As immigrants go, they were rich, used to the good things in life. Donigian was a wealthy Armenian silkworm producer who brought his fortune with him, in gold. Theirs was not a rags to riches story.

They left New York for Texas, where Khatchadour bought a ranch in Fort Bend County, southwest of Houston. Here the Donigians became the Donigans. They sold the ranch in 1896 and moved to Brookshire. When Khatchadour died in 1900, at age 72, one of his sons, Vartan Manasseh Donigan — which he shortened to V. M. Donigan — spent his share of the inheritance to build a hotel in Corpus Christi.

In 1890 V. M. Donigan married Anna Horope Garabedian, the daughter of a family that had been neighbors of his parents in Asia Minor. In 1905 he bought several properties and farms in and around Corpus Christi. He built a hotel in 1907.

This was the State Hotel on Mesquite at the intersection with Starr. It was built on the site of the old Corpus Christi Male and Female Academy. Donigan's State Hotel was considered Corpus Christi's first modern hotel. It even had private bathrooms, which some considered an unnecessary luxury. When a guest at another hotel asked about a bathroom, the proprietor said, "Bathroom? We have no such place in the building. The bay was put here to bathe in and we have never felt like wasting valuable space for a fad like a bathroom."

Donigan leased the hotel for five years and went back to Fort Bend County, where one of his brothers had bought a cotton gin. In 1912, he returned to take over the management of the hotel and brought his family with him. Besides his wife, Anna Horope, there were five children: sons Parnot, Mesog, and Zareth; and daughters Lucille and Nectarine. The Donigan family lived in the hotel.

Over the years, Donigan managed the hotel with the assistance of Mesog and Parnot, after they returned from college. Zareth, the other son, moved to Houston.

Mesog once told a story of his time at the University of Texas at Austin. He was a member of the glee club and on a trip to San Antonio, during a heavy rain, their bus got stuck when a creek flooded the highway. "We all piled out and while our director led we unstuck the bus to the tune of the Volga Boatman. You know how it goes, 'Yo-Ho, Heave-Ho.' "

Another story was told of Mesog. A blind professor, who taught Spanish at the university, was famous for his ability to distinguish his students based on his understanding of their character. He was interrupted in the middle of class by a crackling and crunching noise. The professor turned his head and said, "Someone in class is eating peanuts. And if I'm not mistaken it's Mesog Donigan."

After college, Mesog returned to Corpus Christi to help his brother Parnot and his father run the State Hotel. Parnot was listed as the manager and Mesog the assistant manager. The family owned other commercial properties, including a building on Agnes and another just behind the State Hotel, across from the Federal Building.

The original hotel, built in 1907, had three floors and 25 rooms. In 1916, it was enlarged with a fourth floor added. In 1926, with the opening of the Port of Corpus Christi, the west end of the hotel was added, doubling the original size. The name was changed to the New State Hotel, which advertised 100 rooms, 50 with private bathroom.

It was said to be a pleasant place to stay, right in the middle of town, between City Hall and the Courthouse, with its Billboard Lounge, Apollo Confection Shop, and State Hotel Cafe. Frank Hamer and a detachment of Texas Rangers, sent to quell any disturbances sparked by the Fred Roberts killing in 1922, stayed at the State. For a time, in the 1920s, the La Retama Library was located in the hotel. If a guest at the hotel wanted something to read, he could check out "The Mill on the Floss."

Since V. M. Donigan had taken over the hotel in 1912, the Donigan family lived in the hotel. In 1930, he decided to build a

*V. M. Donigan built a home on Ocean Drive in 1931 (above) which he called Alta Vista Place, but it was better known, as others called it, Donigan's Castle. The photo was taken by Doc McGregor in June 1938. Donigan's State Hotel (below) built in 1907 at the corner of Mesquite and Starr. It is shown soon after the hotel's opening.*

home. Among the many properties he had purchased was the site of the old Alta Vista Hotel on Ocean Drive, at Three-Mile Point, with a brilliant view of the bay at sunrise. In 1931, Donigan built one of the show places of Corpus Christi at 3302 Ocean Drive. He called it Alta Vista Place, but many people in town called it Donigan's Castle.

It was an eye-catching building with a touch of the Mediterranean and Spanish in its design. The Donigan home featured a three-story tower with flanking stucco wings and red tile roofs. It was said to be a replica of the Donigian family home at Geyve, Turkey, where Vartan had happy memories of growing up. Alta Vista Place, or Donigan's Castle, was one of the first fine homes built on Ocean Drive.

Vartan Manasseh Donigan died in 1943, when he was 77, at his home on Ocean Drive. His wife died three years later. Mesog, who never married, died in 1979, when he was 80. His older brother Parnot died in 1992. The house on Ocean Drive was sold in 1979 to Mike McKinnon. The purchase price wasn't disclosed, but was generally believed to be $750,000. The State Hotel, in its later years, became the Town House. It was torn down in 1965.

A parking lot occupies that site today. I walked around it the other day, looking for the message that was etched in the sidewalk on Starr Street that said, "Try the Billboard." Like the hotel, it was gone. The Donigan Castle is still standing, and it still looks exotic, almost as exotic as its history — that silkworm profits from half a world away, brought to this country by an Armenian immigrant, enabled building a red-tiled mansion on Ocean Drive that looks a bit more like Byzantium than Corpus Christi.

*—Feb. 12, 2014*

# Three Courthouses

Nearly 100 years ago, on March 17, 1914, St. Patrick's Day, ground was broken for a new county courthouse, the third since 1855.

Planning for the first courthouse began in 1852. From 1846, when the county was formed, county commissioners held their meetings at Henry Kinney's house or in each other's homes. On April 12, 1853, Kinney sold the county three lots on Mesquite Street for $300. This site became known as courthouse square.

In May 1853, J. B. McCowan began building a structure designed by Felix Blucher. A year later, McCowan was paid $650 for the work done and the job was turned over to James McMartin, who finished it in 1855. It cost $4,000.

In 1861, the courthouse was the scene of hot debates on secession. Judge Edmund J. Davis, who would later become governor during Reconstruction, spoke against seceding in opposition to several pro-secessionist speeches. On Feb. 23, 1861, the vote in Nueces County was 164 for secession and 42 against.

At the onset of war, a ceremony was held on the courthouse steps. A Confederate flag made by women in town was presented to Capt. William Wrather of the Corpus Christi Light Infantry by Mary Woessner. They later married.

After Union warships bombarded Corpus Christi in 1862, the county courthouse sat deserted. County officials evacuated to Santa Margarita on the Nueces River, where they stayed out of harm's way for the rest of the war. Commissioners' court minutes noted that they were "in vacation."

At war's end, Corpus Christi was a virtual ghost town, the streets clogged with dead animals and hardly a light to be seen. Unionists were appointed to re-organize county government and re-occupy the courthouse. Two years later, when a majority of City Council members died during a yellow fever epidemic, county commissioners took control of city affairs. They divided the town into road districts and appointed road overseers for each district. Able-bodied men were forced to work as road hands.

In the 1870s, the courtroom was the scene of the trial of two men charged in the Peñascal massacre. On May 9, 1874, a dozen bandits attacked a store in Peñascal on Baffin Bay, killing the store owner, his brother and two customers. Hypolita Tapia and Andres Davila, two of the 12 robbers, were caught and brought to Corpus Christi for trial.

During the trial, when the prosecutor said Tapia made a voluntary confession, he jumped up, pointing to rope marks on his neck, and shouted, "That's the voluntary confession!" They were found guilty and hanged from a scaffold built on the second floor gallery of the courthouse.

By 1875, the county had outgrown its first courthouse. A new courthouse, built next to the 1854 structure, was called the Hollub Courthouse for Rudolph Hollub, who designed it. The county's first two courthouses were designed by men with a background in mapmaking. Blucher, who designed the first courthouse, was a surveyor and mapmaker who later served in the Confederate Army. Hollub was a mapmaker who served with U. S. Grant in the Union Army. He came to South Texas to work as an engineer building the Tex-Mex Railroad.

The Hollub Courthouse cost $15,000. The old and new courthouses stood side by side on Courthouse Square, facing Mesquite. The old courthouse was used as a jury room and county offices. The 28th District court occupied the second floor of the Hollub Courthouse and on the ground floor were clerks' offices and county commissioners' courtroom.

Of several major trials held in the Hollub Courthouse, one of the most famous involved a shootout 27 years before. Josh Peters, a rancher's son, rode up to a Ranger camp near Banquete and asked who tied a tin can to his horse's tail. It was a prank. Ranger George Talley put gravel in a can and tied it to the colt's tail. The spooked horse almost ran himself to death. Peters said, "Who tied that can to my colt's tail? I'll whip the sorry bastard who did it." Talley shot Peters in the temple; he was dead before he hit the ground.

Talley, indicted for murder, changed his name to Smith and left the state. In 1905, he returned to the area to work on the "Brownie"

*The late Marion Uehlinger, Nueces county clerk, leaves the
1914 courthouse for the last time on July 29, 1977.*

*Nueces County's first courthouse (left) was built between 1853-1855. It was
designed by Felix Blucher. The county's second courthouse (center) was completed
in 1875. It was known as the Hollub Courthouse after designer Rudolph Hollub.*

Railroad and was arrested. When the trial in Corpus Christi began in April 1905, the courthouse filled with old Rangers from Leander McNelly's company. After a mistrial, Talley was found not guilty. He lived the rest of his days on a ranch near Falfurrias.

After nearly four decades, the Hollub Courthouse was too small for the growing county. Voters in 1913 approved a bond issue to pay for a new building. The county's third courthouse was built south of the 1854 courthouse, the Hollub Courthouse, and the County Jail, which were torn down. The Caller praised the new courthouse, which was built in the monumental manner. "Modern architecture is seen to abound in the new courthouse; the massive structure is a credit to the hand of man; one is dazzled as he looks at the tall columns over the doorway."

Five years after it was built, the six-story 1914 courthouse served as refuge during the 1919 storm. Many people escaped the wrath of the storm inside its brick walls. As the wind howled, people slept on floors, desks, judges' benches. Two women gave birth during the night. After the storm, the courthouse was used as a temporary morgue.

The 1914 courthouse — 100 years old this year — has been vacant for 37 years, since the new courthouse was built in 1977. It is a sad old building. It has had a long time to sit and molder and fall to pieces and may have a longer time still. It is protected with an historic building easement and the town remains divided between those who want it restored, with no one willing to pay for it, and those who want it pulled down. When you consider the survival rate of Corpus Christi's historic buildings, the fact that it is still standing is something of a miracle. But standing for what? I have no idea. And no one else does, either. Whatever possibility it may hold — and our imagination fails us — its future seems less interesting than its past.

*—Feb. 19, 2014*

# The Devil's Hat Band

I've written about this more than once, but it's something I've been interested in. Of the many things that brought about an end to the open range, the great cattle drives and the legendary Old West, the main culprit was barbed-wire fencing. But before the coming of barbed wire, plank and mesquite-post fencing was well established in South Texas.

S. G. Miller, a rancher in the Nueces Valley (where Lake Corpus Christi is today) built a 15-mile fence on his ranch. The mesquite-laced fence blocked the road from Corpus Christi to Gussettville and angered Miller's neighbors. Travelers would tear down the fence instead of going through the gate so Miller dug a ditch inside the fence. One night, as related in Mrs. Miller's book "Sixty Years in the Nueces Valley," several wagons ended up in the ditch and "there was such cussing and swearing you never heard."

Mifflin Kenedy built a 36-mile fence of cypress posts and pine boards across a peninsula, from the Oso to Laureles Creek. It cost $4,000 a mile and enclosed 131,000 acres of Laureles Ranch. Kenedy took a keen interest in the fence-building. Isom Thomas, the caporal on his ranch, said if the fence line showed the slightest deviation from a straight line Kenedy made them tear it down and rebuilt it.

Richard King began fencing parts of King Ranch a year later, using planks and cypress posts. Within three years he had 70,000 acres fenced.

In 1873, thousands of cattle starved and froze to death following a drought and "die-up" winter. Kenedy, with his grass enclosed by a fence, didn't lose a single head. That spring, he sent 5,000 healthy cattle up the trail to Kansas. Other ranchers took note. Martha Rabb enclosed her Banquete ranch with pine boards nailed to cypress posts. The 40-mile-long fence took a fence-rider two days to ride.

Soon afterwards, however, Kenedy learned that plank fences would not survive Gulf storms. His very expensive plank fence, barely six years old, was wrecked by the 1874 hurricane. After he sold Laureles and bought La Parra, he had it fenced it with cypress posts and galvanized round wire. Nearby Armstrong Ranch also used round wire and at half-mile intervals installed turning devices to tighten the wire.

In Illinois, Joseph Glidden came up with the idea of thorny wire to keep dogs out of wife's flower garden. Glidden's barbed wire was patented in 1874, but it was slow to catch on in Texas. Some ranchers were afraid that cattle and horses would cut themselves on the barbs and die of screw worms. A sales stunt in San Antonio helped change minds. John W. Gates, a barbed-wire salesman, was also known as "Bet-A-Million" Gates. He convinced San Antonio to let him put up a barbed wire corral in Military Plaza. Longhorns were driven into the corral and, as a crowd of cattlemen watched, the cattle shied away from the sharp barbs. Even when two men entered with flaming torches the longhorns refused to get close to the wire. Those who saw the show were sold on barbed wire. Cowboys called it "bob" wire or, more fancifully, Texas silk.

Good fences did not always make good neighbors. The spread of barbed wire intensified conflicts over land and water rights between ranchers and farmers, cattlemen and sheepmen, free-range cattlemen and enclosed-pasture cattlemen, small stockmen and big ranchers. Many ranchers who grazed their cattle on the open range were furious as grazing land and water holes were fenced off. After a terrible drought in 1883, as water holes and creeks dried up, stockmen found fences blocking their livestock from water. The fences were cut.

Across Texas, gangs of fence-cutters donned gunnysack hoods and roamed nights cutting fences. They called themselves Owls or Javelinas or Blue Devils. In Nueces County, James McBride's fence, five miles from town, was cut. In Victoria, a pasture fence blocks from the courthouse was cut. In Live Oak County, wire-cutters destroyed a fence then dug a grave and left a rope dangling in it with a note — "This will be your end if you rebuild this fence."

As ranch hands rode lonely fence lines to guard against wire-cutters, there were gunfights between masked fence-cutters and ranch hands. A headline in a Chicago newspaper said, "Hell breaks loose in Texas."

*Barbed wire, invented in 1874 in Illinois, came into general use in Texas by the end of the 1870s. Acts of violence connected to fence-cutting escalated after the 1883 drought. Russell Lee photo taken near Marfa, Texas, from the Library of Congress.*

Texas Rangers were sent to quell the violence. Working undercover, they would infiltrate gangs of known cutters to get inside information then stake out fences at night waiting for cutters to start snipping.

The Legislature was called into special session in January 1884 to deal with the crisis. New laws were passed that made fence-cutting a felony, punishable by up to five years in prison. One could carry a loaded gun but it was a criminal offense to be caught at night carrying a pair of wire-cutters, called nippers. With the new laws, the Rangers gained the upper hand, though incidents of fence-cutting violence continued into the 1890s.

J. Frank Dobie wrote that Glidden's barbed wire did for the cattle ranchers what Eli Whitney's gin did for the cotton planters. Fenced pastures meant ranchers didn't have to hire as many hands. Fencing cut down on rustling. And fences reserved the rancher's grasslands for his own herds and made it easier to segregate cattle to improve bloodlines. But for all the advantages of barbed wire, many lamented the passing of an era.

A rhyme put it like way: "They say that heaven is free range land — / Goodbye, goodbye, Oh, fare you well — / But it's barbed wire for the devil's own hat band / And barbed wire blankets down to hell."

"It makes me sick," an old trail-driver said, "when I think that onions and potatoes are growing where mustang ponies should be exercising and where four-year-old steers should be getting fat for market. Fences are the curse of this country."

Barbed wire changed the landscape. It changed the character of Texas. And it divided the old Texas of epic memory from what became the new and modern Texas. It turned free-spirited cowboys into wagon-riding and post-hole-digging hired hands. It brought the open range and the trail drives to a close. And it marked the end of one era and the beginning of another. Nothing has been the same since the coming of barbed wire.

*—Feb. 26, 2014*

# The Boys of '98

One day in the spring of 1898, volunteer militiamen called the Kenedy Rifles marched through Corpus Christi on their way to take part in what would soon be called a splendid little war.

News of insurrection in Cuba had dominated headlines since the beginning of the year. War fever increased after the U.S. armored cruiser Maine exploded in Havana Harbor on Feb. 16, 1898. War against Spain was declared on April 25.

Texas papers were full of chest-thumping rhetoric. When a gun battery was moved to Galveston, the San Antonio Express whooped: "Now the enemy will never get into Texas by way of Galveston." The Corpus Christi Caller reprinted Kipling's poem, "The White Man's Burden," and noted that Spain once ruled half the world but frittered it away on "too many bullfights."

Texas volunteer units being formed included the Belknap Rifles, San Antonio Zouaves, and the O'Connor Guards of Victoria. In Corpus Christi, the Kenedy Rifles, named for rancher Mifflin Kenedy, were already in existence; they were organized 10 years before and held drills in an old warehouse on Lawrence Street.

The most famous Texas unit was the First Volunteer Cavalry, commanded by Leonard Wood, a national hero after the Apache campaign of 1886, with Theodore Roosevelt second in command. The ranks of the First Volunteer Cavalry included former Texas Rangers, Arizona cowboys, Arkansas farm boys and Harvard college boys. They were dubbed the Rough Riders, a name Roosevelt hated.

The Rough Riders trained in San Antonio, at the Bexar County Exposition grounds, and did their drinking at the bar of the Menger Hotel. Before leaving for Tampa, on May 29, the Rough Riders fired their guns into the air. One account said 1,000 rounds were fired. Only half the unit left Florida for Cuba and none of their

41

horses. The Rough Riders' famous charge up San Juan Hill was done on foot.

In Corpus Christi, the 38 members of the Kenedy Rifles had to borrow money to pay for their train tickets to Austin. They left town on the morning of May 3, departing from the SAAP Depot as Jose Crixell's brass band played the national anthem and someone in the crowd yelled, "Remember the Maine!"

The Kenedy Rifles picked up volunteers on the way and arrived in Austin with 84 men. On May 12, 1898, at Camp Mabry near the state Capitol, they were mustered into U.S. service and given a new name, Company E.

While Company E was in training, Admiral George Dewey destroyed Spain's fleet at Manila, the battle of El Caney was fought, the Rough Riders stormed up San Juan Hill, and the U.S. Navy defeated the Spanish fleet outside Santiago Harbor. In the battle before Santiago, Maj. Gen. Joseph Wheeler, a former Confederate, rushed into the fight yelling, "The Yankees are running! The Yankees are running! Damn it! I mean the Spaniards!"

Company E (the former Kenedy Rifles) were moved to Camp Mobile at Mobile, Ala., then to Camp Cuba Libre near Jacksonville, Fla. It was getting too cold to sleep in their tents when they were moved to Savannah, Ga., and issued the new Krag-Jorgensen rifles in preparation for occupation duty in Cuba.

On Christmas Day 1898, the Kenedy Rifles boarded the transport ship Michigan, arrived in Havana Harbor five days later, on Dec. 30, and lined the rails to see what was left of the Maine — the twin smokestacks and white superstructure of the sunken cruiser. As they crossed the bar, with the band playing the Star-Spangled Banner, they waved at departing Spanish soldiers who waved back, glad to be going home.

"We were expecting trouble," Lt. Tobe Fitzsimmons wrote to his parents in Corpus Christi, "but there was nothing but cheers from the natives for 'los Americanos.'" The ships in the harbor, including the battleship Texas, were decorated with American and Cuban flags.

Fitzsimmons described Cuba as being like Mexico with cobbled streets and no sidewalks. When they marched through Havana on the way to their camp, Pvt. Robert "Robby" Hall from Corpus Christi wrote his parents that the Cuban people were very friendly. "They waved and threw us cigars in the parade."

*Corpus Christi's volunteers for the Spanish-American War, the Kenedy Rifles, march through town on the morning of May 3, 1898 on their way to the train depot. After months of training they reached Cuba after the war was over.*

The soldiers of Company E marched on to their camp at the base of a mountain on the Atlantic side of the island. They discovered rum and Cuban girls. "There is some kind of drink here that will set a person wild," wrote Arthur Dear. "Some of the boys got hold of some and nearly went crazy." Sam Tinney wrote that the Corpus Christi soldiers had an advantage over other American soldiers on the island because most of them could speak Spanish and could talk to the Cuban girls.

The soldiers from Corpus Christi did garrison duty all over Cuba. Since the war was over when they arrived, the only fighting they saw was among themselves. The Corpus Christi boys, doing guard duty, were called on to break up a near-riot of soldiers from Indiana and Missouri who were angry at not being allowed to attend a circus.

Almost a year after they had marched out of Corpus Christi, Company E (the Kenedy Rifles) left Dry Tortugas for Galveston, where they were inspected by a health officer to make sure they were not carrying yellow fever or some other infectious disease. They turned in their belts, bayonets, and Krag-Jorgensen rifles and were discharged. Their pockets, one said, were filled with souvenirs from Cuba, mostly Spanish army buttons they had obtained in trade.

When they arrived at the SAAP Depot on Sunday night, April 16, 1899, they were greeted by a large, cheering crowd and the strains of Jose Crixell's brass band, the same band that played when they left the year before. They were supposed to march in ranks through the town but, as the Caller reported, "it was impossible to form them into procession as parents would not give them up."

Three days later, Market Hall was draped in bunting and decorated with a large portrait of Mifflin Kenedy, namesake of the Kenedy

Rifles. The returning heroes from the Spanish-American War were showered with laurel leaves and given the freedom of the city. After dancing, a banquet was served at midnight. For the Kenedy Rifles, the boys of '98, their splendid little adventure was over.

*—March 5, 2014*

# The Cotton Road

Lt. Col. Arthur James Lyon Fremantle of Her Majesty's Coldstream Guards made a three-month tour of the Confederacy in 1863. He arrived at Brownsville, rode up the Cotton Road, and traveled across the South, meeting Confederate generals and leaders. At Gettysburg, on the second day, he watched from the forks of a tree while Robert E. Lee met with his senior generals to confer about the course of the battle.

Fremantle was a London dandy and something of a snob. He hated the American custom of shaking hands and refused to go to parties without his fancy evening clothes. In his tour of the South, at the high tide of the Confederacy, he kept a journal and filled it with vivid and trenchant observations. His chapters on Matamoros, Brownsville and the Cotton Road in South Texas give us an outside perspective of an interesting time.

When Fremantle's ship arrived off the mouth of the Rio Grande on April 2, 1863, he saw some 70 merchant vessels waiting for their cargoes of cotton. The cotton was destined for the mills of England and Europe. Fremantle landed at the Mexican fishing village of Bagdad, which had grown into a thriving port during the war. Fremantle wrote that endless bales of cotton could be seen. Across the river from Bagdad was the Texas town of Clarksville. Upriver were the busy towns of Matamoros and Brownsville.

In Matamoros, Fremantle was taken to a fandango. "A number of benches are placed to form a large square, in the center of which the dancing goes on, the men and women gravely smoking all the time," Fremantle wrote. On Good Friday, he was irritated — he had a hot and dusty walk because "carriages are not permitted to run on Good Friday in Mexico."

When Fremantle crossed over to Brownsville, he found Confederate officers at a fire "contemplating a tin of potatoes" and bragging about a Yankee they had hanged. Fremantle saw the body. He had been partly buried, with his head above ground and the frayed rope still around his neck.

The man was W. W. Montgomery who had been captured on the Mexican side with E. J. Davis, Union leader and former Corpus Christi judge. Montgomery was hanged and the Confederates were about to hang Davis when Gen. Hamilton P. Bee intervened and stopped them, returning Davis to the Mexican side with apologies for the violation of Mexican territory.

A Confederate colonel told Fremantle that he thought the Montgomery hanging was wrong, but "my boys meant well." Fremantle thought Brownsville was probably the rowdiest town in Texas "where the shooting-down and the stringing-up are very much in vogue."

Fremantle left the border in a carriage pulled by four mules and driven by two mule drivers, a man named Sargent and another called the Judge, both much addicted to liquor. Sargent would yell, "Get up, now, you great long-eared (SOB). I wish you was Uncle Abe, I'd make you move." Fremantle said mule driving is an art of itself, "and Mr. Sargent is justly considered a professor at it."

Traveling north, they saw an endless stream of wagons loaded with cotton traveling down the Cotton Road where the prickly pear cactus snagged bits and pieces of cotton from the heavily loaded wagons. "Generally, there were 10 oxen or six mules to a wagon carrying ten bales," Fremantle wrote, "but in deep sand more animals are necessary. They journey very slowly towards Brownsville . . . We are continually passing cotton trains going to Brownsville, also (going the other way) government wagons with stores for the interior."

In the Big Sands, a sand belt 65 miles wide and 100 miles long, they bedded down on a rug by the carriage. "We should have slept very comfortably," Fremantle wrote, "had it not been for the activity of fleas and the incursions of wild hogs." Fremantle was awakened in the night by wild hogs breathing in his face.

On April 20, after six days, they approached King Ranch — "which for several days I had heard spoken of as a sort of Elysium, marking as it does the termination of the sands, and the commencement of comparative civilization." Richard and Henrietta King were in Brownsville, but Mrs. Hamilton Bee, the wife of the Confederate general in charge in Brownsville, was at the ranch.

*A drawing in Frank Leslie's Illustrated Newspaper shows cotton bales lining the banks of the Rio Grande across from Brownsville in 1863 when Lt. Col. Arthur James Lyon Fremantle traveled up the Cotton Road before joining Robert E. Lee's army at Gettysburg.*

Fremantle described her as "a nice, lively little woman, a red-hot Southerner."

Two days after leaving King Ranch, they reached Casa Blanca, where they bought a goat, some corn, and two chickens. At Oakville, wrote Fremantle, all the women were anxious to buy snuff. "It appears that the Texan females are in the habit of dipping snuff — which means putting it in their mouths instead of their noses. They rub it against their (gums) with a blunted stick."

From San Antonio, they traveled to Galveston, where Fremantle met Sam Houston, whom he described as egotistical and vain and "much given to chewing tobacco and blowing his nose with his fingers." Fremantle met Houston in May 1863, two months before Houston's death.

In his journey across the South, Fremantle met many famous people, both statesmen and generals, and made notes in his diary. In Richmond, he had tea with Jefferson Davis, whom he found "full of life and humor." He was a guest of James Longstreet after Robert E. Lee's Army of Northern Virginia invaded Pennsylvania.

On the third day of the battle at Gettysburg, while Longstreet sat on his horse whittling on a stick, Fremantle wrote that the guns opened like the drums of a stirring overture to an opera that told of the struggle of demigods and heroes. After the battle, after George Pickett's failed and fateful charge, he noted the calm and competent rallying by Lee of the shaken Confederate army.

After Gettysburg, Fremantle crossed over the Union lines, traveled to New York and sailed for England. During his sojourn across the South, from April 1 to July 15, 1863, Fremantle became convinced the South would win the war. His account of his travels was first published in London in late 1863. Because of a shortage of supplies, when it was printed in Mobile, Ala., in 1864, it appeared bound in flowered wallpaper. Fremantle's experiences in the wartime boom towns of Matamoros and Brownsville and his trip up the white-fleece-snagged Cotton Road are of particular interest in the history of South Texas.

*—March 12, 2014*

# Salt of the Confederacy

During the Civil War, when Union warships blockaded Southern ports, salt became as valuable as cotton, the white gold of the Confederacy. With foreign supplies shut off, the price of salt rose from 60 cents a bushel to $20 dollars a bushel. It was so scarce people dug up smokehouse floors to sift the dirt for traces of salt.

Without refrigeration, salt was necessary to keep meat from spoiling. There could be no salt pork without salt and the soldiers of the Confederacy fought on a diet of salt meat. At home, salt became so scarce and Confederate currency so worthless that it became a medium of exchange, good as gold.

The great need for salt gave South Texas, rich in saline deposits, a strategic importance. The oldest and largest salt deposit in South Texas was an ancient salt lake, La Sal del Rey (the Salt of the King), in Hidalgo County. White crystals tinged with pink rose to the surface in layers two to four feet deep. Salt blocks cut from the lake were replenished within two or three days. Fifteen miles to the east was another salt lake, La Sal Viejo (Old Salt), in Willacy County.

In Spanish times, a trail stretched from the salt lakes to Laguna Madre. Ox-carts hauled salt to the lagoon, which they crossed on an oyster-shell reef, then traveled down to the tip of Padre Island where ships waited to carry the salt to Spanish ports in Mexico. Mule trains carried salt into the interior as far as Durango and Zacatecas.

When the Civil War began, Texas took possession of La Sal del Rey and the salt of the king became the salt of the Confederacy. The salt was mined and hauled to the Laguna Madre, where it was loaded on flat-bottomed scows with armed guards riding atop the cargo. The salt from La Sal del Rey was controlled by the military board of the state under Pryor Lea of Goliad. Some of the salt was taken to Corpus Christi and loaded on blockade-running ships. In

1863, a blockade runner loaded with salt, the Zion, sank off Ohler's Wharf.

Salt was also gathered on the shores of Laguna Madre. Robert Adams, an early pioneer, worked gathering salt during the war. "When the water came in high, it filled the shallow lakes; when the water receded, the salt could be gathered," he said once in an interview. "It was in small grains, the size of peas, and you had to rake it out of the water. We would pile the salt on the bank and let it drain then put it in sacks and buckets. Wagons used for hauling the salt were pulled by six yoke of oxen. I used to carry salt on my back to the wagons. The salt was wet and the brine ran down my back. I guess I got pickled in those days."

Salt was also gathered along the shores of Baffin Bay, which was called the Salt Lagoon back then. Thomas Noakes of Nuecestown made trips to Baffin Bay to gather salt, which he carried to inland cities to trade for bacon, cornmeal or flour.

The state also established the Aransas Salt Works on St. Charles Bay near the Big Tree on Lamar peninsula. There was another salt production operation at Packery Flat run by James McCarty near the mouth of Mission River, a few miles west of Copano.

At the salt works near the Big Tree, Philip Power in his memoirs said salt was produced by sluicing seawater into open pits where it evaporated. When dry, the glistening salt was shoveled up and ground by a gristmill operated by wind-power. The salt works by the Big Tree were wrecked in 1862 by Union raiding parties operating from the blockading U.S. warships.

The salt traffic in Texas received a ruinous blow in 1863. After Union forces under Gen. Nathaniel Banks captured Brownsville, a Union raiding party under the command of John L. Haynes destroyed the salt-works and the Confederate military depot at La Sal del Rey. In late 1863 and early 1864, as Banks' forces occupied the barrier islands, troops left to garrison Mustang Island spent much of their time trying to disrupt the salt trade. They used launches to try to capture salt barges on the Laguna Madre. The Union soldiers were under orders to dissolve the cargoes of salt if they could not capture it. They dissolved it by dumping it back into the sea from where it came.

One might think an invading army would have higher priorities, but this was a part of the Union strategy to deprive the South of essentials, such as salt. A recent article in the New York Times

*John Anderson's wind-powered grist mill on Water Street ground up salt collected from the Laguna Madre for use in curing meat and hides at beef packing houses along the coast.*

titled "Salt Wars," outlined this strategy. Union raids on Confederate salt production centers were launched in Virginia, North Carolina, Alabama, Louisiana and Texas. "The war over salt," the article said, "was ultimately just one small part of the Union's strategy of economic starvation against the South."

Mining salt didn't stop with the end of the war. After the war came the hide-and-tallow era and beef packing houses along the coast needed huge amounts of salt to preserve the meat and cure the hides.

Salt was hauled from the Laguna Madre on shallow-draft boats to a wind-powered gristmill on Water Street built by Capt. John Anderson, a longtime dealer in salt who owned a salt warehouse in Flour Bluff during the war. At Anderson's gristmill, the salt was ground fine for table use and coarse for the packing houses.

The salt beds of the Laguna Madre and Baffin Bay were wiped clean by the hurricanes of 1874 and 1875. La Sal del Rey, the ancient and once busy salt lake that supplied the Confederacy with salt, was relegated to use as a cattle lick. The extensive salt-works on St. Charles Bay, with its evaporation pits near the Big Tree, were restored and operated by Seth Ballou, who also had a molasses mill. He employed some of his former slaves as workers. Capt. Peter Johnson was quoted in "Refugio" that "the salt works was one place where employment could be had. I often worked there as a boy. Sometimes I had to take my pay in molasses."

*—March 19, 2014*

# Roosevelt's Big Fish

In May 1937 President Franklin D. Roosevelt traveled to Port Aransas to go fishing. It was a tough time. The Supreme Court had overturned elements of the New Deal so he was pushing a plan to gain control of the court. His opponents called it a court-packing plan that would tilt the balance of power. This is no analysis of that scheme; we point it out to put his trip in the political context of the time.

Roosevelt wanted to get out of Washington. He accepted his son Elliott's offer to take him fishing for tarpon. Elliott, who lived in Fort Worth, visited Port Aransas the year before.

The presidential party left Washington by train on April 28. The party included Marvin McIntyre, appointments secretary; Admiral Ross McIntire, Roosevelt's doctor; Edwin "Pa" Watson, military attache; and Paul Bastedo, naval attache. At New Orleans, they had Pompano en Papillotte at Antoine's, described as equal to anything in France. Next morning they boarded Navy destroyer USS Moffett with another destroyer, the USS Decatur, in escort.

The destroyers reached the Aransas Pass channel on May 1 and sighted the Potomac, the presidential yacht. While luggage was being transferred, Roosevelt took a small boat and went fishing off the jetties. He caught a king mackerel. A Navy seaplane brought the mail pouch and he signed letters and documents. After dinner, he fished from the quarter-deck of the Potomac.

On Sunday Roosevelt trolled for tarpon while the Potomac moved to a new anchorage near the lighthouse. That afternoon, he went fishing with Port Aransas fishing guide Barney Farley. The president's legs may have been weak, Farley said, "but his handshake was not. When I told him he could catch a whale with a grip like that, he laughed." Nine tarpon were caught that day but none by the president, though he said he felt four good tugs.

On Monday, Roosevelt went fishing again with Farley. He hooked a tarpon and worked it in. When Farley saw the fish, he had a sinking feeling. "The hook had torn a large hole in the tarpon's mouth. I knew that when I took hold of the leader, the tarpon would jump and the hook would fall out or tear out. I told Mr. Roosevelt I was about to experience the most embarrassing moment of my life — 'I am going to lose your first tarpon.' Sure enough, the fish jumped and shook the hook out. The only thing he said was, 'You called that right.' "

Roosevelt later landed a four-footer. Corpus Christi photographer "Doc" McGregor, in a boat close by, snapped his famous shot of Farley and Elliott holding up the tarpon.

On Tuesday, the Potomac sailed to Port Isabel so the president could visit a friend of Vice President John Nance Garner. At Port Isabel, a passing shrimp boat was hailed so they could buy shrimp for supper. When Farley told the shrimpers the president was on board "two crew members shoveled shrimp on our runabout so fast they nearly covered us up. The president was sitting there grinning with shrimp in his lap."

Back off Port Aransas, Roosevelt played host for friends of Elliott and went fishing with Farley. On Thursday, the Navy mail plane arrived and Roosevelt signed legislation and answered letters.

On Friday morning, Roosevelt received a flash that the German airship Hindenburg had exploded at Lakehurst, N. J., killing 36 passengers and crewmen. He sent condolences to Adolf Hitler. Before noon, Roosevelt and aides, with Farley, left for lunch at Sid Richardson's ranch on St. Joseph's Island. This social call was political; Richardson, the wealthy Fort Worth oilman who owned St. Joseph's, was a major supporter of the vice president.

"When we got there we were faced with the problem of how to get the president in his wheelchair from the boat to the island," Farley said. "Sid didn't have any way to unload him. He didn't have a dock for that. But he did have a cattle chute. We pulled alongside the chute and Sid explained he was going to roll him down." Roosevelt said, 'What in the world, Sid, do you mean you're going to roll me down that bull chute?' Richardson, unfazed, said, 'Mr. President, you're the biggest bull that ever went down that chute.' "

On Roosevelt's last day of fishing — Saturday, May 8 — he went out again with Farley, though Teddy Mathews served as guide. "We were fishing off the south jetty," Mathews said later. "I pulled

*President Franklin D. Roosevelt (with fishing rod) reeled in a 4-foot 8-inch tarpon off Port Aransas on May 3, 1937. His son Elliott and fishing guide Barney Farley hold up the fish. Also shown are Don Farley, steering the boat, Edwin Watson, the president's military aide, in dark cap, and Paul Bastedo, his naval attache. The photo was taken by Doc McGregor.*

around in the open and a northeast wind sent a spray up in the air and it hit the boat. It soaked him. The president said, 'Don't worry, I've been wet before.' "

After a slow morning Roosevelt got a strike at 2 p.m. and an hour later he landed a five-foot tarpon just as photographers and a newsreel camera crew arrived to record it. Farley said the president was excited. He would rub his hands on the tarpon and then on his khaki pants.

The Potomac left on Sunday for Galveston where Roosevelt met, for the first time, Lyndon Johnson, newly elected to Congress. FDR went by train to Fort Worth where he was entertained with a barbecue at Amon Carter's ranch.

Back in Washington, the widening split between FDR and his vice president became permanent. Garner opposed the court plan. Roosevelt asked the vice president about the prospects of Congress passing his legislation to enlarge the Supreme Court and Garner asked if he wanted it with the bark on or off. "The rough way," said Roosevelt. "You are beat," Garner replied. "You haven't got the

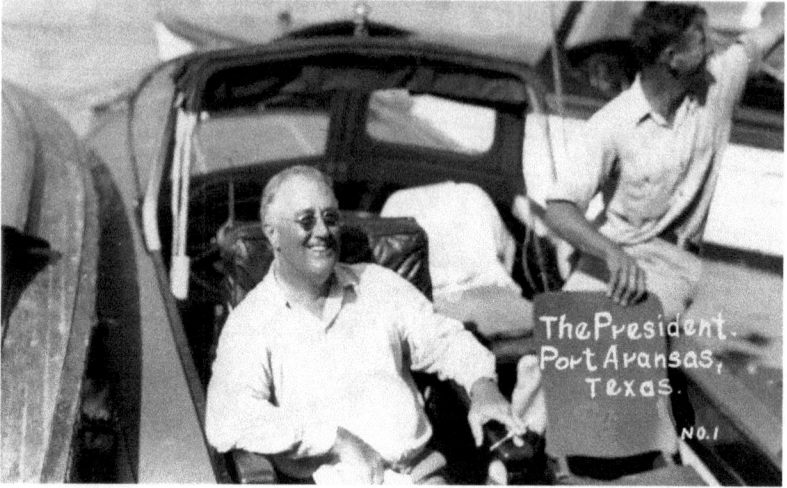

*President Franklin D. Roosevelt poses for photographs after his tarpon fishing trip at Port Aransas.*

votes." When it went down, cartoonists remembered the fishing trip and Roosevelt's plan to reconstruct the court was shown as the big fish that got away.

(Note: The president's trip is well-documented. There is a very good account, from which I have quoted, in Barney Farley's book, "Fishing Yesterday's Gulf Coast," published by Texas A&M University Press. Farley, the legendary fishing guide, died in 1978. More detail can be found in the day to day log of the president's activities at the Pare Lorentz Center of the FDR Presidential Library. The Port Aransas Museum has photocopies of the Potomac's log, which also recorded the president's time on the Texas coast.)

*—March 26, 2014*

# La Quinta and Watsonia

The adobe house on Ocean Drive and the south side of Louisiana Boulevard. looks as though a little piece of New Mexico was plopped down on the bayfront. It was built in 1938 for Mr. and Mrs. Harry H. Watson, who called it Watsonia. It was the second notable house May Watson presided over. For two decades, her home was La Quinta, a mansion on the north shore that was headquarters of the Taft Ranch.

The story of the late May Watson is linked to much of this area's history. She came from Rockport, the daughter of Thomas Henry Mathis and Mary Nold Mathis. She had two sisters and five brothers. Her grandfather Henry Nold built a college at Ingleside before the Civil War. Her father, Thomas Henry Mathis, was one of the founders of the great Coleman-Mathis-Fulton Pasture Company. When the partnership ended in 1879, T. H. Mathis was granted the 24,000-acre Henry Bend Ranch. The town of Mathis sits on part of this ranch.

May Watson once recalled trips from Rockport to Corpus Christi when they would ford the Reef Road across Nueces Bay. "Trips were made by wagon to bring back supplies and often, if the tide was in, it would be dangerous crossing the reef, with the occupants of the wagon having to stand up in their seats while the team was forced to swim."

In 1907, she married Joseph F. Green, manager of the reorganized Coleman-Fulton Pasture Company. This 167,000-acre ranch was one of the most successful ranches in South Texas. One of the original founders, Tom Coleman, sold his stock in the company in 1894 to David Sinton, a wealthy banker, and Sinton's son-in-law, Charles Taft, both of Cincinnati. When Taft became the major stockholder, the ranch began to be called Taft Ranch, though officially it was always the Coleman-Fulton Pasture Company.

When May married Green, the house that would be their home and ranch headquarters was being built on a site overlooking Corpus Christi Bay. The place had been known as Dolan Motts, part of the old Thorpe Ranch. Construction of the mansion was slowed, May recalled, by workers slipping over to Ingleside to sample Hatch's wine.

But the house was finished two months after they were married and they moved in on Christmas Eve 1907. May's mother, Mary Nold Mathis, christened the house La Quinta, Spanish for country house. On Christmas Day, they held a house-warming party for 125 ranch employees. This became an annual event for ranch employees, usually held on New Year's.

The most important guest ever entertained at La Quinta was President William Howard Taft, who came to Texas in November 1909 to visit his half-brother's ranch. Before the president arrived, Charles Taft brought in an expert golfer to design a nine-hole golf course. As a pasture near the house was being converted into a golf course, workers found a snake bed and killed 28 rattlesnakes.

During Taft's stay, ranch hands held a roping and branding competition and dipped cattle in a tick-killing vat "which seemed to fascinate the president." They took the heavyweight Taft riding on an oversized horse. For a general tour of the ranch, they borrowed autos from Beeville, Sinton and Corpus Christi. They also took him jackrabbit hunting, though Taft declined to take a gun. He said later, "I hate to kill things and am content to be a tenderfoot."

The only disturbance during Taft's visit, May once recalled, was a commotion one night when a piece of the ceiling fell in the president's room. "There was a great scurrying about until the cause of the noise was discovered."

May Watson co-authored a booklet titled "Taft Ranch," which outlined the story of the president's visit, the history of the ranch and the founding of the towns of Taft and Gregory. In this booklet, she recalled one tragedy at La Quinta. Her husband's saddle horse "Joy" liked to stand on the bluff gazing out toward the bay. One day, the side of the cliff crumbed and the horse plunged to his death on the beach below.

For 20 years, La Quinta served as the Green family home until Joseph F. Green died on Nov. 20, 1926 during minor surgery to remove his tonsils. He was buried in the Taft Cemetery. May Watson sold the ranch house in 1928 and about that time the ranch

*La Quinta was the headquarters of the Taft Ranch and residence of the ranch manager. The photo was taken by Doc McGregor in 1936, two years before the place burned.*

*The New Mexico-style bayfront home of May Watson, at Louisiana and Ocean Drive, is shown in 1938 soon after construction was completed.*

holdings were liquidated. The house was bought by the Gulf Coast Shrine Club, which operated it as a resort for members until 1935 when it was sold and turned into a hotel. It burned on Jan. 26, 1938. After the fire, two of the four chimneys were all that remained.

After Green's death, May married Harry H. Watson, a retired rancher from Colorado, and they built a new home in Corpus Christi across the bay from where La Quinta once stood. While under construction, May's new house, at the corner of Louisiana and Ocean Drive, got a lot of attention.

The home was built of adobe bricks made on the grounds. The clay was dug out of the bluff in front of the property. The bricks, five times the size of ordinary bricks, were fired in kilns fueled by mesquite and ebony.

I have heard it said that whoever designed the pueblo-style home was immune to art and common sense, however, the architect, William Doty Van Siclen, was quite famous and successful. He designed notable buildings in San Jose, Calif., Seattle and Edmonton, Canada, before he moved to Brownsville. He was 73 when he designed the Watsons' home.

The 15-room house was constructed of 55,000 bricks, each weighing about 20 pounds. Tile from Mexico was laid on stairs, walks, tables and patio benches. The entrance hall was floored with colored flagstones and other floors were made of randomly sized boards secured with wooden pegs. One of the prized furnishings was a large brass bed that William Howard Taft slept in at La Quinta.

Almost 10 years after the house was finished, May's husband Harry died on Dec. 22, 1947. May Mathis Green Watson died on June 21, 1966. She was buried in the Taft Cemetery in a plot between those of her two husbands. The year after her death, the adobe house was sold to Dr. H. Ross Garza. It hasn't been called Watsonia for a long time.

*—April 2, 2014*

# Camp Scurry

When World War I broke out in Europe in August 1914, Corpus Christi and South Texas were focused on events closer to home, along the border with Mexico.

A short précis of the situation in Mexico: Francisco Madero led a revolt against the dictator Diaz in 1910. Diaz fled into exile. Madero was assassinated shortly after taking office and Gen. Huerta became dictator. The revolution kept the border in an uproar. Bandits crossed the river and clashed with U.S. Army patrols. After Pancho Villa attacked Columbus, New Mexico in March 1916, Gen. John Pershing was sent to the border with 10,000 troops. Pershing's Punitive Expedition crossed into Mexico in pursuit of Villa. In 1916, President Wilson ordered National Guard units to the border. Troops poured into the Rio Grande Valley and war seemed likely. Then Carranza and Obregón, moderate leaders within the revolution, gained the upper hand in Mexico.

With tensions easing on the border, the Second and Third Infantry Regiments were ordered to move to Corpus Christi from the Valley. These were Texas National Guard units that were federalized for one year's service. Moving with them would be the headquarters of the Sixth Brigade, known as the Texas Brigade.

To facilitate the move, Corpus Christi Mayor Roy Miller agreed to prepare a 200-acre site in the E. B. Cole tract, at city expense. This area was bordered by Buford, Santa Fe, Louisiana and Ocean Drive, where Spohn Hospital and the Del Mar neighborhood are today.

The city hired 150 workers to clear out the brush. Water lines were laid, electric wires strung, drainage ditches dug, and the streetcar line extended. The site was ready in a week. A trainload of rations (23 boxcars) and 33 new Packard trucks arrived. The camp soon had shell-topped roads, screened tents, and wooden mess halls for 3,500 soldiers.

The Third Infantry Regiment came by train from Harlingen on Thursday, Sept. 7, 1916. They marched through town with Company C from Corpus Christi (the Musketeers) leading the way. The Second Infantry arrived from Pharr the next day. Brig. Gen. John Hulen established headquarters near Ocean Drive, with a good view of the bay.

No sooner had they arrived than some troops were sent on a practice march from Corpus Christi to Calallen, 18 miles away. They camped near the railroad depot at Calallen and when a norther hit in the night, the troops scattered, seeking shelter. Some deserted, catching trains in every direction. Later, the soldiers went on extended marches, as far as Sinton and back.

That Tuesday, Sept. 12, the city held a welcoming reception for the soldiers. Five thousand colas and 600 cakes, baked by women of the town, were served at a big tent. The party ended in a near-brawl between competing bands of the Second and Third Infantry.

The camp was initially called Alta Vista and some suggested it should be named Camp Roy Miller, but army regulations did not allow a base to be named for a living person and the mayor, said the Caller, "is certainly a live one." Hulen named it Camp Scurry after Gen. Thomas Scurry, former commander of the Texas Brigade.

Maj. Gen. Frederick Funston, commander of the Army's Southern Department, visited Corpus Christi. After lunch with Roy Miller, Funston and aides were taken for a swim at North Beach. A regiment of jellyfish drove them out of the water.

At Miller's request, troops were put to work spreading shell on UpRiver Road, as far as Calallen. It was called Shell Road for a long time. Mules bought from King Ranch were used to pack heavy machine guns. The mules stampeded and ran into the heavy mesquite beyond the camp. For days, soldiers tramped through the brush chasing down the mules and retrieving machine guns.

Second Texas fielded a football team made up of former college players, mostly from the University of Texas. They built a practice field at Santa Fe and Booty. The team trounced the country's best military teams, beating them by lopsided scores. They never came close to losing. They ran up 432 points while allowing their opposition 6. That one score was explained by Warren "Rip" Collins: "The game was played in a blizzard and they scored against us when we put the fourth string in." A game against the New York Infantry was also explained: Players on the New York team, made

*Four soldiers stationed at Camp Scurry in 1916 included (left to right) Thomas Hirsch, an unknown soldier, Clarence McCandless and Private Stevens. Some 3,500 Texas National Guardsmen were moved from the Rio Grande Valley to Corpus Christi when tensions along the U.S.-Mexico border eased. The camp later trained soldiers for trench warfare in France.*

up of all-Americans from Princeton and Syracuse, were overheard to say they planned to go easy on the Texans. Second Texas whipped them 102 to 0.

After almost a year, with the border quiet, Camp Scurry was ordered closed and the Second and Third Regiments were demobilized in March 1917. Remaining soldiers were dismantling the camp when new orders stopped the work.

On April 6, 1917, the U.S. entered the war in Europe. The Second and Third Infantry Regiments were called back into service and sent to Camp Travis. Camp Scurry was reactivated as a training base for the Fifth Engineers and the Fourth Field Artillery.

Dermot Meehan, a New Yorker stationed at Scurry with the Fourth Field Artillery, once reminisced about life in the camp. "I remember a bunch of us bought a boat and rented a net. We would drag it around the bay and catch shrimp, then have a shrimp feast. Everybody would donate a nickel for catsup and we'd eat shrimp till

*King Ranch mules were used to haul supplies and munitions at Camp Scurry.*

we were sick. There were lots of pretty girls and there was always a dance somewhere. Whenever you wanted one, there would be one."

Soldiers trained at Scurry fought in many of the major battles in the last year of the war. Besides those killed in action, others died in the Spanish flu epidemic that swept the country. When the Armistice was signed on Nov. 11, 1918, as someone wrote, "a great quiet descended upon the Earth."

At war's end, the last unit stationed at Camp Scurry was a cavalry regiment. A story was told that a soldier pointedly ignored a captain who was walking by. "How long have you been in the army?" the captain asked. "Eighteen months," said the soldier, rather insolently. "Haven't you been taught to salute an officer?" And the soldier was ready with his answer, "Aw, I stopped that stuff when the Armistice was signed." There was no longer a need for Camp Scurry and by 1919 it was closed for good.

*—April 9, 2014*

# The Great Western

Sarah Bourjett, the Great Western, got her nickname in Corpus Christi before she became famous in the Mexican War.

She was born in Missouri or Tennessee about 1813, though details of her early life are vague. Her first husband enlisted in the 7th Infantry at Jefferson Barracks, Mo., and when Zachary Taylor's army was concentrated in Corpus Christi in 1845, Sarah Bourjett was with it.

She was a tall woman, at 6-foot-3, with red hair and blue eyes. She got her nickname when she got off the boat at Corpus Christi and an awestruck soldier said she reminded him of the Great Western, the biggest steamship of the day. "Look at the size of her," he said, "she's as big as the Great Western."

So Sarah Bourjett became the Great Western.

Officially, she was a laundress. In the army, each company was authorized to hire four women to wash and mend the clothes of the soldiers. They were paid with wages deducted from the soldiers' pay. Unofficially, she was a camp follower who provided other services for the men, operating under the official sanction of being a laundress married to a sergeant.

Capt. Daniel P. Whiting of the 7th Infantry wrote in his memoirs that he had a mess composed of the officers of his company which was conducted by the wife of one of his sergeants. "The Great Western, she was called from being a gigantic woman of great strength and hardihood, who afterwards became famous in connection with the service," Whiting wrote. "I was one day attracted by hearing a noise in the campground and looking out saw her pick up a man who had offended her and, as if he were a child, set him down in her wash tub."

It is likely, I think, that the mess she conducted for Whiting and fellow officers was called, after her nickname, the Great Western.

An advertisement in the Corpus Christi Gazette said the Great Western Eating Saloon would serve meals to bachelors at any time day or night, with oysters the house specialty. It was described as a sort of restaurant.

When the army departed for the Rio Grande in March 1846, Sarah's husband was sent by sea to Port Isabel; he may have been ill. By strict orders issued by Zachary Taylor, camp followers could not tag along, but Sarah, as a laundress, was allowed to go. She rode in a cart pulled by mules and filled with provisions. She continued to cook and provide a mess for Whiting and officers of the 7th.

On March 20, at the Arroyo Colorado, they ran into a squadron of Mexican cavalry who taunted them from across the stream. The Great Western left her wagon and shouted that if someone would give her a pair of tongs (meaning pants) that she would wade the river "and whip any scoundrel who dares to show himself."

During the bombardment of Fort Texas (later renamed Fort Brown) Sarah helped to tend the wounded. Some accounts say she was in the thick of the fighting and a fragment of a shell ripped a hole in her bonnet. The first-hand account by Daniel Whiting is probably more accurate. "We had our merriment," Whiting wrote. "Mrs. Bourjett, the Great Western, abandoned our mess when the firing began and resorted with the other women and noncombatants to a shelter."

Whatever the true story, her fame spread. She became the talk of the army and was widely known as the heroine of Fort Brown. When the army reached Monterrey, Sarah went with it and opened a place called the American House, which was described as a "sort of hotel." When the army moved on to Saltillo she opened a second American House there. A painting by Samuel Chamberlain gives us the only known likeness of the Great Western. It shows her in the Saltillo establishment.

During the battle of Buena Vista, it was said that a soldier ran into Sarah's place in a panic and yelled that Taylor's army was all cut to pieces and Mexican troops were headed their way. The Great Western, outraged, cuffed the unfortunate soldier, sending him sprawling, saying, "You son of a bitch, there ain't Mexicans enough in Mexico to whip old Taylor. You spread that rumor and I'll beat you to death."

One of her favorite soldiers, Capt. George Lincoln, who first enlisted her as a laundress at Jefferson Barracks, was killed at the

*Samuel Chamberlain depicted Sarah Bourjett, the Great Western, in her Saltillo establishment. She was holding a pistol but it's unclear for what purpose. The San Jacinto Museum of History Paintings in San Antonio has a large collection of Chamberlain's paintings of the Mexican War.*

battle of Buena Vista. She laid out his body for burial and removed his ring and a lock of hair to send his parents.

After the war, elements of the U.S. Army were sent to take possession of California. The Great Western packed up and was ready to leave with the army. An officer described what happened: "She rode up to Major Buckner and asked permission to go with us. He informed her that if she would marry one of the dragoons, and be mustered in as a laundress, she could go. Her ladyship gave the military salute and then, riding along the front of the line, said, 'Who wants a wife with $15,000 and the biggest leg in Mexico? Come, don't all speak at once — who's the lucky man?' "

A man named Davis accepted the offer, wrote Sam Chamberlain in "My Confessions," even though the Great Western already had two husbands, one in Harney's Dragoons and another one in the 7th Infantry. The marriage lasted until they reached El Paso. The Great Western opened a new place called the Central Hotel, which catered to 49ers on their way to California. Texas Ranger Rip Ford ran into her here and later wrote that "she could whip any man, fair fight or foul, and could shoot a pistol better than anyone in West Texas."

She moved on to Fort Yuma, Ariz., where she died from the bite of a tarantula on Dec. 23, 1866. She was 53. She was buried with full military honors at Fort Yuma. Her last husband was Albert J. Bowman so the name on her tombstone was Sarah Bowman. The Army in 1890 exhumed the bodies at Fort Yuma and moved them to the presidio at San Francisco, which is now the last resting place of the heroine of Fort Brown and the most famous woman of the Mexican War, the Great Western.

*—April 16, 2014*

# Cutting the Herd

Years ago I thought about writing a novel based on a trail drive. I started preparing for the work by studying the distinctive voice of the trail hand, writing down the colorful expressions of cowboys. About that time, I ran across Ramon Adams' lexicon of cowboy phrases called "Western Words." Adams' book had many of the phrases I had in my index box and there were many more.

Trail-driving cowboys had a wry way of defining the world to fit their own experience. Walter Prescott Webb wrote that cowboy language took on the character of the land, close to primal elements. It was also a defining trait. Their colorful expressions, their parody of moral codes, their wit and self-deprecatory humor, set them apart from other westerners.

Everything about the cowboy's existence involved cattle and horses so he drew from that source and his speech reflected that reality. I have read that their originality was due to the solitude, the nearness of the stars and the vastness of the open country.

Since the tools of their trade originated with the vaqueros, their prototype, it is natural that many cowboy expressions were borrowed from them. The lariat came from la reata, chaps from chaparejos, hoosegow from juzgado, and wrangler from caballerango — "he who cares for horses."

As I thumbed through my index file and tried to figure out a narrative structure for this material, nothing suggested itself except the old time-honored list, so here are a selected few sayings from hundreds of cowboy words and phrases that I cobbled together for a novel that was never written.

Air tights — canned goods, like peaches.

Arbuckle — a greenhorn, from green stamps that came with Arbuckle's coffee; a greenhorn was a mail-order cowboy, useful as a three-legged horse.

Angry — someone in a fit of temper was all horns and rattles; someone on the prod.

Bath — washing out the canyon.

Benediction — may you graze with the lead cattle.

Big Sugar — owner of a ranch, a wealthy cattleman, also called presidente or buggy boss.

Breaking a horse — to stay on a bucking horse was to waltz with the lady. Horse-breaking was snapping broncs. To reach for the apple was to grab at the saddle horn, also called squeezing the biscuit. A difficult horse to ride had a belly full of bedsprings. To stay in the saddle was to hug rawhide and to get thrown was to kiss the ground.

Brush thumper — cow hand in the brush country of South Texas.

Clumsy socially — always saddling the wrong horse.

Cold-footed — to act cowardly.

Cook — pot rustler, biscuit shooter, belly cheater, dough-puncher, and coosie.

Confusion — to get your spurs tangled up; also clouding the trail.

Cow chips — compressed hay or prairie pancakes.

Cream gravy — something as good as cream gravy.

Curly wolf — a tough character, a dangerous man.

Cutting the herd — riding through a herd to search for stolen animals.

Dependable sidekick — someone good to ride the river with; a friend chewed tobacco from the same plug.

Die-up — wholesale death of cattle during a drought or blizzard.

Down to the blanket — broke, no dinero.

Dust storm — Oklahoma rain.

Escaping jail — leg bail or rolling one's tail.

Experience — he had wrinkles on his horns, or was bone-seasoned.

Fired — get your saddle or roll your bed.

Fish — an oilskin slicker.

Flexible — adept at all tasks, ready to ride any horse.

Gate — take advantage of an opportunity when the gate's still open.

Greasy sack outfit — a small operation, a cattle drive without a chuck wagon.

Hanging — neck-tie social. A hanged man died with throat trouble or hemp fever.

*Cowboys gathered around a chuck wagon. In cowboy parlance, a cattle drive without a chuck wagon was called a greasy sack outfit. From the Library of Congress.*

Horns sawed off — to tame someone, take the fight out of him.

Hungry — slim at the equator.

Impossible task — to bark at a knot.

Job — each hand has to do his own work; every bull has to carry his own tail.

Kick up a dust — to visit a saloon.

Lazy cowhand — good at covering his back with his belly; someone who was always sitting around the coffee pot.

Leather — those of like mind were cut from the same leather.

Lock horns — to fight.

Marriage — double harness or share the blanket.

Muddy waterhole — you had to chew before you could drink.

On the dodge — avoiding John Law, lighting a shuck, heading for the setting sun, out in the brush, leaving Cheyenne, or riding a tired horse out of Texas.

Opinionated — has a saddle to fit any horse.

Op'ra house — top rail of a corral during bronc-busting; showing off was playing to the gallery.

Outlaw — a mean horse.

Pancake — English-style saddle.

Playing sick — riding the bed-wagon; resting in the shade of the wagon.

Poor — as skimmed milk.

Pretty — as yard flowers.

Putting on airs — riding a high horse.

Riding hard — Burn the breeze or rattle the hocks.

Riding into his dust — following someone's lead.

Roll a cigarette — fill the blanket.

Rope a steer — Put a string on it.

Runt — an acorn calf.

Rustler — a brand artist who packed a long rope.

Saddle is slipping — losing one's touch.

Segundo — second in command.

Sheep — a herd of underwear.

Shut up — hobble the mouth; shut the big bazoo.

Six gun — black-eyed Susan, one-eyed scribe, lead-chucker, smoke wagon, cutter.

Six-gun unloaded — no beans in the wheel.

Slipped his hobbles — a cheating husband, also off the reservation.

Succeed — to get the bacon.

Take the rag off the bush — if that doesn't beat all.

Tense situation — hair in the butter.

Trouble — hell with the hide off.

Ugly — as a rat-tailed horse.

Victim of a saloon shootout — got sawdust in his beard; came down with lead poisoning. A man killed in a gunfight was put to bed or had his lamp blown out. A shootout was a powder-burning contest.

Wassup — an outlaw horse.

Wearing good clothes — rigged out for Sunday.

Whisky — Kill-Me-Quick, Who-Hit-John, Liza Jane or John Barleycorn, bug juice, red-eye or red ink or red disturbance.

Whisky drinking — bending an elbow, painting the tonsils, listening to the hoot owl, getting roistered-up.

Wind up — as in let's wind this up and head for home.

*—April 23, 2014*

72

# Rosita and Meansville

Once promising towns in the Nueces Valley disappeared over time. In their heyday, some were large thriving mercantile centers while others were little more than a store or two. Some are well-known while others are ghostly footnotes. We start near the mouth of the Nueces River and work our way up the Nueces Valley.

Across Nueces Bay was Rosita. How it got its name is lost, but Corpus Christi has always known the area as White Point. How it came to be called White Point is also uncertain. Some believe it was named for the White brothers who moved there in 1856 while others say it was named for the white clay bluff visible across the bay.

In 1857, Frank and Edward White hired a young man to drive cattle from their ranch in east Texas to their new ranch on Nueces Bay. The young man was Darius Cyriaque Rachal, who liked the area and stayed. During the Civil War, he served in Hood's Brigade. After the war, he returned to begin his own ranch, with his new wife Julia Bryan.

Two years later, a yellow fever outbreak hit Corpus Christi and crossed over to White Point. Frank and Edward White and many in their families died. Rachal ripped off boards from his house being built to make coffins.

By 1875, Rachal was sending huge herds up the trail to Kansas. His ranch stretched from White Point to Odem. In 1884, he and a partner bought the 31,000 acre Rabb ranch in Nueces County, which was later sold to Robert Driscoll.

A dance in January 1893 at the Rachal home was an event to remember. Falvella's band played until it played out and another band was brought in. The party that began on Friday lasted until late Sunday. The newspaper said, "They danced all night and danced all day and then danced some more. It was the out-dancingest dance ever held."

*The Rachal ranch house at White Point was built in 1867. A second story was added in 1883. The house faced east with a view of Nueces Bay and Corpus Christi Bay. It was demolished in 1956.*

Keith Guthrie's "History of San Patricio County" includes the story of when Rachal petitioned for a post office and suggested the name of White Point. That name was rejected, so he suggested Rachal, which was also rejected. Then he suggested the old name of Rosita, which was accepted. Rachal died at age 77 in 1918. He was buried in the Rachal family cemetery.

In the 1919 storm, bodies of the dead and half-dead survivors were swept across Nueces Bay and washed up at White Point/Rosita. On Monday after the storm, people on the Rachal ranch rescued survivors and buried the dead in mass graves. In all, 75 survivors and 108 bodies were dumped ashore at White Point.

Guthrie said the White Point/Rosita area had several stores over the years, including a saloon, and the one-room Rosita school operated from 1914 until the 1920s. The Rosita post office lasted from 1892 to 1914.

\* \* \*

Not far inland from Rosita was another community that disappeared — Meansville. It was three miles southeast of Odem, founded by Col. William M. Means before the Civil War. Meansville consisted of a general store run by a Mr. Cherry and a two-story building that was a general-purpose church and school.

William B. Means, an older son of the founder of the community, was elected sheriff of San Patricio County in 1862. He was responsible for the arrest and conviction of Chipita Rodriguez. The body of horse trader John Savage was found in the Aransas River. His head had been split with an ax. Chipita's place was an overnight way station near the San Patricio Road where travelers could get a meal and sleep on the porch. Savage stayed at Chipita's on the night of Aug. 23, 1863 before his body was found in the river.

When Sheriff Means found bloodstains on Chipita's porch, she and her handyman were charged with murder. Means, who investigated the case, served on the grand jury that indicted her. People were rounded up to serve on the trial jury. Four members of the jury had been indicted for felonies, the jury foreman was a friend of the sheriff, and Chipita would make no statements in her own defense.

The trial lasted one morning. The jury brought back a guilty verdict by noon, with a plea for leniency, which was rejected, and Chipita was sentenced to be hanged. Some, doubting her guilt, urged the sheriff not to carry out the sentence. On the day of the hanging, he was out of the county. She was hanged at San Patricio on Friday, Nov. 13, 1863 from a mesquite tree by the Nueces River.

The beginning of the end for Meansville started on Jan. 30, 1876 when three of Means' six sons shot up a dance at Papalote. San Patricio County Sheriff Ed Garner gathered a posse to arrest the troublemakers.

There was bad blood between Garner and Means over the refusal of Means to have his cattle dipped for ticks, as agreed to by all the ranchers. When Means refused, Sheriff Ed Garner hired cowboys to round up Means' cattle and have them dipped. Means was billed $35 for expenses, which he refused to pay.

After the Papalote dance trouble, the posse rode up to Means' place and Garner ordered the hell-raisers to come out. Instead, Col. Means came out in a white nightshirt carrying a rifle and Garner warned him — "I wouldn't do that if I were you." Shots were fired and Means was killed by a shotgun. The family insisted that the old man had buckshot even in the soles of his feet.

Some time later, Garner was killed as he came out of the Meansville church. The sniper who laid in wait was believed to be John Means, a crack shot, but younger brother Alley took the rap for

*Col. William M. Means, the founder of Meansville, was the first victim in what was called the Garner-Means feud.*

it. After Garner was killed, the Means clan was invited to leave. One day in 1879, the family departed in 23 covered wagons, which brought an end to the feud and also brought an end to Meansville. The town withered away after that. The graveyard where Col. Means and Ed Garner are buried is the only hint that there was a settlement there.

*—May 7, 2014*

## Nuecestown and Sharpsburg

Of the once promising settlements of the Nueces Valley, the best-known was Nuecestown near the mouth of the river. Long before it was called Nuecestown, and for a long time afterwards, it was called The Motts for a grove of trees growing along the river. The town was founded in 1852 by Henry Kinney, who also founded Corpus Christi. Nuecetown was 12 miles upriver from Corpus Christi.

In the 1850s, Kinney sought to sell some of his 300,000 acres and sent agents to England to attract settlers. They distributed 20,000 handbills labeled Nueces Valley Land & Emigration. The handbills praised the opportunities in the valley. To each immigrant, Kinney offered 100 acres of land at roughly one dollar an acre. With the purchase of 100 acres, an immigrant would receive a yoke of oxen, a horse, 10 cows, and a lot in Nuecestown. Kinney's efforts produced a flood of immigrants who settled in Corpus Christi and Nuecestown.

Many were disappointed. They had staked all on glowing promises that described the land as rich farmland — "the fairest region of America" — but the land was covered with mesquite brush, had never known a plow, and even if they had planted crops on it there was no market within reach. But Kinney's immigrants adapted to a new life. These were the early settlers of Nuecestown.

When Corpus Christi was threatened by federal ships during the Civil War people evacuated to Nuecestown or, as they called it, The Motts.

The town is famous for a bandit raid that occurred in the last week of March 1875. The bandits arrived on Thursday, March 25, and on Good Friday, they stole horses at two ranch houses above Corpus Christi and killed an old man at Frank's store. They captured travelers encountered on the road and forced their captives to run as they rode toward Nuecestown.

At his store in Nuecestown, Thomas Noakes saw the bandits ride up. He ran to get his Winchester and, as a bandit raised a pistol to shoot a customer in his store, Noakes shot the bandit in the chest. Noakes' wife ran from the store with their children while Noakes hid under the store. When the bandits set the store on fire, the customer made a run for it and was shot. As the fire spread, Noakes left his hiding place and had his rifle ready to fire when Mrs. Noakes yelled that the bandits were gone. As the store burned, a posse arrived from Corpus Christi.

The bandits camped in the brush with their captives. As the posse rode up, shots were fired and a member of the posse, a man named Swank, fell dead. The bandits made their escape, leaving the captives behind. The bandit shot by Noakes was brought into Corpus Christi and hanged on Leopard Street. His body was left hanging until Easter Sunday. The Nuecestown Raid was sometimes called the Noakes Raid.

Noakes rebuilt his store a mile to the west, at a point where the river came closest to what is now UpRiver Road, and the town moved with him. Other stores were Bitterman's, Frank's, and McGregor's. Martin Culver had a meat-packing plant there. The town had a stagecoach inn, a cotton gin, a blacksmith shop, and the second largest school in the county.

Nuecestown was still thriving in the 1880s and 1890s until the St. Louis, Brownsville and Mexico Railroad passed it by in 1905. Rancher Calvin J. Allen gave land to the railroad for right of way three miles from Nuecestown. As a result, the town of Calallen grew up around the depot and the old settlement of Nuecestown, Henry Kinney's second town, withered away. The school and post office were closed.

* * *

Not far from Nuecestown was Sharpsburg, on a slight rise about a mile north of the Nueces River. It was founded by Sidney Gail Borden of the famous Borden family.

John P. Borden, the younger brother of Gail Borden Jr., the inventor of condensed milk, married Mary Susan Hatch of Ingleside and moved to the area in 1855. He started a ranch and the couple had four daughters and one son. The son, Sidney Gail Borden, fought in the Civil War and when he returned he bought land and

*Sidney Gail Borden, founder of Sharpsburg, led a posse after the Nuecestown Raid.*

*The Borden home at Sharpsburg in 1908.*

opened a store on what had been a sheep ranch owned by a man named Sharp.

That marked the beginning of Sharpsburg. It was named for the sheep rancher, but it was Borden's town. As it grew, Sharpsburg gained a gristmill, blacksmith shop, cotton gin, school, post office and a population of about 300. It was a thriving town.

Borden owned a ferry (where I-37 crosses the river near Labonte Park). Borden's business partner was D. C. Rachal, rancher at the White Point/Rosita area. Borden planted grapes and sold wine labeled "Sharpsburg's Best" and "Rachal's Choice." It was said that few visitors to Sharpsburg left without carrying away a prized bottle of wine. These were sold from Corpus Christi to San Antonio.

The river was navigable then. Borden and Rachal owned a flat-bottomed schooner named Nueces Valley which carried cotton and wool down the river and brought back commercial goods for Borden's store. Capt. Andrew Anderson recalled that he often sailed his schooner "Flour Bluff" up the river to Sharpsburg.

After Borden was elected justice of the peace in 1872, he was called Judge Borden. In the Nuecestown Raid, he was one of several people captured by the bandits and held captive until the bandits escaped. Once freed, Borden raised a posse at Sharpsburg and tracked the bandits to Laredo, where the raiders crossed the river to safety. "Boys," he said, "I've brought you on a wild-goose chase. We better head for home."

Borden built a cotton gin at Sharpsburg and subdivided ranch land into farm tracts. He was an early promoter of converting grazing land into cotton acreage. He was elected county judge, county surveyor, and appointed postmaster at Sharpsburg. He died in Sharpsburg on Jan. 31, 1908 and was buried in Corpus Christi. Today, there is nothing to mark the site of Borden's once prosperous river town of Sharpsburg.

*—May 14, 2014*

# Santa Margarita and San Patricio

A gravel bottom made an excellent ford on the Nueces River twenty miles up river from Corpus Christi. It was an ancient place to ford the Nueces that dated back to Spanish and Indian times. This was at Santa Margarita, across the river and just south and west of San Patricio.

For ages, traffic from Mexico crossed the river at Santa Margarita. The Atascosita Road and Camino Real crossed at this place and travelers going to the missions passed by Santa Margarita. In the 1850s, Samuel Reed Miller built a ferry and during the Civil War wagons hauling cotton to the border along the Cotton Road crossed at Santa Margarita.

It was a busy place. John Warren Hunter, a young man hauling cotton to Brownsville, said on the east side of the river there was a congestion of cotton trains waiting for the river to become fordable. The wagons were too heavy for the ferry. On the opposite bank were camped trains returning from the Rio Grande laden with war supplies and merchandise. It was sundown when they rode into this "vast encampment with its bright fires and incessant din of ox and horse bells and shouts of herdsmen."

After Corpus Christi was bombarded by Union warships in August 1862, the town's newspaper, The Ranchero, and Nueces County government were moved to Santa Margarita, safely distant from Union warships.

After the war, Santa Margarita was no longer an important place, though it remained one of the principal stopping places on the San Antonio and Brownsville stagecoach line. Nothing is left of Santa Margarita today. Even the name has been changed. That area is known as the Bluntzer community. There is a bridge where Samuel Reed Miller's ferry operated and county road 666 follows the old Camino Real and crosses the river at this point.

Just across and a bit upriver from Santa Margarita is one of the oldest and most important settlements of South Texas, a town with many lives.

In 1828, James McGloin and John McMullen, Irish merchants in Matamoros, obtained a contract from the Mexican government to bring Irish Catholic settlers to South Texas. For every 100 families that settled, the two would receive 23,000 acres.

The first immigrants arrived at El Copano and Matagorda Bay in 1829. They moved inland and huddled around the old mission of Refugio. McGloin went to pick a spot for the settlement and chose a site near where the Camino Real crossed the Nueces. It was high level land covered with live oaks.

They built a log church and named it St. Patrick's. They built picket houses with thatched roofs and made plaster and whitewashed the houses to resemble their old homes in Ireland. They called the settlement Villa de San Patricio de Hibernia. Then, in the fall of 1835, events began that led to the Texas Revolution.

Two miles west of San Patricio was a crude mud-walled fort named Fort Lipantitlán. One Texan, John J. Linn, described it as looking more like a hog pen than a fort. On Nov. 5, 1835 a force of Mexican militiamen, some from San Patricio, surrendered to 40 Texans under the command of Capt. Ira Westover. Not a shot was fired. Westover's men captured two four-pounder cannons, eight escopetas (old Spanish guns) and several pounds of gunpowder.

Next day, as the Texans were retiring across the river, scouts told Westover that a Mexican force of 80 men was approaching. There was a cold rain as Westover deployed his men. The Mexican soldiers charged and were repulsed with musket fire and shots from two cannons captured at Lipantitlán. After the Mexicans retreated, the Texans threw the cannons into the river.

There was freezing rain at San Patricio on Feb. 27, 1836. A force of 450 Mexican soldiers under the personal command of Gen. José Urrea arrived after making a forced march of 20 miles in freezing rain.

A Texas unit under Col. Francis W. Johnson was sheltering in the town. Urrea's scouts told him that Johnson had split his force of 60 men and that half were waiting out the bad weather in the town, that they posted no sentries. Urrea's troops surrounded houses where the

*A two-story house built by Robert Dougherty at Round Lake near San Patricio housed the St. Paul Academy, a school for boys from 1876 to 1881. The house still stands.*

Texans were quartered. The Texans began firing and, during the confusion, Francis Johnson and five of his men slipped out a back door and escaped. The remaining Texans shot at Urrea's men until their house was set afire. They surrendered and were sent to Matamoros as prisoners.

After the battle, the town was deserted as residents fled east to escape the Mexican army. San Patricio remained deserted for a decade. When Zachary Taylor's army concentrated at Corpus Christi in 1845, in preparation for the Mexican War, he stationed a company of dragoons at San Patricio. With this added protection, residents of the town began to return to reclaim their homes and property.

A post office was established in 1848, Texas Rangers under the command of Capt. J. S. Sutton were headquartered in the town, and San Patricio was incorporated in 1853. During the Civil War, San Patricio profited from traffic on the Cotton Road that crossed the river at Santa Margarita two miles away.

Near San Patricio Robert Dougherty built a two-story house for his family and a school for boys, St. Paul's Academy on Round Lake, which was open from 1876 to 1881.

In the 1880s, in its peak years, San Patricio had several churches, schools, a gristmill and a population of about 400. The decline began after Sinton replaced San Patricio as the county seat in 1894 and the railroads passed it by. The post office was closed in 1930.

What is left of San Patricio holds its annual rattlesnake races on St. Patrick's Day. A replica of the old courthouse of 1872, which burned in 1889, was built in 1985 by the San Patricio Restoration Society. I don't know what the population is today, but what remains of this historic old town is a pale reflection of the time when it was a cultural center of the Irish immigrants and the county seat of San Patricio County, the grandfather of Texas counties which, before statehood, stretched all the way to the Rio Grande.

*—May 21, 2014*

# Lagarto and Gussettville

Of the towns in the Nueces River Valley that flourished and declined, none were more celebrated than Lagarto, which at its peak was the second largest town between Corpus Christi and San Antonio. It was one of the few towns around with its own college, though "college" is a misnomer.

Lagarto was founded four miles from the Nueces River before the Civil War. The town was laid out by a surveyor hired by John Ramey, a Kentucky saddle-tree maker at Fort Merrill. Shortly after the war, William Wrather, a wool merchant in Corpus Christi, moved to Lagarto and opened a store. The place was first called Roughtown then Lagarto, Spanish for alligators in Lagarto Creek.

Lagarto was on the main stage route between Corpus Christi and San Antonio. It was busy enough to support two hotels — the Peters Hotel and the Clark Hotel — two livery stables, two blacksmith shops, a cotton gin and several stores. It had a newspaper, The Echo, then the Informer, which became the Lagarto Times.

One of the unusual things about Lagarto was its so-called college. In 1884, the people of Lagarto issued stock certificates and raised $6,000 to build a two-story structure for the college.

Dr. Alfred G. Heaney, who bought the Valley Ranch and moved to Lagarto from Thomaston, Conn., was president of the college. Heaney later moved to Corpus Christi to practice medicine.

One of the instructors at the college was Ella Jane Byler, who married Richard Dobie and became the mother of the J. Frank Dobie, the famous Texas author. Ruth Dodson, who attended Lagarto College when she was nine years old, said she once asked Mrs. Dobie about the college's status as an institution of higher learning. "She said there was not a pupil in the school who would have been classed beyond the eighth grade." The college closed in 1892.

Dr. Alfred G. Heaney was the president of Lagarto College.

*The Lagarto Bridge built in 1897 spanned the Nueces between Lagarto and Mathis. It was at the site where Miller's ferry operated. When the Wesley Seale Dam was built in 1958, the bridge was cut from its supports and dropped into the channel of the river. It is now at the bottom of Lake Corpus Christi.*

When the San Antonio & Aransas Pass Railroad was building its line to Corpus Christi, ranchers were asked to give or sell land for the railroad right of way. Rancher S. G. Miller secured right of way from Beeville to Lagarto except for one holdout who refused to allow the tracks to cross his ranch. Mrs. Miller in "Sixty Years in the Nueces Valley" wrote that her husband thought the holdout would eventually relent so the land was surveyed for the tracks.

"But when the surveying party reached the land in question," Mrs. Miller wrote, "the owner stopped them. No persuasion, no offer of money, would do any good." Ten miles from Lagarto, Thomas Henry Mathis gave the railroad land for an alternate route, which marked the beginning of the town of Mathis and the end of Lagarto.

A Lagarto storeowner, H. B. Newberry, "tore down his house and moved it piece by piece to Mathis where he rebuilt it. Even a bullet hole above the kitchen door was in the same spot," quoted in Hattie Mae Hinnant New's "Lagarto: A Collection of Memories."

The population of Lagarto dropped steadily and by the 1930s the town consisted of a post office, store and school. By 1940, all three were closed. The impoundment of Lake Corpus Christi in 1959 led to a new residential development called Lagarto, which has little connection to the older town whose ghostly remains are hidden deep in the brush.

Northwest of Lagarto along Ramireña Creek was the old community of Ramireña. It got its name from the Ramirez family who built a fortified ranch house on the south bank of Ramireña Creek, called Fort Ramirez, between 1790 and 1802. After an Indian attack in 1812, the Ramirez family fled back to Camargo.

J. Frank Dobie wrote that the inhabitants of Lagarto were worldly, urbane, and cosmopolitan compared to those of Ramireña. "Eight miles west of our ranch an Englishman named Hughes kept a store with a post office in the back end, the contents of which would fill a fair-sized dry-goods box," Dobie wrote. "This was Ramireña. Everybody called it La Posta, for it had been a stage stand where horses were changed." Besides Hughes' store, Ramireña had a Methodist church and for a short time a school. The post office closed in 1922.

* * *

One of the oldest settlements in what became Live Oak County was Gussettville, 50 miles from Corpus Christi. It was originally called Fox Nation because it was settled by Irish immigrants in the McGloin-McMullen colony named Fox.

The community on the east bank of the Nueces River began to grow when Fort Merrill was built in 1850 above Barlow's Ferry, offering protection to travelers and settlers in the area.

The name of the community was changed from Fox Nation to Gussettville after Norwick Gussett moved in and opened a store. Gussett had been with Taylor's army at Corpus Christi in 1845 as an army freighter. After the Mexican War, in which he was wounded, Gussett returned to South Texas and opened a general merchandise store at Fox Nation. The name was then changed to Gussettville.

When the Texas Legislature created Live Oak County in 1856, carving it out of San Patricio County, Gussett tried to get Gussettville chosen as the county seat, but the new town of Oakville was selected. Two years later, in 1858, Gussettville got the third post office established in Live Oak County.

After his wife Harriet died in 1863, Norwick Gussett sold his store at Gussettville and moved to Corpus Christi where he married Margaret Evans and eventually became the town's wealthiest wool merchant and banker.

Gussettville in 1884 included a church, a school, a general store, and 30 residents. The town lost its post office in 1886 and, after being bypassed by the San Antonio, Uvalde and Gulf Railroad began to fade away. All that remains of Gussettville is St. Joseph's Catholic Church and the old Gussettville Cemetery on its grounds.

Gussettville, like Lagarto, San Patricio, Santa Margarita, Sharpsburg and Nuecestown were river towns and the river was liquid history where people settled, where things happened, where history was made. They disappeared when the railroads passed them by, when competing towns took their trade, or when they simply dwindled away with the passage of time and change in fortune.

*—May 28, 2014*

# The Lost Waterfront

Two powerful Gulf storms, one in 1916 and the more deadly one in 1919, wrecked Corpus Christi's waterfront. The Ladies Pavilion, Loyd's Pavilion and Pleasure Pier, the Natatorium, and the Pavilion Hotel, all popular bayfront structures, were destroyed by the storms.

Corpus Christi was still recovering from the storms when the city built the Pleasure Pier off the foot of Peoples Street. It was built on the site once occupied by Ohler's Wharf, where John Kittredge, commander of the Union blockading fleet, demanded Corpus Christi's surrender in August 1862. When Confederate authorities rejected his demands, Kittredge's warships bombarded the town.

In 1922, the 1,000 foot Pleasure Pier was built at a cost of $8,200, which was money well spent. The pier was one of the first places visited by tourists who wanted to get out over the water and watch the fishing boats and sailboats on the bay. Downtown workers liked to stroll on the pier at noon and guests at the Nueces Hotel would take an evening promenade for a breath of air, with the stars reflected in the waters of the bay.

The Pleasure Pier, despite being near the commercial center of the city, offered relief from the noise and traffic of a growing city and provided a calm, breezy place on the water, with waves lapping at the pier and sailboats gliding in the summer haze. It was a place to watch the passing cavalcade, a place for solace and reflection.

The Japonica docked at the Pleasure Pier, as did the yacht Bettye Lou and a covey of small boats nuzzling the T-head at the pier.

Two years after the pier was opened, in 1924, two civic club leaders, Mrs. G. R. Scott and Mrs. F. A. Tompkins, petitioned the City Council to condemn and demolish two unsightly fishermen's shacks at the entrance of the Pleasure Pier. They said if the city would tear down the shacks, the Federation of Women's Clubs would plant palm trees there. The city declined.

*The Pleasure Pier was built in 1922 from the end of Peoples Street. The pier was a favorite attraction of fishermen, tourists, and downtown workers out for a stroll. Photo from John Fred'k "Doc" McGregor photographic collection of the Corpus Christi Museum of Science and History.*

*The waterfront in 1932 shows the Pleasure Pier, Pier Cafe and the Nueces Hotel's three palms, which it called Tres Palmas. Photo by Doc McGregor.*

Two years later, in 1926, John Govatos opened the Pier Cafe in one of the shacks on the north side of the pier. The Pier Cafe became the most popular restaurant in town. It was enlarged in 1929 and extended 20 feet out over the waters of the bay. It was famous for its family-sized seafood platter, which cost $1, and for its 50-cent fish lunches. Most of the town's 22,000 people got around to eating at the Pier Cafe — "Famous for Seafood Dinners and Plenty of Sea Breezes." The Pier Café was later moved into a fancy new white building on the south side of the pier.

In 1929, when the Plaza Hotel was being built on the bluff, three stately palm trees were rescued and moved to the grounds of the Nueces Hotel, east of Water Street next to the Pleasure Pier. These palms became the emblem of the hotel, used on menu cards, stationery and chair covers. The hotel called them Tres Palmas.

South of the Pleasure Pier, the Municipal Wharf dominated the waterfront. It was built in 1914 at a cost of $50,000 on a rectangular landfill off Cooper's Alley. The Municipal Wharf was the town's primary shipping wharf before the port was opened in 1926. The Municipal Wharf included the San Antonio Machine & Supply Company warehouses, some fish houses, and shacks of retired fishermen and squatters. The 40&8 Arena, with an open-air venue behind it, hosted boxing matches and sports events.

To the north of the Pleasure Pier was the bayfront dock of the Princess Louise Hotel on Water Street, whose east curb was often sprayed by the waves at high tide. Sailboats could practically tie up at the front door of the Princess Louise.

The Pleasure Pier, the Pier Cafe, the famous three palms, the Municipal Wharf and the bayfront facilities of the Princess Louise would shortly become the lost waterfront. The storm this time was one of progress.

Corpus Christi had long dreamed of building a seawall. The Caller in an article on Dec. 22, 1890 speculated on how the city of the future might look and predicted building a seawall 500 feet out from the shoreline, filling up behind the wall and utilizing the ground acquired for commercial development. It was a bold plan ahead of its time.

In 1909, County Judge Walter Timon pushed a seawall plan but he couldn't get the city interested. After the storms of 1916 and 1919, Timon was asked to inspect seawalls along the Atlantic Coast, from Florida to Canada. When he returned, he drafted the Timon plan for the bayfront.

Timon's plan called for the state to give Corpus Christi the state's share of ad valorem (property) taxes from seven South Texas counties for 15 years to pay for the project. This was approved by Legislature and extended twice, each time by 10 years. Locally, however, the Timon plan was shelved.

*Aerial view of the Municipal Wharf shows the SAMSCO warehouse, the 40&8 Arena, fish houses and squatter's shacks. Photo from John Fred'k "Doc" McGregor photographic collection of the Corpus Christi Museum of Science and History.*

*Sailboats almost could tie up almost at the front door of the Princess Louise Hotel on the waterfront. Photo from John Fred'k "Doc" McGregor photographic collection of the Corpus Christi Museum of Science and History.*

One thing could not be shelved. The federal government required a breakwater to be built before it would provide funding to build the port. Work on the breakwater, called the Rocks, started in 1925 and was completed in 1926.

Civic leaders made another push to build a seawall to protect the downtown from powerful hurricanes. In 1928, Gutzon Borglum, who would later be famous as the sculptor of Mount Rushmore, was commissioned to design a seawall for Corpus Christi. Borglum's plan included a 32-foot bronze statue of Christ in the bay, symbolizing the city's name, and a vertical castellated seawall similar in design to the bluff balustrade. There was a fight over the statue of Christ and voters turned down a bond issue to build the seawall.

Borglum was not pleased. When he left for the Black Hills, he had a parting shot for Corpus Christi — "I don't think I have ever seen a town where the crooks and respectable people are so like scrambled eggs."

Once again, Corpus Christi came up short, of money and of the political will, to undertake a big project. The city fell into lethargy and the idea of building a seawall lay dormant for another decade.

*—June 4, 2014*

# Building the Seawall

It was 75 years ago when Corpus Christi finally summoned the political will to build a seawall. It came after decades of dreams, plans and setbacks.

Corpus Christi voters in 1938 approved, by an overwhelming majority, a $650,000 bond issue. There was already $200,000 in the kitty. A second bond issue was later passed for $1.1 million.

There was some opposition. Walter Foster, who owned the Princess Louise Hotel, opposed the project. Foster's hotel was a few steps from the water, but the bayfront plan would push the waterfront back by almost two blocks, leaving the Princess Louise high and dry. But that first bond issue passed by a vote of 1,431 for to 108 against. One explanation for such strong support was because the voters only had to approve the issuance of bonds; they didn't have to pay for them.

After the 1919 storm, the Legislature passed a bill to remit the state's share of property taxes from seven South Texas counties, including Nueces, into a fund for storm protection for Corpus Christi. That was extended several times. Since the fund would retire the seawall bonds, the state paid for the seawall.

Work began on Jan. 1, 1939, the 100th anniversary of the city's founding. Mayor A. C. McCaughan chose a Dallas engineering firm, Myers & Noyes, to design and oversee the project and hired J. DePuy of San Antonio, who built the breakwater, as contractor.

The city almost made a blunder. When the port was built, federal engineers argued that the proposed bascule bridge would be too small for the ever-larger ships being built. The city ignored that advice and built the cheapest bridge it could build, the bascule, which became known as the bascule bottleneck.

On the seawall, city officials opted for the cheapest possible seawall, a straight wall of steel-sheet piling and concrete to separate

*Workers dismantled the Pleasure Pier in 1939 as the project to build the seawall got underway. Photo from John Fred'k "Doc" McGregor photographic collection of the Corpus Christi Museum of Science and History.*

land and water. The city also wanted a narrow 24-foot parkway on Shoreline.

A civil engineer, Edward Noyes of Myers and Noyes, dug in his heels and argued that a stair-step design for the seawall, as he proposed, would cost a little more but would give Corpus Christi a bayfront "second to none" for beauty. He argued for a 200-foot-wide parkway and finally compromised on an 80-foot-wide parkway. Noyes won the argument.

The contractor, DePuy, started work at three points: the bascule bridge, Pleasure Pier, and Municipal Wharf. The Pleasure Pier was dismantled and tenants on the Municipal Wharf were forced to move. DePuy designed a 40-foot-long metal shed on railroad wheels under which the 40-foot lengths of the stepped seawall were poured of reinforced concrete.

In March, local unions picketed the site, protesting that DePuy hired most of his workers from out of town. DePuy countered with numbers showing that three of every four workers on the project came from Corpus Christi.

*The Pier Café, which had been at the water's edge, was surrounded by mud as the café was elevated to meet the new grade for the seawall. Photo from John Fred'k "Doc" McGregor photographic collection of the Corpus Christi Museum of Science and History.*

The bayfront was certainly not a thing of beauty as work progressed. There was a lot more mud than sand. Behind a temporary seawall, the bottom of the bay next to the shore was laid bare.

The bottom clay, called fill, was scooped out by dredges. In time, the fill was pumped into the outlines of the T-heads and L-head and used to raise the elevation between Water Street and the seawall. On top of this reclaimed land would run the parkway, in effect a levee behind the seawall. The parkway was first called Bayshore Boulevard then Shoreline.

The bayfront was a mess, with an army of bulldozers, caterpillars and cement mixers, and a constant thump-thumping of pile drivers driving posts, or piles, into the bay bottom. It was said that if one held a seashell up to his ear instead of the roar of the sea he would hear the thump-thump of the pile drivers. A tourist's postcard from Corpus Christi said, "Town full of mud, sludge and a vile miasma."

Warehouses at the port had been built to the higher grade but some tourist cabins were raised two to three feet and fill pumped in

*An aerial photo shows a wide strip of reclaimed land between Water Street and the seawall. Photo from John Fred'k "Doc" McGregor photographic collection of the Corpus Christi Museum of Science and History.*

*The sun was shining on a gleaming seawall as the Bayfront project neared completion in 1940. Photo by Russell Lee from the Library of Congress.*

under them. The Pier Cafe had to be raised as well as the Nueces Hotel garden. The famous three palms were supposed to be saved, but I don't think they were.

Work on the seawall was completed in March 1941. From scratch to finish, it took two years and cost $2.2 million. The city had been extended almost two blocks into the bay and the bayfront itself had been elevated to 14 feet above sea level — 3.7 feet above the high-water mark of the 1919 storm.

The seawall, from the ship channel on the north end to the foot of Craig Avenue on the south, stretched two miles and every foot, it was said, of the 12,000-foot wall was built to withstand a load pressure of 260 tons. There would be no reprise of the kind of storm surge that wrecked the downtown in 1919.

The yacht basins, the L-head and two T-heads were part of the project. Another L-head, off the end of Twigg, was planned but the state closed its purse, saying it had spent enough on storm protection for Corpus Christi. The plan called for a tube tunnel under the ship channel to be built later but, because of the war, that was dropped.

The seawall was a storm-protective measure. That's why the state agreed to pay for it. But when it was finished, it was clear that it was the greatest beautification program in the city's history. It's ironic that a civil engineer, Edward Noyes, was responsible for the seawall and bayfront design, which was surely an improvement over the parapet wall that was envisioned by sculptor Gutzon Borglum. Noyes' stepped seawall provided seating for the great and scenic amphitheater of the bay.

Though the state paid for it, the people of Corpus Christi assumed a proprietary attitude to the seawall, a strong sense of ownership, which is why the city always stirs up a hornet's nest when it proposes any change to the bayfront. The seawall is a legacy, a trophy, of the time when the city could get things done, and it did it the right way and not on the cheap, all credit to Edward Noyes.

*—June 11, 2014*

# The Cattle Queen of Texas

In 1875, Martha Rabb took over her late husband ranching empire on Banquete Creek, which consisted of 10,000 cattle bearing the famous bow and arrow brand and grazing on the open range.

John Rabb had moved from Helena in 1857 and bought 400 acres on Banquete Creek. His cousin, Sally Skull, had moved to Banquete some years before. Rabb and his wife Martha (Reagan) had six children, three boys and three girls. He died on April 15, 1872 when he was 46 years old.

After John Rabb's death, Martha could see the open range coming to an end. She began to buy land and soon had 30,000 acres of pasture in Nueces County. She enclosed her ranch with a board fence, which took a fence-rider two days to ride. This was called Martha Rabb's Pasture or Rancho Flecha for the bow and arrow brand.

Mrs. P. A. Hunter, daughter of D. C. Rachal, knew Martha when her father bought the Rabb ranch. She said Martha, with a head of tight curls, would sit on the top rail of the corral fence to watch branding and cutting out of stock. She smoked little black cigars — cheroots — and carried a box of them with her. It was also said that she was the undisputed boss of her ranch, with help from her three sons and three daughters. She built the Magnolia Mansion on the bluff at Corpus Christi in 1875.

One night at a dance at Petronila, her son Lee Rabb was shot to death. The killer escaped on Lee's horse. The details of the shooting have not survived, but Lee was known as a violent young man who was a terror to his neighbors.

In 1879, Martha Rabb married a Methodist minister in Corpus Christi, the Rev. Curran M. Rogers. He was 15 years younger, little older than her oldest son, and he began courting Martha Rabb so soon after his wife's death that it was the talk of the town. The Rev.

Rogers and his six children moved into the Magnolia Mansion and relations between Martha and her own children became prickly.

One reason for the bitter feelings was that Martha, after she married the Rev. Rogers, moved a formal portrait of her late husband — an oil painting that showed Capt. John Rabb in his Confederate uniform on horseback — from the front parlor to an outdoor privy.

Martha's sons Green (called Dock) and Frank, it was said, saw it as a betrayal and never forgave her. When she visited the ranch, always with the parson in tow, Frank would disappear and stay gone until she left.

She sold the Rabb ranch to the Rachal brothers, who later sold it the Driscoll brothers. It was the Rabb Ranch that was the foundation of the Driscoll fortune, which was later used to build the Driscoll Hospital. The town of Robstown is located on part of Martha Rabb's old ranch.

Martha sold the Magnolia Mansion in 1885 and she and the Rev. Rogers moved to Austin, where he engaged in politics and spent her money. She died in 1901 and was never reconciled with her sons and daughters. She left what remained of her estate to the Rev. Rogers and his six children. The Rabb sons and daughters contested the will for a time then gave up. The money was mostly gone anyway.

*Martha Rabb, called the Cattle Queen of Texas, built a home on Upper Broadway which she named the Magnolia Mansion. The Magnolia Mansion was moved in 1939 to make way for the Cathedral and demolished in 1952.*

*Mrs. John (Martha) Rabb*

\* \* \*

## CITY LIGHTS

Before Thomas Edison's incandescent lights were installed, Corpus Christi's streets and homes were lit by coal-oil lanterns. The city hired a lamplighter who made his rounds at sunset to light the lanterns and at sunrise to extinguish them.

In October 1889, a contractor for the Edison light system, F. P. McMullen, recommended to the City Council that the coal-oil street lamps be replaced with Edison lamps. The Corpus Christi Caller urged the council to switch to electric lights. It said it would reduce the risk of fire and result in lower insurance premiums.

The City Council made its decision in January 1890. The contract for street lighting went to the Corpus Christi Electric Light Company, owned by Dr. A. G. Heaney, T. P. Rivera and John Stayton. They also owned the city's new telephone exchange.

A visitor to Corpus Christi in 1890, Joseph W. Page, wrote in his diary on Jan. 7: "Went to Corpus Christi today. The town is rather dull, though I understand they will soon have the electric wires up."

On Feb. 15 he wrote: "Notice they are putting up electric light poles." On Feb. 22: "They are putting up the light wires." And on April 12: "They have the electric lights up at last. Everybody is well-pleased with them."

Electricity was available only at night. It cost the city $2.50 per lamp per month and the city had 60 lamps. The newspaper said Corpus Christi "is emerging from darkness and sloth and will take her stand in the dazzling light of commercial push and energy."

The electric company also operated the telephone exchange, although there were few people to call. Dr. Heaney, the founding partner, got telephone number 1 and his son Harry got number 2. There were 15 other numbers. It was deemed permissible for the operator to pass on gossip she overheard but flirting would get her fired.

\* \* \*

## TEXAN OR TEXIAN?

In October 1853, the editor of the Indianola Bulletin wrote: "We have on our table the second edition of the Texan Mercury. Every old Texian we ever heard speak on the subject prefers to be called Texian, instead of Texan. When the Advocate started in Victoria in 1846, 'Texan' was its preface to 'Advocate.' But the editors received so many letters protesting the omission of the 'I' that they at once yielded and, by doing so, gained a hundred subscribers." That was in 1853.

The word Texan began to gain popularity after Texas became a state. Before then, it was almost always Texian. J. Frank Dobie preferred Texian to describe the "strongly individualized breed" that lived in Texas at the time of the Revolution. Gradually, Texan replaced Texian in general usage. Maybe it was like retiring the number of a famous baseball player. The Texians were a breed apart. It's just as well that their own special name died out as they did.

*—June 18, 2014*

# Big Fire in 1892

On July 14, 1892, fire broke out near midnight in the Lay home at 215 Chaparral and quickly spread to the J. B. Mitchell Warehouse and nearby homes.

Volunteer firemen rushed to fill water wagons from the box wells on the bayfront. They were soon directing a stream of water on the fire, but it raged out of control, leaping from the Mitchell warehouse to the William Biggio residence, the Molander and Daimwood homes, then jumped to Royal Givens' grocery store.

Ida Daimwood (Magnenat) once recalled the night of the fire. "It was mother who smell smoke first. My father had just come in and he ran down the street yelling 'fire!' The bell in the old Market Hall began to ring, which was the signal for volunteer firemen to drop everything and come running."

Royal Givens' grocery store, next to the Daimwood home, was shellcrete with a tin roof, which gave the firefighters a good chance to bring the conflagration under control. But while they were fighting the fire in the front of the store, a wooden annex at the rear caught fire and the flames spread to Louis de Planque's photo studio. After an exhausting night, the firemen finally brought the fire under control.

The scene on the morning of July 15 showed many homes and buildings in the 200 block of Chaparral destroyed. Ida Daimwood said their house was gone, but they were able to save the furniture and clothes. Can goods salvaged from Givens' grocery were stacked in the street. The Caller said it was the city's most destructive fire.

After the fire, Corpus Christi got serious about establishing a city water system. The city had wells dug west of town but the water was salty and brackish. Less than a year after the fire, on May 26, 1893, the city celebrated the city's new waterworks. A 12-mile pipeline to the Nueces River brought 200,000 gallons a day.

*In 1895, water carriers called barrileros wait to fill their barrels with water piped in from the Nueces River. The standpipe was at Sam Rankin and Mestina.*

A steam-powered pumping plant at Calallen was fired by wood then lignite coal shipped from Laredo. City officials rode in buggies past cotton fields to see the new pumping plant. "Corpus Christi's waterworks are a grand success," the Caller gushed. "Hydrants are opened and water rushes out with tremendous force. The town is safe against fire."

The new waterworks didn't put the water vendors, the barrileros, out of business. Since piped-in water didn't reach homes for another 20 years, people still relied on their cisterns and when the cisterns ran low they turned to barrileros. But the barrileros did not have to travel to the Nueces River for water. They filled their barrels at a city standpipe.

\* \* \*

## BOHEMIAN COLONY

In 1904, Stanley Kostoryz, a Czech newspaper publisher and storeowner in Nebraska, bought the Grim Ranch southwest of Corpus Christi. It had once been part of Martha Rabb's ranch. Kostoryz paid $52,000 for 7,789 acres and called the tract the Bohemian Colony Lands.

Kostoryz, born in Bohemia (later Czechoslovakia), emigrated and settled in Wilber, Neb., where he owned a combined drug store and

*Stanley Kostoryz bought the Grim Ranch on the outskirts of Corpus Christi to sell to Czech farmers.*

general store. He published a Czech-language newspaper, "Osveta" (Enlightenment). After he sold the paper, he searched the country looking for cheap, fertile land before he found the Grim Ranch outside Corpus Christi.

In Corpus Christi, Kostoryz had A.M. French surveying the land for 160-acre tracts. Later, it was sub-divided into smaller plots. The Caller reported that — "Mr. S. L. Kostoryz has 35 men employed on his property grubbing a clearing and preparing a large acreage for cultivation. This land will be cut into five- and ten-acre farms prepared ready for cultivation of actual settlers."

Czech settlers began arriving in 1906. Since the Aberdeen school was too far away for the settlers' children to attend, the Kostoryz School District was formed in 1907. The first trustees were J. Robertson, John Brandesky, and Park Everhart (for whom Everhart Road was named). The first school was on Kostoryz Road next to Sokol Hall. In 1912, Kostoryz bought the 2,200-acre Robertson Ranch and added it to the Bohemian Colony.

After the death of a son in 1921, a depressed Kostoryz sold the remainder of his 3,700 acres to Longin Folda and he and his wife returned to Europe. Kostoryz died in 1924. Like other communities on the outskirts of Corpus Christi, the Kostoryz settlement was absorbed by the growing city and the Kostoryz school district became part of CCISD in 1952. Not much is left of the Bohemian Colony except the descendants of those original Czech farmers.

\* \* \*

## LADIES PAVILION

Corpus Christi's Market Hall, built in 1871, had market stalls for vendors and butchers, room for city offices, and an auditorium on the second floor where dances were held. It was the social center of the city.

By the turn of the century, the Woman's Monday Club decided the town needed a new entertainment center. The club sold shares of stock to raise funds to build the Ladies Pavilion. It was constructed in 1902 over the water off Water Street, below Peoples Street.

Plays, dances and skating parties were held at the Ladies Pavilion. It was also where the city's first conventions were held. One performance staged at the Ladies Pavilion was called "A Dream of Beautiful Women" with prominent women of the town striking poses in a tableaux of famous historical figures. Clara Driscoll played the role of Cleopatra. Others in the play were Mrs. Leo Kaffie, Mrs. Roy Miller, Mrs. Walter Timon and Mrs. Robert Kleberg.

Most important was a reception given at the Ladies Pavilion in 1904 for members of the Methodist Epworth League who were looking for a place to hold an annual summer encampment. They were delighted with Corpus Christi and when the city offered 18 acres, free of charge, on North Beach, the result became Epworth by the Sea.

The first encampment was held in August 1905 and it was held every year for a decade. Each summer, hundreds of Methodist families and missionaries from around the world gathered on North Beach. The beginning of Corpus Christi as a tourist destination can be traced, at least in part, to the annual Epworth by the Sea encampment, which introduced many Texans to North Beach. As for the Ladies Pavilion, it was destroyed in the 1916 hurricane.

*—June 25, 2014*

# Garner's Our Man

A virtually unknown politician named John Garner beat a Corpus Christi lawyer named John Scott for a seat in Congress. This political race in 1902 changed the future. We can look back and see how much was riding on this one election.

Garner was 34, an attorney, and had been the county judge of Uvalde. He served two terms in the Legislature. As chairman of the redistricting committee he gerrymandered the new 15th district to suit his own ambition. But he put his cards on the table, saying that he was framing a district in which he could get elected to Congress.

The district was enormous, stretching from below San Antonio to Del Rio and from there to Brownsville and Corpus Christi. Garner announced his candidacy in February 1902. He faced stiff opposition in the primary from state Sen. Joe Dibrell of Seguin. "I campaigned in a buckboard, driving a gray mare and a little mule," Garner once said. He had the backing of Jim Wells, boss of bosses in South Texas. Wells sent a telegram to his Corpus Christi allies saying, "Garner's our man."

One of Wells' allies was Pat Dunn of Padre Island. Dunn said, "I got to lambasting around for Garner. Some yahoos made a man out of cement and claimed he was a petrified man they found on Padre Island. They put the petrified man on exhibition in Corpus Christi. The Crony (a Republican-leaning Corpus Christi newspaper) said Pat Dunn and the petrified man were the only men from Nueces County supporting John Garner."

As moderate Democrats, Garner and Dibrell shared the same views. At one appearance, in Sabinal, Garner defended his opponent. "It has been reported that Judge Dibrell is an enemy of organized labor but he told me this is not true and I believe him. I do not want my opponent's position misrepresented. I will never resort to trickery, untruths or half-truths to win votes."

County after county came out for Garner. Dibrell, an old hand at politics, knew when he was beaten. He withdrew and praised his opponent, saying "Garner will make a great congressman. The only thing urged against him is his youth. It is no crime to be young. He may not make a great oratorical display in Congress, but while an unwary antagonist is making a speech Garner will know what he wants, will go out and work for it and get it."

The Republicans nominated a Corpus Christi attorney, John Scott, who had the deep-pockets support of E. H. R. Green, son of the Wall Street tycoon Hettie Green. With Republicans controlling the White House and Congress, the Corpus Christi Crony wrote, "Common sense prompts the idea that a Republican congressman can most efficiently serve his people. If Garner won out, he would be an outsider. Scott would be one of the gang."

Garner captured almost 60 percent of the vote, carrying 18 of 22 counties, including Nueces, although Scott carried Corpus Christi.

On Jan. 26, 1903, Garner and wife Ettie came to Corpus Christi, had dinner at the St. James Hotel (champagne and seafood) and next morning Garner met with citizens and asked for guidance on what he could do in Washington. "What is the one thing dearest to your heart?" he asked.

H. R. Sutherland said, "We want a channel dredged through Turtle Cove into the bay to give Corpus Christi a deepwater connection to the Gulf." Next day, Garner was taken on the schooner Flour Bluff across the bay to show what was needed. With the clarity of hindsight, we know this was an important event for the future of the city.

Garner went to Washington and moved into a boarding house where he kept an office and where Ettie worked as his secretary. Garner quickly learned how Congress worked. He learned that personal relationships were more important than brilliant speech-making. He kept quiet and made friends. Everybody liked Cactus Jack Garner.

The first bill he introduced provided for a survey for an intracoastal canal which would eventually connect Brownsville and Corpus Christi with the Mississippi and Ohio rivers. Garner at a meeting in Victoria said, "It may take 50 years to complete but it will be completed from the Rio Grande to the Mississippi."

He pushed through appropriations for sections of the Intracoastal Canal and included was funding to dredge a channel from the

*John Nance Garner in 1903 after he won election in the newly created 15th congressional district in South Texas. Photo from the Library of Congress.*

Aransas Pass ship channel to Corpus Christi. This was the first crucial step in Corpus Christi gaining a port, though it would take many other steps and another two decades to achieve. In 1926, on Port Opening Day in Corpus Christi, Garner was an honored guest. Forty-five years later, in 1948, the Intracoastal Waterway extended from the west coast of Florida to the Mexican border. The Port of Corpus Christi, the Intracoastal Waterway, improvement of the Port Aransas jetties, were a few of Garner's legislative accomplishments that had great impact on the future of South Texas.

Garner's political career carried him on to the speakership of the House then the vice presidency in the Roosevelt administration. He was the Democratic frontrunner for president in 1940 until

Roosevelt opted to run for a third term. Garner retired, said he was crossing the Potomac for the last time, and went home to Uvalde.

After his wife Ettie died in 1948 he moved out of the main ranch house into a small frame building. His neighbors called him Judge Garner, from his first elected position in Uvalde. He died on Nov. 7, 1967. He was 98 years old.

The citizens of Corpus Christi had once given Garner a gold watch for his help in gaining the one thing dearest to the city's heart. He was carrying it when he died. An editorial in the Caller-Times said, "During his long and full life he witnessed the transformation of Texas from a frontier to a rich and well-developed state, and so effective was his quiet exercise of his mastery of government that no man can truly measure his great contribution to that transformation."

Anyone who thinks politics doesn't matter can learn something from that 1902 race. Without the port, Corpus Christi would never have become a city of any size and it's hard to see how there would have ever been a port without those critical early steps taken in Congress by Cactus Jack Garner.

*—July 2, 2014*

# Webster on Cattle

Shanghai, he was called, though his name was Abel Head Pierce. George Saunders described him in "Trail Drivers of Texas" — "Mr. Pierce was a loud talker, and no man who saw him or heard him talk ever forgot his voice or appearance. He was a money maker, empire builder, and a wonder to his friends and, I believe, to himself."

J. Frank Dobie described him in "A Vaquero of the Brush Country" — "At Tres Palacios, Shanghai Pierce conducted his establishment. Massive-framed, bugle-voiced, infinite in wit and anecdote, Old Shang was known wherever longhorn cows bellowed."

Shanghai Pierce was the most famous of the cattle barons of South Texas, a rough man who made his own way and was as vain of his name and reputation as an opera star.

Pierce grew up in Rhode Island. His father was a blacksmith. He went to live with his mother's brother, Abel Head, after whom he was named, who owned a store in Petersburg, Va. His uncle was a religious fanatic and young Abel tired of the moralizing and sermonizing. In June 1853, the 19-year-old stowed away on a ship bound for Indianola, Texas.

When the ship docked at Indianola, Pierce walked down the gangplank into Texas. He had 75 cents and the clothes he was wearing. At 6-4 and weighing 200 pounds, he was a big, loudmouthed Yankee in pants too short for him. He got a job with cattleman Richard Grimes and asked to receive his first year's pay in cows and calves. He planned to become a cattleman himself.

On Grimes ranch, he split rails until he was promoted to bronc buster. After the rancher's son, William Bradford Grimes, took over, there was a falling out between Abel and the son, and it lasted a lifetime. At the end of the first year, Pierce figured he was due, in lieu of salary, 28 cows and 28 calves. William Bradford gave him four cows and three calves. After that, Abel demanded his pay in dollars, and recorded his own brand, AP.

He was called Shanghai though how he got the nickname is unclear. One version said when he put on his first pair of spurs in Texas, he said, "I look like a Shanghai rooster." He was also known by the carrying capacity of his voice. Chris Emmett in "Shanghai Pierce" wrote that in Indianola, at Daniel Sullivan's store, when someone asked if Shanghai was in town, Sullivan would walk to the door, cup his ears to listen and say, "No, he's not in town."

Shanghai's brother Jonathan joined him in Texas. With the outbreak of the Civil War, they enlisted in the Confederate Army; their regiment fought in the Red River campaign in Louisiana. Shanghai, as regimental butcher, said he was the same as a general — "always in the rear on advance, always in the lead on retreat."

Shanghai and Jonathan established El Rancho Grande on the Tres Palacios River in Wharton County. Shanghai married Fannie Lacy and Jonathan married her sister, making them brothers-in-law. Jonathan ran the ranch; Shanghai took care of the cattle drives and livestock. He was reputed to be opportunistic with a branding iron.

On borrowed money, Shanghai bought cattle to ship to Cuba. George Saunders said he bought cattle all over South Texas. "I remember seeing him many times come to our camp where he had contracts to receive beeves. He would be accompanied by a Negro (Neptune Holmes) who led a pack horse loaded with gold and silver which, when he reached our camp, was dumped on the ground until the cattle was classed and counted out, then he would empty the money on a blanket and pay it out to the stockmen from whom he had purchased cattle. We were glad to sell our cattle at any price as money was scarce in Reconstruction days before the northern trail started."

In 1867, Shanghai and Fannie had a daughter, named Mary but she was always known as Miss Mamie. Three years later, they had a boy named Abel, but he died soon afterwards and Fannie died in December 1870.

Shanghai became one of the first cattlemen to send herds up the trail to Kansas. He would hire a trail boss or do the job himself. Later he would travel with the herd until it was trail-broken and take the train to Kansas to meet the herd and trail-hands.

A large posse led by Shanghai captured a gang of hide thieves near Carancahua Creek in Matagorda County. They were identified

*Abel Head "Shanghai" Pierce arrived at Indianola with 75 cents in his pocket. He became one of Texas' greatest cattlemen.*

as three Lunn brothers, "All-Jaw" Smith and a stranger. All five were hanged from the limbs of a dead tree. When charges were filed against the lynch mob, and Shanghai was summoned to appear as a witness, he left the ranch in his brother's hands and took off for Kansas. He stayed away two years.

At Kansas City, he asked a hotel clerk if there was any mail for him. The clerk looked up, annoyed, and said, "And who (the hell) are you?" Pierce straightened up to his full height and said in that foghorn voice that carried a mile, "I am Shanghai Pierce, Webster on cattle, by God, sir!"

Pierce and his brother Jonathan continued to expand the ranch and cattle operations. Pierce once boasted that — "I got to be a pretty big dog in the puddle. I was borrowing one hundred thousand dollars in Galveston at a time. I stand pat there is not a better cattleman in the state." That's from Emmett's biography of Shanghai.

Shanghai put up a marble statue of himself in Deming's Bridge Cemetery. (The Deming's Bridge community later became Hawley in Matagorda County). Shanghai wrote a friend: "I have put up a statue, an exact likeness of myself. You will recognize it when you see it and say, 'There stands old Pierce.' "

Shanghai died on Dec. 26, 1900 and was buried in the Deming's Bridge Cemetery. Emmett wrote that the rain was falling heavily when his casket was lowered into a deep puddle of water at the bottom of the grave in front of his statue. With that final splash an era was over.

Shanghai Pierce left $1.3 million, a sum considerably grown from the 75 cents he had when he walked ashore at Indianola. As he once described himself, he was the best cattleman around — "Webster on cattle" — and he would have insisted on having the last word.

*—July 9, 2014*

# The Tarpon Club

The Tarpon Club was a two-story hunting resort on St. Joseph's Island that existed just before and after the turn of the 20th Century. The fancy turreted structure was built in the late 1890s by E. H. R. Green, called Col. Eddie or Ned by his friends. He was famous as the son of the rich and eccentric Hetty Green, called the "Witch of Wall Street".

Biographers say that Hetty Green inherited $9 million after her husband's death, then inherited $4 million from an aunt and kept adding to her wealth until she had amassed around $100 million (about $2.5 billion in today's money).

But with all that money, she was a world-class miser. When her young son Eddie broke his leg, she tried to get him admitted into a free clinic for the poor. When she was recognized she reluctantly agreed to pay for his medical care. His leg didn't properly heal and had to be amputated. He was fitted with an artificial leg.

Hetty Green's biography said she lived in a cheap flat in Hoboken that rented for $19 a month, dressed like a street person, and would walk miles to save the nickel streetcar fare. It was said that she would have starved if not for the free buffets. She would go to the bank once a week, fill out a withdrawal slip, count out her assets in a special room, then re-deposit the money.

In 1893, Hetty acquired the Texas Midland Railroad and sent Eddie to take charge of the company. In Texas, he became active in the state's Republican politics and was made an honorary colonel on a governor's staff.

Col. Eddie, as he was called, built the Tarpon Club on St. Joseph's Island. His rich friends would stay at the clubhouse and go fishing and duck hunting. As hunters, Eddie's friends were known to visit island nesting grounds and blast away with high firepower, killing birds indiscriminately.

*Hetty Green (left), called the Witch of Wall Street, amassed around $100 million ($2.5 billion in today's dollars) but would walk miles in the snow to save a nickel streetcar fare. Her son, E. H. R. (Eddie) Green (right), built the Tarpon Club on St. Joseph's Island as a getaway for wealthy sportsmen and their girlfriends.*

*The Tarpon Club on St. Joseph's Island was a hunting and fishing resort for wealthy sportsmen at the end of the 19th century.*

R. K. Sawyer in "A Hundred Years of Texas Waterfowl Hunting" wrote that there wasn't a post office on St. Joseph's and, to justify one, postal regulations required a town, "an inconvenience that club members remedied by creating Sport, Texas. The town of Sport encompassed only one dwelling, the Tarpon Club."

A news item in the Caller on Nov. 25, 1898 reported that — "Col. Eddie Green visited Corpus Christi last week, coming across the bay in his fine yacht, the Mabel. His party spent the night on the yacht before returning to the colonel's clubhouse on St. Joseph's Island." (The yacht was named for his girlfriend Mabel Harlow, a well-known prostitute.)

Green, very active in Republican politics, bankrolled the candidacy of John C. Scott, a Corpus Christi lawyer and Republican candidate for Congress, against the Democratic candidate, John N. Garner, in 1902. Garner won despite Green's war chest.

Col. Eddie left Texas when his mother Hetty died in 1916. She left a fortune of $150 million to Eddie and his sister Sylvia. Eddie Green died in 1936 and left $44 million, including a coin collection valued at $5 million. When it was moved from one bank to another, the transfer required eight armored cars, 16 private guards and seven state policemen.

Green's Tarpon Club on St. Joseph's was closed shortly after the turn of the century. J. J. Copley, who bought the old Alta Vista Hotel at Corpus Christi, with plans to re-open it as a tourist resort, purchased the Tarpon Club. He got it for a bargain, at $8,000, which had cost Col. Eddie $40,000 to build. Copley also bought the gasoline-powered launch Mabel as part of the deal. The Tarpon Club was dismantled in 1905 and was supposed to be moved to the grounds of the Alta Vista, but I don't think it ever was.

* * *

## GRASSHOPPERS HILL

Col. William S. Harney in command of the Second Dragoons was with Zachary Taylor in Corpus Christi in 1845. He returned in the 1850s when he commanded the Department of Texas and the army headquarters were located in Corpus Christi.

In the Mexican War, Harney was in charge of hanging deserters who were part of the San Patricio Battalion that had fought in the Mexican Army. The San Patricio Battalion was made up of Irish soldiers who had changed uniforms. Some were enticed to desert the American army while others were victims of circumstance. Some had gotten drunk and were captured and forced to fight in the Mexican Army.

Near the end of the war, 50 San Patricio men were court-martialed and sentenced to be executed. Others were whipped and branded with a "D" on their cheeks. Harney was in charge of executing 29 of them. Among many accounts of the fate of the San Patricio deserters, the hangings were described in "Captain Sam Grant" by Lloyd Lewis.

Based on Lewis' description, the 29 condemned men were put on Army wagons beneath scaffolds on the outskirts of Mexico City on Sept. 12, 1847. The condemned men stood on the wagons with hands and feet tied and ropes around their necks. Rather than hang the men and get it over with, without ceremony, Harney told them beforehand they would be hanged at the very moment that the American flag — the flag they had deserted — went up at Chapultepec, the Hill of the Grasshoppers, where a battle was underway.

The men were standing on the wagons and watching through the smoke at the distant battle at the top of the hill, two miles away. Harney, sitting on his horse, was "red as a fox about the head and face."

They waited one hour, two hours, then, through the smoke of battle, they could see a flash of red, white and blue (raised by Lt. George Pickett). The wagon drivers cheered and even the doomed men cheered and through the cheering came Harney's order for the execution to proceed. The wagons rolled from under 29 of the San Patricio deserters, leaving their bodies dangling from scaffolds in the hot September sun.

After the war, Harney lived in Corpus Christi in the 1850s. He bought thousands of acres of property along the bayfront south of town. Much of that area along today's Ocean Drive was part of the old Harney tract.

*—July 16, 2014*

# Spanish Place Names

Texas was an unexplored wilderness, not even a name on a map. Some in Mexico thought it was part of Florida. What little they knew came from Pineda's voyage and Cabeza de Vaca's amazing tales. It took the arrival of the French for New Spain to explore what came to be called Provincia de los Tejas.

In 1519, Capt. Alonso Alvarez de Pineda's fleet sailed past Cuba and followed the Gulf coastline. He may have anchored in a horseshoe-shaped bay on June 4, 1519, the feast day of Corpus Christi, and named the bay for that holiday. He called Padre Island Isla Blanca (White Island) and the Rio Grande the Rio Palmas, River of Palms.

The man who sent Pineda exploring, Francisco Garay, led his own expedition and sailed into the pass separating Padre and Brazos Islands on July 25, 1523, St. James Day. He named the pass Brazos de Santiago — the Arms of St. James.

In 1528, survivors of the Narváez expedition washed ashore on a barrier island, probably St. Joseph's. Alvar Núñez Cabeza de Vaca called it Malhado, Isle of Misfortune. Cabeza de Vaca and three survivors lived with fierce coastal Indians for six years, walked across northern Mexico to the Gulf of California and made their way to Mexico City, a journey of 5,000 miles. It was an incredible journey and tale of survival.

In Mexico City, they could hardly stand to wear clothes. During their long trek, they shed their skin like snakes and the under skin became so sensitive they could not bear the abrasive touch of clothes. Their story remains an epic of adventure and endurance. Spanish Mexico now knew that a great land lay to the north.

Officials in New Spain and Spain turned their attention and energy toward Texas after Robert Cavelier, Sieur de la Salle, landed on the coast in 1685. The French explorer had discovered the Mississippi

121

River and claimed the land it drained for France. He returned to France and prepared to establish a colony at the mouth of the river.

La Salle sailed from France with four ships filled with soldiers and settlers. By mistake or design, they made landfall not at the mouth of the Mississippi but on a creek on Matagorda Bay, which turned out to be a tragic miscalculation.

La Salle lost three ships (one was captured by the Spanish, one wrecked in Pass Cavallo, and one turned back to France) leaving him with one ship. The French salvaged timbers from the wrecked vessel and built Fort St. Louis. When the last ship, the La Belle, sank in Matagorda Bay, they were stranded.

La Salle took a company of men to search for the Mississippi, which they could follow to French Canada. His men turned mutinous and killed him. Those left at Fort St. Louis died in a smallpox epidemic followed by a Karankawa massacre. Only a few children survived as captives of the Karankawas.

News of the French landing led the Spanish to launch expeditions to find and destroy La Salle's colony. One expedition was mounted in 1689 by Alonso de León, who crossed the Rio Grande and followed an old Indian trail. De León came to a river with no name on April 4, 1689. He called it Rio de las Nueces (river of nuts) for pecan trees on its banks.

On the Atascosa, De León's men opened a cask of wine to celebrate Holy Saturday; De León called the stream Arroyo del Vino. He named the Guadalupe River — Nuestra Señora de Guadalupe, Our Lady of Guadalupe.

At the deserted French fort on Garcitas Creek, De León found a macabre scene of skeletons in rotted clothing. The following year he returned and burned Fort St. Louis. He explored Matagorda Bay, which he called La Bahía del Espíritu Santo (Bay of the Holy Spirit). It had been called San Bernardo.

De León's men found Indian canoes and named the creek there Arroyo de las Canoas, Canoe Creek. Around the pass from the Gulf, their horses stumbled in the deep sand so the pass became Paso Caballo, the Pass of the Horse.

Over the years, New Spain's interest in Texas waxed and waned. In 1746, José de Escandón was commissioned to colonize an area from Tampico to the San Antonio River, called Seno Mejicano. One expedition sent to explore the region was led by Capt. Joaquin Orobio Basterra.

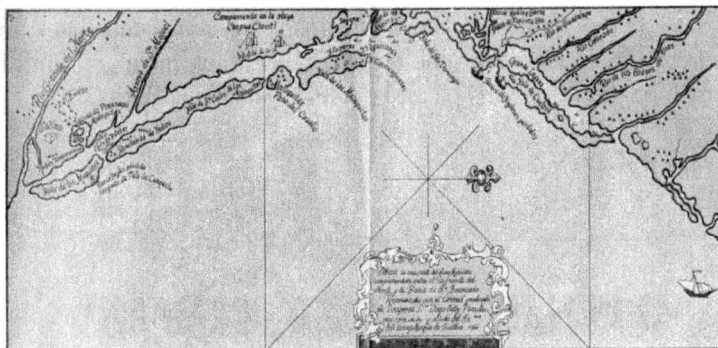

*An enlarged detail from Diego Ortiz Parrilla's 1766 map of the Texas Coast shows his encampment on the beach, labeled "Campamento en la playa Corpus Christi" (encampment on the beach at Corpus Christi). From the Caller-Times Archives.*

Orobio Basterra with 50 soldiers set out on Jan. 29, 1747. He followed the Nueces to its estuary and reported: "This river of Las Nueces, which until now was thought to join the Rio Grande del Norte (Big River of the North), enters the sea at this place, where a great bay is found, to which I gave the name San Miguel Arcangel."

Orobio Basterra explored the Cayo del Oso (Watershed of the Bear) and called Oso Creek La Purisima Concepción (the Immaculate Conception). Baffin Bay he named Lago de la Santisima Trinidad and Los Olmos Creek (Creek of the Elms), he called Arroyo Concepción. He may have been the first to name the Laguna de la Madre (Mother Lake), but we don't know that.

One aspect of Escandón's colonizing was the establishment of ranches in South Texas. The first ranch in what is today's Nueces County was built on Santa Petronila Creek, founded by Blas Maria de la Garza Falcon. The rumors of another foreign incursion, this time by the British, led to an expedition under the command of Diego Ortiz Parrilla in 1766.

Parrilla established a base camp at the Santa Petronila ranch and sent a party to explore Padre Island, which he called Isla de la Malaguitas. Parrilla's map showed his encampment on the beach at Corpus Christi.

Parrilla called Copano Bay Santo Domingo. His recommendation led to building Fort Aránzazu to guard the entrance to the bay. After the port of Copano was established, named for Copane Indians, the bay was called Copano. Parrilla considered Matagorda and St. Joseph's one island, which he called Isla de Culebra (Snake Island).

Many of the Spanish place names on the coast date back to a hundred-year stretch from the time of the French incursion until the Spanish began to establish a real presence in South Texas.

*—July 23, 2014*

# A Curtain of Green

Many Spanish place names were given during a hundred-year stretch that began in 1685, the year of the French which also marked the beginning of Spanish Texas. Some names from that period are still with us while others came soon afterwards.

—Aransas. The name of the bay, pass and river originated with Fort Aránzazu, built to guard the entrance to Copano Bay. The Handbook of Texas attributes the name to an Indian tribe called Aransuas; however, the origin of Aránzazu and its derivative Aransas has not been pinned down.

—Baffin Bay was called Lago de la Santisima Trinidad by Orobio Basterra in 1747. Later it was called Salt Lagoon. The name Baffin Bay has been attributed to Mifflin Kenedy. His Laureles Ranch bordered the bay. He supposedly named it as a joke after Baffin Bay near Greenland, one of the coldest places on Earth, but there's no evidence for that.

—Cayo del Oso. The origin of the Watershed of the Bear is unknown. It probably came after Orobio Basterra visited the area in 1747 because he called Oso Creek Purisima Concepción (Immaculate Conception). The land grant that included Corpus Christi was called Rincón del Oso. If rincón is translated as corner or remote place, the grant was for Bear Corner or Bear Place.

—Copano Bay was named for the Copanes, a Karankawa tribe. In 1766, Diego Ortiz Parrilla called the bay Santo Domingo. After the port of Copano opened in 1785, the bay was called Copano.

—Corpus Christi. It has long been an article of faith that the bay was named by Alonso Alvarez de Pineda in 1519, the first European to explore the coast. Some believe he anchored in the bay on the feast day of Corpus Christi and gave it that name.

Pineda's records were lost, so we may never know for sure if he did indeed name Corpus Christi Bay. However, the legend is so old

125

and so persistent that it may contain some truth. Some old legends and fables do turn out to be true.

What we know for a fact is that in 1766 Parrilla explored the area. His map showed his encampment at "Campamento en la playa Corpus Christi" and thus emerged the name Corpus Christi.

—Lavaca and Matagorda bays were called La Bahía del Espíritu Santo (Bay of the Holy Spirit). Lavaca (the cow) was believed named for buffalo, not cows.

Henri Joutel, one of La Salle's lieutenants, saw herds of buffalo ("beeves," he called them) on the coast north of Matagorda Bay.

Juan Enriquez Barroto in 1687 called Matagorda Bay San Bernardo, but it later gained the name Matagorda, Spanish for the heavy cane found there. The Lavaca River was known for a time as Río Caña, or River of Canes. Today, Espíritu Santo survives as the name of a small bay between Matagorda and San Antonio bays.

—Mustang Island. An earlier Spanish name of obscure origin was Isla de General Mina. The later name obviously came from the abundance of wild horses on the island. Settlers shot the mustangs to keep them from luring away ranch stock.

—Nueces River. In 1689, Alonso de León, on his way to the coast in search of La Salle's French fort and settlement, crossed this river and called it Rio de las Nueces (nuts) for its pecan trees. The Nueces is one of the few old names that hasn't been changed in more than 300 years, though the pecan trees have long been gone.

—Padre Island has had many names. It was called Isla Blanca for its white beaches, Isla de Santiago, Isla de Corpus Christi, San Carlos de los Malaguitos, and Isla del Padre Ballí. Pineda called it Isla Blanca (White Island) and Parrilla in 1766 called it Isla de la Malaguitos for the Malaquite Indians on the lower end.

In 1804, Padre Nicolas Ballí established a ranch on the southern end of the island, called Santa Cruz (Holy Cross). Though the ranch was abandoned in 1844 the name Isla del Padre survived.

—Paso de los Brazos de Santiago (the Arms of St. James) separates Padre and Brazos islands. It was named by Francisco Garay in 1523.

—Paso Caballo, between Matagorda Island and Matagorda Peninsula, was named by Alonso de León in 1690 after the horses of his men stumbled in the sand near the pass. Paso Caballo became Pass Cavallo in English. As with the Nueces, it is one of the old names that stuck.

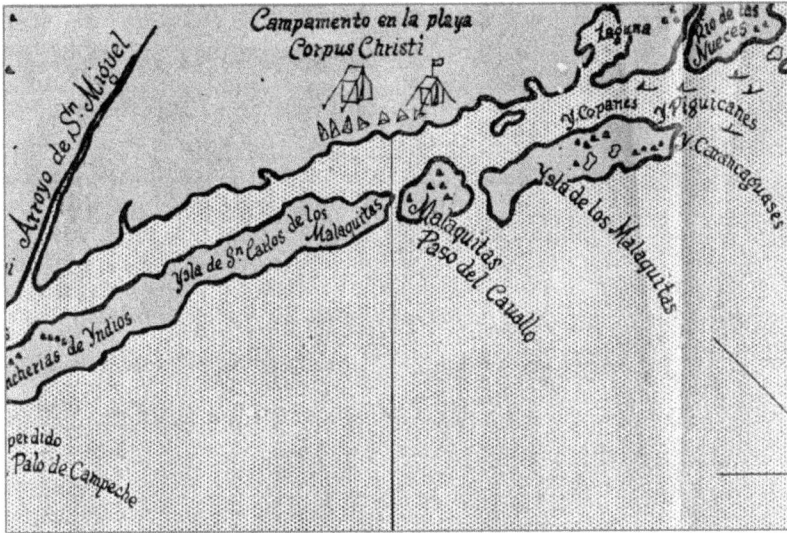

*An enlarged detail from Diego Ortiz Parrilla's 1766 map of the Texas Coast shows his encampment on the beach, labeled "Campamento en la playa Corpus Christi" (encampment on the beach at Corpus Christi). From the Caller-Times Archives.*

—St. Joseph's Island. If it is the same island, Cabeza de Vaca called it Malhado, or Isle of Misfortune. St. Joseph's fits the size, location and the general description of Cabeza de Vaca's island.

Parrilla in 1766 called St. Joseph's and Matagorda together as Culebra (Snake) Island for its rattlesnakes. An English map of 1792, which relied on Spanish sources, identified the island as Ysla de San Josef and showed it as one long island. Some old Spanish maps showed it as Isla de Aránzazu or Isla de San José. Early settlers, beginning in the 1830s, called it St. Joseph's. The name was changed in 1973 to San José.

The origin of many place names along the coast is a complicated story which I have only touched upon. And I haven't addressed the fact that Karankawa place names have been lost. Most likely they were related to distinctive geographical features, but, sadly, the Karankawan names disappeared long ago, like the Karankawas themselves. Nothing is ever lost if there are some to remember, but there were no Karankawas left to remember.

A perusal of old maps will show that South Texas was liberally sprinkled with names connected to past events in the area's rich history. Spanish expeditions left us with names that evoke visions of the past.

You can almost see De León's men crossing the Nueces, with shady pecan trees lining its banks, or see their horses stumbling in the deep sand near Pass Cavallo, or the buffalo grazing near the shore of Lavaca Bay, or the wild mustangs kicking up their heels among the dunes of Mustang Island. And, perhaps, in the mind's eye you can picture a solitary and elusive bear withdrawing behind a curtain of green on the Cayo del Oso.

*—July 30, 2014*

# Ada Wilson

You will have noticed the stone house on Ocean Drive at Doddridge with a strange round turret tower that looks as if it were built to repel Viking raiders. The story behind it is even stranger. It was Ada Laverne Rogers Wilson's tower.

When she died in 1977, the obituary noted her two big achievements — the establishment of the Ada Wilson Hospital for Crippled Children and her legal battle that forced Texas to buy her Mustang Island land for a state park. There was a third achievement — the creation of Ada herself as a character in her own story.

Let's make a large assumption. Let's say that everything she said about herself was true. She was born in Randolph, Tenn., in the family of a lumberman. She was a musical genius. By nine she was playing Bach fugues — "not etudes, honey, fugues." She graduated at 18 from Cumberland University, studied at Julliard's, and had her debut as a concert pianist at Carnegie Hall — "I was great!" — then performed in concerts for year.

In 1921, at age 22, she married Sam Wilson Jr., an oil lease broker in El Dorado, Ark. Wilson drilled dry holes before he and Ada moved to Corpus Christi in 1936. Wilson's luck turned and he was credited with bringing in the Aransas, Agua Dulce, Wilson and Refugio oilfields. He formed his own oil companies, bought the Nixon Building on the bluff, renamed it the Wilson Building, and bought Mustang Island except for Port Aransas.

Meantime, Ada founded the Ada Wilson Hospital of Physical Medicine and Rehabilitation. It began in a small house on Chaparral before it was moved to a cluster of houses on Third Street. She later helped build a new facility next to Driscoll Children's Hospital. The Ada Wilson clinic was recognized as a pioneer in rehabilitation.

After Sam's death in 1957, she traveled to England where she had a nice visit with the Queen "even though they said it was a cocktail party, but honey, all they serve over there is tea." She discovered that her late husband was related to royalty, somehow, and decided to build a round tower next to her home on Ocean Drive to give it a castle-like appearance. It was designed by architect Richard Colley and was used to store her antiques and china.

In 1976, a Caller-Times reporter, Mary Alice Davis, interviewed Ada for two long stories. From that interview we learn that Ada was staying in a hotel because rats had invaded her home on Ocean Drive. "I've got rats in my house, honey. Tails long as cat's tails. But I think they are out now." We also learned that:

—She was a child prodigy in music. "My music education, now that's the thing to play up. I was great in music! Great!" And she was recognized as a potential movie star — "They said I was beautiful!"

—She was successful before she met Sam Wilson. "Honey, my picture and what I had done went all over the world. I made $2 million and everybody knows it."

—She was the brains in their oil business. "Sam never could make a deal. He was good-looking and honest and crazy about me. And he could bring in a well. He could do that."

The reporter mentioned the rivalry between Ada and the late Clara Driscoll, pointing out curious parallels shared by the two doyennes or dowager queens.

Mrs. Wilson founded the Ada Wilson Hospital. Clara Driscoll left money to found the Driscoll Children's Hospital. After Clara built the 20-story Driscoll Hotel, Ada and Sam bought the Nixon Building nearby; the two structures dominated the city skyline. Clara wrote two books and an operetta. Ada wrote a short story and several musical compositions, including the city's official song. Clara's husband Henry Sevier served as U.S. ambassador to Chile. Mrs. Wilson said her husband had been appointed ambassador three times "but they never came through because of changes of administration or something."

Whenthe reporter asked Ada if she and Clara had been rivals, she said, "Oh, no, honey, not at all. That's a mistake. Let me tell you about poor Clara. I felt sorry for her. She would go on and on about my brilliance and what I had done . . ."

The late publisher of the Caller-Times, Edward Harte, wrote a column in 1976 that detailed Ada Wilson's long fight with the state. She had decided to sell Mustang Island — she called it "my island"

*Ada Wilson during an interview in February 1976. She died a year later. Both photographs are from the Caller-Times Archives.*

*Ada Wilson's home on Ocean Drive at Doddridge, with its added turret tower, from 1977.*

— to private developers and she would have made a lot of money. "Sissy Farenthold, then in the Legislature, took the lead in trying to convince Ada that a state park was the highest and best use for Mustang, or at least part of it."

But the state didn't want it, or least the chairman of the Parks and Wildlife Commission didn't want it. So Ada took her case to court and eventually it reached the U.S. Supreme Court, where she won. "From a monetary point of view," Harte wrote, "Ada would have been better off to drop the whole thing and sell to private interests. But we can all be glad that she didn't." It was a fine thing.

When Ada Wilson died on Feb. 17, 1977, an editorial in the Caller-Times described her as a flamboyant original. "Many South Texans, young and old, are alive and walking today because of the hospital she built. Hundreds of thousands will enjoy the public beaches of Mustang Island in future years because she believed strongly enough in an idea to fight government bureaucracy and win."

In life, Ada Laverne Rogers Wilson craved attention and knew how to get it. She would always seek the center of the stage. Whichever gene contributes to a sense of discretion and modesty and self-deprecation, Ada didn't have it. She was always improving and adding to her life story, enlarging her role and manufacturing supporting details as needed, but who would challenge her? Whatever she was, she was never ordinary; as she told Mary Alice Davis, "Honey, I've been unusual all my life." If part of her life story was a creation of her own fantasy, then many were enriched by that fantasy and the deeds of a very great heart.

*—Aug. 6, 2014*

## Shootout at Bessie Miller's

A resurgent Ku Klux Klan in the 1920s was active in local politics and political battles sometimes descended into real ones. In the 1922 election in Nueces County, Klan-backed candidates captured many county offices and one Klan candidate almost won the sheriff's race. The anti-Klan candidate was Frank Robinson, who won by only 64 votes. His opponent was W. F. "Wildfire" Johnston, who accused Robinson of stuffing ballot boxes in Robstown. Texas Rangers were rushed to Corpus Christi to keep the peace.

That October, Sheriff Robinson harassed a storeowner and suspected Klan member, G. E. Warren, by slapping him and calling him a Kluxer. Warren phoned Fred Roberts, a Klan leader, to ask for help. Roberts was still in his car in front of Warren's store when he was shot and killed by Sheriff Robinson and two deputies. The sheriff said he thought Roberts had a gun. He was acquitted in a trial in Laredo but, fearing Klan retaliation, he decamped for Mexico.

Three years later, in 1925, the worst shootout in city history was Klan-related. It was a hot and sultry summer evening on July 5, 1925, a Sunday, when Deputy Constable R. R. Bledsoe received a drunk and disorderly complaint from Bessie Miller. Bessie's place was a stucco house at the north end of Sam Rankin Street where she specialized in renting girls by the half-hour.

After Bledsoe got the call, he drove to the First Methodist Church to get his boss, Constable Carl Bisbee, who was attending services with his wife and daughters. Bisbee left church and went with Bledsoe. It was the last call they would ever make.

Bisbee, from Gilmer, Neb., was well liked. He had been a clerk before he was elected constable, with Klan support. He was known as a calm person with a polite demeanor. His deputy was the opposite. Bledsoe, a former Ranger, was considered a bully who liked to pistol-whip drunks and slap shoeshine boys. Like Bisbee, he was suspected of being a Klan member. But, then, who knew who belonged to the Invisible Empire?

Bledsoe and Bisbee arrived at Bessie Miller's at 8 p.m. and parked in front of a Ford coupe on the street in front. Two men were about to get into the car: George Ryder, a 31-year-old from a ranching family in Alice, and his friend Paul McAllister, a deputy game warden who was also a former Texas Ranger. McAllister had been a deputy sheriff in Cameron County when he killed Brownsville City Marshal Joe Crixell in 1912. He was acquitted and later hired as a policeman in Corpus Christi. He was known to belong to the anti-Klan faction in local enforcement.

Bisbee and Bledsoe, the constable and deputy constable, approached the Ford coupe. Ryder was about to open the driver's door; McAllister was already in the car. Bledsoe asked Ryder where they were going and Ryder said San Diego. "No, you're not," said Bledsoe. "You're under arrest." "What for?" asked Ryder. "It don't make no difference what for," Bledsoe said. "I can lock you up for any reason I want to."

Ryder told Bledsoe and Bisbee they had better go back to town before there was trouble. Bisbee said to Bledsoe, "Well, let's go back and leave them alone." He got back into the patrol car, but Bledsoe pulled his pistol and shot Ryder in the leg.

Bisbee fired shots from the patrol car. McAllister tripped as he tried to get out of the Ford coupe. Bledsoe shot him to death as he was on the ground. Ryder returned fire at Bledsoe and Bisbee. Another man on the scene, Rufus "Big Boy" McMurray from Three Rivers, was shot, either as a participant or innocent bystander.

In a few minutes, five men had been shot: constables Bisbee and Bledsoe, Ryder and McAllister, and McMurray from Three Rivers. McAllister was dead at the scene. Ryder died 24 hours later. Bledsoe died at 10:40 in the emergency room and Bisbee died at 12:15. All had many gunshot wounds.

Before he died, Bisbee said he tried to stop the shooting, but that the men had been drinking and didn't know what they were doing. He was anxious about the condition of his colleague in the fight and also asked about McAllister. His last words were, "Poor Paul, poor Paul."

In the days that followed there were conflicting accounts of who fired first. One said George Ryder claimed that he fired first. "He (Bledsoe) called me a bootlegger and I fired the first shot." But

*Ku Klux Klan members turned out for the burial of W. F. "Wildfire" Johnston at Rose Hill Cemetery in June 1925. Johnston was the Klan candidate for sheriff in 1922. Several confrontations between Klan and anti-Klan factions ended in bloodshed, including the worst shootout in city history on July 5, 1925. Photo is from the Corpus Christi Central Library.*

Ryder's brother, who talked to him before he died, said he told him that Bledsoe started shooting. And that was confirmed by a woman who worked for Bessie Miller and was watching from a window. She said Bledsoe fired first, shooting Ryder in the leg and then shot McAllister. Sheriff Ben Lee's investigation reached the same conclusion.

"The constable (Bisbee) hired a deputy (Bledsoe) who had a mania for killing people," Sheriff Lee said. "By the time the thing was over, there wasn't anybody left to try for the killings. They were all dead."

George Ryder's body was shipped to Alice for the funeral. Services for his friend McAllister were held at the home of Corpus Christi Police Chief J. B. Shaw. Sheriff Lee was a pallbearer. The sheriff and the police chief belonged to the anti-Klan faction.

Short services were held for Bledsoe at the David Peel Mortuary, a meeting place of the Klan. Bisbee's funeral was reported to be one of the largest the city had seen in a long time. Thirty robed members of the Knights of the Ku Klux Klan, No. 225, held ceremonies at the grave at Rose Hill Cemetery.

The fifth man who was shot, McMurray from Three Rivers, survived. An investigation into the causes of the shootout was conducted by a justice of the peace, but the results were never published. On matters relating to the Klan, the custom was that some subjects were better left unmentioned, and people probably wanted to put that dismal incident to rest.

Bessie Miller's place continued to operate for another 16 years, until 1941, when similar establishments in the red-light district were all closed, at the request of the new Naval Air Station. As for the Klan, the Invisible Empire became less influential and more invisible in local politics.

*—Aug. 13, 2014*

# The Skeleton That Testified

It was a hot day in the office of Sheriff Ben Lee in the Nueces County Courthouse on Sept. 1, 1931. In came Matt Dunn and a vaquero named Juan. "This is the sheriff's office, Juan," Dunn told the vaquero, "tell them what you saw."

Juan said he was working cattle on the Dunn ranch on the Oso near the Don Patricio Causeway when he noticed cattle shying away from something in the brush. He thought it was a rattlesnake but he found a human skeleton.

Deputies Ike Elliff and Jim Shaw went to check it out. At the site they saw the bleached bones of a skeleton near an automobile top. A closer look revealed blond hair and a hole in the back of the skull.

Who was the blond man? Who was the killer? What was the motive? The clothing offered no clues. The elements had erased any laundry marks. Near the bones they found a scrap of a Houston newspaper and an envelope addressed to Fred Sinclair of Sinclair Metal Works in Corpus Christi.

They took the skeleton to undertaker Maxwell P. Dunne. The coroner's exam revealed that the murdered man's left arm was shorter than his right. Elliff had a vague memory of dealing with a man with a shorter left arm, but the details escaped him. When he looked through notes of old cases the name of Alfred Steinbach caught his eye. That was the man he was thinking of. He had investigated that young man.

A girl named Mary Moulter told Sheriff Lee that Steinbach was a suspicious character, that he didn't have a job but always had money. When Elliff questioned Steinbach he said that he was writing a book, his home was in Cincinnati, and his father sent him an allowance. Elliff concluded that Mary Moulter's suspicions were groundless. But when he talked to him he had noticed that Steinbach's left arm was shorter than his right.

137

At Steinbach's rooming house, the landlady said she hadn't seen him since early July. She said he had roomed with a man named Don Carlis and that Carlis told her Steinbach left for San Antonio. Elliff didn't mention finding the skeleton.

The deputies went to see Fred Sinclair. He told them Carlis had worked for him but now worked at the Binz Garage. They went to the garage and asked for Carlis. "I am Carlis," said a tall man. They told him they were looking for a man named Steinbach. Carlis showed no surprise. "I am looking for him, too," he said. "He owes me $125."

Carlis said he thought Steinbach left for Canada. They took Carlis to the county jail for further questioning. By nightfall, the deputies had been working since they found the skeleton that morning. They had Carlis in jail but no evidence. If they told him about finding the skeleton and accused him of murdering Steinbach, they would probably not get very far with the interrogation.

Steinbach's father in Cincinnati said he would bring his son's dental chart. Elliff and Shaw went back to the Binz Garage. Frank Binz's son Henry said he went with Carlis to the Don Patricio Causeway to put an axle on a car. He said Carlis told him he had been hunting near the causeway and found a human skeleton.

The deputies were startled because they had kept the news of the skeleton quiet, yet Carlis knew of human bones in the brush where Steinbach, they believed, had been found.

The case was taking shape. They knew Carlis roomed with Steinbach, that Carlis had worked for Sinclair and an envelope addressed to Sinclair was found by the bones, and that Carlis had told about seeing a skeleton in that same area. When the suspect's tools were examined, a hammer was found that perfectly fit the hole in the skull. On it were bloodstains and a strand of blond hair.

The deputies learned that Carlis had been in prison and had several aliases. Now they were ready to talk to their suspect.

They told Carlis that Steinbach was dead and accused him of killing him. Carlis said he was ready to make a statement. He said he and Steinbach were out riding when his car broke down. Another car came along, three men jumped out, one of them shot Steinbach, and they took off. He said he didn't think anyone would believe his story so he hid Steinbach's body.

When a dental chart showed the skeleton was Steinbach, Carlis was charged with murder.

The courtroom was packed when the trial began on Nov. 9, 1931. Halfway through the trial, there was a scream when Dunne, the undertaker, wheeled in a gurney with the skeleton on it. District Attorney D. S. Purl told the court that Steinbach had returned from the dead to tell of his fate.

" 'Look at my teeth. Look at my left arm. Look at these pictures. You see, I'm Alfred Steinbach,' the bones of the dead man seemed to be saying. 'Now look at these nicks in my ribs. That's where I was shot. See this round hole in my skull. That's where the murderer hit me with a ball-peen hammer.' "

The jury found Carlis guilty and he was sentenced to 99 years in prison. The case of the talking skeleton got national attention. It also got reversed. Bringing the body into the courtroom had so prejudiced the jury, the appeals court ruled, that Carlis did not receive a fair trial. They sent the case back for retrial. In the second trial, Carlis was found guilty but sentenced to only eight years in prison.

A curious thing happened while Carlis was waiting for that second trial. He somehow convinced Sheriff Lee that he could prove his innocence if the sheriff would take him to San Antonio.

The sheriff took Carlis out of jail and drove him to San Antonio, where he escaped. He was recaptured in Missouri and returned to Corpus Christi. Sheriff Lee said in explanation that, "We went to San Antonio and he prevailed upon me to take him to a certain address. He went in the front door and out the back door. I guess I shouldn't have trusted him."

(A detailed account of the investigation and trial was told by Deputy Ike Elliff to Forrest Beck, which was included in the "Pathfinders of Texas" by Mrs. Frank DeGarmo.)

*—Aug. 20, 2014*

# The St. James Site

The Union Theater was there, at the southeast corner of Chaparral and Lawrence, then the St. James Hotel, then Lichtenstein's fourth and final downtown location. Now something else is going up on this historic site.

The Union Theater was there first. It was one of the oldest structures in Corpus Christi, built in 1845 when Zachary Taylor's 4,000 troops were concentrated at Corpus Christi preparing for the Mexican War. The theater was built to entertain the troops. It could seat 800.

The builder, Charles Bryant, was an exiled architect from Maine. He became involved in a rebellion in Canada and crossed the border with Maine volunteers. When the rebellion failed, Bryant came close to being hanged. He left for Texas.

Two months after Bryant's theater opened, Taylor's army departed for the Rio Grande, in March 1846. The theater sat empty. Bryant went to Galveston where he got a commission to design St. Mary's Cathedral, a beautiful building that's still standing.

Bryant returned to Corpus Christi with plans to reopen the Union Theater as a hotel. He became mustering officer for the Texas Rangers and was on his way to Austin when he was killed by a raiding party of Lipan-Apaches. He was killed on the Chocolate Bayou not far from Refugio. John Grumbles' company of 23 Rangers chased the Indians 300 miles before giving up.

Bryant left a widow, six children, an estate of $1,500, town lots in Corpus Christi, and architect's tools worth $5. His family later received 640 acres of land from the state in recognition for his services. No sketch or photograph of Bryant or his Union Theater has survived.

The Union Theater was torn down in 1868 to clear the site for a new hotel called the St. James, being built by cattleman J. T. "Tom"

James but named for a famous hotel in Kansas City. Edward Sidbury was in charge of constructing the St. James. It had a wide porch gallery on the east and south sides, facing Chaparral and Lawrence. At the back of the hotel were clumps of mesquite and cactus.

Before it was completed, James sold the hotel to William Long "Billy" Rogers, who is a story in himself. Rogers survived a massacre on the Arroyo Colorado in 1846, at the beginning of the Mexican War, in which his father and a brother were killed.

Billy had his throat cut and was thrown in the Arroyo Colorado, but survived. In later years, Rogers and his brother Lieuen were said to prowl the border looking for the killers and, one by one, took revenge. A slit throat on the Rio Grande was called Billy's mark.

Rogers was a rancher and sheriff of Nueces County before he bought the hotel. He was a legislator, built Market Hall, and was the founder of the city's fire department. He died on Dec. 17, 1877 at age 56. A reporter's funeral note said, "Star Rifles, escort. Fire Department. Music (provided by Masons). Hearse. Family. Citizens on horseback. Citizens in carriages."

After Rogers' death, a Confederate veteran, William Biggio, became the manager of the St. James. Biggio was born in Italy and immigrated to Mobile, Ala. During the Civil War, he was the pilot of the Confederate ram Webb which tried to run the gauntlet of Union gunboats blocking the mouth of the Mississippi. The Webb was captured and Biggio became a prisoner. After the war, he moved to Rockport and in 1877 came to Corpus Christi to manage the St. James.

Under Biggio's management, the St. James became known throughout Texas. It was the headquarters of gamblers and gunmen, ranchers and politicians. John Wesley Hardin, who once backed down Wild Bill Hickok in Abilene, stayed there. So did Ben Thompson. When Leander McNelly arrived in April 1875, his Rangers camped a mile from town while McNelly put up at the St. James. Congressman John Garner stayed at the St. James and so did Gov. Jim Hogg.

An article in the Caller once said, "While governors and congressmen banqueted in the dining rooms of the St. James, gamblers and happy-go-lucky cowboys faced each other across tables in backrooms, with poker chips drawn up in neat stacks before them and loaded revolvers beside them."

*The St. James Hotel at the corner of Chaparral and Lawrence was built in 1869 by cattle rancher J. T. "Tom" James. It was Corpus Christi's most famous hotel in the late 19th and early 20th century. It was demolished in 1937 and Lichtenstein's was built on the site. The Doc McGregor photo was taken in 1936, the year before the hotel was torn down.*

In the 1880s, after the Tex-Mex railroad was built to Laredo, Corpus Christi got its first transit system, horse-drawn herdic coaches, which stopped at the St. James to pick up passengers. In the evenings, prominent citizens would lounge on the porch of the St. James and talk about the events of the day.

Anna Moore Schwein in her memoirs said the hotel hired a trio of Italian musicians from Cuero — Billy Falvella, Frank Pelligrino, and Tony Demarco. Judge Walter Timon said one of their favorite songs was "Listen to the Mockingbird." They would finish the evening by playing "Home Sweet Home."

Biggio, a generous man, would never turn a man away hungry, whether he could pay for a meal or not. When he became too feeble to run a hotel and retired in 1905, the Caller said the hotel under another manager would never be the same. Biggio kept the hotel ledgers, which ran from 1877 to 1905, until they were destroyed in the 1919 hurricane. When he died, soon after his retirement, the district court adjourned in respect.

In later years, the St. James was operated as a rooming house serving a motley clientele before it was finally closed. The Caller in an article on Jan. 4, 1937 called it a wreck and a firetrap, with yellow-stained wallpaper hanging from sagging walls. It was torn down in 1937.

Three years later, Lichtenstein's was built on that site. Now Lichtenstein's has been demolished to make way for a new apartment building, called the Cosmopolitan, which is going up fast. It will occupy one of the prime spots in downtown Corpus Christi, the site of the old Union Theater, St. James Hotel, and Lichtenstein's last location.

Tearing down the old and replacing it with the new removes the visual context of our history. People will soon scratch their heads and ask, "Where was the old Lichtenstein building?" The Union Theater and the St. James already are mostly forgotten. How quickly the past becomes overlaid with, uh, progress.

*—Aug. 27, 2014*

# J. W. Moses, Mustanger

In his last years J. Williamson Moses wrote articles about his early experiences in Texas that were published in the San Antonio Express between 1887 and 1890. His byline was Sesom, Moses spelled backwards. Moses was a surveyor, Ranger, mustanger, storekeeper, soldier and judge. He was wounded by an Indian arrow and almost hanged by an intolerant posse. He was a Confederate expatriate in Mexico following the Civil War.

Moses was born in 1825 in South Carolina on the family plantation, which he remembered as a place of great beauty. He joined a group of volunteers for the Mexican War and arrived in Texas in 1846. Moses came down with a fever and was left behind when the others traveled to the border.

Moses spent the winter of 1846 in Houston. One day, David Burnet sent him to find Sam Houston. He found the hero of San Jacinto in a saloon engrossed in a bar bet. The bet was that Houston couldn't lift a heavy chair and hold it aloft by the lower rung without the chair wobbling. Houston won the bet. It took several drinks before he would agree to leave to see Burnet.

Once, traveling near Bastrop, Moses stopped at a tavern called Hell's Half Acre where some saloon toughs tried to pick a fight and they had Moses, with his gun drawn, pushed against a wall. An old man came in and, without raising his voice, asked what the ruckus was all about. The saloon toughs slunk off like whipped hounds. The old man was Edward Burleson, ex-vice president of the Republic.

In 1848, Moses went to work with James Giddings' surveyors in the region of the Pedernales, Llano and San Saba rivers. Since they could take only a small amount of cornmeal and flour on the overloaded pack horses, Moses wrote, they usually went without bread. But they had plenty of meat, including bear, deer, antelope

*David Burnet (left) dispatched Moses to find Sam Houston. Moses found him in a saloon engrossed in a bet over whether he could lift a heavy chair without it wobbling. Edward Burleson (right), former vice president of the Republic of Texas, came to Moses' rescue when he was threatened by rowdies in a bar near Bastrop.*

and wild turkey. Moses said, "We used to eat our partially dried lean meat as bread and the fresh and fat meat as meat."

When they were least expected the Comanches would turn up to disturb their peace. One day Moses ran into a Comanche war party. He didn't see them until he was almost on them. They shot a shower of arrows as he whipped his horse toward a cedar mott. One arrow hit him in the side, pinning him to the saddle, but he escaped to rejoin the rest of the party as they formed a defensive line. When the Comanches charged, the surveyors responded with a fierce fire. The Indians shouted insults and rode away. Moses described Comanches as bloodthirsty, murderous cowards and great villains. That was after he was hit by a Comanche arrow.

He lost his favorite horse Selim in another Comanche scrap. When he last saw him, he was being ridden by two braves. Moses left word with Indian agents that he would swap three or four good ponies for Selim, but he never saw him again. Forty years later, he wrote, "I never call to mind old Selim without regret."

Moses joined Sutton's company of Rangers, which made camp at San Patricio. Not long afterwards, frontier protection was turned over to the Army's mounted infantry stationed at a string of new forts. The army was in the saddle, so to speak, even if it couldn't ride. The Rangers were mustered out in San Antonio.

Moses said San Antonio was more like a Mexican puebla than an American town. Chili vendors, their charcoal fires burning, held forth nightly on the Main plaza, three-card monte was dealt, and every man carried a sidearm. Most days there was a horse race or cockfight which ended in a fight.

Moses turned to mustanging in the Wild Horse Desert. He was the captain of a crew of mustangers who made their living catching and selling wild horses. In the early 1850s the prairies of South Texas were overrun with mustangs. Within a decade, however, they were mostly gone, like the buffalo they were hunted to near extinction.

Corpus Christi in the early 1850s, Moses wrote, had two or three buildings on the bluff and the beach part of town consisted of two or three stores, the largest being William Mann's red-brick store. Mann's trade in hides was a big business. During this time, he wrote, a man named Tom Parker served as bailiff in district court. Parker stepped before the bench one day and told Judge M. P. Norton, "Here is your venereal, judge." The judge scolded his bailiff. "Venire, Mr. Parker, venire. Really, you must learn the law terms better."

Moses married in 1854 but divorced his wife a year later over some domestic situation he never explained. He opened a store in Banquete and married Victoriana Cuellar in 1857. Soon afterwards, Moses was almost hanged by a posse that thought he was guilty of, as it was said, being Jewish. He was rescued by Banquete cattleman John Rabb.

During the Civil War, Moses served as a lieutenant in Rabb's militia company on the border. After the war, he moved to Mexico with other diehard Confederate expatriates where he got work operating a sawmill near Saltillo. Moses loved Mexico, which he always called "the land of Dios y Libertad." "I have yet to see an American who traveled to or worked in Mexico who will not freely admit that the people of Mexico are generally, almost universally, kind and considerate."

Moses moved back to Texas and in 1871 he was elected chief justice (county judge) of Aransas County and admitted to the bar. He moved to San Diego where he became county judge.

As Moses recalled the old days, there was a spaciousness we no longer have and always the sense of lurking danger. "San Diego —

*J. Williamson Moses, a surveyor, Texas Ranger and mustanger, said they often went for months without eating bread or vegetables. Their diet consisted of bear, antelope, deer, wild turkey, goose and small game.*

where but a short time ago we chased herds of mustang horses, lassoed wild cattle and fought the fierce and savage Comanche — is now a thriving town."

Moses died on April 28, 1893. An obituary said that "another old Texas landmark is gone, lamented by all." A few years ago I re-edited Moses' Sesom articles into a book titled "Texas In Other Days," which was printed by the Corpus Christi Friends of the Library. This gave me a greater appreciation of Judge Moses, the old mustanger who belongs to the history of South Texas.

*—Sept. 3, 2014*

# The Red Rovers

Because of the epic story of David Crockett, we are all familiar with the Tennessee volunteers who fought in the Texas Revolution. Not so well known is the story of the Alabama volunteers who met a similarly tragic fate.

There was a strong connection between South Texas and Northwest Alabama before the revolution. As John Henry Brown tells us, "The largest and most remarkable addition to Austin's colony, arriving by land in December 1830 and by water in February 1831, was a self-organized group of kinsmen and friends from Decatur and Tuscumbia, Ala."

The group traveled by water from Decatur in two flat-bottomed boats, one loaded with cotton and the other with household goods. They traveled up the Tennessee River to the Ohio then down the Mississippi. At New Orleans, the cotton was sold. They chartered a ship which took them to Cox's Point on the Texas coast and joined what became known as the Alabama Settlement in Jackson County.

After the Texas revolt began in 1835, public meetings were held in Alabama to drum up support for Texas. While this was done all over the South, Alabama was particularly responsive.

A mass meeting was held at Shakespeare's Theatre in Mobile. Those who volunteered to join the fight in Texas were called the Mobile Greys, under the command of David Burke. They reported at San Felipe on Nov. 30, 1835.

At Montgomery, a number of men formed a company called the Alabama Greys under the command of Isaac Ticknor. They landed at Copano in January 1836.

At Huntsville, a company of volunteers was organized under the command of Peyton Wyatt. They were furnished with muskets from the Alabama state armory. They traveled overland and reached Washington-on-the-Brazos in December 1835.

At Courtland, a small town near Decatur in North Alabama, men volunteered for Texas under the command of Dr. Jack Shackelford. He had a military background, owned a cotton plantation and had been trained as a surgeon. Among his 55 volunteers were a nephew and his oldest son, Fortunatus.

Shackelford's men were dressed in uniforms made by the women of Courtland. These were fringed shirts patterned with red, green and brown checks and pants dyed red; the dye was made from the red clay of North Alabama. The red pants gave them the name the Red Rovers. They landed at Matagorda Bay on Jan. 19, 1836.

After the fall of the Alamo, four Alabama companies — the Mobile Greys, Huntsville Volunteers, Alabama Greys from Montgomery and Red Rovers from Courtland — were assigned to the command of Col. James Fannin at Goliad.

Shackelford of the Red Rovers knew something about military tactics; he had served on Andrew Jackson's staff in the War of 1812. Before the battle of Coleto Creek, Shackelford begged Fannin not to tarry on the open prairie, with good cover a few miles away and Mexican Gen. José Urrea somewhere in the vicinity.

Fannin ignored the advice and Urrea caught them in the open. For infantry facing cavalry, Fannin's men had to fight in the worst place possible. During the fight, the Red Rovers were on the extreme right front of Fannin's hollow square. They fought like veterans. Shackelford said his men "would have done honor to Rome and Sparta in their proudest days of military glory."

After Fannin surrendered, the men were marched back to Goliad and herded into the church. On March 27, Palm Sunday, they were led out under a pretext; they believed they were being taken to Copano where they would board a ship to return to the United States. They were all shot. The dead were stripped and their naked bodies were covered with brush and burned.

Of the 165 Alabamans at Goliad, 141 were killed in the massacre. A few were spared and several others escaped. Of the 35 Mobile Greys, 28 were executed. Of 34 Huntsville Volunteers, 27 were killed. Of 41 Alabama Greys from Montgomery, 35 were killed. Of 55 Red Rovers from Courtland, 51 were executed, including Shackelford's son and nephew.

Shackelford survived because his services as a doctor were needed. He was taken to San Antonio with Dr. Joseph Barnard where they treated wounded Mexican soldiers.

*The monument at Goliad where the bones of the massacred are buried.*

As Shackelford wrote, he and Dr. Barnard remained in San Antonio until the Mexican forces began their retreat after the battle of San Jacinto. "We procured horses and made off, passing the Mexican Army in the night." At Goliad, Shackelford went to the scene of the slaughter and saw the bones of his men and the other victims of the Goliad massacre bleaching on the prairie. He asked Gen. Thomas Rusk to make sure that "the bones of our fallen companions were interred with all the honors of war."

When he arrived back home at Courtland, Dr. Shackelford was greeted by a large crowd. They were the fathers, mothers, brothers and sisters of the Red Rovers. They came to congratulate him on his escape. As one account (Henry Foote, "Texas and Texans") related, Shackelford gazed on the large crowd, planning to give them some idea of how it was. But as he remembered all that had passed he was so overcome by emotion that he began to cry. And those gathered before him began to shed tears in their shared remorse for all the Red Rovers slaughtered at Goliad. Their bones are still there, buried in Texas.

*—Sept. 10, 2014*

# On Water Street

Where were the old buildings on Water Street in the 19th Century? They were pulled down long ago, swept away by storms or improvements. Not only are the old buildings gone but we don't always know where they were. And of course Water Street no longer is lapped by high tides, not since the seawall was built. It lost the waterfront and even the smell of water.

In the 100 block of Water was Mann's red house on the beach side at Cooper's Alley near where Blucher's Creek emptied into the bay. It was one of the most notable places in early Corpus Christi. Mann's structure got its name from the color of its shellcrete bricks.

William Mann's place was a complex built around a central courtyard and surrounded by a high wall made of shellcrete. During threats of an Indian attack, Mann's became the town's fort-like sanctuary. The main structure was three stories high. It included a store, the Mann family residence, and places for traders from Mexico to stay. A pier for loading and unloading trade goods was in front of the buildings.

In the 200 block was Conrad Meuly's bakery at the intersection of Laguna (renamed Sartain). Meuly, an immigrant from Switzerland, came to Corpus Christi at the time of Zachary Taylor's encampment. He built his home on Chaparral behind the bakery. The Education Service Center building occupies the site today.

Down from Meuly's bakery was Cornelius Cahill's place, built in 1848 of shellcrete bricks with wood facing. It sat directly across from the Central Wharf, facing the bay. Cahill's two-story building housed a store and family dwelling on the first floor and the City Hotel on the second. City aldermen held their meetings at Cahill's in the 1850s.

Cahill's was demolished after it was damaged in the 1919 storm. It was not easy to pull the old building down. Several charges of dynamite were used, but the explosions left only small breaks in the walls, hardly larger than the space made for the dynamite sticks. Finally, by undermining the foundation, workers were able to bring down the old walls.

In the 300 block, between William and Lawrence, were several buildings on the water side. In the middle of the block was an ice plant built in 1878 by Richard King. Before, blocks of lake ice packed in sawdust were brought in each spring from Maine and New York. After King's death in 1885, the ice plant passed into the hands of George Blucher.

Near the ice plant on the water side was John Superach's oyster shop. Across the street was James Hunter's Livery. In the 400 block, at the Lawrence intersection, were two wool warehouses owned by Doddridge and Davis. Elizabeth Hart's store, built in 1848, was in this block.

Past the Schatzel intersection was the old Byington house which was used by Zachary Taylor for his headquarters in 1845. It was torn down in 1910.

On the south side of the Peoples Street intersection was the Hunsaker Building where E. J. Davis had a law office after the Civil War. Davis was elected governor during Reconstruction. The Nueces Building occupies this site. Edward Ohler's building, on the north side of Peoples, was an identical twin to the Hunsaker building. Stretching into the bay in front of Ohler's was Ohler's Wharf. When Henry Kinney held the Lone Star Fair in 1852 Maltby's Circus was on the beach in front of Ohler's.

Edward Ohler was one of Corpus Christi's principal merchants after he arrived from Veracruz in 1848. His two-story building had a store and warehouse downstairs with living quarters upstairs. Ohler sold groceries, dry goods, and Colt Navy pistols for $25. Ohler's store was torn down in the 1860s. After that, George Evans built a hide and wool warehouse there.

Next to the Evans warehouse was John Anderson's windmill and cottage. Across the way was Anderson's wharf where his ships docked. Anderson's mill was used to grind salt and corn and saw timber into firewood. The Anderson home and windmill were torn down after his death. In 1913, the Nueces Hotel was built on the site of the Evans warehouse and the Anderson home and windmill.

Between Starr and Taylor, on the south side of Taylor, was the office for architects Carroll and Iler. Charles Carroll designed St.

*Robert Ritter's hotel and bathhouse, which opened in 1891.*

*A postcard from Jan. 19, 1907 shows the Seaside Hotel at the east end of Taylor Street, facing south, with its arbor of salt cedars next to the bay.*

Patrick's Cathedral in 1881. One of his daughters was Mary Carroll, who became school superintendent; Carroll High School was named for her.

Past Taylor, on the water side of the street, was the home of Capt. John Dix, built in the 1850s. Dix, a retired sea captain, wanted a view of ships coming in. The Dix home was sold to Jack Ennis who converted it into the Seaside Hotel. At the hotel's popular arbor, guests could sit in the shade of salt cedars and watch the coming and going of boats on the bay. Ennis built the Seaside Pavilion on a pier off Taylor Street in front of the old Dix home.

In 1891 Robert Ritter built the Ritter Hotel and Bath House on a pier over the water, a popular gathering place in the 1890s. A ball was held at Ritter's on Jan. 8, 1893. An article said the pavilion was decorated with evergreens, flowers and bunting. The Falvella orchestra from the St. James Hotel provided the music. After dancing, a curtain was drawn to reveal tables loaded with delicacies. Supper lasted for an hour then the dancing resumed.

Further north, past the Stanley Welch home, was the wooden Brooklyn Bridge over the slough between Corpus Christi and Brooklyn. That was before it became known as North Beach.

*—Sept. 17, 2014*

# On Chaparral Street

Chaparral was called Front Street. It was Corpus Christi's main street. Whether it was named for the chaparral thicket beyond its southern limits I am unable to say.

In block one at Cooper's Alley was William "Billy" Rogers' home. Rogers survived a wagon-train massacre at the beginning of the Mexican War. His throat was cut but he survived and supposedly tracked down the bandits who killed his father and brother and, one by one, slit their throats. Rogers' home at 101 Chaparral burned on Oct. 1, 1871. After the fire, he organized Corpus Christi's first fire volunteer department. His replacement home was torn down in 1941.

Past Laguna (now Sartain) was Belden's Warehouse, a shellcrete building that stored supplies for Taylor's army. Frederick Belden, a merchant in Matamoros, moved to Corpus Christi to engage in the Mexican trade soon after the town was founded in 1839.

Across from Belden's was Conrad Meuly's house built in 1851. It sported fancy iron grillwork from New Orleans. That site is now occupied by the Education Service Center. Mifflin Kenedy's office in the 1880s was at the southwest corner at William Street. It is easy to imagine Kenedy, the cattle rancher and former steamboat captain, walking down the hill from his opulent mansion on the bluff — an olive-green Italianate building — to his shed-like office on Chaparral.

Diagonally across the intersection was the Gravis boarding house (it was called the California House) built in 1846 by J.A.F. Gravis. After he died of yellow fever in 1854, his widow Irenah married H.W. Berry. She ran the Berry boarding house and would send a boy out with a bell on a pole to beckon boarders at meal times. The Executive Surf Club occupies what was once known as the Berry Corner today.

Across from the Berry boarding house was the Noessel building. Originally it was the Kinney House hotel, built in 1845, then Kinney sold it to George Noessel. At the other end of the block was Prokop Hoffman's grocery store.

North of the Berry boarding house on the east side were Hirsch's wool house, the Crescent Hotel, the Favorite Saloon, and Frank & Weil's store. The Hirsch wool house was built in 1860 by David Hirsch, who became a major wool dealer and founder of Corpus Christi National Bank. For ox-cart drivers bringing in wool, his store was identified by a Star of David on the building.

Next to Hirsch's was the Crescent Hotel. Capt. Fred Steen and wife Nevada bought the Crescent after 1883 and it became the Steen Hotel. Next to Steen's was George Roberts' Favorite Saloon, which had been John Fogg's Saloon. On the corner was a store where E. Frank and Charles Weil sold dry goods and ranch supplies.

Across the Lawrence intersection on the west side was the St. James Hotel built in 1869. Across Chaparral from the St. James was the Doddridge and Davis Bank. The bank was downstairs with various offices upstairs. The bank closed in 1890.

North of the Doddridge Building on the east side was Wheeler's shoe store followed by Julius Henry's store, Friend and Cahn's Bank, Blumenthal & Jordt furniture store, and Headen & Son. Three identical homes were remodeled to house Blumenthal & Jordt. The three gables gave the building an unusual appearance.

At the corner of Schatzel was William Headen's wool store in a wood-frame building that had belonged to Mayor William Grace of New York. Grace was Headen's partner in the wool business. The structure was dismantled and put on a schooner and brought to Corpus Christi. The building was later occupied by ship chandler J.W. Westervelt.

Between Schatzel and Peoples on the west side was Dreyer's candy store, next door to Bob Berry's cottage with a large mulberry tree in the yard, followed by George Mew's ship chandlery. The Sierra Madre Hotel was on the corner, where the old Montgomery Ward building is today.

Across from Dreyer's on the east side was Keller's Saddlery, Morris' dry goods, and the La Retama Saloon. The La Retama building was remodeled to become Norwick Gussett's wool store and bank. Gussett was probably the city's wealthiest wool merchant. He was called Col. Gussett but he had been a sergeant during the

*Girls ride their bikes past the Doddridge and Davis Bank, which was across the street from the St. James Hotel. The bank was downstairs with various offices upstairs.*

*The DeRyee and Westervelt drug store was at the corner of Peoples Street and Chaparral. Dr. William DeRyee made the building's shellcrete blocks and collected mahogany driftwood on the island to frame the doors and windows.*

Mexican War. He founded the town of Gussettville before he moved to Corpus Christi. Gussett's store sported a rooster weathervane.

Diagonally across the Peoples Street intersection was DeRyee's drug store. Dr. William DeRyee made the building's shellcrete blocks and collected mahogany driftwood on the island to frame the doors and windows. DeRyee's was torn down to clear the way for the four-story City National Bank, built in 1908, and still standing.

Down from DeRyee's was John Hall's tin shop, decorated with a stove mounted on a pole. Past Hall's were two boarding houses run by Eli Merriman's mother. Across from DeRyee's on the east side of the street was Lichtenstein's first department store.

Past Lichtenstein's was J. B. Mitchell's hardware store, later sold to E. H. Caldwell. Mitchell sold fencing material, plows, Studebaker wagons, harrows and Buckeye mowers. His store was followed by George French's grocery store then the Kearney cottage which was used as the U.S. Customs Office.

At the end of the block at Starr was John Woessner's place. At the corner was the Woessner store and wool warehouse, where dances were held upstairs. People remembered that Woessner's had a good dance floor — "springy and fine."

In the next block, at the corner of Taylor, was the old Ranahan home built of shellcrete in 1853. During the federal bombardment of Corpus Christi in 1862, a shell smashed through the front wall, leaving a three-foot hole. It was torn down in 1938 to become a parking lot for the Ritz Theater.

Across Taylor, on the east side corner, was the home of Royal Givens, a fish dealer known as the Drumfish King. During the occupation after the Civil War, the house was used as Union headquarters, where Confederates had to swear to uphold the Constitution. Since that was called the Ironclad Oath, the house was known as the Ironclad Oath House.

*—Sept. 24, 2014*

# On Mesquite Street

While Chaparral was Front Street, Mesquite was known as Back Street. From reading accounts of pioneers and looking at old street maps, one can get a good idea of where some of the buildings were located and form some idea of what Corpus Christi was like more than a century ago.

At the south end of Mesquite in the 100 block, between Cooper's Alley and Laguna, was Frederick Belden's store. The Belden home was a two-story house at the corner of Mesquite and Laguna. Belden Street was named for him.

In the 200 block was a shellcrete building used as a Catholic school run by the Rev. Bernard O'Reilly. At the end of the block at the William intersection was the home and studio of Louis de Planque, a talented photographer who came to Corpus Christi in 1868 after stints in Mexico and Indianola. People would stroll by his studio to see photos of the town displayed in his windows.

Across William Street was Thayer's "Yankee Notions" store and on past Thayer's, in the middle of the block, was John Fogg's Livery. Fogg, a Confederate veteran, at one point operated a stagecoach line to Brownsville. At the livery, he boarded horses and rented buggies, surreys and hacks. Fogg's became Pitt's Livery, which sold and serviced the town's first automobiles.

On the west side of Mesquite, just past Lawrence, was Robert Ritter's Bazaar, a racket store that opened in a two-story building in the late 1880s. It was called a racket store because it sold kids toys that made a loud racket. This was a forerunner of the five-and-dime. Ritter also owned a hotel and bathhouse on a pier in the bay. Past Ritter's was the bakery of John Uehlinger, whose bread carts made the rounds of the town's homes and restaurants.

Across from Ritter's on the corner was the Constantine Hotel. When it was remodeled and renamed the Bidwell, one of its 25 bedrooms was turned into a bathroom. The Constantine/Bidwell Hotel became Lichtenstein's furniture showroom in 1940. It was torn down in 1999.

In the block between Schatzel and Peoples was Conrad Uehlinger's Saloon, set back from the street, as if it were shy, with a hitching post and room for horses. This had once been the old Ruby Saloon run by Peter Benson, Nueces County's wreckmaster. Past Uehlinger's Saloon, on the corner of Peoples, was the McCampbell Building. Upstairs was the law firm of John McCampbell and John Givens and downstairs, in the 1880s, was W. S. Rankin's grocery store.

Across from Rankin's Grocery, on the west side of Mesquite, was the civic center of the city, Market Hall, which was the equivalent of a town square. It was built in 1871 by Richard Jordan and William Rogers. They gave the city space for municipal offices and leased out the lower floor to butchers and vegetable vendors. To sweeten the deal, the city made it illegal to sell meat or vegetables anywhere inside the city except at Market Hall.

On the Mesquite Street side of Market Hall was the meat market of H. L. Dreyer, who was known as the boss butcher because he was responsible for keeping the other butchers in line. On the west end were quarters for the Pioneer Fire Company No. 1.

Major social events were held at Market Hall. At a Christmas ball in 1876 the town was outraged that someone scattered cayenne pepper on the dance floor. One of the most popular events held at Market Hall was the annual Firemen's Ball. Market Hall was torn down in 1911 and a new brick city hall was built on the site. Now there is a pocket handkerchief of ground called a park.

Next to Market Hall was a large building occupied by Heath & Son, which sold groceries, crockery, and iron stoves.

Diagonally across the street was R. G. Blossman's grocery. It was where the Furman building is today. Blossman sold wine, liquor and fancy delicacies, like pressed pigs feet.

Down from Blossman's was the home of John Timon, a fine old house built in 1885. In February 1891, Mrs. Timon and daughter returned from Beeville to discover a wrecked house and the body of Timon. There was evidence of a struggle but no obvious signs of how he had died or been killed. The justice of the peace ruled that death was due to unknown causes. The Timon house was in shambles and had been ransacked. Eyebrows were raised by the fact

*Robert Ritter's Bazaar was on the west side of Mesquite past the Lawrence Street intersection. Ritter's was called a racket store, a forerunner of the five-and-dime. It opened in the late 1880s.*

*Heath & Son Emporium, which sold groceries, crockery, and iron stoves, was north of Market Hall, on the west side of Mesquite Street before the intersection with Peoples Street.*

that the last person to see Timon alive was a delivery boy, who happened to be the stepson of the justice of the peace who made the ruling. If it was murder, it went unsolved. The Timon house was demolished in 1955. The Furman parking garage is on that site today.

Across from Blossman's, on the northwest corner of Mesquite and Peoples, was Matthew Headen's home. It was torn down to build the Hatch & Robertson building, later known as the Lovenskiold building. This was where farmers bought Rock Island plows and Birdsell wagons. The structure had many tenants over the years, including the Times' newspaper office and Bingham's drug store. The century old building, long vacant, is still there, looking as if it had eczema or some awful disease.

Down Mesquite, across Starr Street, was the Corpus Christi Male and Female Academy, run by Professor J. D. Meredith and his wife from 1880 to 1896. The State Hotel was built on this site. A parking lot is there today.

The next block, between Taylor and Twigg, was dominated by Artesian Square, which got its name from a well drilled in 1845. Two blocks down was the Nueces County Courthouse. The first courthouse was built in 1854 and the second in 1875, known as the Hollub Courthouse. It was designed by Rudolph Hollub who had been a mapmaker in the Union Army on the staff of Gen. U.S. Grant.

The old buildings of the 19th Century on Water, Chaparral and Mesquite — Mann's red house, Ohler's, DeRyee's drug store, the Ironclad Oath house, Ritter's racket store, Market Hall and Hollub's Courthouse — are gone and almost forgotten. Almost.

—*Oct. 1, 2014*

# Boom and Bust in 1840s

John Linn, a Victoria merchant, landed a cargo of tobacco on a beach on Corpus Christi Bay in 1829. Henry Gilpin that year brought a schooner filled with trade goods for Mexico and landed at the same place, called the old Indian trading grounds. This was where Henry Kinney built a trading post in 1839, which marked the beginning of Corpus Christi.

Kinney's Rancho stood on the frontier of what was called Western Texas. It was the only settlement between the Nueces and Rio Grande, a no-man's land claimed by Texas and Mexico and governed by neither. After Kinney, other traders arrived, including Gilpin, Frederick Belden, J. P. Kelsey, and Henry Redmond. They sold leaf tobacco, cotton prints, manufactured products and bought hides and wool from Mexico.

Kinney in those years kept in touch with friends in Mexico and Texas. He would write President Mirabeau Lamar in Austin and Gen. Mariano Arista in Matamoros. With Mexican cavalry operating in no-man's land, Texas created "spy" companies to patrol the region and keep an eye on Mexican forces.

Some spy companies preyed on Mexican traders. In 1841, John Yerby's company attacked a caravan and killed eight merchants. Troops from Mexico encountered Yerby's band south of Corpus Christi. Most of Yerby's men were killed. In a letter to President Lamar, Kinney warned that if the activities of the spy companies were not suppressed all would be lost at Corpus Christi, whose existence depended on the Mexican trade.

In May 1844, a Comanche raiding party attacked Corpus Christi. Kinney and 11 men chased the Indians west of town. In the fight, many Indians and three Corpus Christi men were killed. When Kinney appealed to Lamar for help he was authorized to raise a company of Rangers for protection.

One day Comanche raiders were chased to the Rincon (North Beach). The Indians were up against the water and it was gathering twilight. The men confronting the Indians decided to wait until daylight to attack. Next morning, to their surprise, the Comanches were gone. They had crossed over an underwater natural reef and made their escape. That's how Corpus Christi discovered what was known as the Reef Road.

After Kinney was elected to the 9th Congress of the Republic, he helped ratify terms of annexation to the U.S. As Texas moved toward statehood, war with Mexico threatened. The U.S. began to assemble an army and Kinney wrote the U.S. envoy in Austin that Corpus Christi was a good location for the army. His letters helped convince Zachary Taylor to bring the army to Corpus Christi.

On Aug. 1, 1845, the first companies of Taylor's army landed on North Beach, where they were greeted by congregations of rattlesnakes angrily buzzing in the tall grass. Within three months, 4,000 men were concentrated at Corpus Christi, representing half the strength of the army. Besides the soldiers, the settlement swelled from 100 inhabitants to about 2,000.

When the army departed for the Rio Grande in March 1846, the town almost disappeared. A month after the army left, Nueces County was created by the new legislature. The county stretched from Corpus Christi to Laredo and south to the Rio Grande. At the first commissioners meeting held in January 1847, they established ferry tolls on the Rio Grande and Nueces and appointed an overseer to stake the Reef Road.

A Houston paper noted the town's downfall after the army left. "Since the removal of the U.S. Army from Corpus Christi, the town has fallen almost as rapidly as it rose. The population has dwindled from 2,000 to a few hundred. The 200 grog shops that were the glory of the citizens a few weeks since, the faro banks and roulette tables have disappeared. A few stores are all that is left of the late flourishing town of Corpus Christi."

Even Kinney left with the army and his business partner, William Aubrey, traveled south with a wagonload of whisky. A soldier on his way to Mexico, William McClintock, wrote, "The town is situated on a low beach containing some 30 houses and on the hill are 15 or 20 Mexican huts now deserted. Corpus Christi was a poor insignificant place until the army took up its quarters there. I think its existence will be an ephemeral one."

*Sketch of Zachary Taylor's army encampment at Corpus Christi was drawn in October 1845 by Capt. Daniel P. Whiting. Almost half the total strength of the army was concentrated at Corpus Christi until March 1846 when army units left for the Rio Grande and the coming war with Mexico.*

After the Mexican War ended in 1848, Kinney returned with plans to improve the town's fortunes. He wanted to establish a trade corridor with the Chihuahua region of Mexico.

Kinney bought surplus army wagons and formed a partnership with William Mann and William Cazneau to open a trade route with northern Mexico. Kinney put up $10,000 for the venture. Cazneau began to assemble a train of wagons filled with goods destined for Chihuahua. Corpus Christi filled with wagons and ox-carts as the Great Chihuahua Train took shape.

When gold fever spread across the country, Kinney placed ads in eastern newspapers claiming that the best route to the California goldfields started at Corpus Christi. Steamers and packet boats brought in prospective miners heading west. Kinney bought a steam dredging machine to deepen a channel through the mudflats of the bay. He opened the Corpus Christi Hotel, advertising rates of $30 a month — "the same for man or horse."

Gunsmiths, blacksmiths, coopers set up shop, along with cobblers, barbers and chandlers. The California-bound gold-seekers, eager to get to the diggings, were organized into companies with names like the Essex Mining Company, the Carson Association, and the Mazatlan Rangers.

Cazneau's trade caravan departed in April 1849. The Corpus Christi Star reported that Cazneau intended to establish two trading posts on the Rio Grande, one at Presidio del Norte and one at El Paso "where the traders will buy goods and themselves convey them into Mexico."

The effort in 1849 to establish a trade corridor to Chihuahua fizzled; Kinney and his partners lost money on the Great Chihuahua Train. The traffic of gold-seekers through Corpus Christi soon ceased after word spread that the route across northern Mexico was very difficult. For Corpus Christi, the gold rush ended in late 1849 and Kinney's town began to languish again.

*—Oct. 8, 2014*

# Army Returns in 1850s

The big news in Corpus Christi in January 1850 was the death of Charles Bryant, killed and scalped by Indians. Bryant, an architect from Bangor, Maine, took part in a rebellion in Canada, was sentenced to be hanged, and escaped to Texas. He built the Union Theater in Corpus Christi in 1845 to cater to the army. In 1848, he joined the Rangers and was called to Austin in January 1850. Bryant was killed near St. Mary's by a band of Lipan Apaches.

Corpus Christi's first census at the beginning of the 1850s showed the town had 551 free citizens, 47 slaves, and 112 soldiers.

Henry Kinney, the town's founder, was in financial straits and wanted to sell 300,000 acres of land. He circulated handbills in England and Scotland offering land for farming. Many immigrants left for Texas as a result of Kinney's campaign. They settled in Corpus Christi or Nuecestown on the Nueces River.

In early 1852, Kinney began promoting the Lone Star Fair, billed as the first state fair in Texas, and probably inspired by Paxton's Crystal Palace. Kinney expected 20,000 people would attend the fair at Corpus Christi beginning on May 1, 1852. Corpus Christi's newspaper, the Nueces Valley, reported that Kinney was untiring in efforts to make the fair a success. He sent "Legs" Lewis to New Orleans to buy silver cups and chalices to award as prizes.

As May 1 approached, ships from New Orleans and Texas ports departed for Corpus Christi. Kinney had a steam-powered packet boat, the Major Harris, built to convey passengers across Corpus Christi Bay. Henry Maltby's Circus arrived from San Antonio. If the streets were filled with visitors, the numbers were nothing like the 20,000 Kinney expected. Less than 2,000 people came, probably because Corpus Christi was a little too far from civilization. The Indianola Bulletin reported that the fair fell infinitely short of what was expected and was, in the main, a failure.

Kinney lost $50,000 on the fair. His creditors closed in. He gave up his Mustang Island ranch and mortgaged other holdings.

Richard King, a steamboat captain on the Rio Grande, came up to attend the fair. On the way King and party camped by a small stream called Santa Gertrudis. In July 1853, King bought 15,300 acres, part of the Santa Gertrudis grant, at two cents an acre. He signed on "Legs" Lewis as a partner in a cattle ranch. The land was surveyed and deed filed in Corpus Christi on Nov. 14, 1853. That was the beginning of King Ranch.

The Eighth Military District in Texas manned forts on the frontier. Supplies came in by sea and were hauled by wagons to the government depot at San Antonio and on to the army forts. Gen. Persifor Smith, commander of the Eighth Military District, decided to move his headquarters from San Antonio to Corpus Christi. The army established warehouses, saddler's shops, wheelwright and blacksmith shops, a wagon yard, and quarters for soldiers and muleskinners. Army supplies came in by ship to be freighted overland to frontier forts.

Soldiers had hardly arrived before there was a riot on New Year's Day 1854. A fight between the inhabitants and soldiers at a fandango resulted in a soldier being stabbed to death and four others hurt. Angry soldiers set fire to jacals in an area of town called Little Mexico.

One July day in 1854 a Mexican vessel loaded with fresh fruit docked at the wharf. It was believed that the ship also brought yellow fever and the town was soon a fever ward. A wreath of black smoke hung over the city, which came from burning the clothes and bedding of those who died and from smoldering tar buckets in front of homes that were thought to neutralize noxious vapors. The outbreak ended with the first frost, but it claimed many of the town's 700 inhabitants.

Corpus Christi in the 1850s was a transit point for officers assigned to frontier forts. Lt. Phil Sheridan stopped on his way to Fort Duncan. Lydia Spencer Lane, wife of a lieutenant, wrote about their arrival in 1854. They stayed in tents on North Beach. Mrs. Lane wrote that a spacious wall tent had been floored for her and her husband, as newlyweds, but an unmarried officer with higher rank claimed it. "We only saw the outside of it," she lamented.

The town's hopes were raised by gossip that the army would move its supply depot from San Antonio to Corpus Christi. Those

170

*A silver cup awarded at Henry Kinney's Lone Star Fair held in Corpus Christi in May 1852.*

hopes were dashed by a report that said Corpus Christi was unsuitable due to its lack of fresh water and the mudflats in the bay that made navigation difficult. The army recommendation was to use the port of Indianola and freight goods to San Antonio and from there to frontier forts.

In 1856 and 1857, the army moved Eighth Military District headquarters back to San Antonio. Corpus Christi was in a bad way again, as it was 10 years before when Zachary Taylor's army marched away. Its once busy stores became idle and many who depended on the $15 a month army paychecks were forced to look elsewhere for a living. Many became stockmen and some, especially Kinney's immigrants from England and Scotland, turned to sheep.

This marked the beginning of the sheep era, during which Corpus Christi became one a thriving wool market, eventually shipping out millions of pounds of wool each year. And, with the King Ranch, the cattle era began at about the same time in almost the same location, Santa Gertrudis Creek.

In 1858, a volunteer militia organization called the Walker Rifles was established in Corpus Christi. Charles Lovenskiold was captain, Henry Maltby first lieutenant, and Joseph FitzSimmons second lieutenant.

Maltby, who brought Maltby's Circus to the Lone Star Fair in 1852, began publishing the Ranchero in Corpus Christi in October 1859. The Ranchero on Dec. 17, 1859 reported that a dance was held at Cornelius Cahill's building and that "the beauty of Corpus Christi never appeared to better advantage. Parties of this character are conducive to much good and make one feel a much happier and better person."

*—Oct. 15, 2014*

# War Brings Blockade, Misery

The decade of the 1860s was a bad time. Corpus Christi's strategic location made it a battleground during the Civil War and to compound the miseries of war the region suffered one of the worst droughts ever. After the war, a yellow fever epidemic decimated the city and filled the graveyards.

The big news in August 1860 was the murder of Deputy Sheriff Tom Nolan, who was shot trying to arrest a violent drunk. His brother Mat Nolan, the sheriff, would be shot down himself four years later.

The talk in early 1861 was of the looming conflict. Nueces County had voted 142 to 42 in favor of secession on Feb. 23, 1861. The first of several volunteer troops organized in Corpus Christi wore gray uniforms with red silk sashes made by wives and sweethearts of the soldiers.

Henry Kinney, the town's founder, was shot to death in Matamoros on March 3, 1862 under mysterious circumstances. There were conflicting accounts but he was probably shot in the early hours at the front door of his former lover, Genoveva Perez, by her new husband. Kinney's will was filed for probate in Corpus Christi in March 1862.

Union blockade commander Lt. John W. Kittredge was a small sallow man with a fearsome reputation. His armada of four warships sailed into Corpus Christi Bay on Aug. 12, 1862. Next morning, he landed under a white flag and met Confederate Major Alfred Hobby on Ohler's Wharf. Kittredge gave Hobby 48 hours to evacuate the inhabitants. Did they want to evacuate? They did. They streamed out of town and camped on a sheep ranch west of town or at Nuecestown where they could hear the distant thunder of guns.

The battle began on Saturday Aug. 16, 1862. Confederates fired three cannons from behind a sand-bank battery. A shot passed through the mainsail of Union ship Corypheus and another tore a gaping hole in the gunboat Sachem's side. The ships returned fire.

After a lull in the battle on Sunday Kittredge landed a shore party to attack the Confederate battery. They were turned back by a cavalry charge. Kittredge reclaimed the shore party, moved his ships out of range then spitefully bombarded the city as he sailed away. — a drive-by shooting. Returning evacuees collected spent cannonballs and called them Kittredges.

A month later, Kittredge went ashore at Flour Bluff. Confederates had been forewarned and laid a trap for him. Kittredge and his gig's crew were taken without a shot fired. To capture the man who had so recently attacked the town was a victory indeed. Kittredge gave parole and was sent North.

In 1863, the ship Zion sank off Ohler's wharf with a load of salt. Saline crystals mined from the Laguna Madre constituted Corpus Christi's main contribution to the war effort, along with its men and boys. Conscription laws were rigidly enforced. Boys who reached 18 were sent away to fight; males too young or too old were forced to drive cotton wagons down the Cotton Road.

In November 1863, Union forces under Gen. Nathaniel Banks captured Mustang Island and the 20th Iowa took over the Confederate fort on the island. That Christmas, Commander of the 20th, Maj. William Thompson, led a scouting party into Corpus Christi. He found many in town were starving.

Confederate soldiers butchered stray cattle at the Salt Lake and distributed the meat to starving families. During the winter of 1863, federal troops came to Corpus Christi and pulled down vacant houses for the lumber to build huts on Mustang Island. Union forces were pulled out before war's end.

Cecilio Balerio, a Nueces County rancher, commanded an irregular Union cavalry outfit that attacked Confederate wagon trains carrying cotton on the Cotton Road. Early in 1864, Balerio's son Jose was captured in Corpus Christi. He was taken before a firing squad before he agreed to divulge the location of his father's camp. On March 13, 1864, Confederate Maj. Mat Nolan led a force to Balerio's camp, near San Diego. In the fight in a mesquite thicket, two of Nolan's men were killed and five of Balerio's. Jose was allowed to escape as payment for leading the Confederates to his father's camp. Balerio crossed over into Mexico where he remained for the rest of the war.

*Thomas Noakes' painting shows the high point of the battle of Corpus Christi on Aug. 18, 1862. Union ships fired at a Confederate battery of three guns located near where the ship channel is today. Union forces landed and were repulsed by Confederate cavalry (lower left). Noakes was a member of Capt. John Ireland's infantry company, which participated in the battle.*

At war's end, Corpus Christi was in a state of desolation, dead animals littered the streets and the smell of decay hung over the nearly deserted city.

That July, two Union regiments of black soldiers arrived to begin the occupation. Union sympathizers were appointed to local government positions. One of the first acts of a newly organized county government was to replace the stakes marking the Reef Road.

On July 1, 1867 a man named Snyder arrived at Ziegler's hotel. Within two days he was dead. He came from Indianola where yellow fever was in full fury. Three weeks after the Indianola traveler's death, Corpus Christi was stricken. People fled the city to escape the pestilence. San Patricio County posted armed deputies at ferry crossings with orders to stop anyone from crossing from Corpus Christi.

The death toll climbed. Dressed lumber stacked on the bluff to build a new church was diverted to make wooden box coffins. On Aug. 14, William Maltby, editor of the Advertiser, described the calamity. "There is scarcely a house in the city that has escaped sickness or death. Our pen is inadequate to the task of describing the distress that prevails among us." His wife and sister died in the outbreak.

175

In early September, a cold front brought relief. No new cases were reported and the death toll began to drop. Joseph Almond, a carpenter and sheep rancher, kept a diary and recorded the deaths each day. Almond's tally was that 135 people died in the yellow fever summer of 1867.

The last year of a calamitous decade marked the election as governor of Edmund Jackson Davis, who had been a judge in Corpus Christi. The stage carrying him to Austin stopped at the home of an old friend in San Patricio, out of respect for the conventions of the time, and the message quickly came back. "Mrs. Sullivan is not at home to a traitor."

*—Oct. 22, 2014*

# Bandits Burn Noakes' Store

In the 1870s Corpus Christi was one of the largest wool markets in the world, a time when longhorns were trailed to Kansas and cattle were killed at hide-and-tallow factories. It was a time of bandit raids and reciprocating violence. It was unsafe to travel the roads and no one ventured beyond town limits without being armed to the teeth, pistols cocked and rifles ready.

In 1871 the greatest cattle drive in history was made with 700,000 head going up the trail. South Texas recovered from the war on the strength of cattle sales in Kansas.

On Oct. 1, 1871, people rushed to the corner of Chaparral and Cooper's Alley where a new house built for William Rogers was burning. The sun came up over a charred lot. Rogers lost no time in organizing the city's first fire department, the Pioneer Fire Company No. 1, which fought its first fire when the Colored Baptist Church burned.

Edmund J. Davis, Union general and Republican governor from Corpus Christi, visited his hometown and sold his home on the bluff to Norwick Gussett. Davis, throughout his term as governor, was pursued by furious controversy. Former Confederates saw nothing to like in Davis.

The most important news in 1871 was the approval of a bond issue to dredge an eight-foot channel across the bay.

In July 1871, the city agreed to a proposal by William Rogers and Richard Jordan to build a structure to house city offices with rental stalls for butchers and vendors. The result was Market Hall, which became the town's social center for 40 years. That October, the lighthouse on the bluff was torn down.

After the great trail drive in 1871, beef prices fell to nothing and beef slaughter houses were built along the coast, with three on North Beach and one at Flour Bluff.

On a trip to Corpus Christi, Ingleside's George Hatch, 83, was slain by robbers north of the reef. Rancher John Rabb, one of the first cattlemen in Nueces County to drive cattle to Kansas, died in 1872. His widow Martha became known as the Cattle Queen of Texas.

In 1872, Richard King donated land on Carancahua as a site for a public school. There had been private schools but no public ones in Corpus Christi's 30-year history. Two small buildings, one for white and one for colored students, were erected. There were 146 pupils that first year. Parents could buy McGuffey's readers for their scholars at Herman Meuly's News Depot.

In October 1872, Louis de Planque arrived from Indianola to hold a photo exhibition at Market Hall. City Marshal P. Whelan warned in a public notice that dogs had to be tagged and hogs penned. That year, many of the town's horses and mules died after being fed spoiled corn.

Hispanic mutual benefit clubs, the beginning of political awareness, were formed in the 1870s. Club Reciproco was founded in Corpus Christi in 1873. Its avowed purpose was to protect the poor, provide mutual benefits for its members, and elevate all those "who may wish to associate with members of the club."

Public road construction began in 1873 with the building of a trunk road from Corpus Christi to Nuecestown. This became UpRiver Road. A survey by Lafayette Caldwell showed three majorroads leading out of Corpus Christi, the UpRiver, Laredo, and Brownsville roads.

On Nov. 24, 1873, the schooner Fountainbleu wrecked in the Aransas pass channel. The ship broke apart and lost its cargo of shingles. Two other ships went down in the pass during the decade, the Reindeer and the steamer Mary. Shipwrecks were so frequent the state appointed wreckmasters to oversee salvage operations. Peter Benson was wreckmaster for Nueces County in the 1870s.

Livestock froze to death during the frigid winter of 1873. Hides taken from dead cattle in Nueces County amounted to more than $500,000. Cowboys called this the Great Die-Up.

In 1874, Morris Lichtenstein arrived from Indianola and opened a dry goods store on Chaparral. The completion of the Morris & Cummings Cut allowed ocean-going ships to reach Corpus Christi. The Morgan Line steamer Gussie docked at the Central Wharf on May 31, setting off a big celebration.

*Nueces County's new courthouse built in 1875 was called the Hollub Courthouse after the architect, Rudolph Hollub, a former mapmaker in the Union Army. The County Jail is at the far left.*

On Good Friday 1875, a band of 50 bandits from Mexico pulled a raid on Nuecestown, 12 miles from Corpus Christi. The raiders took hostages they met on the road and burned Noakes' store. A wounded bandit left behind was taken to Corpus Christi and lynched. After the raid, Corpus Christi formed the Star Rifles to defend the city and Leander McNelly's Rangers were unleashed on border-crossing bandits.

A new courthouse completed in 1875 was called the Hollub Courthouse after the architect, Rudolph Hollub, a former mapmaker in the Union Army. Surveying and brush-clearing began on Uriah Lott's railroad to Laredo. Track-layers followed behind brush-choppers as the railroad moved west. The line eventually became the Tex-Mex.

A hurricane hit on Sept. 16, 1875, destroying Staples Wharf and washing away salt deposits on Laguna Madre. The storm almost destroyed Indianola, killing 176 people. The port city was rebuilt, but another hurricane finished the job.

On July 4, 1876, as the city celebrated the nation's 100th birthday, Stanley Welch's arm was blown off. Two 12-pound howitzers were being fired and Welch was sponging a gun and driving the cartridge home when it backfired, taking off his hand. Dr. Spohn had to amputate the arm.

179

Richard King built the city's first ice plant in 1878, a red-brick warehouse off Water Street next to Cooper's Alley. George Blucher was hired to drive the ice wagon.

By the end of the 1870s, there were more sheep than cattle in Nueces County, the beef packing era and trail drives were coming to an end and fencing would soon finish off the open range. The 1870s were a time when Corpus Christi began to realize its dream of becoming a port city, when railroads were being built across South Texas, and when McNelly's Rangers put a stop to cross-border forays like the Nuecestown Raid.

*—Oct. 29, 2014*

# Making Tracks in 1880s

After the calamities of the Civil War and Reconstruction, the 1880s looked to be a decade in which nothing much happened. But important changes were taking place. Railroads were being built, fences were closing off the open range, and the sheep era and trail drives were coming to a close.

Uriah Lott was building a railroad from Corpus Christi to Laredo when he ran out of money and was forced to sell. The Texas Mexican Railway acquired the project and finished the line to Laredo in 1881. The new company allowed the former owners to celebrate the inaugural run. Lott, Richard King, and Mifflin Kenedy, the principal backers, invited friends to ride to Laredo in a private car. It was first scheduled for Sept. 22, 1881, but was postponed five days due to the death of President James Garfield.

When the inaugural run was made, someone spiked the punch with 12 quarts of champagne and three gallons of Rose Bud whisky (King's brand, a clue). As the train rolled toward Laredo, with ice tinkling in punch glasses, the guests were in high spirits. When they reached Laredo, the engineer said, the train and the passengers were fully loaded.

The Texas Mexican Railway, the Tex-Mex, was said to be the most unusual railroad in the world. If an engineer spotted a buck near the tracks, he would stop the train and let passengers take a few shots. Ranch wives would give conductors shopping lists to be filled. The train stopped when cattle wandered onto the tracks, which made for a leisurely schedule.

The first edition of Corpus Christi Caller was printed on Jan. 21, 1883, an unusually cold night. A bucket of oyster stew bought to feed the pressmen froze solid. Printing ink had to be thawed for the press. News in that first edition included the birth of triplets, two boys and a girl, in the Mark Downey family and a report on the prospects of a railroad being built from San Antonio to Corpus Christi.

E. J. Davis, Reconstruction governor of Texas, died in Austin on Feb. 27, 1883. His monument, an obelisk, was the tallest in the State Cemetery. A former Confederate said that was entirely appropriate since Davis was "the biggest SOB Texas has ever seen."

On July 4th, 1883, James McPherson, the city engineer, was killed when a cannon exploded as the city celebrated the holiday. Seven years earlier, on July 4th, 1876, Stanley Welch's arm was blown off when a howitzer backfired. The 1883 incident may have been the last Civil War cannon fired to celebrate the Fourth.

The first pictures published in the Caller came in the presidential campaign of 1884. The newspaper printed the photos of Democratic candidate Grover Cleveland and running mate Thomas Hendricks.

In 1884-1885, Corpus Christi had 48 businesses, with 40 of them below the bluff in the beach section of the town. Top firms and property owners in the city included Doddridge & Davis Bank, with property valued at $115,500; Norwick Gussett's bank, 111,000; lumberyard owner E. D. Sidbury, $71,550; J. B. Mitchell Hardware, $45,000; banker and wool merchant John Woessner, $43,050; and rancher Mifflin Kenedy, $34,250.

For three decades, the Corpus Christi region was sheep country. Carts loaded with wool from as far away as Mexico rolled into Corpus Christi, one of the world's great wool markets. After the Civil War, tax rolls showed there were 1.2 million sheep in Nueces County. In shearing season ox-carts loaded with wool came to Corpus Christi to sell to the town's wool merchants, Norwick Gussett, David Hirsch, Ed Buckley, Perry Doddrige, William Headen, John Woessner, and Uriah Lott, before he turned to railroads.

The wool era came to an end in the 1880s. A parasite decimated the flocks, fencing closed off the open range, and Grover Cleveland was elected president in 1884. Cleveland promised to lower the tariff on cheap Australian wool. Domestic wool sold for 26 cents a pound the day before he took office and dropped to seven cents a pound the day after. Wool warehouses in Corpus Christi closed. Sheep ranchers of the Nueces Valley turned to cattle. And that was the end of the sheep era in South Texas.

Richard King, founder of King Ranch, died at the Menger Hotel in San Antonio on April 14, 1885. He was 61. Most of the family was

*An 1887 map of Corpus Christi was drawn by Augustus Koch who drew similar views of cities around the country. It was called a bird's-eye view because it was sketched as if seen from a high perch. The Corpus Christi's bird's-eye view shows the steamship Aransas at the Central Wharf and another ship at the Sidbury Wharf. Streets, houses, and stores were drawn with meticulous detail.*

by his bedside, along with Mifflin Kenedy, who had just buried his wife Petra. The eulogy of a ranch hand who worked for King summed up the cattleman: "He was a rough man but he was a good man. I never knew a rougher man or a better man." King started with 15,500 acres in 1853 and left his wife Henrietta 614,000 acres.

The Kansas Legislature, afraid of the spread of tick fever, passed a law in 1885 preventing Texas cattle from entering Kansas. That and the coming of railroads ended the great trail drives out of South Texas.

The Aug. 30, 1885 Caller reported that Morris Lichtenstein left on the steamship Aransas for New York to buy his fall goods. Besides Lichtenstein, the Aransas carried 16 other passengers, 102 bales of hides, 11 bales of cotton, five bundles of wet salted hides, 1,913 bars of lead, and 147 bags of istle.

Corpus Christi got its second rail line in 1886 when the San Antonio and Aransas Pass Railroad (SAAP) built a trestle bridge across Nueces Bay. Some 300 visitors from San Antonio, Floresville, Beeville and other points arrived on a seven-coach special. To celebrate, Corpus Christi held a beach party that featured baked oysters and fish chowder.

On Aug. 20, 1886, Indianola was hit by another powerful hurricane. It was followed by a fire that consumed what the storm left standing. Two catastrophic storms a decade apart spelled the end of Indianola.

On Dec. 11, 1886, the Corpus Christi Daily Gazette reported that the city had seen "all kinds of weather this month: cold and hot, dry and wet, calm and windy, cloudy and clear, pleasant and unpleasant," which just about covered the weather for the decade.

*—Nov. 5, 2014*

# Century Ends With Crash

An unusual experiment was conducted in Corpus Christi in 1891 based on the theory that clouds could be bombarded into dropping moisture. On Sept. 26, 1891 experimenters fired shells from two howitzers west of town. When the guns were fired raindrops fell and people watching the show got soaking wet. Resolute scoffers pointed out that thunderclouds were over the city and it had rained the day before.

Corpus Christi at the beginning of the 1890s had no municipal water supply. Residents relied on collected rainwater stored in cisterns. Each house had its own little reservoir. They cooked in, washed in and drank rainwater. When it didn't rain and cisterns ran low, they bought water from street vendors called barrileros who hauled water from the nueces River.

On July 14, 1892, fire destroyed homes and stores in the 200 block of Chaparral. A year later, on May 26, 1893, the city celebrated a new waterworks, with 200,000 gallons a day piped in from the Nueces River. Since water pipes didn't reach homes, the new waterworks didn't put the barrileros out of business. People still relied on cisterns and barrileros.

The city's first high school was built in 1892. Professor Moses Menger was lured from Austin to become the principal of the new school. Graduation ceremonies for the first graduates were held at Market Hall in June 1893.

Elihu Harrison Ropes, from New Jersey, developed big ideas for Corpus Christi which created the boom times of the early 1890s. Ropes hired a crew to dredge a pass across Mustang Island; he planned to build a port next to the pass. He planned to build a railroad to Brownsville and bought land for a development called "The Cliffs," built a resort hotel, the Alta Vista, and had a streetcar line run out to the hotel.

Land values soared. In Flour Bluff, land that sold for $8 an acre before Ropes sold for up to $1,000 an acre at the height of the boom. The crash came in 1893 during what they called a money panic. Ropes' sources of capital dried up and he left town. The pass across Mustang Island silted in. Lots in "The Cliffs" were sold for delinquent taxes and the streetcar line was sold at auction. The Alta Vista stood vacant. Elihu H. Ropes, bankrupt and in near poverty, died in New York City in 1898. Corpus Christi hardly noted his passing.

"Blacksmith Bob" Fitzsimmons rented a house on North Beach in 1895 to train for a bout with "Gentleman Jim" Corbett. Fitzsimmons ran wind sprints on the beach with his pet lion loping beside him. The fight with Corbett was called off after the Legislature made prize-fighting illegal. In 1897, the fight was finally held in Carson City, Nev. People in Corpus Christi gathered outside the newspaper office as the results came in by telegraph. A cheer went up when it was announced that Fitzsimmons knocked out Corbett to become the heavyweight champion.

In 1898, the Kenedy Rifles marched through Corpus Christi on their way to "a splendid little war." When war against Spain was declared on April 22, volunteer units were formed all over Texas. The Kenedy Rifles were formed into Company E of the First Texas Volunteer Infantry. Another volunteer unit, the Longview Rifles, was moved to Corpus Christi for coastal defense. They camped on North Beach. When they left town, the Caller editorialized that, "It is needless to say that there were a good many tears shed when the time came to tell the boys goodbye. While it is not likely that the company will have to go to Cuba, one cannot always tell when a war is going to end."

The Kenedy Rifles were in training when war ended. They were assigned garrison duty during the occupation. When they marched through Havana, Robert Hall wrote home that the Cuban people "threw us cigars and gave us stuff to drink."

Almost a year after they had marched out of Corpus Christi, the Kenedy Rifles arrived back in Corpus Christi at the SAAP Depot on Sunday night, April 16, 1899. Three days later, Market Hall was draped in bunting and the returning heroes were showered with laurel leaves and given the freedom of the city.

The worst-recorded cold front in Texas history occurred in 1899. It struck on Saturday night, Feb. 13, 1899. Temperatures plunged to

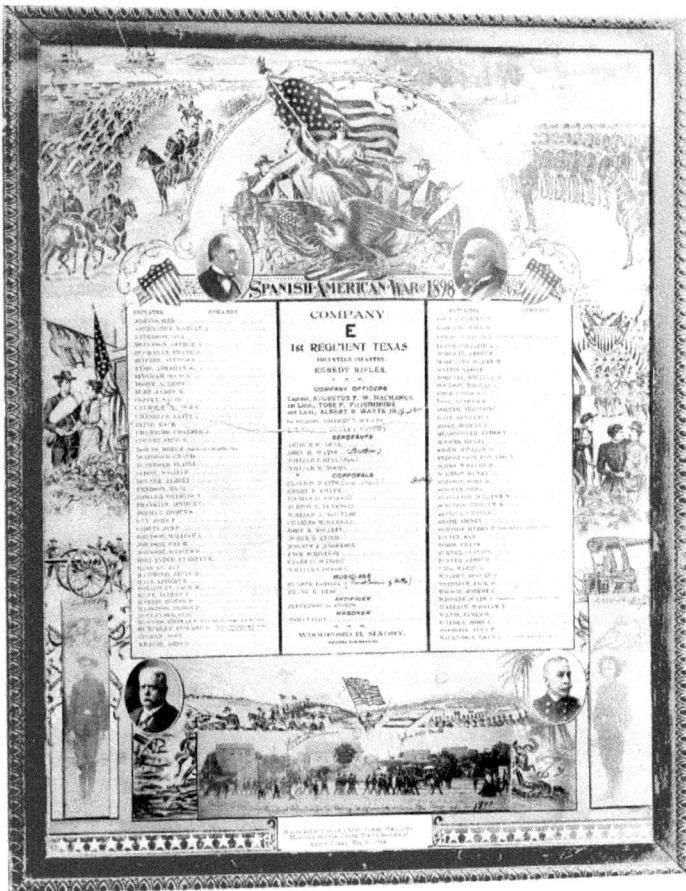

*A Spanish-American War memorial dedicated to the Kenedy Rifles, or Company E, once hung in the Nueces County Courthouse. The bottom portion of the memorial plaque showed a photo of the Kenedy Rifles marching through Corpus Christi on May 3, 1898.*

Siberian levels. In the Panhandle, they fell to 31 degrees below zero. Corpus Christi was the hot spot at 11 degrees above zero.

Across Texas, cattle froze to death by the thousands. For those still alive, their breath condensed and hung in clouds over their heads. At Port Aransas, called Tarpon, the boat harbor froze solid with boats encased in ice. The storm froze the river solid at Nuecestown, froze Nueces Bay, and froze the saltwater in Corpus Christi Bay out past the piers. The blizzard of 1899 was the coldest weather Corpus Christi ever experienced.

The concluding decade of the 19th Century is a good place to sum up the city's six decades of progress and setback, boom and bust. Kinney built a trading post on the old Indian trading grounds in 1839. When Texas joined the U.S., Zachary Taylor concentrated an army at Corpus Christi to prepare for war with Mexico. When the army left, Corpus Christi became a virtual ghost town. After the war, it became a transit point for 49ers going to California. In the 1850s it was made headquarters for the Eighth Military District.

The blockade in the Civil War stopped trade. In August 1862, the town was evacuated before the battle between Union warships and a Confederate shore battery. Much of the activity of the war related to the blockade and hauling cotton down the Cotton Road. At war's end, Corpus Christi was in a ruinous state. It was beginning to recover when yellow fever struck in 1867.

The 1870s brought trade based on the sheep and cattle industry. It was also a time of cattle rustling and bandit raids, culminating in the Nuecestown Raid. The Ropes-inspired boom in the 1890s crashed during a depression and the economic doldrums that followed lasted well into the next century.

*—Nov. 12, 2014*

# First Sheriff Left Mystery

Who was Henry Berry? Was his name Henry or Harrison? He used both. He also used the initials H. W. and sometimes W. H. Where was he from? Just Ohio. Being vague about name and background suggests he had something to hide. The mystery doesn't matter much except it would be nice to know if the county's first sheriff was a wanted man.

Henry or Harrison or H. W. or W. H. Berry came to Corpus Christi in 1843. He had been a member of a ranging company and was associated with Robert Moore, one of the original members of the Alabama Settlement in Jackson County. They came from around Decatur and Tuscumbia, Ala., in 1831 to settle the western part of Stephen F. Austin's colony.

In Corpus Christi, Berry worked as a gun hand for Henry Kinney. In May 1844 Comanches raided the town and were chased by 11 men, including Berry. In the battle west of town Berry was hit in the groin with an arrow, which he pulled out and kept as a souvenir.

After that attack, the Republic of Texas authorized Kinney to establish a company of 56 men for protection. Berry was named captain of the company.

In 1845, when the U.S. army concentrated in Corpus Christi before the Mexican War, Berry was a rival of Lt. U. S. Grant for the attentions of a girl named Elizabeth Moore. It's not certain, but she was probably the daughter of Robert Moore, Berry's friend from Alabama who moved from Jackson County to Corpus Christi.

Berry would take Elizabeth riding on his black pacing mare. One day Grant asked to borrow the mare and Berry saw him riding with Elizabeth. Berry then refused to loan Grant his horse, realizing the lieutenant was winning his girl away.

The next time Berry was to take Elizabeth riding, he found his mare's mane and tail had been cut off, a trick played by Grant.

Elizabeth refused to ride such an ugly horse. When the army moved on to the Rio Grande, it gave Berry a clear field for Elizabeth's affections. They were soon married.

After the Legislature created Nueces County in 1846, Berry was elected sheriff. He served two years then became a builder; he had been trained as a bricklayer and mason. His building partner was John A. F. Gravis, a veteran of San Jacinto.

Berry and Gravis built Mann's red house on the waterfront, so called because of the red shellcrete bricks. They built the Ohler and Hunsaker buildings, Cornelius Cahill's place on Water Street, and Forbes Britton's house on the bluff.

An early resident described how they made shellcrete, an adobe-like brick. To make lime, they dug a pit and piled shells on top of wood, set it on fire and let it burn for days. They shoveled the lime off the top. To make bricks, they mixed crushed shell, lime, clay and water in a vat then poured this slurry into wooden molds. The bricks were sun-dried then Berry built a kiln to fire them.

In January 1849, Berry's wife Elizabeth gave birth to a son, Robert Henry. She died not long afterwards.

During the gold rush, when gold seekers stopped off in Corpus Christi, Gravis built a small hotel on Chaparral called the California House. His wife Irenah ran it. Gravis died during the 1854 yellow fever epidemic. His estate consisted of a Spanish pony, two-wheeled gig, and six-shooter. At auction, the estate brought $27.

In 1854, Berry took the four minor children of Dwight Brewster to bring up after their appointed guardian declined the responsibility. Berry married Irenah Gravis and became stepfather of the four Gravis children. In 1857 he was elected mayor, but soon resigned to protest the city's plans to issue bonds to dredge a channel across the bay. He returned to the building trade.

In 1860, Berry and Irenah re-opened the old California House. They called it the Sierra Madre Hotel, but it was known as the Berry boarding house. That same year Berry joined James Barnard as co-owner of the La Retama Saloon. When Deputy Tom Nolan was shot to death by an unruly drunk, Berry was appointed deputy by Sheriff Mat Nolan.

During the Civil War, Berry, a native of Ohio, spoke against secession at a meeting at the courthouse. Confederates called him a renegade. After Corpus Christi was shelled by Union warships, Confederates began to threaten the pro-Unionists in their midst.

190

*Henry W. Berry came to Corpus Christi in 1843, worked as a hired gun for Henry Kinney, and was elected Nueces County's first sheriff in 1846.*

Berry said later he had to leave the country or be subjected to mob violence. He took his large family and joined the exodus of pro-Unionists to Matamoros. They stayed a year.

When the Union Army under Gen. Nathaniel Banks captured Brownsville and forts on Mustang and Matagorda islands in late 1863, the pro-Unionists came out of hiding. Berry moved his family back to Corpus Christi.

Confederate Major Mat Nolan, still sheriff, reported to his superior Rip Ford that three Corpus Christi "renegades" were seen helping Union soldiers load confiscated cotton. He identified them as John Cody, Thomas Tinney and Henry Berry. Nine local men were indicted for treason by the Nueces County grand jury, but Berry's name was not among the nine.

At sundown on Dec. 22, 1864, Maj. Mat Nolan was talking to a horse trader on Mesquite Street when Berry's two stepsons, Frank and Charles Gravis, walked up and started shooting. The horse trader was killed outright and Nolan was mortally wounded. Nolan identified the shooters and said he knew why they shot him. He died without saying more. It was speculated that Nolan had orders to arrest Berry and this led Berry's stepsons to shoot him.

The war soon ended and no action was taken against Frank and Charles Gravis. When Union supporters were put in positions of authority, Berry was appointed sheriff and he made his stepson Charles Gravis a deputy.

Capt. H. W. Berry, Nueces County's first sheriff and sheriff again during Reconstruction, died on May 15, 1888 when he was 69. Every business in town closed as the funeral procession passed. The last of his and Gravis' buildings, called Centennial House today, still stands as a monument to its builders. As for whatever secrets Henry W. or Harrison W. Berry may have been hiding, they were buried with him in old Bayview Cemetery.

*—Nov. 19, 2014*

# Peeling and Tanking

South Texas was overrun with longhorns following the return of Civil War soldiers. Within five years, by 1870, trails to Kansas were well beaten when 300,000 head of cattle were pointed out of Texas and trailed across Oklahoma to Kansas railheads. By 1871, 700,000 head were trailed north, a flood of cattle that glutted the markets, with the price of beef dropping so low that fewer herds were driven north.

Within three years from 1870, the value of the longhorn was reduced to the value of its hide, the tallow that could be rendered for candles, and horns and bones that could be fashioned into buttons and knife handles. Almost overnight, beef slaughter houses — called packeries or hide and tallow factories — were built and put into operation along the coast.

Entrepreneurs set up big sheds with iron vat boilers, hired butchers and cowboys to round up steers. They made great profits from the sale of hides and tallow.

Rancher Richard King and Nelson Plato built a beef slaughter house inside the city limits of Corpus Christi, south of downtown. John King and W. N. Staples built a packing house on Padre Island on what today is called Packery Channel. Mifflin Kenedy built a packery at Flour Bluff and John Wade built another at Nuecestown, which was sold to Martin Culver.

Three packeries operated on North Beach. John Hall, from England, established Hall's Packery on the slough that was called Hall's Bayou (his son, Bob Hall, became a longtime county commissioner). The Corpus Christi Advertiser reported that Alonso DeAvalon would commence "peeling and tanking" at his packery on North Beach. (Because the hide came off like a shuck the process was called peeling and because the meat was boiled in a giant vat to get the tallow it was called tanking.)

John Anderson and sons hauled salt aboard their schooner Flour Bluff to Kenedy's packery. Andy Anderson said Kenedy told them, "You can have all the tongues you want, boys, but don't get in the way." It was said the meat from Kenedy's packery had a distinctive flavor because they put wild bay leaves in the cooking vats.

John "Red" Dunn, who worked in a packery on North Beach, described how the process worked in "Perilous Trails of Texas."

Cattle were driven from a large pen into a small chute. A man with a spear standing on a walkway above the cattle stabbed them in the back of the neck to sever the spinal cord. The bodies were hauled to the skinning floor by a block and tackle pulled by a horse. Butchers skinned them. The gut man cut the carcass open and took out the entrails. The hide man took the hide to a vat to be salted down. The marker cut the hams and shoulders, marking where the bones were to be broken.

The ax man broke the bones where they were marked. Meat was pitched onto platforms near the tanks until there was enough to fill the tanks. Steam was turned on and the meat cooked so thoroughly the large joint bones became soft. Tallow was skimmed from the top by bucket-sized ladles. Dunn said they would sometimes run out of cattle and the meat would lie on the platforms two or three days in the hot weather. The stench was suffocating.

The greatest concentration of slaughter houses was in the Rockport-Fulton area. The first was built by William Hall, from Maine. James Doughty located a slaughterhouse on a rocky point on Aransas Bay, which became Rockport. Other large packeries in the area included American Beef Packery, West and Weiser Company, Boston Packing Company, and Cushman and Company.

The Cushman packery was at Frandolig Point, the site later developed into Key Allegro. The Cushman packery hired 10 cowboys to supply it with 1,000 head of cattle every two weeks.

Across South Texas, the longhorns were driven to the packing houses. A packery employing 40 workers could process up to 250 head of cattle a day. The men were paid well to work — from $1 to $4 a day. Hides were salted down and rolled into bundles for shipment. Carcasses were put in boilers and the tallow skimmed off and put in 300-pound barrels. Tallow was a lucrative commodity. Cow fat was used to light the street lamps of many cities and it was used to make candles. Bones were used to make knife handles, buttons and combs. Some of the meat was dried into fertilizer cakes.

*Packing house operations smoked like volcanoes in John Grant Tobias'*
*romanticized painting depicting the waterfront at Fulton in front of the*
*Marion Packing Company in 1875. This painting, which was largely conjectural,*
*was done in the 1920s; the palm trees would not have been there in 1875. But it*
*gives a good idea of the scale of packing house operations in the Rockport-Fulton*
*area.*

Meat that couldn't be sold or given away was dumped into the bays or heaped on mountains of flesh that attracted scavengers.

The appeal of the packing houses must have diminished the closer one got to them. Odor from discarded meat is pre-eminent in the accounts of the packery era. Mrs. George Fulton Jr., who lived near the Fulton packery, said the meat was burned, which made a terrible odor. J. Frank Dobie said a mountain of waste meat near one of the Rockport packeries "stank to high heaven. Flocks of seagulls and other birds gorged on it. Those must have been the fattest seagulls in Texas."

Coastal schooners took the hides and tallow from the packing houses at Corpus Christi to Rockport. At Rockport, ocean-going vessels docked at the Big Wharf, where there was always at least one ship and sometimes as many as six loading hides, horns and tallow. It was reported that in 1874, 102 million pounds of tallow and $2 million worth of hides were shipped from the coast.

There may be no calculation of the numbers of cattle that were slaughtered during the hide and tallow era, but within a decade the packery business declined. Drought and winter die-ups, not to mention the operations of the packing houses, depleted the longhorn herds across South Texas. Beef prices rose and it was no longer profitable to slaughter cattle for their hides and tallow and dump the meat. The great slaughter was over. The big iron tanks were hauled away to be used as cisterns and the peeling and tanking business came to a dead end.

*—Nov. 26, 2014*

# Roy Miller, Go-Getter

Once upon a time, as stories used to go, a young man wearing a fancy suit and derby hat arrived in Corpus Christi. Henry Pomeroy Miller, soon known as Roy, was the new p.r. man for the St. Louis, Brownsville and Mexico Railroad. He stayed at the Constantine Hotel and went to work in an office across from Market Hall. His job was to produce a railroad magazine.

Roy Miller was already known as a go-getter. He was born in Blue Rapids, Kan., in 1884. After the family moved to Houston, he sold papers for three Houston newspapers, worked as a soda jerk, and graduated as valedictorian of his class when he was 15. At the University of Chicago, he waited tables and tutored other students to pay his way. He graduated after three years with a bachelor's degree in philosophy. He returned home to work as a reporter for the Houston Post.

Two years after Miller arrived in Corpus Christi he courted and married Maud Heaney, daughter of prominent doctor Alfred G. Heaney. He left his railroad job to become editor of the Corpus Christi Caller. He took on added responsibilities as secretary of the Commercial Club — forerunner of the Chamber of Commerce — and this led to his involvement in city politics. He left his editor's job, opened a real estate office, and ran a successful campaign for mayor in 1913.

Miller's tenure as mayor marked great progress for the city. At the time he was elected, a magazine named American City described Corpus Christi as an ill-lighted, poorly served, and run-down tourist resort with no paved streets, few sidewalks, an ineffective water system, an inadequate fire department, and an unsightly bluff frowning on the business district in the beach section below.

During his administration, the first 12 miles of streets in the city were paved. Twenty six miles of sewer lines were laid. A municipal wharf was built and a city garbage incinerator installed. A modern water system was installed and a new professional fire department, with modern equipment, was created to replace the horse-drawn wagons of the volunteer firemen. The unsightly bluff was terraced and topped with the bluff balustrade. Miller was the first mayor to have an office in City Hall and keep regular office hours. After a year in office, the Caller said he had given the city the best administration in its history.

In 1916, his lobbying brought Texas National Guard units stationed in the Valley to Corpus Christi in a new army base named Camp Scurry.

After serving three terms, Mill lost in the 1919 city election to Judge Gordon Boone, a surprising upset. He went back to work as publisher and part owner of the Corpus Christi Caller. After the devastating 1919 storm, Miller was chosen chairman of the Citizens Relief Committee.

As publisher of the Caller (managing director, they called it then), Miller used the disaster as a starting point to preach the need for a deepwater port. A month after the storm, he wrote a series of page one editorials entitled "Now is the time." In his first editorial, he wrote: "Corpus Christi today, now, this very minute, has the opportunity to fix and secure her future. The one thing which will ultimately place Corpus Christi in the forefront of great American cities is deepwater. Because of the recent storm, the whole question of port facilities is to be reopened . . . We say to Congress, as we say to ourselves, now is the time."

In 1920, as Miller led the campaign for a deepwater port, he spent a lot of time in Washington lobbying Congress. He was a man of striking character, a forceful and persuasive advocate.

Harvey Weil, who served for years as the port's attorney, once told the story of how Corpus Christi beat out competing cities for the port designation. One December day in 1920, Weil wrote, Miller took Major L. M. Adams, of the Army Corps of Engineers at Galveston, on a hunting trip on King Ranch. The two men drove around all day before Adams shot a buck. That night at the ranch's Big House, Miller took a bottle of bourbon to Adams' room. After a few drinks, Miller came out and whispered to banker Richard King, grandson of the ranch's founder, "We've got it." Adams returned to Galveston and recommended Corpus Christi as the best place for a new port. When Adams retired from the Corps of Engineers in

*Roy Miller's home at 1224 N. Chaparral took a beating in the 1919 storm. Before the storm hit, Miller took his family to the Nueces Hotel where they spent several days as refugees. He lost the home and most of the furnishings in the storm.*

*A group photo on King Ranch house steps: Roy Miller, bottom left and Robert Kleberg Sr. Henrietta King, widow of Capt. King, was in a chair at the top of the steps. Roy Miller's wife, Maud Heaney Miller, is at the upper right, sitting.*

1930, he was named director of the port of Corpus Christi. That suggests a deal was struck at the King Ranch.

When President Warren Harding signed legislation authorizing the construction of the port of Corpus Christi on May 22, 1922, Miller sent a short telegram to the Caller saying, "We win!"

Seven years to the day after the 1919 storm struck, Corpus Christi celebrated the opening of the port. Roy Miller, with his keen blue-gray eyes and hair turned silver, delivered the dedication. "While it cannot and ought not be said that the Port of Corpus Christi is a creature of circumstance or the child of disaster," he said, "it is undeniably true that the realization of a dream of more than half a century was hastened by the disastrous storm of Sept. 14, 1919."

In 1929, Miller sold his interest in the Caller and went to Washington as a special representative of the port and the city. In the 1930s, he worked to promote the Intracoastal Canal and lived long enough to see the canal near completion in World War II.

Miller became ill in December 1945 with an intestinal disorder and died on April 28, 1946. He was 62. Corpus Christi High School was renamed Miller High in his honor.

Henry Pomeroy Miller's three terms as mayor marked a time of prosperity and growth, with streets paved and the bluff beautification projected completed. He turned the litany of death and destruction from the 1919 storm into a successful campaign to obtain a deepwater port. He remained the most dedicated champion of the port and Intracoastal Canal. As mayor and the city's greatest promoter, he compiled a record of achievement matched by no other leader in Corpus Christi's history. Much praise was heaped on his memory. Much praise was earned.

*—Dec. 3, 2014*

# Louis de Planque, Photographer

It's a shame that Louis de Planque's name is not more familiar. He was a craftsman, if not an artist, and one of the most important photographers in Texas from the Civil War into the 1890s.

De Planque (pronounced plunk) was born in Prussia in 1842, though little is known of his early life. He and wife Eugenia arrived in Matamoros in 1864, a turbulent time when that city was considered the back door of the Confederacy. Their arrival from France may have been connected with the landing of French forces protecting the Emperor Maximilian.

However he got there, in 1864 de Planque opened photographic studios in Matamoros and then Brownsville. He advertised in Henry Maltby's newspaper, the Ranchero, which had been moved from Corpus Christi to the border.

During the war, de Planque photographed civilian and military leaders, Confederate and Union. He took a photo of Rip Ford, commander of the Cavalry of the West that fought the last battle of the Civil War. He photographed Confederate Major Mat Nolan, the sheriff of Nueces County, and ranchers Richard King and Mifflin Kenedy, who were busy on the border overseeing the shipment of Confederate cotton.

At this point, something should be said about the nature of photography in de Planque's time. As I understand it, photography was invented in the late 1830s by Louis Daguerre, whose daguerreotypes took minutes to expose and were one of a kind; no duplicates could be made.

In the 1850s, the wet-plate process was invented, which was far superior to daguerreotypes. Exposure time was almost instantaneous and there were no limits to the prints that could be made from glass-plate negatives. Once exposed, though, the plate had to be developed immediately, which made outdoor shots difficult. The photographer had to carry along a portable darkroom and the chemicals needed for developing.

Despite the difficulties, many of de Planque's surviving photo copies from the Civil War were taken in the field. (This would later become easier when dry-plate photography was invented in the 1870s; photographers no longer had to carry a portable darkroom and developing chemicals. The dry plates could be exposed and taken back to the studio to be developed.)

Also invented in the 1850s was the carte-de-visite camera, which could take multiple poses of the same person on a single plate. These were printed and cut into small photos the French called cartes-de-visite — or visiting cards. They were very popular. It was almost a social obligation to have one's photo taken for cartes-de-visite to give friends and relatives, kind of like posting selfies in Facebook. Many, if not most, of de Planque's surviving photos are of the cartes-de-visite style.

After the war, on Oct. 7, 1867, a hurricane struck Matamoros and Brownsville. De Planque's studios and archives of glass-plate negatives were destroyed. Soon afterwards, he moved to Indianola, jumping from the frying pan into the fire. From Indianola, he took extended business trips to Corpus Christi and Victoria where he would establish a temporary studio in hotel rooms.

William Maltby wrote a puff piece on de Planque in the Corpus Christi Advertiser on April 8, 1870. "Louis de Planque, the photographer, has arrived at last. He has fitted up rooms at the Ziegler Hotel and tomorrow will be ready to receive visitors. We first became acquainted with de Planque in Mexico in 1865. He has not met his superior in the South as an artist." De Planque stayed four weeks before returning to Indianola.

In the hurricane of 1875, the first of two devastating storms that wiped out Indianola, de Planque's studio and collection of glass-plate negatives were once again destroyed. He moved to Corpus Christi, where he opened a studio and his business prospered. Few people of standing failed to have their portraits made by de Planque. Strollers would pass by his studio windows, at the corner of Mesquite and William, to see the latest display of street scenes.

De Planque was partial to display and parade. He loved dressing up in an outlandish costume for the annual Columbus Day festivities. A newspaper article said he would arm himself with knives and guns, decorate his hat with a feather, drape an Indian

*The photographer Louis De Planque dressed up for a Columbus Day parade in Corpus Christi. His wife Eugenie probably took the photo. For the parade, De Planque carried guns and knives and decorated his hat with a feather, draped an Indian blanket over his shoulder, and carried a lariat. He wore a large bowtie and leather leggings to represent, well, nobody could ever figure out what.*

blanket over his shoulder, and carry a lariat. His wore a large bowtie and leather leggings that reached the knees. Asked what he was supposed to represent, he would smile and say it satisfied him.

His last Columbus Day appearance was in 1897. He died of a stroke on May 1, 1898. He was 56. An obituary in the Caller said: "Mr. de Planque was an artist, one of the best photographers in the state. Like many others, however, he never accumulated much of this world's goods. A more kind-hearted and polite man than Mr. de Planque was not to be found and he will be missed."

His work of a lifetime is also missed. A few of his Civil War photographs were found in 1999 at a landfill in Monterrey. They were rescued and compiled in a book by Jerry Thompson and Lawrence T. Jones III, "Civil War and Revolution on the Rio Grande Frontier." Other copies of his photos came from the daughters of William Maltby, who kept 48 de Planque shots, half of them taken in Corpus Christi. These make up the de Planque collection in the Corpus Christi Central Library.

De Planque was unlucky with storms. The glass-plate negatives taken in the Civil War were destroyed in the hurricane of 1867. Later negatives were lost in the Indianola storm in 1875. What happened to the thousands of negatives taken in Corpus Christi disappeared after his death, perhaps dumped — years of work gone. Very little was left, to our great loss. That's why the name of Louis de Planque remains virtually unknown.

*—Dec. 10, 2014*

*Carte-de-visite photos of the Empress Carlota, wife of Mexico's ruler Emperor Maximilian, and Gen. Juan Nepomuceno Almonte. These date from the time Louis de Planque had photo studios in Matamoras and Brownsville. He later moved Corpus Christi. Both photos are from the De Planque collection at the Corpus Christi Central Library.*

*Carte-de-visite photos of Amanda Allen and Martha Rabb's Magnolia Mansion on the bluff by photographer Louis de Planque. Both photos are from the De Planque collection at the Corpus Christi Central Library.*

# First Decade of 20<sup>th</sup> Century

In the first year of the 20th Century, Corpus Christi was a coastal village of 6,000 people, with unpaved streets and one resort hotel. The town had languished after the collapse of the Ropes boom in 1893 but it was waking from a long slumber.

Josiah "Si" Elliff, who founded the 44 Ranch near Banquete, died. He came to Texas as a runaway and worked on Martha Rabb's ranch until he started his own. On July 3, 1900, he went out to pick ears of corn for supper and suffered a heart attack.

In 1901, George Blucher bought a new Oldsmobile, the first automobile in Corpus Christi. It cost $650, had a motor under the back seat and a tiller instead of a steering wheel. The following year Dr. Alfred Heaney bought a one-cylinder Cadillac and his rival in all things, Dr. Arthur Spohn, bought his own. Peter McBride, a dairyman, was riding in a mule cart when he encountered Dr. Spohn in his new motorized monster. "I kept trying to hold the mules back," McBride said, "but they were scared and there was no stopping them." McBride could see no use for so much speed.

In 1901, Clara Driscoll, 22, wrote a letter to the Corpus Christi Caller describing the plight of the Alamo, about to be sold as a site for a hotel. Her letter sparked a campaign to raise $75,000 to buy the property. When the campaign came up $50,000 short, she signed five notes for $10,000 each. She was called the savior of the Alamo.

It was also in 1901 when Alex and Moise Weil opened a grocery store on Mesquite. Meats sold at the store came from the Weil Ranch.

Perry Doddridge died on June 11, 1902. He was orphaned at seven when his parents died and at 14 he went to work for the riverboat line operated by Richard King and Mifflin Kenedy. He moved to Corpus Christi, became a wool merchant, served as mayor, and built the town's first bank.

The Ladies Pavilion opened on Aug. 7, 1903. It was a wooden structure built where Ohler's Wharf once stood off Water Street. It got its name because ladies of the Woman's Monday Club raised money to build the facility. One of the first stage presentations at the pavilion was a tableau titled "A Dream of Beautiful Women" in which Clara Driscoll played Cleopatra.

Morris Lichtenstein died on Aug. 12, 1904. Lichtenstein, a Confederate veteran, moved his department store from Indianola to Corpus Christi in 1874. The store grew into the town's premier mercantile establishment. Lichtenstein died after he got blood poisoning from an amputated toe.

In 1905, the first summer revival of the Methodists' Epworth League opened on Aug. 8 on North Beach. When the Methodists arrived, Corpus Christi had three railroads, six automobiles, 10 churches, one cistern factory, three lumber yards, a fire department, and a three-man police force.

In 1905, the long-vacant Alta Vista Hotel, built during the Ropes boom, was restored for reopening. As part of the project, a new shell-top road called Ocean Drive was built. That year, Corpus Christi's Board of Trade traveled to Brownsville on the new St. Louis, Brownsville & Mexico Railroad, Uriah Lott's third railroad. Also that year, Chaparral and Mesquite were being graded and at the high school commencement at the Ladies Pavilion, Marie von Blucher was valedictorian.

It was also in 1905 that Spohn Sanitarium (hospital) was built on North Beach where the old Miramar Hotel had burned. Before the hospital was built, doctors performed surgeries in the homes of patients. The $15,000 hospital was built with contributions from the people of Corpus Christi.

A trial began in December 1905 of George Talley, a former Ranger charged with murder 26 years before. The shooting was the result of a prank at the camp of Texas Rangers near Banquete. Talley tied a tin can to the tail of a colt owned by Josh Peters. That led to a gunfight with Peters shot to death and Talley leaving for New Mexico. When Talley returned to Corpus Christi, he was arrested. The trial made for a reunion of Leander McNelly's Rangers from the 1870s. Talley was eventually found not guilty.

This was a time of great change as crops replaced cattle on old grazing lands and ranches were broken into tracts for farmland. The railroads helped the ranchers and land promoters by offering low-

*President William Howard Taft visited Corpus Christi on Oct. 22, 1909. The president is sitting in the back seat of a seven-passenger Rambler, with city officials, during a parade down Chaparral.*

cost rates to homeseekers. The land boom was on. The greatest of land promoters was George H. Paul from Iowa, who perfected the art of selling land. In one year, as the boom advanced, Paul sold 56,000 acres of Driscoll ranchlands north of Robstown. When the boom had reached its apex, Paul had sold half a million acres of South Texas ranchland. Between 1900 and 1910, homeseekers came by the thousands. After buying their plots, they built homes and cleared fields for cultivation. New towns sprouted up.

President William Howard Taft visited Corpus Christi in October 1909. He was a guest at the ranch of his half-brother, Charles Taft, and stayed at the Taft ranch house, La Quinta.

In planning for the president's visit, Corpus Christi's welcoming committee ordered matching outfits for the occasion: knee-length Prince Albert coats, stovepipe hats, kid gloves and shoes of the same color. On Oct. 22, a Coast Guard cutter ferried Taft across the bay to the Central Wharf. Members of the welcoming committee, nifty as bridegrooms, were there to greet him. The portly president was wearing an old alpaca coat and wrinkled gray trousers, presenting a down-and-out look next to the elegantly dressed welcoming committee. Taft was amused at their discomfiture.

The president spoke from a stage built on the side of the bluff. When he noticed men in Civil War uniforms in the crowd, he asked them to join him on the stage, forcing the welcoming committee to stand under the hot sun. Taft returned to La Quinta where he stayed for four days. For the first decade of the 20th Century, Taft's visit in October 1909 represented, in Churchill's later phrase, the end of the beginning.

*—Dec. 17, 2014*

# A Stormy Decade

In 1910, the beginning of a new decade, Daniel Hewitt from Tyler built Corpus Christi's first trolley line. He laid tracks on wooden blocks with copper wires strung overhead. The line had four cars. The inaugural run was made on March 28, 1910.

In 1911, as the Madero revolt gained momentum against the Porfirio Diaz regime in Mexico, a peace conference was held in March in Corpus Christi.

Representing the revolutionaries was Alfonso Madero, brother of Francisco Madero, the leader, and his father. Representing Diaz were Rafael Hernandez and Ernest Madero, an uncle of the revolutionary leader. There was no agreement. The Diaz government wanted the "insurrectos" to lay down arms with no concessions. While in Corpus Christi, the elder Madero attended church at St. Patrick's Cathedral. His son, Francisco Madero, became president of Mexico later that year but was assassinated two years later.

The first airplane flights at Corpus Christi thrilled large crowds on July 3 and July 4, 1911. Aviator Oscar Brindley flew a Wright brothers' plane over North Beach, part of a July 4th program.

One of the first acts of the Corpus Christi Independent School District, created in 1909, was to build a new high school, which was completed in 1911. People called it the brick palace because it cost so much.

Market Hall, in its 40th year, was torn down to make way for a new three-story brick City Hall built in 1911 on Market Square.

In 1912, John Dickenson built the Beach Hotel on North Beach. A streetcar stopped at the front door and the grounds ran down to the water. The six-story Nueces Hotel opened in 1913. It boasted more than 200 rooms, an elegant ballroom, Sun Parlor and Tropical Gardens.

In 1913, after Roy Miller was elected mayor, the unsightly bluff was terraced to prevent erosion and topped with a white balustrade. Among other improvements made during the Miller administration was the asphalting of major streets. Also, voters that year passed a $250,000 bond issue to build a new courthouse. The new six-story courthouse became, as the newspaper called it, "a credit to the hand of man."

On June 6, 1914, Loyd's Pavilion and Pleasure Pier opened on the bayfront. Loyd's had bathing facilities, a room for picture shows, a restaurant, saloon, ballroom, and cold drink stands. The new slogan in town, said the Caller, was "Meet me at Loyd's."

Nueces County, in 1915, dedicated an arched causeway across Nueces Bay, which replaced the old Reef Road.

A federal grand jury indicted County Judge Walter Timon for plotting to "corrupt the ballot" in the 1914 election. Indictments were also brought against other county officials.

During the trial, one witness testified that it was discussed in Timon's office how much it would cost to bribe voters on the Hill (meaning the Hispanic community). A witness testified that Timon said it would take $2,500 to $3,000 "as the other side will spend money like water." On the stand, Timon said he had never had to buy a single vote in Nueces County. The jury convicted five but could not agree that Timon was implicated.

Passions were raised to a fever pitch in the wet-dry campaign in 1916. Families that had been friends for generations quit speaking and there were fisticuffs in the streets. On March 10, 1916, Nueces County voted dry by 218 votes out of 3,377 votes cast. The following Saturday night, the town's 37 saloons were closed and dark. Saloons would be closed all over the country four years later when national Prohibition took effect.

On Aug. 17, 1916, a storm in the Gulf moved inland at Baffin Bay. In Corpus Christi, the storm destroyed the Ladies Pavilion, badly damaged Loyd's Pleasure Pier, wrecked the Natatorium, washed away the Seaside Pavilion's pier, and wrecked the new causeway. The 1916 storm turned out to be a harbinger of a far deadlier storm.

Construction of the long-delayed federal building was completed in December 1916. The Post Office, Customs office and federal courts were moved into the new building on Starr Street, a tan-brick structure with a red tile roof.

*Men check the depth of water on Peoples Street in the first wave of the 1919 storm. The water rose two feet in the first 20 minutes of the storm. The storm tide downtown reached a depth of 11.5 feet. The death toll for Corpus Christi, officially, was 284, but many believed the actual total was far higher.*

In 1916, with the Mexican revolutionary troubles spilling over the border, President Wilson ordered National Guard units to the Valley. When tensions on the border eased, the Second and Third Infantry Regiments were moved from the Valley to Corpus Christi. These were Texas National Guard units federalized for one year's service. They set up camp in a 200-acre site in the area around where Spohn Hospital is today. The base was first called Alta Vista then named Camp Scurry after Gen. Thomas Scurry, former commander of the Texas Brigade. After a year, Camp Scurry was ordered closed. Then, on April 6, 1917, the U.S. entered the war in Europe and Camp Scurry was reactivated as a training base.

With Spanish flu raging in 1918, businesses and schools closed. On Oct. 18, city government closed theaters and public dances. Poolrooms, domino parlors, and soda fountains were closed. Cafes could stay open if they moved tables five feet apart. On Oct. 26, there were 475 people stricken with the flu in Corpus Christi; 21 deaths had been recorded in two weeks. Camp Scurry was placed under quarantine; soldiers could not leave and civilians could not enter.

The epidemic ended about the same time that World War I ended, on Nov. 11, 1918. In Corpus Christi on Armistice Day, church bells were ringing and horns blowing as people took to the streets to celebrate. With the quarantine lifted, Camp Scurry held a dance to celebrate the end of the war and the end of the epidemic.

A year later, on Sunday, Sept. 14, 1919, Corpus Christi was hit by the worst storm in the city's history. Hundreds of bodies washed up across Nueces Bay. The downtown and North Beach were devastated. Each empty lot, where homes and businesses once stood, spoke of personal tragedies. The official death toll in Corpus Christi was 284 but many believed the toll was far greater because many unidentified bodies were buried in mass graves. The decade came to an end with much of Corpus Christi in ruins.

*—Dec. 24, 2014*

# 1920s Came Roaring Back

Corpus Christi entered the 1920s trying to recover from the worst disaster in its history. It was devastated by the 1919 storm. It showed a determination not only to recover but to improve, an indication of the indomitable spirit of the city. This determination led to building the breakwater, the port and eventually the seawall. Out of tragedy came dynamic change.

Nueces County had been "dry" for four years, since 1916, when Prohibition took effect across the nation on Jan. 16, 1920. National Prohibition opened the era of bootleg liquor, backyard stills, and whisky smugglers called tequileros.

The first traffic rolled across the temporary Nueces Bay Causeway on Oct. 21, 1921. It was a makeshift wooden bridge built close to the water to replace the first causeway, a concrete structure wrecked in the 1919 storm. A fire on Nov. 20, 1921 destroyed the generating plant leaving the city without electricity. After the fire, the Caller hooked up a tractor to the press and with a steady foot on the accelerator got the press to operate, a trick learned after the 1919 storm. The city was without electricity for months.

The Saxet Company in 1922 brought in the first producing gas well in Nueces County off Shell Road west of the city.

Big news came on May 22, 1922 when President Harding signed legislation authorizing the Port of Corpus Christi. A bond election in October to establish the navigation district passed ten to one. In 1922, the city built the Pleasure Pier off Peoples Street for $8,200. It became a favorite place for strolling and fishing. The Pier Café opened four years later.

In October 1922, Klan leader Fred Roberts was shot to death in his car on Railroad Avenue. Sheriff Frank Robinson and two deputies were tried for murder on a change of venue to Laredo. They were acquitted. Robinson, fearing retaliation, never came back to Corpus Christi. Three years later, on July 5, 1925, a shootout in front of a house of sporting girls also had Klan connections. The shootout at Bessie Miller's left four men dead and another wounded. "By the time the thing was over," Sheriff Ben Lee said, "there wasn't anybody left to try for the killings; they were all dead."

On Nov. 9, 1924 a train called "The Blackland Special" pulled out of Corpus Christi with 105 farmers and businessmen, all wearing pearl-gray Stetsons, on board. The group toured north and central Texas to promote blackland farming of South Texas.

The widespread destruction of the 1919 storm led the city to build a protective breakwater. A railroad trestle was built into the bay in the curved shape the breakwater would become. Granite rocks were hauled to the end of the line, where a barge-mounted crane dropped the boulders to the bay floor. As the breakwater took shape, the rail lines were pulled up and the work backed its way toward town.

The great event of the decade came seven years to the day that the city was hit by the 1919 storm. On Sept. 14, 1926, the Port of Corpus Christi was opened, making the city a gateway to international trade.

Port opening day, a dramatic moment, was the biggest celebration the city had ever seen. Excursion trains brought 25,000 visitors to double the city's population. Boat races, a beauty contest, and an historical pageant were held. The downtown was draped in bunting for a parade. Three U.S. destroyers arrived for the port opening.

The port led to the greatest growth in the city's history. The year after the port opened, Corpus Christi was filled with cotton producers, cotton buyers, cotton brokers, cotton exporters. One result of this boom was the need for office space. Maston Nixon built the Nixon Building at Leopard and Broadway. The 12-story structure was filled with offices of cotton buyers. When the 14-story Plaza Hotel went up two years later, it gave the city skyline twin towers.

A derelict from the Ropes boom went up in flames in 1927. The Alta Vista Hotel, built in 1890 at Three-Mile Point, was destroyed by fire. A bucket brigade couldn't save it. On July 4, 1927, the Don Patricio Causeway across the Laguna Madre was opened to traffic. Crossing the open troughs built on wood pilings cost motorists $3 for a round trip.

Corpus Christi High School (now Miller) was built in 1928 at a cost of $320,916. Gutzon Borglum, later famous as the sculptor of

*A crew in late 1924 works on the wharf and transfer sheds during construction of the Port of Corpus Christi.*

*The official program for port opening day on Sept. 14, 1926. Activities included a parade, dedication ceremonies, motorboat races, a beauty contest, and an historical pageant. The city spent more than $50,000 on the celebration.*

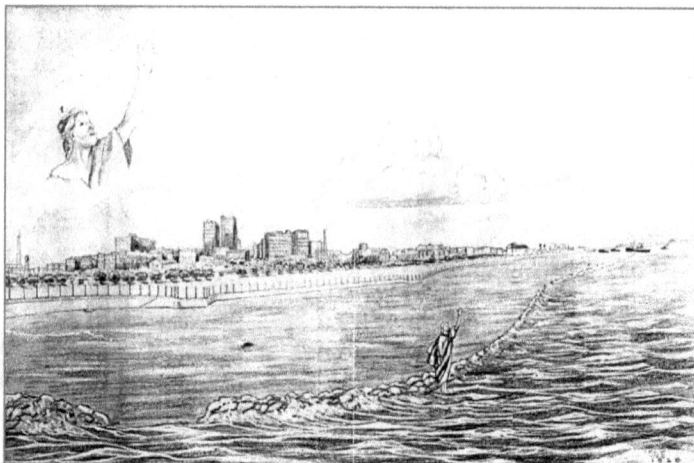

A sketch of Gutzon Borglum's bayfront improvement plan shows an inset image of Christ. The plan called for a statue of Jesus with upraised arm in front of the breakwater.

Mount Rushmore, was brought to Corpus Christi in 1928 to design a bayfront plan. Part of his plan called for a huge statue of Christ with arm raised to still the raging waters. His plan also called for a seawall, boulevard and landscaped parks. The plan was scrapped.

On Feb. 17, 1929, Ben Garza, owner of the Metropolitan Café, forged a compromise among separate Hispanic civil rights organizations to form the League of United Latin American Citizens (LULAC). The organizations were the Order of the Sons of America, Council No. 4; Knights of America, San Antonio; the League of Latin American Citizens, formed in Harlingen in 1927. The meeting was at Obreros Hall at Lipan and Carrizo. At the first convention in May, at Allende Hall, Garza was elected president and Luis Wilmot from Corpus Christi was elected treasurer.

Billy Sunday, a former baseball pitcher, opened a five-week revival in Corpus Christi on March 3, 1929 in a warehouse at the port. Most sessions drew from 5,000 to 6,000 people.

The port in 1929 led the nation in cotton tonnage. It was approaching 600,000 bales shipped out each year. On any given Saturday during cotton-picking time, Leopard Street became the main drag for cotton-pickers and families. Corpus Christi at the end of the decade was a prosperous place but hard times were coming.

*—Dec. 31, 2014*

# Hard Times in 1930s

At the beginning of the 1930s, banks folded, farms were repossessed, jobs disappeared, and families lost their homes as a depression turned into the Great Depression.

The decade got a cold start on Jan. 19. Temperatures dropped to 12 degrees and the bay near the shore froze solid. It was the coldest weather seen since 1899.

At the beginning of the decade, the port was growing, the Intracoastal Canal was being dredged, and oil was discovered in Saxet Field, followed by discoveries in the Minnie Bock and Clara Driscoll fields.

In January 1930, for five cents, one could see Harold Lloyd in "Welcome Danger," the first talkie at the Palace. At the Nixon Building, housewives were offered a free salad with vegetables "freshened" in the new Frigidaire Hydrator. The new Erskine model Studebaker cost $895 at Winerich Motors.

"Doc" Mason opened the Dragon Grill on North Beach, the first of three nightclubs named Dragon Grill, two on North Beach and one on Water Street.

The dance marathon craze hit Corpus Christi in July with a contest at the Crystal Beach Ballroom on North Beach. It began on July 24 with 19 couples who danced 40 minutes of every hour to the music of Clarence Schenk's Rio Grandians playing tunes like "I Love You Truly." People paid 50 cents to watch the tired dancers shuffle their feet. After 31 days two couples, one from Corpus Christi and one from the Valley, were left. The Valley couple got married while they danced. On the last day, the boy from Corpus Christi forgot to move his feet and the Valley couple won $675, a sizable sum when few people were acquainted with folding money.

On Nov. 23, 1930, the La Fruta Dam on the Nueces collapsed and Lake Lovenskiold, the city's reservoir, emptied into the flooding river. The Mathis Dam was built in 1935, creating a new reservoir named Lake Corpus Christi.

In 1931, cotton prices fell from 18 to five cents and calf prices dropped from 9.3 cents a pound to 3.6 cents. The falling beef and cotton prices hurt Corpus Christi more than the Wall Street collapse two years before.

For those who had a job, pay was low. The salary at a dry-cleaning firm was $4 a week. Farm hands earned 40 cents a day. If pay was low, so were prices. Steak sold for 15 cents a pound at Cudd's Grocery and hamburgers at Bunk's Cafe on Leopard cost five cents.

In February 1932, the USS Constitution visited the port. The frigate from the War of 1812 stayed nine days and was visited by 100,000 people. (Nueces County population was 51,779 in 1930.)

In 1932, the city began to observe "Prosperity Days" on Sunday, Monday and Tuesday. On June 1, American Airways inaugurated passenger service to Corpus Christi with a 10-passenger Fairchild.

In March 1933, banks were closed and deposits frozen. The Chamber of Commerce issued trade certificates valued at $1 each, to be redeemed for cash when the banks reopened. Montgomery Ward announced that bids were being sought to construct a new department store building at the corner of Chaparral and Peoples, the site of the old Uehlinger Building.

The first farmer in the country to get a check for plowing up his cotton crop was a Nueces County farmer, W. E. Morris, who was given an expense-paid trip to Washington where, on July 28, 1933, President Roosevelt handed him a check for $517. Morris plowed under 80 acres of cotton on his farm in the London community.

Three hurricanes caused damage in 1933. The worst was the Sept. 5 storm, which destroyed the Don Patricio Causeway to Padre Island, swept away tourist cabins on North Beach, and damaged the temporary Nueces Bay Causeway. The city ran out of yeast because of the storm; a plane was sent from Dallas with yeast supplies for local bakers.

On Dec. 3, 1933, Corpus Christi, like the rest of the country, celebrated the end of Prohibition and the return of John Barleycorn and Johnny Walker. It had been a long drought, since Corpus Christi went bone dry in 1916, though dry it never was.

The South Texas Exposition, an agricultural fair, was held in 1934 at a warehouse at the port. The exposition was held again in 1935

*One of many tin and cardboard shacks on North Beach during the Depression years of the 1930s. The woman in the doorway was the wife of an out-of-work World War I veteran. Photo by Russell Lee, Library of Congress.*

and 1936. A big hit was radio personality W. Lee O'Daniel and his Light Crust Doughboys. Pappy O'Daniel would be back four years later running for governor.

In 1934, the city gained its first major industry, Southern Alkali, which became Pittsburgh Plate Glass. The plant made soda ash from crushed oyster shells. It hired 1,800 workers in a city desperate for jobs.

In 1935, the city annexed North Beach, with its shacks of tin, tarpaper and scrap lumber. The following year, a small zoo opened in South Bluff Park. The menagerie included two small black bears, a lioness, some monkeys, a deer, owls, a goat that died, and a coyote that was killed. It was soon closed.

In 1937, Pat Limerick built a grocery store out in the country. In the early morning he could hear coyotes howl and ducks would land on a nearby puddle. That area became Six Points.

In May 1937, President Roosevelt was fishing for tarpon off Port Aransas with guide Barney Farley. When Roosevelt landed a tarpon, Farley said, the president was so excited he would rub his hands on the fish and then on his khaki pants.

Ben Garza, the first president and founder of LULAC, closed the Metropolitan Café and entered a sanitarium for treatment of tuberculosis. He died at the age of 44 in 1937. Flags at the City Hall and Courthouse were lowered to half-mast and the governor and the White House sent representatives to his funeral.

There was a hard-fought city election campaign in 1937 between Dr. H. R. Giles and A. C. McCaughan. McCaughan won. Work began in 1939 on building the seawall. In 1939, the city won the competition for a naval air station. Building the base at Flour Bluff would bring "Prosperity Days" for real. For Corpus Christi, the depressed thirties came to a welcome end.

*—Jan. 7, 2015*

# City Was Booming in 1940s

As the 1940s began, 9,000 workers were building the Naval Air Station at Flour Bluff at a furious pace. Hotels were packed. A migrant camp on North Beach was crowded with poor people looking for a job at the base. The city was a huge construction site and it was slow going, anywhere in town. Sewer lines were being laid, streets paved, and the seawall was under construction. As the bayfront work progressed, the 20-story Driscoll Hotel was rising on the bluff, and Corpus Christi was under construction.

The naval air station was dedicated on March 12, 1941. Navy aviators trained at NAS would play a major role in winning the coming war in the Pacific.

The red-light district was shut down on Aug. 1, 1941. Moving vans hauled away fancy furnishings from 39 houses of sporting girls. The new Lichtenstein's on Chaparral opened in December.

On Dec. 7, a placid Sunday, people heard the shocking news that Japanese planes had attacked U.S. bases in Hawaii. On Monday, at the cavernous Assembly & Repairs hangar, sailors listened to Roosevelt's day-of-infamy speech. The city's first war casualties were Billy Jack Brownlee, killed at Hickam Field, and Warren Sherrill, killed on the Arizona.

With rationing, civilians were allowed two pairs of shoes a year, men wore pants without cuffs, and housewives registered for sugar coupons. To save gasoline, Central Power & Light wheeled out a fleet of bicycles for meter readers.

In 1942, six air-raid sirens were installed around the city and the Navy opened a secret radar training school on Ward Island. The first blackout drill was held on Jan. 19, 1942. The city was almost completely dark except for two pinpricks of light from homes of blackout violators and, without the hazy blur of city lights, the starry sky was brilliant. Ten days later, the next blackout was no drill. It

*Lichtenstein's new store on Chaparral, built on the old St. James Hotel site, opened on Dec. 1, 1941, seven days before the Japanese attack on Pearl Harbor.*

was the real thing after a German U-boat was sighted lurking off the shipping lane near Port Aransas.

Sheriff John B. Harney went on trial in 1942 in district court. The Attorney General's office sought his removal from office for misconduct, based on the shooting death of a man from West Virginia. Harney claimed he shot him in a scuffle over a gun. The jury found him not guilty and on the next election he was returned to office for another term.

On April 21, 1943, President Roosevelt and Mexico's President Avila Camacho and their wives visited the Naval Air Station. It was Roosevelt's second visit to this area of the Texas coast, after his tarpon-fishing trip in 1937. At NAS, Roosevelt delivered a speech to the assembled aviation cadets and watched an aerial display of dive-bombing.

In 1944, two German POWs escaped from a POW camp at Mexia and fled to Corpus Christi, setting off a big manhunt. They were caught at a tourist court on North Beach. At war's end, German POWs were housed at the Naval Air Station in a compound near the South Gate.

What seemed at first to be a routine case reached Judge Joe Browning's court in May 1945. Bush Jackson leased the Elks Club building to "Doc" Mason, who wanted to establish the Dragon Grill there. The building was already leased to Joe Mayes' Playboy Club. Browning instructed the jury to bring in a verdict for Jackson. The jurors refused. The judge ordered them confined to the courthouse until they brought back a verdict he wanted. A jury statement said the verdict was ordered against the conscience of the jurors.

When Caller columnist Bob McCracken criticized the judge for his handling of the case, the judge had McCracken, a reporter and the publisher jailed. The Supreme Court reversed Browning in a landmark decision (Craig v. Harney) which noted that a judge cannot use the power of his office to insulate himself from criticism.

When victory over Japan came on Aug. 15, 1945, the town went wild, with cars racing through the streets, hooting and honking, as policemen tried to control the crowds. A reporter wrote that, "Everyone was shouting and singing and hugging each other. The joy of peace exploded and everybody loved one another." Everyone talked to everyone else. There were no strangers that day.

With the war over, returning veterans would find a changed city, with the new Driscoll Hotel on the bluff and the old Dragon Grill burned and gone. "Saddest of all the changes," the Caller wrote, "will be those missing faces. Many are gone and many who will return will never be the same."

The war was over but rationing was not. Corpus Christi butchers appealed to the Office of Price Administration for relief from the "meat famine" and there were bread lines in April 1946. Private yachts that had been drafted to patrol the Gulf looking for U-boats were returned to their owners in 1946.

Former mayor Roy Miller died on April 28, 1946 after he underwent surgery for an intestinal disorder. No other leader in the city's history compiled a comparable record of achievement — from paving downtown streets, building the bluff balustrade, successfully lobbying Congress for the port of Corpus Christi and much else besides.

On June 18, 1946, a crowd estimated at 10,000 lined Chaparral for a parade honoring Fleet Admiral Chester W. Nimitz. The Naval Air Station became a shadow of its wartime self; Cabaniss, the last of the auxiliary fields, closed in 1947. There was some consolation in 1949 when the Blue Angels moved to Corpus Christi.

Dr. Hector P. Garcia returned to Texas from the battlefields of Europe. When he came to Corpus Christi to practice medicine in 1946 there were no Hispanics in local government. He and men like him, who helped to win the war, came home to this? In 1948, Garcia founded the American GI Forum, which became the nation's largest Hispanic veteran's organization. The struggle for recognition for Hispanics, veterans and otherwise, became Dr. Hector P. Garcia's life work.

*—Jan. 14, 2015*

# Building Harbor Bridge

At noon on June 17, 1950, under a blue sky and bright sunshine, the new Padre Island Causeway opened the once isolated island to thousands of visitors and gave Corpus Christi a new playground. The causeway's $1.2 million cost would be repaid through a $1 toll.

At the end of June 1950, President Truman ordered U.S. troops to Korea to enforce, in his words, a police action, whatever that meant, but the reality was a new war in a distant land. The reserve Company B of the 15th Marine Infantry, composed of 80 young men from Corpus Christi, left for the conflict. Richard Garza was the first man from Corpus Christi killed in the Korean War.

The new W. B. Ray High School opened in September 1950. Only the library was air-conditioned.

An ice storm struck Corpus Christi in January 1951, rupturing water pipes as the temperature dropped to 18 degrees, the lowest since 1899 when the temperature dropped to 11 degrees. It was freezing, cold, and miserable. Buses and taxis were parked, airline flights halted, and telephone circuits knocked out. The frozen rain caused traffic accidents, closed schools and ruptured water pipes. It was freezing, cold, and miserable.

In 1951, a new concrete causeway replaced the old temporary causeway across Nueces Bay. A new City Hall opened on Shoreline in 1952. Memorial Coliseum opened two years later. In 1952, a two-million-bushel grain elevator, the first to be built in 20 years on the Texas coast, went into operation at the port. Dr. Hector P. Garcia, founder of the GI Forum, led a campaign to clean-up almost 3,000 open pit privies in the city. Driscoll Children's Hospital, legacy of Clara Driscoll, heiress of the Driscoll ranching dynasty, opened in 1953.

A popular song said, "It ain't gonna rain no more" which seemed to be true as another severe drought punished South Texas, with cattle dying and drifting sand covering ranch fences. In 1953, the Mathis reservoir ran low and water rationing was instituted. The reservoir, built in 1936, was one tenth the size of the larger reservoir (renamed Lake Corpus Christi) after the Wesley Seal dam was built in 1958.

When King Ranch observed its centennial in July 1953, the Caller-Times editorialized — "Perhaps no area other than the vast stretch of land lying between the Nueces and Rio Grande could have provided the setting for so challenging an operation as Capt. Richard King started a century ago."

On Dec. 3, 1953, the Palace Theater on Chaparral, built in 1926, burned in a spectacular fire. Guests on the top three floors of the nearby Nueces Hotel were evacuated while others watched as firemen fought the great conflagration. It was the last show at the Palace.

Pioneer oilman Gus Glasscock filled in 22 acres of the bay in 1954 with plans to build a resort hotel and office complex. The plans fell through and the reclaimed land was put up for sale. Corpus Christi's first TV station, KVDO, nicknamed K-Video, went on the air on June 20, 1954. Also in 1954, La Retama Library moved from the W. W. Jones mansion into the old City Hall on Mesquite.

In 1955, Lichtenstein's bought out Perkins Brothers and, two years later, opened a branch store in the new Parkdale Plaza shopping center.

A big question was how to replace the bascule bridge, built in 1926. The bascule's 97-foot opening was a tight squeeze for the larger cargo and tanker vessels. When a ship approached, the bridge was raised, stopping traffic, and this bottleneck became a nuisance for motorists, especially as the volume of ship traffic grew.

But the question of the times was how to replace the old bascule bridge. The town debated whether to dig a tunnel under the port entrance or build a high bridge over it. To make sure it went the way they wanted, state highway officials in 1954 offered $9 million to build a bridge but not a dime for a tunnel. The City Council quickly voted for a bridge. At one point in the debate, Mayor Albert Lichtenstein, leader of the tunnel faction, resigned in protest.

Construction of the bridge began in June 1956. It took three years and four months to build. Harbor Bridge opened to traffic on Oct. 23, 1959. The old bascule bridge was sold for scrap.

*Construction of the Harbor Bridge was started on each side of the ship channel. When the two spans met they were off by a few inches, which had been expected. One side was jacked up until the two spans fell into line. The new bridge dwarfed the bascule bridge under it. Harbor Bridge opened to traffic on Oct. 23, 1959.*

The completion of Harbor Bridge was not a good omen for North Beach. In its heyday, the North Beach Amusement Park would attract up to 4,000 visitors on an average weekend and 20,000 or more on holidays. After the causeway opened up the island, the numbers began to drop and the amusement park was closed. Harbor Bridge served to bypass and isolate North Beach. The city changed the name to Corpus Christi Beach, but that didn't solve the sense of separateness nor stop North Beach's steady decline.

Just before Christmas 1958, the Navy announced it would close the Overhaul & Repair Department, which employed 3,000 civilian workers. It had been in operation since World War II. The closure was a severe blow, but despite protests from civic leaders the O&R was shut down in 1959.

A lot happened from 1900 to 1960. The 1919 storm left a wake of devastation but, destructive as it was, that ordeal pushed the city into making greater efforts to revivify itself and obtain a deepwater port. It was no coincidence that the port was opened seven years to the day — Sept. 14, 1926 — of the terrible storm. In the depressed 1930s, people got by, they endured. Corpus Christi weathered the hard times with the help of oil and gas discoveries. Like the rest of the country, Corpus Christi began to recover with the onset of war. The city played its role in World War II, with Navy pilots trained at NAS and with shipments of oil, the lifeblood of war, through the port. The economic downturn after the war was short-lived as Corpus Christi grew on the strength of the port and port-based refineries and chemical plants. If building the seawall was the great civic accomplishment of the 1940s, building Harbor Bridge was the high point of the 1950s.

*—Jan. 21, 2015*

# The Dobie Ranch

When I moved here the first book I read on South Texas was J. Frank Dobie's "A Vaquero of the Brush Country" followed by more Dobie books. No other writer captured the essence of this place like Dobie.

James Frank Dobie was born on Sept. 26, 1888, a Wednesday, in Live Oak County. He was the first of six children of Richard J. and Ella Byler Dobie. His people were ranch people, cattle people and horse people. His grandfather Robert Dobie and his brother Sterling were ranchers in Harris County in 1846. After Robert drowned, leaving a wife and three sons, a fourth son, Richard, was born four months later. That was J. Frank's father.

Sterling Dobie moved to Live Oak County in 1859. He started a horse ranch, partly owned by his brother's widow. She moved to Live Oak County with her sons. In 1886, Jim and Richard bought a ranch, then Richard bought Jim's share and married Ella Byler.

The Dobie ranch was seven miles west of Barlow's Ferry, six miles south of Lagarto. The 7,000-acre ranch was too small, said Dobie's father, to have a name. J. Frank described the house where he grew up, which sat among live oaks overlooking Long Hollow. The house had a paling fence, vegetable garden, flower beds, smokehouse and stables with rooms for saddles.

Of his childhood, Dobie wrote, "No play world could have been more interesting than the one I, my sister and brothers made . . . With pegs, twine and sticks we built pastures and stocked them with spools, from which my mother's sewing machine had used the thread, for horses; with tips of horns, sawed off in the branding chute, for cattle; with oak galls for sheep and snail shells for goats. The goats could not be branded but we branded the other stock with baling wire heated red-hot." Ranch kids learned to make their own entertainment.

231

Whenever his father was away, Dobie's mother kept a Winchester rifle within reach. She remembered, from growing up in the Bluntzer community, the famous Nuecestown Raid, but she was never fearful and would say, "Don't trouble Trouble until Trouble troubles you."

The timeless rhythm of ranch life enfolded J. Frank until he went off to school. He was taught at the ranch until 16 when he was sent to live with his Dubose grandparents and attended high school in Alice. When he left for college, to seek his fortune in the wide, wide world, Ella cautioned him — "Remember where you came from." And he remembered.

In front of the stables at the ranch the ground was paved with caliche. Red ants made their mounds underneath the caliche. In the early mornings when horses were being saddled they would stamp the caliche to knock the ants off their hooves. "After I went off to college," Dobie wrote, "I half awakened before daylight every morning to the sound of those horses stamping their feet on the caliche. The memory is a part of me."

He remembered the milk cows — Pet, which the children would ride, Old Paint, with a crumpled horn, and Hookey, who once threw his sister Fannie into the air. He remembered the time a vaquero dried out his wet rawhide leggins at a campfire and they became stiff as armor. The vaquero stood them up "and talked to them and had them talk back to him. Everybody was laughing."

Dobie graduated from Southwestern University, where he met Bertha McKee. They married in 1916. After college, he worked for the San Antonio Express then became an instructor in English at the University of Texas. He was sent to France during World War I, but was never at the front. After the war, his uncle Jim Dobie hired him to manage the 250,000-acre Olmos Ranch in lower South Texas. It was here where Dobie decided to collect the legends, tales and folklores of the past.

Dobie returned to the University of Texas to teach a course called "Life and Literature of the Southwest." When colleagues joked that there was no such thing as literature in the Southwest, Dobie said, "Well, I'll teach life then." And he began to write. He had a talent for telling stories, whether they were made-up or true, fiction or folklore or history. His writing style was that of a storyteller sitting before the glowing red of a dying campfire. "The way to spoil a story," he would say, "is to talk about it rather than tell it."

232

*J. Frank Dobie in 1955. People sometimes remarked that he resembled the poet Carl Sandburg and cowboy humorist Will Rogers. The South Texas storyteller, who grew up in Live Oak County, died in 1964.*

Dobie's books include a mixture of history and legends tinged with personal experience and written in his unique storytelling style. His books include "A Vaquero of the Brush Country," "Coronado's Children," "Tongues of the Monte," "The Longhorns," "The Mustangs," "The Voice of the Coyote," "I'll Tell You a Tale" and many others.

A friend visited Dobie at his home on Waller Creek near Austin. He found him sitting under a Spanish oak, boots off and hat pushed back, passing time with a mutual friend, Jack Daniels. Dobie had been in bad health and said he could hear the summons from up there. There were no stories left to tell.

Dobie died on Sept. 18, 1964. His funeral was held at the University of Texas and he was buried in the State Cemetery. Of all famous Texas writers, Dobie came closest to the skin of the people.

The brush country of Live Oak County and the ranch people of South Texas became part of his DNA, part of his identity as a writer.

In a piece written for the Caller-Times in 1959, Dobie described his ranch memories:

"The calves sucking their mothers and playing about them in pasture . . . coyotes serenading after dark . . . my horse Buck pointing his ears when I walked into the pen to rope out a mount and seeming to ask if I were going to ride him or Brownie . . . the green on the mesquites in early spring . . . the stillness of day and night broken by windmill lifting rods . . . the rhythm of a saddle's squeak . . . these the land gave me . . . "

Like the people he wrote about, J. Frank Dobie was out of the old rock.

*—Jan. 28, 2015*

# Up the Trail

From 1779 to 1781, longhorn cattle from South Texas missions were driven across the swamps of Louisiana to feed the army of Bernardo de Galvez, who mounted a campaign against the British to assist the American Revolution.

Sometime in the 1820s Martin de Leon drove a herd from Victoria to New Orleans. After the Texas Revolution, cattle in the Nueces Strip were driven east and in the 1840s they were trailed to Ohio, Missouri, and even California after gold was discovered. During the Civil War, cattle were trailed east to feed Confederate armies. W.D.H. Saunders was 17 when he drove a herd from Goliad to Mississippi in 1862.

This was a prelude to the great cattle drives that began after the war. Returning Confederate soldiers were broke, few jobs were available and money was scarce. However, the ranges of South Texas were teeming with half-wild longhorns that had proliferated during four years of war and neglect. They were chased down, branded and walked to market.

Small herds went north to eastern Kansas in 1866, but the drovers ran into trouble from Jayhawkers and Redlegs. When the railroad reached Abilene in western Kansas, where herds could be sold and shipped to the stockyards of St. Louis and Chicago, drovers turned in that direction and eventually to other Kansas railhead towns.

Some 75,000 head of cattle went up the trail in 1867. The herds grew larger every year thereafter. In 1869, 600,000 cattle went north and the greatest drive in history was made in 1871 when 700,000 head went north from Texas.

With the first signs of spring, Texas cattlemen began rounding up herds for the drive, which would take three to four months. They wanted to get to Kansas before winter. Herds were moved up the Texas, Western and Chisholm Trails. Besides trail hands, there was a trail boss, horse wrangler and cook. The hands were paid $30 to $40 a month based on experience.

Cattle were driven hard at the beginning of a drive to rush them away from their familiar home ranges. After a herd was trail broken, it averaged 10 to 12 miles a day. In the morning, the cattle would graze in the direction of the drive and in the afternoons cowboys moved them along at a faster pace. They would reach bedding ground at sundown.

When they moved away from the well-beaten trails, looking for grass and water, drovers followed the stars. At night the tongue of the chuck wagon would be pointed toward the North Star and next morning the drive would take that direction.

The chuck wagon carried food and cooking utensils. The bed wagon, also called the hoodlum wagon, carried extra saddles, branding irons and bedrolls.

With a herd making 10 to 12 miles a day, cowboys could ride along dozing in the saddle. The top hand rode point. On either side near the front were swing riders, near the rear were flank riders, and at the rear were drag riders. Cowboys worked long hours, ate beans, drank Arbuckle's coffee, and sometimes were rewarded with a raisin dessert called spotted dog or son of a bitch in a sack. At night they played poker, told tall tales, and slept on a blanket with their saddle for a pillow.

It was dangerous when there were flooded rivers or when the herd stampeded. Personal accounts of the trail days can be found in "Trail Drivers of Texas." "We took the river route," one wrote, "since we must have crossed every damned river in the country." Worse than crossing a river on the rise was a stampede. Thomas Welder of Beeville said his herd pulled "a big show" 10 nights in a row. Cattle would run for any reason — a sudden noise, the flare of a match — but they often ran in a storm. A flash of lightning and crack of thunder and off they went, running like race horses.    A cowboy from San Antonio wrote that in one violent electrical storm he could see lightning on the brim of his hat and the tips of his horse's ears. Cowboys killed on the trail were rolled up in their blankets and buried with a grave mound shaped over them. One cowboy wrote that the saddest sight he had ever seen was a mound of fresh earth topped with a pair of old cowboy boots.

Cowboys grew excited as they left Indian Territory and crossed into Kansas. On reaching the outskirts of the typical Kansas cow

*From the 1860s into the 1880s more than five million head of cattle were driven up the trails that stretched from South Texas to Kansas. This was a world-crossing journey for young men who had never been more than a few miles from home. The cattle drive era represents an epic chapter in the history of Texas. Photo from the Library of Congress.*

towns — Newton, Hays, Wichita, Abilene or Dodge City — herds were held outside town until buyers looked them over. After they were sold, the longhorns would be shipped on railroad cars to eastern slaughter houses.

Once in town, as a matter of policy, Texas trail hands did not always behave at a high level. After they were paid they would take a bath with lilac soap, get their hair cut, buy a rig of fancy clothes, and get ready to cut a shine.

One described his arrival in Dodge City. "I went to a barber shop, got my face beautified, put on some new clothes, and went forth to see the sights in the toughest town on the map. At the first saloon, a girl came up, put her hand under my chin, and said, 'Oh, you pretty Texas boy, buy me a drink.' "

After a big time in one of the cow towns, some of the cowboys traveled home by railroad and then by steamboat. Others sometimes rode over the same trail, nursing hangovers and telling each other of their experiences on the way up. Riding home on the trail, they said, saved money for the bartender.

One cowboy, after he graduated from his first trail drive, said he would never forget the feel of the saddle, the heavy pull of weight of a six-shooter on his belt, or what a blessing on a rainy night was that yellow slicker they called fish. After resting up in the winter, many cowboys would be ready to take the trail again the next spring. That is, until times changed and the coming of railroads, wire fences, shorthorns, and the man with the hoe put an end to that epic chapter in Texas history.

*—Feb. 4, 2015*

# Steamer Mary Wrecked in 1876

The sidewheel steamship Mary, with eight passengers and crew of 30, ran aground and sank in the Aransas pass channel on Nov. 30, 1876. An eyewitness account of the wreck was provided by Susan East Miller, wife of rancher S. G. Miller. Mrs. Miller, her children and a brother were returning on the ship from a trip to Louisiana to visit her parents. She wrote:

"From New Orleans our party went to Morgan City (called Brashear then) to embark on the Mary for Rockport. Before we left we loaded my two horses that brought us overland to Louisiana. Little did I know the fate ahead for the valiant animals nor the harrowing experience we would face before we saw land again.

"We had a rough sea. The rolling of the ship sent me to bed with seasickness, leaving the children in the care of my brother and the chambermaid. We were traveling over a choppy sea, with the wind shifting, which made hard going for the ship. My brother, Dr. East, reported that the captain was uneasy. The cargo was heavy and the vessel was so old it was not fit to run any longer. The captain did not dare venture out to sea where it would be smoother sailing for fear the ship would be swamped in turning.

"The night we reached the bar (off the Aransas pass channel) a freezing norther swept out from land and struck the vessel. The boat racked, plunged, and dipped from side to side. It was difficult for me to stay in my berth. Yet I never felt uneasy because I had such confidence in the captain's skill.

"Next morning I noticed water in my room. I heard terrific noises and the room began to crash and pull apart. The chambermaid came running and cried, 'Get up! The boat is sinking!' Dr. East told me to run for my life to the pilot's house, explaining that Aunt Sophia and the children were already there. He caught my hand and we waded through water pouring through the ship like a mighty river.

"Everyone was huddled in the pilot's house. As a last resort we were to try the lifeboats, a dangerous undertaking in such a sea. Waves dashed over the sides of the ship as though they were great monsters angered at the delay in engulfing our frail boat.

"The captain told us that he had signaled the pilot (on Mustang Island) to come pilot the ship across the bar. When the pilot did not answer, the captain decided to take the boat across himself. In attempting the crossing, however, the boat ran into a buoy, which ripped her side open and she began to sink.

"Signal guns were fired and the flag of distress hoisted. We saw the pilot coming and our hopes began to rise. My poor horses were trapped in their stalls. I begged the captain to have their ropes cut so they could swim to shore, but he said it was impossible for anyone to get to them. I could hear them struggling until the water reached them. How my heart ached.

"About seven in the morning the pilot reached us, only to be confronted with the task of getting close enough to throw a rope to us. Trial after trial was made to get near us. Each time the waves carried our rescuers beyond reach.

"We watched the desperate efforts of the brave men in the pilot boat, risking their lives to save us. After three or four hours of hard work, the rope was caught by one of our men and the small boat was lashed to the Mary. To reach the gangplank we waded through water waist-deep on deck.

"The children were carried to safety then the rest of our party went into the pilot boat. As I started across the gangplank, the Mary broke away and down I went into the sea. As I went down, the heel of my shoe caught on one of the slats, which broke my fall and enabled me to catch hold of the two sides of the plank. Scrambling to a sitting position on the gangplank, I bobbled up and down as each big wave struck. The sailors caught hold of it again and I was helped into the rescue boat. Our trip in that small boat was another ordeal, but we managed to get across the bar while waves that seemed mountain-high lashed the Mary.

"To reach the pilot's house we walked the length of a 300-foot wharf made of two planks. We suffered an agony of cold as the blizzard whipped about us in our wet clothing. On our arrival we found our good hostess awaiting us with a roaring fire in the fireplace, where we sat and dried our clothes. Afterwards she served us a hot meal.

This is believed to be the Morgan Lines steamship Mary that served the Texas coast from her home port at Brashear (now Morgan City). The sidewheel steamer, built in 1866, wrecked in November 1876. The artist's depiction comes from the Corpus Christi Museum of Science and History. The original art is at the History Museum of Mobile in Mobile, Ala.

Susan (East) Miller with her husband S.G. Miller about 1905. She recalled the wreck of the Steamer Mary in her book, "Sixty Years in the Nueces Valley." (Miller family photo from James Collins.)

241

"All the next day we waited for a boat. At last, evening brought a glimpse of one coming our way. After taking us aboard, it headed for Rockport, where a crowd of people came to hear the story of our escape. I learned that Mr. Miller was in Corpus Christi, where he had been waiting three days, almost crazed with grief following news that the Mary had been shipwrecked and all aboard lost.

"After a 12-hour trip to Corpus Christi, we reached our destination about nine the next night. Mr. Miller was waiting at the wharf. There are no words to describe our happy meeting, after he had mourned us as dead and we had given up hopes of seeing our loved ones again."

* * *

At the scene of the wreck, barrels of flour, bolts of calico, wagon wheels, even a dentist's chair, washed ashore. The Corpus Christi Gazette warned people not to sample the contents of unlabeled bottles found on the beach since the Mary's cargo included a large supply of strychnine.

Susan Miller's first-hand account of the wreck was taken from her memoirs published in 1930, "Sixty Years in the Nueces Valley." Exploratory dives in 1989 and 1993 found the Mary to be in poor condition after more than a century of time's work. What remains of the old side-wheeler still lies in its watery grave near the mouth of the pass off Port Aransas.

*—Feb. 11, 2015*

# Trade Route to Chihuahua

One morning in 1821, at Boone's Lick, Mo., a man named William Becknell loaded his string of mules with trade goods and left for Santa Fe. He returned with rawhide bags filled with silver pesos, which marked the beginning of the Santa Fe Trail. This led indirectly to the founding of Corpus Christi.

The Santa Fe Trail ran from St. Louis and Independence to Santa Fe and northern Mexico. In due time, it became a great trade route. Goods shipped from St. Louis sold in Mexico for up to four times their cost and brought back profits into the hundreds per cent. Northern Mexico, the size of France, was a merchant's paradise. Trade on the Santa Fe Trail was estimated, in today's dollars, at $150 million a year. Immense fortunes were made.

In New Orleans, the merchants took note. Since New Orleans was much closer to Mexico than St. Louis, why couldn't they take a large share of this flourishing trade? The New Orleans merchants sent commercial agents to Matamoros. But Mexico was concerned about American immigration into Texas. It sought to hinder trade from the U.S. by imposing high tariffs on foreign goods, which were enforced only on American traders.

Seeking another entry into the lucrative Mexican market, the New Orleans merchants hired forwarding agents along the Texas coast, which was strategically located to become a conduit for trade. Several Texas coastal towns started as places where small boats with contraband cargo could land and unload goods for transport inland.

Henry Kinney, newly arrived from Illinois, opened a store at Aransas City on Live Oak Peninsula as an agent for New Orleans merchant J. H. Blood & Company. Kinney was engaged in the Mexican trade, as was James Power, founder of Aransas City. Both men were frontier merchants who dealt in tobacco, calico, wool, hides, sheepskins, goatskins and anything else they could buy or sell.

It was in late 1839 when Henry Kinney moved his store from Aransas City to a high bluff overlooking Corpus Christi Bay. It was a beautiful site but that wasn't what brought him there. It was a better location for the Mexican trade. Goods had been landed on the wide beach at this site since 1829 for overland shipment into Mexico. Kinney's Rancho, as it was first called, was a trading outpost, a place through which the commerce of Mexico could pass.

The Corpus Christi Star on Oct. 17, 1848 noted why the town was founded. "The object of Col. Kinney, when he first settled here, was to establish commercial intercourse with Mexico, which his penetrating genius showed could be accomplished better from this point than any other."

Henry Kinney was followed by John P. Kelsey, Frederick Belden, Henry Gilpin, Henry Redmond, William Mann, J. R. Everitt, and other Mexican trade merchants. There were others, comprising a B-list. Because these traders were avoiding Mexico's unfair tariffs, the trade was on the shady side, though the traders did not consider themselves smugglers. Technically, they were and, technically, from Mexico's point of view, Corpus Christi was a smuggler's outpost.

Corpus Christi merchants bought and sold Mexican goods. There was no other market for them. The population of Kinney's settlement in its first five years was about 100 people. The surrounding area was mostly unpopulated, with a few widely scattered ranches. Kinney, Belden, Kelsey, and Mann became wealthy merchants; they didn't gain that wealth by selling to the locals. Everyone in town — from butchers, bakers, and candlestick-makers — lived on the Mexican trade.

Traders from Mexico arrived with trains of pack mules and ox-carts. From Mexico came wool, hides, goat skins and crude silver bars molded in sand. The wool and hides brought money to buy domestic cloth, tobacco, and manufactured articles for sale back in Mexico. It was this commercial traffic from and to Chihuahua, Coahuila, and Nuevo León that kept schooners sailing between Corpus Christi and New Orleans. This was the economic pulse of early Corpus Christi.

Trade was brought to an abrupt halt during the Mexican War but after the war ended in 1848 it was resumed. Kinney, in an effort to revive the trade, established a partnership with William Cazneau

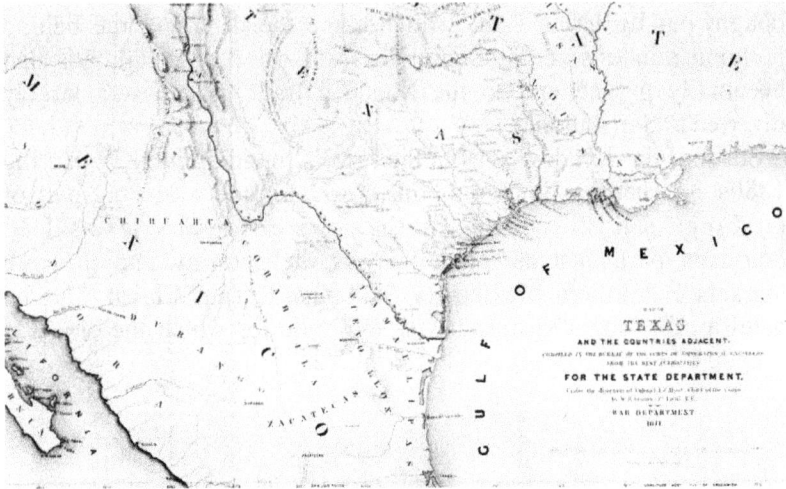

*An 1844 War Department map produced for the State Department shows South Texas and northern Mexico.*

and William Mann to send a caravan filled with goods to northern Mexico. The caravan of 50 wagons and ox-carts, called the Great Chihuahua Train, departed in March 1849.

Reports in the Corpus Christi Star testify to the steady commerce between Corpus Christi and the markets in Mexico. One of many such items in the Star reported that a party of traders arrived from Guerrero on the west bank of the Rio Grande. "In a few days, we understand, another party from the same place will be here."

The Civil War disrupted trade, but after the war it resumed in the late 1860s and early 1870s. On any given day, ox-cart trains loaded with wool, hides and skins arrived from Mexico.

When Mary Sutherland first saw Corpus Christi, in May 1876, Chaparral was crowded with ox-carts and wagons. "Some of the vehicles had as many as six yokes of oxen, and the patient animals were lying down in a seeming tangle, reaching from curb to curb, chewing the cud and waiting the crack of the whip, the signal to begin the long hot journey across the prairies to and beyond the Mexican border, carrying in their wake a whiff of civilization. Clothes, shoes, hats, cook stoves, sewing machines, oil lamps, clocks, any and everything, bought with the proceeds of sales of hides, tallow, dried meat, wool."

In the 1870s the shipment of Mexican ore through Corpus Christi was begun by wool merchants Edey & Kirsten. The firm was bought out by Uriah Lott, who became the driving force behind building railroads across South Texas. It was Lott's railroads that eventually put an end to the Mexican trade, which was largely diverted to San Antonio.

But for four decades — from the town's founding in 1839 into the 1880s — what was known as the Mexican trade was a big part of the Corpus Christi economy. In the city's early years, it was THE dominant part. Just as Santa Fe was the gateway into the rich markets of northern Mexico for St. Louis, Corpus Christi was the gateway for New Orleans. It was the trade for which the city was founded.

*—Feb. 18, 2015*

# The Skinning War

A bad drought in 1871 and 1872 was followed by a cold winter. Where there was water, there was no grass; where there was grass, there was no water. Cattle were too weak to travel between the two and they died by the thousands. Cowboys called it a die-up.

Spring brought the skinning season. Every man with a horse and knife went looking for dead cattle. Anyone could take the hide of a dead animal, no matter the brand, and the hide was ready money. When it was sold, the owner was due the value of the skin less the amount owed the skinner for his work. Ranchers hired their own skinners or used ranch hands for the grisly task.

Hide thieves also worked the ranges. Bandits from below the border had been stealing cattle for years, especially after the end of the Civil War. Then the value of beef dropped so low the hide was worth more than the cow. Instead of rounding up herds and driving them across the border, hide thieves killed cattle and skinned them where they fell.

They didn't wait for them to die, but helped them along. Some hide thieves used a long knife fixed to a pole to cut the tendons to immobilize the cattle. They were shot or stabbed to death. Hamstrung cattle were sometimes skinned while still alive, poor creatures.

The hide thieves hauled the hides to disreputable buyers or took them back to Mexico for sale. Two notorious hide thieves were Pat Quinn and Alberto Garza, known as Segundo Garza or Caballo Blanco.

The ranchers believed — and we suppose they would have known — that Gen. Juan Cortina, the Mexican folk hero and their longtime border antagonist, was more than a little implicated in the stealing of hides and the rustling of cattle. Garza was his second in command, which gave him the nickname of Segundo.

The hide thieves rode in heavily armed gangs — from 10 to 100 men — and could take on any force they ran up against and if truly threatened they could escape to Mexico.

The conflict between ranchers and hide-peelers was called the Skinning War. In the 1870s, J. Frank Dobie wrote in "The Longhorns," the waste of cattle for hides in South Texas was equaled only by the slaughter of buffalo on the Great Plains.

The Nueces Valley in 1872 reported, "We learn of the wholesale slaughtering of cattle by Alberto Garza and party. At one place there were 275 carcasses, at another 300, and at another 66. These robbers seem to be well-supplied with arms and ammunition, rodeo the cattle and shoot them down in their tracks until a sufficient number is killed for the day."

The newspaper urged vigilantes to get busy. "Let the mesquite branches show the fruits of their labor." "Red John" Dunn's company of Rangers, led by Warren Wallace, chased Garza in Live Oak County but could never corner him. Dunn in his memoirs wrote that lookouts warned Garza when the Rangers got too close.

"Garza's signalman kept him well posted and he always gave us the slip. One day Lieutenant Ferguson said, 'I am going to get one of those birds.' We rode toward a large hill and saw smoke curling up. Ferguson got off his horse and handed me the reins, telling me he was going to slip up on the signalman. I heard his sharpshooter boom and he yelled, 'Come on! I've got him!' The signalman was as dead as a nail. We found a sack with old pieces of bootlegs, shoes, and a can of tallow used to color the smoke."

Segundo Garza, or Caballo Blanco, had 60 men at work killing and skinning in Nueces and Duval counties. He boasted that, "The armed men of Texas mean nothing to me." In one account, he sent a taunting message to the town of San Diego demanding that they bring enough money to buy the hides his men had amassed or to send men to fight.

A posse composed of Jasper Clark, James F. Scott and nine others took up the challenge and attacked Segundo Garza's camp. Garza and his men escaped in such a hurry that they left their saddles, bridles and bloody hides behind. The vigilantes found the carcasses of 80 skinned cattle. Soon afterwards, Dobie wrote in "A Vaquero of the Brush Country," Caballo Blanco and his crew were "settled."

Following another die-up in 1873, the hide thieves were busy. After "Red John" Dunn's company of Rangers was disbanded he

*Sketch of a cattle raid on the Texas border appeared in Harper's Weekly in 1874. From the Library of Congress.*

joined a vigilante outfit that went after the outlaw skinners and merchants engaged in buying stolen hides.

"In the lower country called the Sand," Dunn wrote, "thousands of head of cattle belonging to the stockmen were killed and their hides sold to merchants who built stores for the purpose of disposing of stolen goods."

Dunn called the places "Mexican ranches." (A ranch did not always mean a cattle ranch; a store with a few houses around it was sometimes called a ranch.) Many of the hide-buying "ranches" were below Baffin Bay in today's Kenedy County, identified as La Travisada, La Mesa, La Prieta, and El Mesquite.

Dunn's vigilante outfit, led by Banquete cattleman T. Hines Clark, burned these ranches and according to some reports killed all the men they encountered. This led Nueces County Sheriff John McClane to send a telegram to Austin: "Is Capt. McNelly coming. We are in trouble. Five ranches burned by disguised men near La Parra last week. Answer."

Capt. Leander H. McNelly and a company of Rangers headed for the lower country. They ran into Clark's vigilantes, including the two Dunn brothers, John and Matt, and cattleman Martin Culver. In a tense standoff, McNelly ordered them to disarm and threatened to attack them if they refused. Dunn put a different slant on the story. He said McNelly "informed our captain that he had orders for us to disband, explaining that he had been sent there to take charge of that territory. Our captain told him that this was agreeable as we were on our way home."

The Skinning War lasted half a decade, from 1871 into 1875. T.R. Fehrenbach in "Lone Star" wrote that the hide thieves and the vigilantes who chased them cut a furious swath across the land. The bloody actions of these outlaw flayers and the arbitrary reprisals of the hard-riding vigilantes kept blood feuds alive for generations.

*—Feb. 25, 2015*

# Vigilantes in the Saddle

It was the end of shearing season at Thad Swift's place. He was a deaf sheep man who lived at a small ranch on Saus Creek, between Refugio and St. Mary's. On Monday, June 7, 1874, he took his spring wool clip to St. Mary's and was paid $700 in silver dollars, which he carried home in leather sacks.

That night, Swift was murdered. He was cut to pieces, the killers trying to make him tell where he hid the silver dollars. His wife Irene was stabbed 25 times. Their hacked-up bodies were left in the yard and mangled by hogs.

Three young daughters knew nothing of the slayings until they woke and found the bodies of their parents. Mattie, the oldest, was eight; she took her sisters, leading one and carrying the other, to a cousin's house three miles away.

Men turned pale at the terrible sight on Saus Creek. The scene was imprinted forever on the mind of John Young, who worked at a nearby ranch. "What I saw at the Swift Ranch changed me from a simple-hearted country boy to a hard-nerved man boiling for revenge."

It was a violent time. Committees of Public Safety — vigilantes — were organized all over. They were called minutemen because, in an emergency, they were required to drop whatever they were doing and be in the saddle in a minute, armed and ready to ride.

The minutemen turned out after the Swift outrage. One posse was under the command of a ranch hand named Edward Fennessey, one was led by Robert "Coon" Dunman, and another was led by rancher Henry Scott, a former Confederate officer.

Henry Scott's minutemen followed the trail of Juan Flores, considered a prime suspect. He was with Swift when he sold his wool clip and knew about the silver dollars. 'Coon' Dunman's "Regulators" checked on the whereabouts of every Mexican-

American in Refugio County while Fennessey's posse headed for Goliad, directed there by John Young.

Young told them he knew of a "bad Mexican" named Moya (he called him Moyer) who might have been involved in the killings. The evidence was weak. One of the Moya brothers was seen riding near the Swift Ranch before the murders and he was known to have a sharp knife. Any doubts were quashed when it was remembered that "old man Moyer" had remained loyal to Mexico during the Texas Revolution.

Fennessey led his posse toward the Moya Ranch. The Moyas saw the posse coming and barricaded themselves inside the ranch house, which was built of palings, with chink holes here and there. They refused to come out. One shouted to the posse, "What do you want?"

Dan Holland peered into a chink hole and shouted, "We want you!"

One of the Moyas shot Holland under the left eye, killing him instantly. The posse fired at random through the chink holes, trying to hit moving shadows inside.

Phil Fulcord, the sheriff of Goliad County, arrived and shouted through the door, urging the Moyas to come out. He promised them full protection of the law. They came out. There were two brothers, Antonio and Marcelo, and their aging father, Agustin. The sheriff convinced the Refugio minutemen to let him take the Moyas to Goliad.

After the sheriff left with his prisoners, the minutemen held a hurried conference. They were angry over the killing of Dan Holland and not inclined to wait on the slow workings of the law. John Young described what happened in "A Vaquero of the Brush Country."

"A lot of us did not propose to put off a punishment we knew the Mexicans deserved. The guard and prisoners (Sheriff Fulcord and his deputies) had only gone three miles when we surrounded them. The guard offered practically no interference. In the melee that followed, Marcelo was shot dead. Old Moyer (Moya) was wounded and down on the ground. A maddened ranch boy rode his plunging horse over him, emptying his six-shooter at him. Another man dismounted and cut the Mexican's throat."

The Moyas were left dead in the dust of the road. The action was extreme, even in those violent times, since the Moyas had no known

*Henry Scott, the grizzled old vigilante leader from Refugio, led his company of minutemen on the trail of Juan Flores, the main suspect in the Swift murders on Saus Creek.*

connection to the Swift killings. But no lawyers or judges were riding with the vigilantes to ensure fair play.

Several other Mexican-Americans suspected of complicity in the Swift murders were chained in the Refugio courthouse. One night a lynch mob took three prisoners and hanged them on Saus Creek.

Henry Scott's minutemen trailed Juan Flores, the prime suspect, to Laredo, where he crossed to the river. Scott sent a man across to bargain with Mexican authorities. That story is also told in "A Vaquero of the Brush Country."

"Late one evening, 15 of Scott's men struck camp on the east bank of the Rio Grande. About midnight, we saw a skiff coming over to our side. When it landed, two men with a prisoner between them jumped out. The prisoner was Juan Flores. By the light of a little fire, Captain Scott counted out $500 in gold to the Mexican captors. After we had seen them row back across the river we put Flores on a pack horse and started with him for Refugio."

Juan Flores was tried and convicted. Before he was hanged he admitted his guilt and expressed remorse. "Goodbye, boys," he told the spectators, "don't be bad like I was." Flores was hanged on the outskirts of Refugio, across from the cemetery.

This was a terrible time. As the retaliation following the Swift murders showed, the vigilantes were not particular about whether their victims were guilty or innocent. Refugio Judge W. L. Rea said Scott's minutemen restored order in Refugio County and ranged into Goliad, Bee, San Patricio, and Nueces counties. "They tracked down and liquidated skinners, rustlers, bad men, desperadoes and common criminals." But some were killed, like the Moyas, merely on the suspicion of being "bad."

Besides the Swift murders, this savage era produced the Peñascal massacre at Baffin Bay and the Nuecestown Raid a year later. It produced retaliation killings, like that of the Moyas, and the lynching of "suspects" whose bodies were found hanging on lonely trees throughout South Texas. The bitterness from those lawless days lasted a long time. Blood memories die hard.

*—March 4, 2015*

# Hanging Chipita

It was past high summer, a bad time in the war, after the defeat at Gettysburg and fall of Vicksburg. It was not a festive time. A man who bought horses for the Confederate Army was riding to Mexico with $600 in gold to buy more horses. He was a big man with a beard. His name was John Savage.

On Sunday night, Aug. 23, 1863, Savage stopped at a ramshackle cabin at Aldrete's Crossing, where the San Patricio Road reached the Aransas River. The cabin next to a dense thicket was a place where a traveler could get a meal and sleep on the porch.

The woman who ran the place was named Josefa, but people called her Chipita. She came to Texas as a young girl, arriving with her father Pedro in the 1830s. Her mother died in Mexico and her father was killed fighting on the Texas side in the revolution.

John Savage spent the night at Chipita's. Next morning, a servant from John Welder's ranch was washing clothes in the Aransas River when she found a body wrapped in burlap bags. It was Savage. His head had been split open with an axe.

Sheriff William Means was summoned. At Chipita's cabin, he found blood on the porch. She said it was chicken blood. With prodding, her handyman Juan Silvera, of limited intelligence, said he helped Chipita dump the body in the river. The sheriff did not establish a motive. It was not robbery. Savage's $600 in gold was found in his saddlebags.

Sheriff Means arrested Chipita and Juan Silvera. There was no jail at San Patricio; they were chained to a wall of the courthouse.

The man who would sit in judgment was Benjamin F. Neal, a lawyer and newspaperman. He was elected chief justice of Refugio County in 1840 before he moved to Corpus Christi. He established the Nueces Valley newspaper and in 1852 was elected the first mayor of Corpus Christi.

255

At the start of the war, Neal organized an artillery company that was stationed on Mustang Island. On Feb. 25, 1862, sailors and marines from Union blockading ships raided the settlement on Mustang and St. Joseph's, burning homes and slaughtering cattle.

Neal retreated to Shellbank Island and offered no resistance. The Mustang Islanders accused him of cowardice, which he called a dismal slander. He said he had no infantry to repel the incursion and his battery was short of ammunition. The criticism had to be troubling for a man with unconcealed political ambitions.

But Neal was popular in Corpus Christi. When District Judge John McKinney of Goliad died, Neal defeated three candidates to fill the vacancy. He turned over his artillery company to his second in command, Capt. William Maltby, and began his duties as judge of the 14$^{th}$ District Court. The most important case on the fall docket was the State vs. Juan Silvera and Chipita Rodriguez.

The prosecutor was District Attorney John S. Givens. Pat O'Docharty and William Carroll represented the defendants. The trial was irregular. Sheriff Means served on the grand jury that indicted Chipita. On the trial jury were four members under indictment for felonies, one for murder. The foreman, Owen Gaffney, was a friend of the sheriff. Chipita would not help in her defense.

The trial lasted the morning of Friday, Oct. 9, 1863. The jury quickly brought back a verdict by noon. Juan Silvera was found guilty of second-degree murder. Chipita was found guilty of first-degree murder. The jury urged the court to show mercy for Chipita — "on account of her old age and the circumstantial evidence against her."

Judge Neal sentenced Silvera to five years in prison. He ignored the jury's plea for mercy and sentenced Chipita to be hanged on Nov. 13, 1863.

The Ranchero, Corpus Christi's newspaper, noted that the investigation and trial were conducted under trying conditions and said, "We are decidedly pleased with our neighbors in San Patricio County." The newspaper praised Neal's handling of the trial and said he gave every promise of making an excellent judge.

While Chipita counted her remaining days, Gen. Nathaniel Banks' invasion fleet arrived at Brazos San tiago on Nov. 1, 1863. After capturing Brownsville, Banks' soldiers headed for Fort Semmes, the Confederate garrison on Mustang Island. When Union soldiers

*Benjamin F. Neal, Corpus Christi's first mayor, was judge of the 14th District Court when he ordered Chipita Rodriguez to be hanged on Friday, Nov. 13, 1863.*

approached Fort Semmes, Neal's battery under Capt. Maltby surrendered. That was on Monday, Nov. 16, 1863.

Three days earlier, while the coast was in a panic over the invasion, Chipita's execution day arrived. Judge Neal was gone and Sheriff Means was delivering Juan Silvera to Huntsville. The responsibility to carry out the execution was left to John Gilpin, the hangman.

On the day of the hanging, the weather was cool, with a wind from the north, but it was a dark and gloomy day, whatever the weather. Gilpin, the hangman, borrowed a new wagon at the home of Betty McCumber. Chipita sat on a rough box of undressed planks for the short ride to the river. She was wearing a new dress and her hair had been brushed. The wagon was pulled by oxen and people walked behind.

A mile from town, the wagon stopped at a mesquite by the river. A rope was fixed around her neck and when a lash of the whip moved the oxen forward, Chipita's body was so slight and the oxen so slow that the fall did not snap her neck. She strangled to death. The village was sick at heart over Chipita's cruel death. One elderly man said, "It's a black day for San Patricio."

A later account said people cried and did not feel foolish for their crying. As the hangman hunched over a shovel digging her grave, a young boy, Jack McCowan, would later recall that he heard noises from the coffin, a thump and moan as if she was trying to get out. For years, people said they saw, or thought they saw, Chipita in ghostly form walking the river bottoms, groaning, with a piece of rope around her neck.

Chipita Rodriguez was the only woman legally hanged in Texas. No doubt it was a grievous error that the judge failed to grant her clemency, especially since the evidence was so flimsy and the proceedings so irregular. Many believed she was innocent of the murder of John Savage, but death was everywhere that year of the war and one more hardly seemed to matter.

*—March 11, 2015*

# Summer of Yellow Fever

It was on the first day of July in the summer of 1867. A visitor named Snyder got a room at Ziegler's Hotel. He died two days later. He came from Indianola where yellow fever was in full fury.

Corpus Christi knew about the yellow fever outbreak in Indianola, brought by refugees from Veracruz. They showed the dreaded symptoms — a fever, reddened eyes, headaches, and black vomit caused by internal bleeding. Near the end, faces turned yellow.

They didn't know what caused yellow fever or where it came from. They thought it came from a noxious vapor or evil miasma in the air. They knew it came during the hot months of summer, but had no idea it was spread by mosquitoes.

It was a time of drought, with fearful heat and cloudless skies. Day after day, a scorching sun beat down. On July 26, Helen Chapman wrote in her diary: "Almost everyone in town sick. Mr. Mitchell died at noon . . . all of us weak and miserable . . . Sickness increasing . . . Three deaths today . . . The weather hot and sultry."

Stores were closed and streets were empty as commercial, social and civic activity all but ceased. Smoke rose from tar buckets with smoldering charcoal, but nothing kept the fever away.

Some tried to escape the pestilence by going to the Curry settlement on Padre Island and others went to White Point. San Patricio County posted armed guards at ferry crossings with orders to use deadly force to stop anyone from Corpus Christi.

As deaths increased, lumber stacked on the bluff to build a new Presbyterian church was diverted to make coffins.

Three doctors and druggists in town, G. F. Johnston, Eli Merriman, and George Robertson, worked until they took the fever and died.

Helen Chapman listed the sick and the dead in her diary. "July 25: Mr. Drinkard died in the night. July 29: Several deaths in town;

much distress. July 31: Mr. Eastwood died this morning. Aug. 2: Mr. Mitchell was buried at midnight Thursday. Aug. 4: Mr. Palmer, a native of Canada, died this morning, buried this evening. Aug. 5: three deaths today, a young man at Mr. Scott's, Samuel Clymer, a carpenter who worked for Palmer, and a child on the hill."

Anna Moore Schwien, a former slave, recalled the death of Dr. Johnston's eight-month-old baby. "When I took the baby's clothes to Mrs. Johnston, the baby was sick with the fever. Mrs. Johnston put it in my arms and it died while I held it. She took it from me and laid it on the bed. But I didn't take the fever. Mrs. Johnston also escaped."

On Aug. 14, six weeks after the fever began, William Maltby, editor of the Corpus Christi Advertiser, described the calamity. "There is scarcely a house in the city that has escaped either sickness or death of some of its inmates. Our pen is inadequate to the task of describing the distress that now prevails among us."

The week before, Maltby's young wife, Mary Grace (Swift) died, along with his sister. In the Aug. 14 edition, he listed the names of the victims. The spread of the fever was undaunted and the August heat unabated.

In the common suffering, old animosities were forgotten. When Helen Chapman, a fierce Unionist, came down with the fever she was visited and comforted by William Maltby, a die-hard Confederate.

In late August, a hero of the epidemic was stricken. Father John Gonnard, a Catholic priest from France, had worked night and day with ministering hands. When he caught the fever, two black men in town — Chandler Johnson and Joe Whitlock — cared for him in his sick-bed until he died. He was mourned by the entire city.

Corpus Christi had a new chapter of the Howard Association, named for British philanthropist John Howard. The president of the association, Rev. J. P. Perham, was one of the first victims of the fever. His successor, E. J. Davis, later the governor of Texas, was one of three men who built and paid for a pest house at the corner of Antelope and Carancahua. Victims with no family were taken to the pest house to get well or die. The Howards also hired undertakers and paid to have coffins built.

A fever-stricken sailor who worked for John Anderson was taken to the pest house. Andy Anderson, a boy then, took some clothes to the sick man. When he reached him, the man was lying on the floor.

*William Maltby (above), editor of the Corpus Christi Advertiser, wrote on Aug. 14, 1867 (below) that scarcely a house in Corpus Christi had escaped sickness or death in the yellow fever epidemic that spread to the city from Indianola. Among the victims were Maltby's wife and sister.*

"He yelled, 'You little fool. What are you doing here? Can't you see these people died of yellow fever?'

He referred to seven or eight corpses in the room. 'Well,' I told him, 'We have it at home, so what difference does it make?' "

As with the epidemic in 1854, deliverance came with cold weather. There was a chill in the air at the end of August as a cold front brought relief from the heat wave and the epidemic. No new cases were reported and the death toll dropped as the fever died out. Thanksgiving that year went unobserved in Corpus Christi.

In the epidemic, parents lost children, children lost parents, and in some cases entire families died. Many orphans were adopted by families that lost their own children. Cornelius and Catherine Cahill, who lost two children to the fever, adopted two nieces and a nephew who were left orphaned. J. B. Murphy and wife adopted two girls, unrelated to them, who lost their parents. Martin Kelly and his wife adopted his brother's five children, all under 12, left orphaned by the fever.

Many accounts of the epidemic estimated that 300 of the town's 1,000 inhabitants died. This was an exaggeration. Joseph Almond, a sheep rancher and cabinet-maker, recorded each day's deaths. When it was over, his tally showed 135 people died in the outbreak; a later account reduced it to 127.

After the town's doctors died, E. J. Davis brought Dr. Thomas Kearney to Corpus Christi from Havana. Dr. Kearney sent back for four rose bushes, which he planted in his yard on Chaparral. They were cabbage roses, with pale pink petals, that would long be remembered as the roses that came in 1867, the year of yellow fever.

*—March 18, 2015*

# Replacing the Reef Road

One day in the early 1840s a Comanche war party struck Corpus Christi and Texas Rangers, who were visiting in town, chased the Indians to the Rincon (North Beach). They faced each other in a wary standoff as the sun set.

The Rangers decided to keep the Indians hemmed in against the bay and send for reinforcements. They could attack them in the morning. At first light, the Indians were gone. They had escaped, as the Rangers discovered, by following an oyster-shell reef that led to the other side of Nueces Bay. The Indians knew — perhaps had always known — about the ancient reef passageway. That discovery was to have a long and useful life.

When Zachary Taylor's army was concentrated at Corpus Christi in 1845, soldiers made a cut in the reef to allow boats to travel up the Nueces River to carry supplies to a dragoon camp at San Patricio. This cut later forced horses to swim across the deeper water at high tide.

The first work ordered by the Nueces County Commissioners Court, on Jan. 11, 1847, was to mark the reef, with its twists and turns. The average depth of Nueces Bay was two to three feet, but off the reef was bottomless mud that would bog horses and wagons and the sharp-edged oyster shells would cut up a horse's legs. Toward the middle, the reef made a sharp turn, forcing travelers to go a mile out of the way. Those who tried to take a shortcut across this dogleg would get a good soaking or their teams would get bogged in heavy mud.

Near the end of the century, people from across the bay who came to shop in Corpus Christi had to leave early to cross the reef before dark. Those who overstayed would have to hang over the side of the wagon and look for the post markers in the phosphorescent glow kicked up by horses' hooves.

Wallace Clark, a teacher, recalled that his friend from White Point was late leaving Corpus Christi and lost his way after dark on the reef. "To make matters worse, one of those blue northers struck in the night. The team was a pair of excellent gray horses. Passersby discovered the wagon and team stranded on one of those oyster shell islands the next morning, the man almost frozen and the horses covered with heavily caked mud."

When it was proposed to build a trestle bridge across Nueces Bay for the San Antonio and Aransas Pass Railroad, Capt. Andrew Anderson was hired to make a survey. He found such a depth of mud leading from White Point that the railroad crossing had to be located on the solid footing of the old reef.

After 1886, when the railroad bridge was built, boys would walk across it to go duck-hunting at Gum Hollow. If a train arrived while they were in transit, they would drop down and sit on the wooden crossbeams until the train passed and then climb back on the tracks.

In August 1914, Nueces County let a contract to build an arched concrete causeway across the bay, after voters approved a $165,000 bond issue. The causeway would connect Corpus Christi to fast-growing San Patricio County. Much of the old reef was dredged up for fill material for the new causeway.

On Dec. 10, 1915, the first trip across the causeway took 29 minutes in a seven-passenger Cadillac. The causeway was not open to the public until the paving was completed in late January 1916.

A hurricane on Aug. 18, 1916 damaged the new causeway and railroad trestle. It was a portent of worse to come. While the causeway was being repaired, travelers drove around Nueces Bay and crossed the river at Borden's or Bitterman's Ferry, a 40-mile trip instead of seven miles across the causeway.

After the causeway was repaired, eight-year-old Theodore Fuller and a friend rode a bicycle to Portland. "We asked for a drink (at a house in Portland). I don't think there was any pretense in the astonishment of the lady who gave us a drink. Two little boys had ridden a bicycle from Corpus Christi six miles away."

The 1919 hurricane delivered a greater blow than the 1916 storm. The terrific force of the storm carried away the causeway except for the bascule lift bridge, which was left standing like a lonely sentinel. Some concrete girders were knocked as far away as 200 feet to the west. Afterwards, citizens of San Patricio again had to drive 40 miles around Nueces Bay to reach Corpus Christi.

In 1921, Nueces County built a temporary causeway. This replacement bridge was a timber-pile structure built almost at ter-level; it was not as stylish as the 1915 causeway. A celebration was held in Corpus Christi on Oct. 8, 1921 to observe the opening of the new causeway.

Another hurricane, on Sept. 5, 1933, put the "temporary" causeway out of commission. This same storm also destroyed the Don Patricio Causeway to Padre Island. The deck of the Nueces Bay Causeway was washed away by storm tides, leaving only the pilings and, once again, the bascule bridge segment.

A proposal was considered to operate a shuttle train with flatcars to carry automobiles across the trestle, which was damaged but had survived. That plan was dropped in favor of a ferry service that operated for three months while the causeway was being rebuilt. The ferry made a round trip every hour.

After the causeway was repaired, it carried traffic across Nueces Bay throughout the war years until the first of two concrete structures was built in 1950. Traffic began flowing over the new elevated causeway on Nov. 28, 1950. The second causeway was completed in 1963, providing twin spans across the bay. Traffic across the old SAAP railroad trestle was stopped in 1961. Removal of the pilings was completed in the 1970s.

But long before the modern twin causeways spanned Nueces Bay, from the 1840s until 1915, Corpus Christi had the only underwater road in the world, marked and maintained at county expense. It must have been quite a sight to see buggies and wagons and men on horseback moving across the bay, looking as if the horses and mules were walking on water, as they slowly made their way along the old oyster reef road.

*—March 25, 2015*

*Two men ride bicycles on the rails across Nueces Bay in 1903.*

*An artist's perspective of the 1915 causeway shows the bascule draw span, arched concrete bridge, and shell-fill roadway on the north end.*

*The new Nueces Bay Causeway was opened for traffic in late January 1916. Postcard photo by Karl Swafford.*

*The railroad trestle bridge was twisted out of shape and the Nueces Bay Causeway, less than a year old, was damaged in the 1916 storm. While the causeway was being repaired travelers were forced to make a 40-mile detour around Nueces Bay.*

*An attendant waits for traffic to raise the lift bridge on the "temporary" causeway that replaced the original concrete causeway after it was destroyed in the 1919 storm.*

*The temporary causeway, shown in 1942, was built in 1921 to replace the original concrete structure. It survived until the modern elevated causeway opened in 1950.*

# Norwick Gussett, Wool Merchant

Norwick Gussett, the founder of Gussettville on the Nueces River, became one of Corpus Christi's richest wool merchants in the 19th Century.

Gussett, from North Carolina, was reared in Ohio. By family accounts, he came to Corpus Christi in 1845 with Zachary Taylor's army. Accounts say he was a muleskinner whose job was to haul water from the Nueces River. The soldiers dug an artesian well but the water was brackish and undrinkable, so drinking and cooking water was transported from the river.

Family stories relate that Gussett served in Lt. U. S. Grant's company at Corpus Christi and with Robert E. Lee in Mexico. These stories may be incorrect. Army records show that he enlisted on May 26, 1846 at Hamilton, Ohio, which was two months after Taylor's army left Corpus Christi for the border. The official record says that after he enlisted Gussett was assigned to the First U.S. Infantry, which was not at Corpus Christi. We leave the matter for further advisement.

Gussett fought in the battles of Monterrey and Buena Vista. Afterwards, the First Infantry was transferred to the command of Gen. Winfield Scott. Gussett was wounded at Cerro Gordo and for the rest of his life kept a piece of polished bone that was taken from his hip.

After the war, Gussett was discharged at Ringgold Barracks and returned to Corpus Christi. He married a woman from Detroit named Harriet Elizabeth Jamison and they had a daughter, Clara Matilda. They moved to Oakville where Gussett started a freight line then moved to what was called Fox Nation on the east bank of the Nueces River, a stagecoach stop on the Corpus Christi to San Antonio run. It was called Fox Nation because it was settled by Irish immigrants named Fox. Gussett opened a general store there.

After Fort Merrill was built across the river, the community began to grow and the name was changed to Gussettville. When the Legislature created Live Oak County in 1856, Gussett lobbied to have Gussettville named the county seat but Oakville was chosen. In 1858, Gussett was appointed the first postmaster at Gussettville. He handled the mail in his store. During the Civil War, Gussett enlisted in the Fort Merrill Guards, a militia company, and later served in Capt. John Rabb's company of Confederate militia.

His first daughter, Clara Matilda, died in 1854. Another daughter, Josephine, was born in 1860. Gussett's wife Harriet died at Gussettville in 1863.

After the war, Gussett moved to Corpus Christi and married Margaret Evans. He opened a store on Chaparral, became a buyer of wool and hides, and established his own bank. There were two banks in town, Gussett's and Perry Doddridge's.

Gussett's first store in Corpus Christi was on Chaparral, his second was at the corner Chaparral and Peoples, and his third was at Chaparral and Schatzell. Mexican traders called Gussett's place "tienda del gallo," the rooster store because of the rooster weather vane on the roof.

Besides engaging in the Mexican trade, Gussett operated his own fleet of schooners (named for his daughters) to take wool and hides to New York and bring back merchandise. In one year, 1873, he purchased more than three million pounds of wool. Though he never achieved a rank higher than sergeant in the army, out of respect he was known as Colonel Gussett.

In the 1870s, when the Morris & Cummings Cut was dredged across the bay, the City Council agreed to establish a monopoly at the Central Wharf. The monopolists would pay the city $1,000 a month for control of Central Wharf for 30 years. The deal was made and wharf fees were raised. Gussett built his own wharf off North Beach, outside city limits, and this put a quick end to the Central Wharf monopoly.

Besides Josephine, who was born in 1860 to Gussett and his first wife Harriet, Gussett and his second wife Margaret had five children. They included daughters Susie, Leona, and Elise; sons Norwick Jr. and Horatio de Columbus, known as H. D. C. Norwick Jr. died from a brown recluse spider bite. H. D. C. joined his father's business. The four daughters married George Reynolds, W.H. Brooks, Royal Givens, and C. J. McManus.

*Norwick Gussett's first store on Chaparral (far left) sported a rooster as an identifying symbol for ox-cart drivers. His place was called the rooster store, "tienda del gallo." Gussett, the founder of Gussettville, later became one of Corpus Christi's richest wool merchants.*

Norwick Gussett died on Sept. 28, 1908. The Caller obituary said, "Colonel Gussett's demise, like the passing of all good and great men, is viewed with regret by a sorrowing community."

\* \* \*

## WRECKMASTER

Capt. Peter Benson in 1867 was appointed wreckmaster for Nueces County. He succeeded Robert Mercer on Mustang Island. Benson was from Ireland and liked to tell about the time he saw Daniel O'Connor. Benson's family lived on Padre Island in the 19th Century but kept a house in Corpus Christi for school purposes.

Before a channel was dredged through the Aransas pass at Port Aransas, frequent shipwrecks were caused when ships got caught in a storm or when captains tried to cross the bar without the services of a bar pilot so they could pocket the fee themselves.

Because the depth of water varied from five to 10 feet, depending on wind and tide, crossing the bar could be a dangerous undertaking and the pass was constantly changing, shifting, silting and moving to the south.

It was the wreckmaster's job to safeguard goods washed up on shore or salvaged from a stricken vessel. He would get five percent of the value of the cargo. The wreckmaster appointed deputies called "wreckers" to search the shoreline with long poles to probe the sand, looking for buried cargo. Some island residents would bury goods that washed ashore in the hopes of reclaiming the merchandise later. Among the major shipwrecks of the Benson era was the Reindeer, which went down in 1870, the Fountainbleu, a lumber schooner that foundered in 1873, and the steamer Mary, which sank in 1876.

The Mercer logs, kept by a family of bar pilots on Mustang Island, noted on Nov. 24, 1873: "Schooner Fountainbleu arrived from Sabine, crossed the bar, and tried to make a tack in the pass. She lost ground. Dropped one anchor. It did not hold her. She let go the other but it was too late." The ship filled with water, lost its cargo of shingles, and broke apart, with pieces of the vessel washing ashore.

Peter Benson, the old wreckmaster, died when he was 94.

*—April 1, 2015*

# The Greatest Ranger

John Coffee Hays, the greatest of all Texas Ranger captains, stood 5-8 and weighed 150 pounds, looking too small and frail to fight. But he became the ideal of what a Ranger captain should hope to be.

Jack Hays was born near Nashville, Tenn., on Jan. 28, 1817. When his parents died, he lived with an uncle, Robert Cage, in Yazoo, Miss. The uncle wanted him to clerk in a store but Hays, who longed to be a soldier, left home for Texas. At Nacogdoches, a bar bully tried to pick a fight with the slender 19-year-old. Hays shot him dead.

He arrived in South Texas after the battle of San Jacinto and joined the Texas Army. He was a member of the fatigue party sent to dig graves for the remains of 400 of Fannin's men killed at Goliad. After Hays joined a Ranger company, he was promoted to sergeant and led patrols in search of bandits, horse thieves and hostile Indians. In 1838 and 1839, he worked as a surveyor.

In 1840, the 23-year-old Hays was appointed captain of a Ranger company headquartered in San Antonio. John Wilbarger wrote — "With this small company, for it never numbered more than three score men, Jack Hays protected a vast scope of frontier, reaching from Corpus Christi on the Gulf to the headwaters of the Frio and Nueces Rivers."

As a Ranger captain Hays showed remarkable qualities. He never got rattled. Even in the confusion of a battle, he was cool, calm and impervious to alarm. His first rule of fighting was never to back down and his second was to never show fear. He seemed to know how a battle would turn out and that certainty inspired his men. T.R. Fehrenbach said Hays became a leader because he was the best thinker under stress, the deadliest man around.

In 1841, Hays with 40 Rangers rode up the Medina River on the trail of a Comanche raiding party after women and horses. The

Comanches had seen the Rangers first and lay in ambush, hiding among the steep rocks of Bandera Pass. At 11 in the morning, when Hays led his Rangers into the pass, they were fired at from both sides. The Rangers were close to panic, with dead and dying men and plunging and frightened horses. Hays yelled, "Steady, boys! Get down and tie those horses." In hand-to-hand fighting, five Texans were killed and six were wounded, heavy casualties for the Rangers. It was one of Hays' toughest fights.

In June 1841 Hays took 30 Rangers up the Sabinal River toward an Indian camp in Uvalde Canyon. When Hays led an attack on the camp, the Comanches took cover in a dogwood thicket. Hays took a Ranger with him to drive out the Indians. The men heard shots; Hays came out carrying the wounded Ranger. He went back into the thicket and after several shots Hays' men found their captain with eight dead Comanches.

What may be true or may be legend, embroidered over time, was a fight in 1841 at the Enchanted Rock, a prominent landmark that overlooks the Llano Valley, near today's Fredericksburg. Hays was out scouting alone, away from the Ranger camp, when Comanches came up behind him. He raced to the Enchanted Rock, slapped his horse on the rump, and scrambled to the top. As Comanche warriors ran up after him, Hays took pot-shots at them, picking them off from his crater at the top. When Hays' rider-less horse arrived at the camp, the Rangers rode to his rescue. The Indians took off, leaving 15 warriors dead on the Enchanted Rock, all killed by Hays. This was war and they were the enemy.

The following year, Hays was instrumental in defeating and turning back Mexican Gen. Adrian Woll after he captured San Antonio in September 1842. This incursion was known as the Woll Raid. While Hays was not in charge — Gen. Matthew "Old Paint" Caldwell was in command — it was Hays who drew Woll's forces out of San Antonio to Salado Creek, a place Hays chose for the battle. Woll took a beating and retreated back to Mexico.

In 1844, Hays obtained a supply of Colt "five-shooter" revolvers from the Texas Navy, which was being dismantled. They came in handy in a fight on the Pinta Trail, midway between San Antonio, Austin and Gonzales. It was one of the hardest fights Hays had since the ambush at Bandera Pass. Hays and 14 Rangers were scouting on the Pedernales. They were camped on the Pinta Trail, an old Indian route, when they observed Indians following them. When the

*The fearless Jack Hays led Texas Rangers in the last years of the Republic and Texas volunteers in the Mexican War. He died in California.*

Rangers advanced, the Indians feigned alarm and made for the cover of a wood at the top of a hill.

Hays made no move to chase them. He could see a larger force partly concealed on the ridge. The Indians made for the top of the hill and waited for the Rangers to attack. Hays led the Rangers into a ravine, which was concealed from the Indians' view, and they rode around the base of the hill and came up behind the Indians, taking them by surprise. The Rangers used their new Colt five-shooters in the fight.

Hays said in his report, "Whenever pressed severely, the Indians were making the most desperate charges. Had it not been for the five-shooting pistols, I doubt what the consequences would have been."

When war loomed with Mexico, Hays raised a regiment of Rangers, which trained at Corpus Christi with U.S. troops in 1845 and early 1846. Many of Hays' Rangers enlisted. During the war, an Army officer pointed to "a little fellow" at the head of the First Regiment, Texas Volunteers, and asked who he was. He was surprised when someone said it was Jack Hays, the famous Ranger captain.

If the war had lasted longer, Rip Ford wrote, Hays would have been in line to be promoted from colonel to brigadier general for his actions at Monterrey and Mexico City, quite an accomplishment for the boy who left home to become a soldier.

Hays married Susan Calvert of Seguin in 1847 and they left for California in the gold rush of 1849. He became the first elected sheriff of San Francisco and helped found the town of Oakland. Jack Hays died on April 21 (San Jacinto Day) in 1883. He was the greatest of all Ranger captains, whose fighting reputation was never equaled in the long history of the Texas Rangers.

*—April 8, 2015*

# E. H. Caldwell

Edward Harvey Caldwell was 21 when he came to Corpus Christi from Tennessee to join his father, who was pastor of the First Presbyterian Church, and Caldwell's eight brothers and sister. He arrived on the mail boat from Indianola on Sunday morning, March 24, 1872. The preacher's son promptly went to church where he played the organ and taught Sunday school. We know much about his life from memoirs he wrote in his later years.

Caldwell studied law in the McCampbell law office but the law didn't suit him and he got a job as a bookkeeper for wool merchant and banker Perry Doddridge.

In his memoirs, Caldwell said that as a freight collector for Morgan Line ships it was a heavy chore to carry the silver coins which served as currency. "I would tire from lugging them around to the point that $1,000 in silver seemed to weigh a ton (actually, it weighs 65 pounds) . . . Silver was drayed around city streets by the wagon-load. Such shipments came from the mint in New Orleans and were packed in kegs like any other merchandise."

Caldwell described the social life in the 1870s. "Our group enjoyed moonlight drives in one-horse buggies rented for $2.50 per trip. We always had a chaperon to lead our party in her own buggy. We would leave town and go about seven miles out, then return to arrive within the time limit set by the rental agency, 11 p.m. To stay out beyond this time limit, well, it just wasn't done."

"Dancing was also popular," he wrote. "Market Hall was the site most frequented for this activity. Many balls were put on at the hall. It was also the site of high society weddings, since private residences were not large enough to accommodate all the guests."

One day a yellow dog spooked his horse and Caldwell took out his pistol and shot the dog dead. A district court judge fined him $50 for carrying a concealed weapon. "I thanked the jury and added the

277

observation that I had no doubt that more than half of them at that very moment were carrying concealed weapons."

As a bank clerk, Caldwell saw how much money sheepmen were making. In 1875, he and a younger brother, Willie, a clerk in Mitchell's hardware store, invested in a sheep venture. They leased the Borjas Ranch west of San Diego and bought 1,200 sheep.

On Caldwell's first night at the ranch, he and his herder were in camp. By firelight, they saw three men ride up on horseback. One man, apparently the leader, asked to be shown where to water their horses. Caldwell refused and instead told them where to find water. He believed they were bandits because he recognized the horse the leader was riding. He had seen the horse at George Reynolds' ranch near Orange Grove.

After the men left to water their horses, the leader returned and Caldwell kept his rifle pointed at his heart. The man again demanded that Caldwell lead the way to water, but Caldwell could hear their horses splashing in the water tank.

"I told him they knew very well where the water was," Caldwell said. "He insisted I show him. I said I wouldn't. He asked why. I replied, in Spanish, 'porque' (because)." Caldwell kept his gun pointed at the man's heart until they finally departed.

As he had suspected, Caldwell discovered next day that the men were bandits, members of the same bunch that raided Nuecestown and burned Noakes' store. This was the famous Noakes Raid.

On Easter Sunday, March 28, 1875, a posse led by Sidney Borden, from Sharpsburg, arrived with lathered horses. They were chasing the bandits. The posse captured and hanged two luckless men from Laredo, who had no connection to the raid.

Caldwell's ranch house, built of caliche rock with loopholes for defense, became headquarters of other sheepmen in the area.

Caldwell wrote that they spent a lot of time in target shooting, showing off their skill. One day while riding with Don Vicente Vera, a neighbor, Caldwell saw a deer venture out of the brush 500 yards away. He fired his carbine and the deer dropped. An affidavit like that, Caldwell wrote, was useful in a place where constant vigilance was needed to stay alive. "This was not frivolous bragging, but cheap insurance."

At the ranch house, the men took turns cooking. A house rule was that if anyone complained about the food he would get kitchen duty for a week. One morning a man said, "This oatmeal is too damn

*Edward Harvey Caldwell owned a sheep ranch in Duval County and hardware store in Corpus Christi.*

*Wagons hauling casing for artesian wells on King Ranch in front of Caldwell's Hardware on Chaparral in 1901.*

salty" before he remembered the rule and quickly added, "just the way I like it."

Caldwell was elected to the county commission of the newly formed Duval County. The Borjas Ranch became a mail stop and Caldwell was named postmaster, with a salary of $12 a year.

In 1880, he married Ada Lasater, the sister of Ed Lasater, later the famous rancher at Falfurrias. Caldwell met her during a game of croquet at her parents' ranch near Campbellton in Atascosa County. She was home from school in Ohio and Caldwell thought she was from the North — "where the wind didn't spoil their fresh complexions."

Caldwell decided to get out of the sheep business. A parasite was killing the sheep flocks and the price of wool plummeted after the tariff on Australian wool was lifted. Since there was no market for sheep in South Texas, Caldwell and two men drove 5,000 sheep to San Angelo and then on to Abilene where he sold them at a heavy loss.

In 1884, Caldwell returned to Corpus Christi, invested in the Mitchell hardware company, and built a home at 715 S. Broadway. In 1895 he started his own hardware firm, the Caldwell Farm and Ranch store.

Caldwell's hardware store was a prosperous concern until it was wrecked in the storm of 1919. On the morning after the storm, the store was in ruins. Caldwell kept the business going long enough to pay off his creditors.

Caldwell, during his 40 years as a merchant in Corpus Christi, was a leader in the effort to gain a deepwater port and he was one of the founders of the Commercial Club, the forerunner of the Chamber of Commerce. Edward Harvey Caldwell, sheep rancher, hardware merchant, civic leader, longtime elder of the First Presbyterian Church, died at his home on South Broadway on March 14, 1940. He was 89.

*—April 15, 2015*

# Seaside Hotel

A hundred years ago, to use a nice round number, if you stood at the end of Taylor Street with your back to the bluff, you would have been in front of one of the finest resort hotels on the Gulf of Mexico, the Seaside Hotel. The Seaside was famous for its view of sails and fishing boats and its arbor of wind-shaped salt cedars by the bay.

The Seaside in 1915 included the original building, the Seaside Pavilion, built on a pier in the bay, the Seaside annex and several cottages. The original structure was the Dix house, built about 1850 by John Dix.

Dix was a seafaring man. As a boy, he served on a privateer in the War of 1812, journeyed to the South Pacific, and once was shipwrecked on the rugged coast of New Zealand. He came to Texas in 1834, fought in the Texas Revolution, and settled in Washington County.

Dix moved to Corpus Christi in 1849 and built a large shellcrete home at the bay end of Taylor Street. He planted a grove of salt cedars by the water's edge and settled down to an old mariner's coveted view of ship traffic on the bay.

In the Civil War, Dix was an outspoken supporter of the Union, though John J., his oldest son, was a Confederate officer. Mary Sutherland in "The Story of Corpus Christi" related that the elder Dix, though she didn't name him, was signaling Union ships in the bay from an upper window of his home. Local Confederates threatened to hang him.

Another Dix story took place during the bombardment of the city by federal warships in 1862. Mrs. Frank DeGarmo in "Pathfinders of Texas" wrote: "At the Dix home, the entry of these troops was viewed with fear and trembling by the wife of Captain Dix (the son) while his parents were elated, so much so that his father seized his

281

Union flag and started for the roof, but he was met at the foot of the stairs by his daughter-in-law carrying a shotgun. She said, 'My husband, your son, left me here with you to protect and take care of, not to insult. While I am here if you attempt to raise that flag over this house, I will shoot you off the roof.' The flag was not raised."

When the war ended, Dix was appointed chief justice (called county judge today) of the reorganized Nueces County government.

A school for former slave girls was operated in the house by Dix's wife. The Dix home was operated as a boarding house, usually called the Dix House or Dix Hotel. In 1866, Eliza Ann Sullivan, who ran a well-known boarding house in San Patricio, moved to Corpus Christi to keep the Dix House.

Dix was serving as chief justice of Nueces County when he died in 1870. Soon afterwards, John J. sold the old homestead to William DeRyee.

While the historical record is filled with gaps on this subject, I believe the old Dix House was converted into the Seaside Hotel just after the turn of the 20th Century. An ad in the Caller in June 1904 said the Seaside "is the only hotel on the beach." It was run by A.R.A. Brice, formerly the manager of Eddie Green's Tarpon Club on St. Joseph's.

In 1905, Brice sold the Seaside and bought the Bayview Hotel in Rockport. W. A. Fitch bought the Seaside, giving him three hotels in Corpus Christi, including the old St. James and the New Constantine. Fitch had the Seaside remodeled and refurnished.

It's not clear when Jack Ennis bought the hotel (another gap) but it was after 1906 and before 1908. Ennis gained wealth as a pioneer in the development of early oil fields in East Texas.

Ennis expanded the Seaside's footprint. He added the annex at the water's edge and the Seaside Pavilion on a pier in the bay. He hired J. H. Hopkins as manager, soon followed by George S. Beard. The Pavilion included guest rooms on the third floor, a dance hall on the second, and bathing facilities on the first floor. The Seaside Electric Theater was built on the south side of Taylor Street.

A story was told of Ennis. One day, he was sweeping the concrete floor under the salt cedars when a woman guest, mistaking him for the janitor, asked how much he earned. He took out his pipe and said, "Oh, just enough to keep me in tobacco." She gave him two dollars and told him to buy something for himself. When she checked out, she was told that her bill had been taken care of by the

*A postcard from Jan. 19, 1907 (top) shows the Seaside Hotel, at the bottom of Taylor Street, facing south, with its arbor of salt cedars next to the bay.*

*The popular Seaside Pavilion was built on a pier in 1908.*

owner. Ennis told her, "No woman as kind-hearted as you will have to pay a cent at my hotel."

Among the more famous guests of the Seaside were William Jennings Bryan and wife. They stayed there two weeks after Bryan

*The Seaside dining room is also shown from 1907.*

lost the 1908 presidential election to William Howard Taft. Bryan came to Corpus Christi to attend the Inland Waterway Convention on Nov. 17, 1908. Land promoter George H. Paul, who brought thousands of homeseekers to South Texas, always stayed at the Seaside.

The Seaside was famous for its cuisine. It was noted for its Stuffed Redhead Duck with French Dressing, Broiled Oysters a la Maitre d'Hotel, Green Turtle Aux Quenelles, Chicken a la Creole, and Green Apple Pie with Swiss Cheese. These were a few choice items on the 1908 menu. An ad said, "The sea breezes never fail to create that hungry feeling that is handled so thoroughly and so well at the Seaside table."

When Jack Ennis died in 1909 or 1910 (newspaper archives are missing for that period), he left the Seaside to Nancy Ferguson, daughter of Cy Ferguson, a close friend. While she owned the hotel, it was managed by B. Otis Johnson and his wife Mollie.

The Pavilion lost its pier in the 1916 hurricane and, three years later, like so much else on the waterfront, the Seaside Hotel and Pavilion were destroyed in the terrible 1919 storm. Before that, for two decades, the Seaside Hotel was at the heart of Corpus Christi, known for its fine cuisine, its home-like atmosphere, and its salt-cedar arbor sculpted by that ever-present breeze coming off the bay.

*—April 22, 2015*

# Laguna Madre Murders

A bizarre crime occurred on April 12, 1965 when three fishermen were killed on the Laguna Madre. The trail of circumstances began in California with Paul Eric Krueger, 17, and John Phillip Angles, 16, sons of well-off parents in California. They met at school and agreed to run away and join a rebel movement in Venezuela. They stole a car, guns, money and headed for Mexico, then decided to hijack a boat at Corpus Christi.

Krueger had an AR-15 rifle and an M-1 carbine. At the JFK Causeway, they rented a small boat and traveled down the Laguna Madre. They drank a bottle of wine they found at a fishing shack.

Traveling down the Laguna Madre in their boat, Krueger and Angles saw three men fishing from a pier. Krueger said, "I'm going to kill those people." He opened fire on the men. They were hit and toppled over into the Laguna Madre. Krueger continued shooting until his rifle was empty, then took the M-1 and emptied that into the lifeless bodies. The boys returned to their car and drove to San Antonio, where they split up.

The bodies of the three fishermen were found by the pier. They were all from Corpus Christi, identified as Noel Little, Van Dave Carson, and John David Fox. All were married with children. The bodies were so riddled an autopsy couldn't tell how many times they had been shot.

Angles was picked up in Kerrville and Krueger was picked up in Mexico, somewhere between Juarez and Chihuahua. Angles, a juvenile at 16, was not brought to trial; he was cleared of taking any active role in the shootings. He was released from the State School for Boys at Gatesville in 1968.

Krueger was tried in Dallas on a change of venue. He entered a guilty plea and was sentenced to life in prison. The widows of the slain fishermen were in court for the sentencing. They were stay-at-

*Paul Eric Krueger (center) and his parents leave the courthouse in Dallas in May 1966. He pleaded guilty to killing three fishermen on the Laguna Madre and was sentenced to life.*

home housewives, each with three children, who had to take jobs to support their families after their husbands were killed.

Krueger was released after serving 12 years. He earned three degrees in prison and was hired as a professor at Penn State University until his past was revealed in a TV documentary in 2004.

It was the most violent and mindless of crimes — two runaway boys with high-powered weapons and vague ideas of joining some revolutionary movement in Venezuela. It was one of the worst crimes in South Texas history, a crime as random as they come, without motive or reason except deep in the psyche of the killer.

*A White Point gas well blowout in November 1914 resisted all efforts to bring it under control. Hope of capping the well ended when the gas ignited and the well caught fire.*

## WHITE POINT GASSERS

The oil and gas era in the Corpus Christi area began with a bang. A test well in the White Point area on the Rachal Ranch across Nueces Bay blew out on Sept. 6, 1913.

Bill and Marjorie Walraven in their book "Wooden Rigs — Iron Men" quoted Chris Rachal, who had seen the blowouts when he was growing on the Rachal Ranch. "The White Point Oil and Gas

Company rig was coming out of the hole when she went," Rachal said. "There was no drilling mud in those days to control pressure. The drill pipe came straight up through the derrick. It went several hundred feet into the air. The rig, except for the boilers, was lost. It burned until it cratered over. Mud and water mixed together to choke off the gas flow."

The drillers knew that where there was gas there was oil. They kept drilling. There was another White Point blowout in 1914. Hope of capping the well ended when it caught fire and exploded, leaving a hole 50 feet deep and 150 feet across. The J. M. Guffey Petroleum Company (later Gulf Oil) drilled several test wells around White Point and they all blew out.

In 1916, what was considered the biggest strike of gas in the world was made at White Point. This was the Guffey No. 1. The San Antonio Light said the roar of the escaping gas "can be heard easily for seven miles . . . A stick of mesquite cordwood thrown into the stream went at least 500 feet high." When the escaping gas ignited, the monster well caught fire. "It shook windows in Sinton 14 miles away," said Chris Rachal, "and lit up the skies in Sinton and Corpus Christi." The well finally burned itself out, leaving a huge black scar.

Another gas well was struck in 1923 four miles west of town in the Saxet area. They found oil on Aug. 16, 1930 in the Saxet field. A banner headline in the Caller proclaimed — "John Dunn No. 6 Near City Comes In As Oil Well." It produced only 1,440 barrels of oil, but it was the forerunner of wells in Nueces and San Patricio Counties that produced millions of barrels of oil. For Corpus Christi, the discovery of oil in the 1930s eased the plight of the Great Depression.

*—April 29, 2015*

# First Newspapers

The first newspaper in Corpus Christi was the Gazette established in 1846. It was followed by the Star in 1848, the Nueces Valley in 1851 and the Ranchero in 1859. The Advertiser made its appearance after the Civil War and the Caller was born on Jan. 21, 1883, a Saturday night so cold the ink froze solid.

The Gazette was a consequence of the coming war with Mexico. When Zachary Taylor moved his command to Corpus Christi in 1845, Samuel Bangs, originally from Boston, publisher of the Galveston Daily Globe, came to Corpus Christi to review the situation.

Bangs formed a partnership with Corpus Christi physician George Fletcher and hired an influential member of the Hispanic community, Jose de Alba, to edit the paper. Bangs left his Galveston newspaper in the hands of Benjamin F. Neal.

Bangs set up a printing office near Taylor's camp. He was one of the outstanding early printers in Texas and the first of many notable publishers and editors who printed the news in Corpus Christi.

The first edition of the Corpus Christi Gazette was published on Jan. 1, 1846. It was a biweekly, with four pages, and included a section printed in Spanish. The paper featured new type and woodcuts and cost 10 cents a copy.

That first issue listed the units and officers in Taylor's army. It was filled with advertising. The slogan of the Gazette was adopted from a Davy Crockett quote, "Be Sure You Are Right Then Go Ahead." The New Orleans Times-Picayune announced its arrival: "A new and spirited paper just started by Bangs and Fletcher."

In early March 1846, Taylor prepared to move his command to the Rio Grande. The general's marching orders were published in the Gazette. On March 8, 1846, the Second Dragoons marched out of Corpus Christi. The Third Infantry was the last to leave. As the soldiers marched away, drummers beat out the army's farewell tune, "The Girl I Left Behind Me."

Thousands of white tents were gone, along with 4,000 soldiers and nearly 2,000 of the town's transient inhabitants. Before Bangs left for the border, he sold the Gazette to Jose de Alba. But with the army gone and Corpus Christi reduced to a virtual ghost town, there was no market for the paper and the Gazette ceased to publish.

After the war, John Peoples, a well-known war correspondent, moved to Corpus Christi to found the Corpus Christi Star. The first edition was published on Sept. 5, 1848. The Star followed the example of the Gazette and included a section in Spanish, called La Estrella.

It must have been dull for Peoples. Instead of describing battles, he wrote of the town's shortage of soap, which he reported was caused by a New Orleans merchant who, instead of filling an order for 120 boxes of soap, only sent 12. Peoples visited the army's old camping grounds. "The gutters can still be seen where the tents were struck, and if the government established a military depot here, we would like to see this pretty spot selected."

The Star was filled with reports of the California gold discovery. Henry Kinney, the town's founder, ran ads in eastern newspapers claiming that the best route to the gold fields started at Corpus Christi. The route promoted by Kinney was by ship or packet boat to Corpus Christi, then overland across Chihuahua and Sonora to southern California then a march up country to the goldfields.

Gold seekers began arriving in January 1849, brought by fast-sailing packet boats plying between Galveston and Corpus Christi. The town filled with emigrants going west. In the Star, Peoples advised them to learn Spanish "or they will be puzzled when they get into Mexican country, where even the mules understand no other language."

Peoples came down with the gold fever himself and in February 1849 he joined a group of organized gold-rushers heading west. He wrote letters to the Star describing the misadventures on the way. Peoples didn't make it to the goldfields; he drowned crossing the Gulf of California.

Charles Callahan, another Mexican War correspondent, took over the Star when Peoples left. He also took off for California later in the summer of 1849 and James Barnard, still another war correspondent and tramp journalist, bought the Star.

When the word spread that the route across Chihuahua and Sonora was difficult and dangerous, the gold-seekers fell back on more established routes and the Star soon ceased to publish.

Another early editor in Corpus Christi was Benjamin F. Neal, who took over Bangs' Galveston paper when Bangs started the Gazette. Neal moved to Corpus Christi to practice law and in 1851 he established the Nueces Valley, the town's third newspaper.

Big news in the Nueces Valley was Henry Kinney's Lone Star Fair. Kinney spent lavishly to promote the fair and hoped to draw thousands of visitors. His main purpose was to attract settlers who would buy some of his 300,000 acres.

In early 1852, Neal's paper reported that Kinney was untiring in efforts to make the fair a success. He sent Legs Lewis to New Orleans to buy silver cups and chalices to award as prizes. The fair opened in the first week of May 1852. There were bullfights, cockfights, exhibitions of local products and livestock, and a circus. But fewer than 2,000 people came and Kinney lost $50,000 on the fair.

When Neal was elected mayor of Corpus Christi in 1852, he sold his interest in the Nueces Valley to Legs Lewis and others, but he resumed control of the paper in 1856 when Corpus Christi fell on hard times.

The town began to languish when the Eight Military District moved its headquarters from Corpus Christi to San Antonio in 1856. Warehouses, saddler's shops, wheelwright and blacksmith shops were closed and once busy stores became idle.

In lean times, the Nueces Valley passed from Neal to James Barnard. He published the Nueces Valley for about year before departing for Brownsville, where he founded the Brownsville Flag. The Democratic South, published by Clinton Bryant, appeared briefly in Corpus Christi but soon folded, leaving the city without a newspaper until the fiercely partisan Ranchero filled the vacuum in 1859.

*—May 6, 2015*

# Maltby's Ranchero

Corpus Christi for a time in the late 1850s was without a newspaper after the Nueces Valley folded in 1857 and the short-lived Democratic South shut down in 1858.

Into this vacuum came a man of extreme views, Henry Maltby, who practiced a style of personal and partisan journalism with a vengeance. Maltby was never neutral and never colorless.

Maltby came from Mansfield, Ohio. He brought a circus to Corpus Christi to perform at Henry Kinney's fair in 1852. He returned to Corpus Christi in 1855, was elected mayor, and traveled to Nicaragua where Kinney was embarked in a futile effort to establish an empire on the Mosquito Coast.

Maltby came back to Corpus Christi to found the Ranchero. The first edition was printed on Oct. 22, 1859. It was violently partisan like Maltby himself. Despite his Ohio origins, Maltby was fiercely pro-Democratic and anti-Republican. The Southern cause was oxygen to him.

Maltby, with his dark eyes and immense black beard, was called the most handsome man in Texas. He was joined by his younger brother William. Eli Merriman, the later Caller editor, described the brothers as "expert printers and newspaper men of the highest class — ready writers, brilliant and well-informed; Democrats always." Norman Delaney, former history professor at Del Mar, wrote a book about the Maltby brothers published by Texas A&M Press several years ago in 2013.

William liked verse. In 1861, as the South moved toward secession, he wrote a piece of poetic fancy — "What will teach northern fanatics a lesson? Secession. What will make a man frisky? Whisky. What will build the graveyard fence? Pence. What is sweeter to us than honey? Money. What is needed by the Ranchero? Dinero."

In the first year of the war they felt the bite of the blockade. Publication of the Ranchero became unpredictable as newsprint was hard to get. Henry wrote in a "War Extra" — "This is the first time we have missed an issue. We trust the Devil will lay malevolent hands on Old Abe and anchor him in the middle of the lake of fire and brimstone." The Ranchero printed a second "War Extra" on Aug. 19, 1862, reporting the bombardment of Corpus Christi by Union warships.

William joined a volunteer artillery company and was captured when Mustang Island fell to Union forces. His older brother Jasper, a Union general, made life easy for him as a POW in Vicksburg. Meanwhile, Henry moved the Ranchero to Santa Margarita on the Nueces River then to Brownsville and later Matamoros.

After the war, William returned to Corpus Christi and started his own newspaper, the Advertiser. His columns were signed "Bro. Bill." Like the Ranchero, the Advertiser was anti-Republican and diehard Confederate. This was a bad time, following a crippling war and in the poisoned atmosphere of Reconstruction.

In the summer of 1867, the Advertiser listed the victims claimed in a yellow fever outbreak, which included Maltby's wife, Grace Swift Maltby.

E. J. Davis, who would be elected governor, formed a company and began printing a pro-Republican paper, the Union Record, which survived only a few weeks before it was destroyed by fire.

In 1870, Benjamin F. Neal, the lawyer and former judge, revived his old journal, the Nueces Valley. He published the paper from his home on Artesian Square. Eli Merriman began his career working for Neal.

Neal soon sold the Nueces Valley to Republican backers who were allied with the E. J. Davis administration. The paper was edited for a time by Nelson Plato, who printed his seriocomic rules for visitors of the newspaper — "1. Enter softly. 2. Sit down quietly. 3. Subscribe to the paper. 4. Pay for it in advance. 5. Don't touch the type. 6. Keep six feet from the devil. 7. Don't talk to the compositor. 8. Hands off the manuscript. Gentlemen observing these rules will greatly oblige the editor and not fear the devil."

William Maltby, the constant nemesis of the Nueces Valley, decided to back off from the fight and lay down his pen. In a grumbling farewell message on Jan. 4, 1873 he wrote: "This week we sever our connection with that dear old Advertiser, having

*Henry Maltby, a native of Ohio, founded the Ranchero newspaper in Corpus Christi in 1859. Plausibly or not, he was called the handsomest man in Texas. Maltby printed a "War Extra" on July 20, 1861. His paper was passionately pro-Confederate.*

disposed of the office, with all its good and bad will. Worn out by toil, trouble, affliction, anxiety, we seek respite."

James Barnard, who worked for newspapers all over the country, had published the Corpus Christi Star for a brief time in 1849. He returned to Corpus Christi and he and his brother Frank began the Corpus Christi Gazette, the second paper by that name.

The office of the Gazette was on William Street. The first edition appeared on Jan. 4, 1873. When Maltby retired, the Barnards purchased the Corpus Christi Advertiser and merged it with the Gazette. The Gazette's rival was the Nueces Valley, but when Republican fortunes began to wane and Gov. Davis lost his bid for re-election, the Nueces Valley ceased to publish.

It was bought by Horace Taylor, a former postmaster, who changed the name to the Valley Times. He also and changed the political alignment from pro-Republican to "independent always — neutral never." When Taylor died in 1875, the Valley Times was continued for another three years by Charles Beman.

When D. McNeill Turner was editing the Gazette, owned by James and Frank Barnard, he kept a six-gun on his desk and a shotgun within reach. A buzzer connected to James Barnard's desk warned him of the approach of any irate reader. In 1877, Turner bought the Gazette from the Barnards. He suspended publication in 1879.

In 1876, Eli Merriman was laid off from his job as a printer at the Gazette. He went to see William Maltby, who opened a job-printing operation on Water Street after he sold the Advertiser.

Merriman and Maltby agreed to start a new paper. Maltby put up his printing shop as his share of the investment and Merriman added $700. Maltby took passage on the ship Leona for New York, where he purchased a new Washington hand press.

The first edition of Maltby's and Merriman's Free Press was printed on Feb. 21, 1877. When Maltby died in 1880, Merriman continued to publish the paper until the Corpus Christi Caller was established three years later.

*—May 13, 2015*

# Born On Cold Night

The Corpus Christi Caller was launched in 1883 by W. P. Caruthers, Ed Williams and Eli Merriman. It was chartered with capital stock of $10,000 with shares valued at $100 each.

Major stockholders were cattle barons Richard King and Mifflin Kenedy, with 10 shares each, while Caruthers had seven shares, Ed Williams five and Merriman three. Other stockholders were Morris Lichtenstein, T. P. Rivera, and John Welder.

The Caller Publishing Company paid Merriman $2,500 for his Free Press, which had 703 subscribers, and it paid $2,500 for the Ledger, with a circulation of 345, founded in 1879 by James Barnard and Ed Williams. This cleared the field for the Caller of two rival publications that were popular in the city.

The reason the name "Caller" was chosen, Merriman wrote, was that as newsboys called out the paper for sale the hearer would think of the paper as being a 'caller' of news. He compared it to earlier times when a town crier would 'cry out' the news. Merriman's explanation didn't stop jokes about the Crawler, Brawler and Bawler.

The first edition on Jan. 21, 1883 was late getting to press. It was the coldest January that many could remember. "The night was so bitterly cold," Merriman wrote, "that scuttles of coal were placed under the press to warm things up. The ink was so hard it could hardly be cut with a knife. Coal oil was used to soften it. Oysters ordered from John Superach's place on Water Street for oyster stew for the night crew were a solid cake of ice when they arrived."

T. P. Rivera, a local stationer, waited with other stockholders near the hand-cranked Cottrell press. The Caller office was in the old Noessel building on Chaparral. As they waited for the first issue, someone ran in and yelled, "Stop the press! Triplets have been born at Mark Downey's home." This was big news. The press was held.

In 1884, Ed Williams, one of the Caller founders, left the paper to run for mayor. After he lost he went to Mexico to go into the oil business and was killed in Mexico City in a streetcar accident. W. P. Caruthers remained with the Caller a few years before he sold his share of the paper to Merriman; he moved to Denver to buy and sell property. Of the three founders only Merriman remained.

The Caller became a daily on June 2, 1891 but after the collapse of the Ropes boom it retreated back to a weekly. It switched to a steam-powered press in 1893.

Among the Caller editors who figure prominently in the city's history, none were better known, or better liked, than Eli Merriman and Roy Miller. Both were unique as positive spokesmen for the city.

Eli Merriman was born in 1852, the son of a doctor and rancher in Banquete. As a boy, Eli remembered seeing Sally Skull, woman freighter and gunslinger who, he thought, had the fierce staring eyes of a hawk.

During the Civil War, young Merriman attended the Hidalgo Seminary in Corpus Christi. The yellow fever epidemic of 1867 claimed the life of Dr. Merriman. After Dr. Merrman's death, Eli's mother sold her land at Banquete and opened a boarding house on Chaparral, later known as the Oriental Merriman Hotel.

In 1870 Merriman, at age 18, got a job as a typesetter for Benjamin Neal's Nueces Valley. He later worked for the Gazette and in 1877 he and Bill Maltby started the Corpus Christi Free Press. Merriman rode from Corpus Christi to Nuecestown to Oakville selling subscriptions. He would fill out the form on the horn of his saddle. Merriman married Ellen Robertson, whose father, a pharmacist, had died in the 1867 epidemic, like Merriman's father.

When J. P. Caruthers and Ed Williams planned to start a new paper, Mifflin Kenedy, a principal investor, insisted that he would invest in the enterprise only if Merriman could be induced to take part. Merriman was persuaded to sell the Free Press and join the venture.

Merriman, after 29 years as editor and publisher, sold his interest in the Caller to Henrietta King in 1912. He kept one share of stock and served on the board of directors and continued to write for the paper. He died in 1941 at age 88. A former newsboy, J. W. Falvella, said Merriman "was always heart and soul behind every movement

*The Caller's first home (left) was Felix Noessel's two-story building on Chaparral. The first edition of the paper was printed on Jan. 21, 1883, a night so cold the ink froze and had to be thawed out. Eli Merriman (right) was one of three men who founded the Caller in 1883. He sold his interest in the newspaper to Henrietta King in 1912. He died in 1941*

that had for its purpose the making of a greater city of Corpus Christi."

Another premier newspaperman in the Caller's early history was Henry Pomeroy Miller, better known as Roy. Miller arrived in Corpus Christi in 1904 as a public relations promoter for the St. Louis, Brownsville and Mexico Railroad. He married Maud Heaney, a doctor's daughter, and left his railroad job to become editor of the Caller.

When he was 29, in 1913, he was elected mayor. During his administration, downtown streets were paved, sewer lines laid, a municipal wharf built, a modern water system installed, and the unsightly bluff was terraced and topped with the bluff balustrade.

Miller's lobbying in 1916 lobbying brought Texas National Guard units to Corpus Christi in a new army base named Camp Scurry. When Miller lost the mayor's race in 1919, he returned to the Caller as publisher. After the 1919 storm, Miller was named chairman of the relief committee. He wrote a series of page one editorials using the disaster as a starting point to preach the need for a deepwater port.

In the 1920s, Miller fought against the Ku Klux Klan and he fought for the development of the city. He went to Washington to lobby for a deepwater port and when President Harding signed legislation authorizing the construction of the port of Corpus Christi on May 22, 1922, Miller sent a two-word telegram to the Caller — "We win!"

Roy Miller sold the Caller and went to Washington as a special representative of the port and the city. He died in 1946 when he was 62. While Miller was editor of the newspaper for three years and publisher for 10 years, he was better known for his successful efforts to build and establish the port of Corpus Christi and the Intracoastal Canal.

*—May 20, 2015*

# Dead or Alive

The Caller in its early years did not lack for competition from rival journals. Soon after it was established in 1883, the Daily Critic emerged, lasted a few months and moved to Lagarto. The Christian Advocate surfaced in 1890 and lasted for a year. The Ocean Wave, also begun in 1890, was published for two years before it moved to Laredo. The Gulf News, also born in 1890, went broke two years later.

The Sun began to publish in 1891. It went out of business but was later purchased by John Hardwicke, who changed the name to the Texas Sun. After he died in 1906 his widow ran it for another three years.

There were others but not one of the roughly two dozen papers the town has seen come and go was anything like the Corpus Christi Crony, edited by James Henderson. Henderson wrote in the Crony's first edition on March 9, 1901 that the paper was originated solely for his benefit and he offered one year's subscription to anyone who would bring in 100 boll weevils "dead or alive."

Henderson wrote that a dance at Banquete was a tame affair — "nobody killed and only a few injured." The oldest street in the world in ancient Babylon was dug up, he wrote, and it was in better condition than Leopard Street.

Henderson drowned while bathing in the bay off Central Wharf.

J. W. Falvella, a typesetter at the Caller, started the Herald in 1907 with Jeff McLemore, W. G. Blake, and John B. Armstrong. It was printed from an office on Mesquite. The nearby Constantine Hotel won an injunction preventing the Herald from running its press late at night. In 1910, the Herald was sold to the Caller and the papers consolidated as the Corpus Christi Caller and Daily Herald.

Eli Merriman, editor, publisher, and soul of the Caller for three decades, retired on Jan. 10, 1912. He was 60. He kept one share of

*The Daily Herald staff in 1907 with delivery boys in front of Joe Mireur's building at 409 Mesquite. The Herald was sold to the Caller and the papers consolidated as the Corpus Christi Caller and Daily Herald.*

stock so he could remain on the board of directors and he continued to write a regular column.

The Corpus Christi Democrat, founded in 1911, was purchased in 1917 by Walter Pope, state legislator known as "Uncle Elmer." He changed the paper's name to the Times.

The Times had one reporter, Victor Hugo Herold. This was not all that unusual. Most early newspapers got their news by reprinting items from other papers, not by sending reporters out to report from the scene. In earlier times, ship captains who brought papers from other cities were prized by newspaper editors as a source for their "news." Papers were filled with items reprinted from other papers. But the Times found it cheaper to reprint items from its competitor than to hire its own reporters.

A story in the Caller-Times Centennial edition in 1983 recalled that Vic Herold's job was to rewrite local news from the morning Caller for the afternoon Times. Herold said the Caller got tired of that bare-faced theft. "On April 1 the Caller carried an item that Mr. A.P. Rilfirst of San Antonio was a visitor in our city. I rewrote this news and it went back to the composing room. Pretty soon the linotype operator came in and said, 'Can't you see what they are doing to you? This man's name spells April First, and they are trying to make a fool of you.' " That item went into the wastebasket.

The next trick the Caller pulled was to report that a big onion farm project would be located near the city. Foreign investors included Count Nelots and Baron De Hclif. Herold, now wary, figured out that Nelots was "Stolen" and De Hclif was "Filched."

Roy Miller was back running the Caller after he was defeated for re-election. In February 1919, the newspaper was moved from the old Noakes building to the old Doddridge Bank building a block to the north. Months later, the Caller handled the biggest story in the city's history, the Sept. 14, 1919 storm, which caused widespread destruction in the downtown and North Beach and claimed at least 284 lives, possibly 400 or more.

The newspaper offices in the Doddridge building suffered severe damage from the 11.5 feet tidal wave. The press and business office on the first floor were under water for several hours. Editorial offices and the composing room, with the linotype machines, on the second floor escaped major damage.

On Monday, the day after the storm, the Caller did not publish. It was the first time it had missed an edition since it was founded. It managed to publish a broadsheet on Tuesday after the staff found some undamaged newsprint and cleaned off an old hand-press that had been covered with water on the first floor. They put together a one-page broadsheet with hand-set type and printed a few copies on the hand-press.

That Sept. 16 paper gave a partial list of the dead, a proclamation by Mayor Gordon Boone requiring everyone to register at City Hall, some facts about the storm, and an eyewitness account by Ben Whitehead, editor of the McAllen Sun who was a patient at Spohn Sanitarium on North Beach during the storm.

The Caller missed publication only on Monday and Thursday. It printed a one-page broadsheet for the rest of the week. No attempt was made to try to deliver the paper, with so much of the city destroyed, but carrier boys pasted the scarce copies on fences and walls of major buildings.

The following Monday, Sept. 22, a week after the storm, the Caller began using the composing room and press of the Kingsville Record. The Caller staff stayed at the Casa Ricardo Hotel and took their meals at the White Kitchen, paid for by Henrietta King, the majority stockholder of the Caller. The Caller was printed at Kingsville until Sept. 30.

**Corpus Christi Caller**

*The Caller's front page two days after the storm, on Sept. 16, 1919, gave a partial list of the dead, a proclamation by the mayor, and a notice that the Caller would publish on small hand-press until the big press could be repaired and electricity restored.*

The big duplex press in the Doddridge building was cleaned up and repaired, but the city light plant that provided the power had been destroyed by the storm. The Caller got a Fordson tractor from the Glover Johns dealership and used a long belt to connect the drive shaft to the press. With some careful "driving" the Caller's press was back in operation.

—*May 27, 2015*

304

# Trying Times

On Thanksgiving Day after the 1919 hurricane the Caller published a "Come Back" edition filled with rosy and upbeat stories but the paper was going through hard times. Roy Miller had borrowed $31,000 to make the move from the Noessel building to the Doddridge building and the paper's finances, like the city's downtown, was in ruins.

One employee, Gilbert Vetters, recalled that he had just been promoted to the mailroom. As a carrier boy he was paid in dollar bills but with his promotion he received a check. When he went to the bank to cash it, he found it was no good. A co-worker told him to take it to Lichtenstein's. Lichtenstein's cashed his $10 check, as it did for other Caller employees. The store paid its advertising bills with them. In those days, reporters were charged for their pencils — a nickel each — although copy editors were given pencils free.

Henrietta King bailed out the cash-strapped paper. The doyenne of King Ranch paid $20,000 for the paper's assets and two months later sold the paper to Roy Miller on credit.

In 1928, Houston Harte, Sr. and Bernard Hanks came to Corpus Christi to see about buying the Times from Walter Pope. Harte was the publisher at San Angelo and Hanks published the Abilene paper. It was raining and they found the Times' flatbed press in a vacant lot. It was under a tarpaulin to keep out the rain. As the two men took a stroll on the Pleasure Pier, Harte was very low about what he had seen and offered to call it a day. Hanks said, "If you want to buy linotypes, the place to go is Brooklyn. I think this town has a future and I like this water." They bought the Times. Another newspaper group bought the Caller from Roy Miller for $250,000 ($3.4 million in today's dollars) and sold it to Harte and Hanks.

On May 27, 1945, a landlord-tenant dispute case was heard in County Judge Joe Browning's court. Bush Jackson was the agent for

*Tom Mulvaney, Bob McCracken and Conway Craig have coffee with Sheriff Harney (right) on Aug. 3, 1945 after they were arrested and jailed on the orders of Judge Browning. The case of Craig v. Harney eventually went to the Supreme Court and resulted in a landmark decision for press freedom.*

owners of the Elks Club building at Starr and Water. He leased the building to Doc Mason, nightclub operator, on condition he break the lease held by Joe Mayes, who ran the Playboy Club on the ground floor. Mason wanted to establish the Dragon Grill there.

When the case came up for trial, Mayes had been drafted and was stationed at Fort Hood. His wife was operating the Playboy Club. On Saturday, Judge Browning instructed the six-man jury to bring in a verdict for Bush Jackson.

The jurors balked. Twice they returned verdicts for Mayes. The judge sent them back each time with orders to return with a verdict in favor of Jackson. Late on Saturday night, the jurors were locked up for the night, confined in the jury room.

On Sunday morning the judge told the jurors to bring back a directed verdict for Jackson or he would keep them locked up. After 15 hours, the jury brought back a verdict in favor of Jackson, with a statement: "It is to be understood that this verdict is rendered and recorded on the order of this court against the conscience of the jury."

The Caller-Times reported on the case and columnist Bob McCracken criticized the judge, who promptly cited for contempt

*Ed Harte was named publisher of the Caller-Times in 1962. He said he always knew he would get to be publisher "if I behaved myself." In later years Harte donated $46 million to Texas A&M University-Corpus Christi to establish a research center, later named the Harte Research Institute for Gulf of Mexico Studies.*

the publisher of the Caller-Times, Conway Craig, the managing editor, Bob McCracken, and reporter Tom Mulvaney. Judge Browning ordered Sheriff John Harney to arrest the publisher, managing editor and reporter. At the county jail, Harney gave them a breakfast of huevos rancheros. McCracken took his portable typewriter to write his column from the jail. They were released after five hours.

Craig v. Harney reached the U.S. Supreme Court. On May 28, 1947, the high court reversed Judge Browning and the Court of Criminal Appeals. The high court ruled that a trial is a public event, that what happens in a courtroom is public property, that a judge cannot use the power of his office to protect himself from criticism. This landmark decision remains a cornerstone of constitutional law.

I am going to skip a big chunk of the Caller-Times' later history, including the end of the separate afternoon paper, the Times, and the sale of the Harte-Hanks chain, including the Caller-Times, to the E.W. Scripps Company. I started this series with the idea of sticking to the 19th and first half of the 20th century, but I can't leave the subject without mentioning Edward H. Harte, who died in 2011.

Ed Harte, when he was named publisher of the Caller-Times in 1962, said he always knew he would get the job "if I behaved myself." He had worked at the family paper at San Angelo as a reporter and editor and apparently behaved himself.

Ed Harte, as I knew him, had that rare ability to see the other point of view and he never forgot that his great privilege in life carried with it great responsibility. He retired in 1987 and in 2000 he donated $46 million to Texas A&M University Corpus Christi to establish the Harte Research Institute. Such an act of generosity was not surprising for Ed Harte.

Newspapers have had a presence in Corpus Christi for 169 years, since 1846, but these are trying times for the Fourth Estate and who knows what the future of many newspapers may be. Corpus Christi's first newspaper, the Gazette, lasted only a few months in 1846. The next newspaper, the Star, lasted a couple of years, as did the Nueces Valley, the Ranchero, Advertiser, Free Press, Ledger, Herald and Crony. They have all come and gone. The Caller, the lone survivor, has lasted 132 years. It must have been doing something right.

*—June 3, 2015*

# Zoom Town

The Naval Air Station in Corpus Christi was built in seven months beginning in June 1940, representing an investment of $100 million by the government, an investment that paid off when naval aviators trained at Corpus Christi played a major role in winning the war in the Pacific.

It started in November 1939 when Navy officials recommended Corpus Christi for a new naval air training base because it offered nearly ideal training weather, its activity could easily be coordinated with the older base at Pensacola, and the skies over South Texas were not congested.

The Navy eventually settled on a site at Flour Bluff bounded by the Cayo del Oso, Corpus Christi Bay and the Laguna Madre. Congress allocated money in 1940 to begin construction on a 2,050-acre tract of land covered with scrub brush and sand dunes. The contract was awarded to Brown & Root, W. S. Bellows of Houston and Columbia Construction of Oakland, Calif.

One of the first Navy officials to arrive was Cmdr. L. N. Moeller, the public works officer at Pensacola, who was in charge of constructing the new base. One of his first acts was to order 13,700 tons of structural steel to build aircraft hangars and other facilities. It was said to be the largest single order for steel ever placed in Texas, three times more than what the city ordered to build the seawall. The cost, at $1.3 million, was more than was spent later to build Corpus Christi's largest building, the Driscoll Hotel.

With war threatening, contractors raced against time to build the base. The sounds of bulldozers vied with the cries of seagulls. Sand dunes that reached 40 feet were leveled. Millions of tons of clay were pumped in to raise the elevation. A ship channel was dredged and docking facilities built. A seawall around the waterfront was extended. New roads were built. Seaplane hangars on the waterfront and land hangars near the Oso were built. Barracks, mess halls, repair shops, and ground school buildings followed. Four runways of 5,000 and 6,000 feet were built. A 13-mile water line to the base was completed in 30 days. A 19-mile railroad spur was built from the Texas-Mexican Railway to the base. It was all done at a frenzied pace.

With long lines of trucks delivering construction material and 5,000 workers riding buses or driving to the base, the volume of traffic on Ocean Drive and Alameda was heavy. One day in September 1940 policemen counted 10 cars a minute on Ocean Drive. Traffic on Alameda and Ocean Drive approaching the base was made one-way going south in the morning and one-way going north during the evening rush hour — strategy of a high order for the traffic department.

While the base was being built, Corpus Christi, a small town with a population of 57,000, was expanding rapidly. New water and sewer lines were being extended, streets paved, with a mountain of dredge material from the seawall project piled on the bayfront. You couldn't get within hailing distance of the bay without crossing a sea of mud. The Driscoll Hotel and Lichtenstein's new store were being built. An article in Collier's about the new base and the city called Corpus Christi "Zoom Town."

Construction conditions were far from ideal. With rainfall twice that of normal, Corpus Christi streets turned into canals in the wettest spring in 40 years. Construction workers at the base struggled with standing water and drifting sand. One day there would be blowing sand and the next day torrents of water, sending workers scurrying for shelter like half-drowned rats. One man said, perhaps apocryphally, "This is the only place in the world where a passing truck can splatter mud in your eye and at the same time throw dust in your face."

Despite these adverse conditions, the base was 70 percent built, a year ahead of schedule, when it was dedicated on March 12, 1941. The ceremony was held on March 12, 1941. Frank Knox, the Chicago newspaper tycoon and Secretary of the Navy, was the main speaker.

Capt. Alva Bernhard read the orders appointing him commander of the base, ordered the colors raised and set the watch, the same as a captain would do aboard ship. After the ceremonies, the day was further punctuated by a dinner banquet at the White Plaza Hotel.

*A sailor walks near Building One, headquarters of Corpus Christi Naval Air Station, in early 1941. Because many took off their shoes to walk through the sand, water faucets and towels were provided at the entrance of buildings so people could wash their feet before putting their shoes and socks back on.*

*Base security personnel check cars entering the Naval Air Station for dedication ceremonies on March 12, 1941. After war came in December, the base quickly grew to become the largest Navy air-training center in the country.*

Lyndon Johnson, whose political influence with President Roosevelt helped locate the base at Corpus Christi, was on hand for the occasion.

A week later, on March 20, 1941, the first class of 52 cadets started classes. They would have to cram a year's study into seven months. In that first class was Don Hager, who had been a star football player at Rice University, the only Texan in the group.

In coming months three auxiliary fields were rushed to completion. Rodd Field was commissioned on June 7, Cabaniss on July 9, and Cuddihy on Sept. 9.

The first group of 52 cadets began flight training on April 7. The early cadets were trained in an open cockpit biplane — the N3N and N2S — called the Yellow Peril for its canary yellow color. They advanced to the SNV, made by Vultee in California, which was nicknamed the Vultee Vibrators because they shook so badly. They finally progressed to the SNJ Texan, a single-wing training craft that on some models had arrester hooks for carrier landings.

The first fatal training accident happened on July 10. An ensign, L. J. Shudde, was killed and a cadet, Donald Lesher, was seriously injured.

It was a hot day on Nov. 1, 1941 when the first class of cadets graduated. Corpsmen were kept busy picking up those who keeled over from the heat.

Capt. Bernhard told the graduating class they had had to endure acres of sand and mud to march through "but I am proud of the fact that 45 of you out of 52 have completed the full course of training. When I finished my aviation training, I was told that if I remembered these three rules, I would live to be an old man. One: Keep your flying speed. Two: Keep your flying speed. Three: Keep your flying speed."

*—June 10, 2015*

# Joe's Sister

The day after Pearl Harbor a civil service worker at the Naval Air Station's Assembly & Repair Department went to see the officer in charge, Lt. Comdr. Herman Halland, to resign. Two days later, a young woman came to the department seeking a job. When she told Halland her name he said, "Do you have a brother named Joe who used to work here?'

"Yes," she said, "he joined the air corps so I would like to take his place." She got the job. Women would be needed to fill jobs on the base when the men went off to war.

The job Joe's sister applied for was classified as mechanical learner. She would work six days a week, eight hours a day, and earn $104 dollars a month. After three to six months of working by day and studying by night, she would be eligible to be promoted to "helper trainee" with a salary of $140 to $150 a month.

This was part of a much bigger story. The nation in World War II was being altered in a striking way. Because large numbers of men went off to fight and war production demanded even more workers to produce the weapons of war, a new supply of labor had to be found. This led to a social revolution as six million women or more joined the civilian workforce.

Like the sister who took her brother's job, women filled jobs left vacant by men in uniform. They kept production moving on assembly lines, in aircraft factories, and in Corpus Christi at the huge Assembly & Repair Department at the Naval Air Station.

Some women workers were recruited through the Depression-era program, the National Youth Administration. These were young single girls, recent high-school graduates, sent to train and work at NAS from all over the country. Others were older married women, some whose husbands were away fighting and some who were war widows. One woman in the Assembly & Repair Department, whom

313

the girls called Mom, had one son fighting in the Pacific, a son-in-law with Patton's army in France, and a daughter in the WAVES (Women Accepted for Volunteer Emergency Service).

Women workers in the Assembly & Repair Department were instantly recognizable with their regulation coveralls, identity badges and hair cut short so it wouldn't get tangled in machinery. At the mid-point of the war, in 1943, 20,000 civilians were employed at the Naval Air Station, many of them women. Most of them worked repairing Navy planes used to train student pilots. They did Navy-wide overhaul and repair of all types of airplanes.

Due to wartime censorship, there are not many stories in newspaper archives about the women who worked at the base. There are photographs. Years ago I ordered a batch of photos from the Library of Congress of women workers at NAS. Most of them were taken in 1942 by Howard Hollem, a Farm Security Administration photographer.

In looking at the photographs it struck me that they all looked so confident, so sure of themselves. These were the faces of a new idea, that women could easily handle jobs once done exclusively by men, and they did. Behind the faces were the stories.

Eloise Ellis was a sociology major at the University of Southern California before she joined the Assembly & Repair Department and became a supervisor . . . Jo Ann Whittington worked as a telephone operator before she was trained in electrical overhauling at the base . . . Mabel Carmen left her home in Mississippi to train as a machinist repairing Navy planes . . . Mrs. Doris Duke, housewife and mother, worked reconditioning sharp plugs . . . Mary Josephine Farley, rated as a top-notch mechanic, had a pilot's license and made cross-country flights. These were a few of the 20,000 workers at the Naval Air Station during the war.

Something else struck me. The government's language in World War II would be hooted down as condescending today. A pamphlet aimed at encouraging housewives to join the workforce said, "If you've sewed on buttons or made buttonholes on a machine, you can do spot welding on airplane parts. If you've used an electric mixer in your kitchen, you can learn to run a drill press." The Caller-Times was no better. A story on Oct. 29, 1943, about women guards at the Assembly & Repair Department called them "pistol-packing mamas" and said, "Even the men admit that the ladies can pack a pistol along with the best." Oh, well, it was a different time.

*Eloise Ellis, a former sociology major at the University of Southern California, was a supervisor in the Assembly & Repair Shop at NAS. Photo by Howard Hollem, from the Library of Congress.*

*Two women workers in the Navy's Assembly & Repair Department take a lunch break. Photo by Howard Hollem in 1942 from the Library of Congress.*

The war in the Pacific ended on Aug. 15, 1945. I can't pin down what happened in the Assembly & Repair Department at the Naval Air Station, at least not through the newspaper archives, but all over the country women were laid off. They were laid off not only because the jobs they were doing were no longer in great demand but because returning veterans were hired to take their places.

One cartoon showed a supervisor handing a termination notice to a woman looking upset. "Now that the war is over," he told her, "so sorry, have suddenly remembered you are incapable of working in a factory." That was cited in Doris Kearns Goodwin's book "No Ordinary Time." Women who had worked so hard to meet the labor needs of the war were no longer needed. Goodwin also quoted a woman war worker named Mary Smith who said, "Now that the war is over, I've lost my job, for no other reason apparently except that I am a woman."

That was a national disgrace. But the social revolution enacted by the war meant irrevocable change and the women would soon be back in the workforce, in the vanguard of a new era.

There is a statue in Vancouver, Wash., of Rosie the Riveter that honors the working women of World War II and there may be others I don't know about, but I have always thought that we have, at least so far, missed a chance in Corpus Christi to repay part of an enormous debt to the civilian women workers who kept the planes flying at the Naval Air Station during the war. Do you think perhaps a statue should have been erected in their honor?

—*June 17, 2015*

316

# University of the Air

In Corpus Christi in December 1941, most shopping was done downtown. More than 15,000 people attended the grand opening of Lichtenstein's new store. Downtown parking was free; there were no parking meters. Outside the downtown area, streets were dirt or gravel. Cars could get stuck on Louisiana at Menger Elementary and Santa Fe was a gravel road beyond Louisiana. Ocean Drive was paved but in poor condition.

The Tower Theater at Six Points was playing "When Ladies Meet" with Greer Garson and Joan Crawford. Young couples danced to "Chattanooga Choo Choo" at the Palmero, El Rancho or Swingland on North Beach. The City Council was considering an ordinance to prohibit high-school students from hitch-hiking home after school. The school board asked for bids to build new classrooms under the stands at the new Buccaneer Stadium at Corpus Christi High School.

It was a lovely day on Dec. 7, 1941 when, shortly after noon, people heard on radio that Japanese planes had attacked U.S. bases at Pearl Harbor and destroyed much of the Pacific fleet. At the new Naval Air Station, leaves were cancelled and Capt. Alva D. Bernhard, commander of the station, said, "We will post more guards, and take other precautions we can't talk about, and we will continue to turn out as many pilots as we can as fast as we can. That's our job."

Hundreds of sailors and civilian workers gathered the following day in the cavernous Assembly & Repair Department hangar to hear FDR's war speech, which was delivered with unusual gravity, every word kept distinct as if underlined: "Yesterday, December the seventh, nineteen forty-one, a date which will live in infamy . . ."

The Naval Air Station, nicknamed the University of the Air (Pensacola was known as Annapolis of the Air), quickly moved from choice to necessity. The training schedule was expanded to seven days a week and elevated in intensity and tempo. From graduating 300 pilots each month, it rose to 600 a month. In time, new fields were built at Kingsville and Beeville, along with Rodd, Cuddihy and Waldron to meet the demands for Navy aviators.

The base filled other roles. Boot camp training was added to relieve the Navy's overcrowded training bases. The air station became the supply point for the Gulf inshore patrol, composed of sub-chasers and minesweepers charged with guarding the vital shipping lanes. The base also hosted a torpedo bomber training squadron and at Ward Island it supervised a secret radar-training school.

Hollywood stars Tyrone Power and Robert Taylor were among those stationed at the base during the war. Power, a lieutenant in the Marines, went through flight training at NAS while his wife Annabella put up at the Driscoll Hotel. Power, despite his celebrity status, refused any special treatment. Robert Taylor, already a pilot, was at NAS in 1942 for refresher training. George Bush, the future president and father of a president, earned his wings at NAS in 1943. John Glenn, the first man to orbit the Earth, graduated from flight training at NAS in 1943.

Not so well-known was Gerald F. Child. He was in the first class to graduate at the station weeks before Pearl Harbor was attacked. Less than a year later, Child and his PBY crew were the first to locate the Japanese fleet steaming toward Midway. Before his plane was shot down, Child kept visual contact with the Japanese carriers, which helped give the U.S. Navy a great victory, considered the turning point of the war in the Pacific.

On April 21, 1943, President Franklin D. Roosevelt and Mexico's President Manuel Avila Camacho arrived by train from Monterrey, where they had conferred for several days, to visit the base. They were welcomed by the base commander, Rear Adm. A.E. Montgomery, and had lunch with cadets in the mess hall.

The following month, on May 31, the largest war-time class of cadets graduated with 331 members, more than seven times the number of that first class of 45. In 1944, 21,067 pilots graduated at the base. There were more than 25,000 Navy personnel at NAS and auxiliary fields and 40,000 civilian workers. The training of pilots was so accelerated that by war's end more than 35,000 pilots had earned their wings at the Naval Air Station.

Aviation cadets check the flight board before going to their planes. The board showed the plane number, take-off time, and the instructor assigned to each cadet for that day's flights. Photo by Howard Hollem, Library of Congress.

Lt. E. W. Allen presents "wings" to the first cadets to solo in flight training at the Naval Air Station. Toward the end of 1941, Corpus Christi NAS was turning out 300 aviators each month. After the attack on Pearl Harbor, the number was doubled.

319

The base took on a new function. German POWs were housed in a compound enclosed with barbed wire near the South Gate. The POWs worked at manual labor jobs for which they were paid 80 cents a day. People found them to be good, cheerful workers. In one chore, they dug up hackberry trees from the banks of the Nueces River and replanted them at the base. In the evenings they were shown movies. They particularly liked Walt Disney films. The POW camp was in operation from August 1945 until March 1946.

When the war in the Pacific ended on Aug. 15, 1945, people jammed the streets and cars streamed down Chaparral, tooting their horns and making a hullabaloo of noise and commotion. There was dancing in Artesian Park and the bands played on, until well past midnight.

With the war over, Navy planes were mothballed and fields deactivated. Less than 10 percent of the pilots needed during the war would be needed in peacetime. Auxiliary fields Waldron, Rodd, Cuddihy, Kingsville and Chase were closed in 1946 and NAS went through a slimmed-down metamorphosis. And Corpus Christi lost the buzz and excitement of thousands of servicemen stationed at the Naval Air Station.

During World War II, it was said that there was probably not a pilot in the Navy who had not at one time or another landed at Corpus Christi. Either he took flight training at NAS or stopped at the base on a cross-country flight. Many of the aviators who fought and died in the great naval battles in the Pacific, the battles that ultimately won the war, were trained at the Corpus Christi Naval Air Station. When the base was being built in 1940, people said it would make Corpus Christi important, or at least more important, but they didn't know at the time just how important it would be.

*—June 24, 2015*

320

# Independence Day

The largest Fourth of July celebration held in Corpus Christi came in the centennial year of 1876. It began at midnight July 3 and lasted until dawn July 5. People had never seen the like.

The celebration of the nation's hundredth birthday included the firing of cannons, parades, a baseball game, speech-making, singing, dinner on the school grounds, and dancing the night away. A cannon mishap took a man's arm but did not end to the festivities.

At midnight on the third, James Downing supervised the discharge of two guns on the bluff. The 12-pound howitzers were borrowed from King Ranch. The men were supposed to fire 13 shots for the original 13 states but they lost count and fired 14. After the guns were fired, bell-ringers kept the church bells pealing until their arms gave out. The city went back to sleep for a few hours.

At first light, the bell-ringers began again and the howitzers were fired, the correct 13 shots this time. At 7 a.m., people gathered near the Congregational Church for a review of the Star Rifles under the command of Capt. S. T. Foster, who ran a livery stable. The Star Rifles were organized the year before, after the Nuecestown Raid, and turned out once a week to practice marching and small-arms drill. On this morning, wearing new black-and-white uniforms, they presented arms between two flags emblazoned with 1776 and 1876.

An hour later, near the Courthouse, 500 people watched a baseball game between Corpus Christi and Fulton. Up on the bluff a reception was held for invited guests by the mayor, City Council, and Centennial Committee. Afterwards, students and teachers from the Presbyterian and Methodist schools formed at Artesian Square and marched to Market Hall. The program there began with the reading of Scripture, followed by prayers, the singing of "America" and "Shall We Gather at the River" — a rich mixture of the New Testament and American history.

The town was full for the holiday, the streets crowded with carriages and men on horseback. Galloping horsemen ran impromptu races. One man, Pat Lawler, was riding a splendid horse and waving a flag inscribed with "Hard Money," the war cry of the Democrats.

When the noonday sun reached its zenith, it was time for firing the howitzers again. The plan was to fire 100 shots for 100 years of the Republic.

One man at the guns was Stanley Welch, editor of the Valley Times. His job was to sponge the gun and ram home the cartridge. Besides Welch, the two guns were manned by Charles Beman, publisher of the Valley Times, Larry Dunn, J. J. Boerum, and T. P. Rivera. After the tenth shot was fired, Beman put in the powder and Welch was ramming it home when the gun prematurely discharged. The rapid firing had overheated the piece and set off the powder.

As smoke cleared, Welch was holding what was left of his right arm. The explosion tore off his right hand and broke his arm below the elbow. One of his fingers, with a ring on it, was found a block away. Welch was taken to Mrs. Merriman's boarding house, where he had a room, and Dr. Arthur Spohn amputated the arm below the elbow.

Welch urged them to carry on with the celebration as if nothing had happened, though the gunners, after consultation, decided to discontinue the firing of the howitzers. From his bed the invalid could hear the ringing of the bells that signaled the assembly for the grand parade.

It was scorching hot as parade units formed at Market Hall, moved south on Mesquite to William then north on Chaparral to Mann and up to the bluff to the school grounds. The order of procession included musicians, Star Rifles, ladies in carriages, government officials, clergy, volunteer firemen, members of the bar and medical association, baseball clubs, men on horseback, children on foot, wild with excitement , and loose dogs that joined the parade or were just headed in the same direction.

At the school grounds there was the reading of the Declaration of Independence, the singing of "America" and Mayor William Headen delivered the prepared speech of Stanley Welch, who was supposed to be the day's main speaker.

There may have been a groan or two when Richard "Dickie" Power was called on to recite his centennial poem. Power always

*Judge Stanley Welch, when he was younger, lost his right arm when a 12-pound howitzer misfired in the 1876 July Fourth celebration. He was later assassinated during a political turmoil in Rio Grande City. Photo from the Corpus Christi Central Library.*

had a poem ready for every occasion; some of the boys thought he was a head case. His centennial poem ended with the lines, "So, glory to Washington / And his compeers of old / Who fought to gain the liberty / We value more than gold."

A slight shower came up before supper but the sky soon cleared. Long tables that could seat 700 people were set with dishes cooked by women in the town, more than enough to satisfy every glutton, and the benches were crowded. In the shade of a tree were barrels of ice water and cold lemonade. The grounds were lit by Chinese lanterns and, from the windows of the schoolhouse, lamps provided by J. B. Mitchell Hardware. Toasts were made to Our Country, the Heroes of '76, George Washington, Texas, the Central Government, and the Women of America.

After supper, one major event was left: a dance at Market Hall. There was fiddling and dancing until daylight broke on the morning of the fifth. This brought Corpus Christi's celebration of the nation's centennial to a close. Except for the frightful cannon accident, nothing went awry to mar what people said was the best, most glorious Independence Day ever — which it was.

While Stanley Welch recuperated from the amputation of his right arm, he studied law and was admitted to the bar. He was elected county attorney and then district judge. He was a political ally of the Democratic boss of bosses, Jim Wells. The one-armed judge was assassinated on election day, Tuesday, Nov. 6, 1906 as a result of political violence between Republicans and Democrats in Rio Grande City. He was shot to death in his sleep. The man convicted of killing him, Alberto Cabrera, a former bartender, escaped from a Texas prison and joined Carranza's revolutionary forces in Mexico. Judge Welch's son, Arthur Spohn Welch, who was six years old when his father was killed, died in 1976.

*—July 1, 2015*

# Twelve-Mile Motts, 1858

Thomas John Noakes left his home in Sussex, England when he was either 16 or 18 (accounts differ), crossed the Atlantic and reached Texas in 1846 or 1848. He got a job as a ranch hand for Corpus Christi founder Henry Kinney and worked on a dredge boat digging a channel across the bay. He bought land in Nuecestown, 12 miles from Corpus Christi, and worked to establish a ranch.

Over the years Noakes developed skills as a saddle-maker and innovator. He could fix clocks and musical instruments and kept a diary. The first volume which began in 1848, the green book, was lost, but later volumes tell us much about life in South Texas just before, during and after the Civil War. What survives of Noakes' diary begins in 1858 and continues through the summer of 1867, with gaps during the Civil War.

Because of his diary, we know Thomas John Noakes as well as it is possible to know someone from 150 years ago. He was well-educated, artistic and had a talent for making things, but he was often sad and unhappy and, when life was really trying, inclined to self-pity.

Noakes lived outside Nuecestown, known as Twelve-Mile Motts or simply the Motts, close to where Calallen is today. Noakes was one of the first settlers at the Motts. Other English immigrants, attracted to Texas by Kinney's land promotions, settled nearby. Noakes was a bachelor homesteader, struggling to make a living, and life on the Texas frontier was a hard struggle, as Noakes' diary shows. It has the clarion ring of experience itself.

On Thursday, Jan. 7, 1858, Noakes intended to go to Corpus Christi with his cart to fetch various things but a cold driving sleet kept him home. He worked around the house, planted a few seeds, and boiled a pot of rice, which he mixed with a fish, for Peter, his puppy. Peter, Noakes wrote, was loose-limbed and big-boned and

325

had the appetite of a lion. He hated the cold and would get so close to the fire that it burned off his eyebrows.

Noakes spent much of January on organized cattle hunts, riding with George Reynolds, Joseph Wright and neighbors to find strayed cattle, which they would round up, brand and return to the home ranges. When the cattle were found, they had to be herded closely or they would run away.

Noakes rode to Corpus Christi on Feb. 5 to try to collect money due him for his work for a dredging company. Noakes wrote that the mudflat people owed him $160 but he couldn't collect. He also checked on his property in town. He owned a house and lot he had purchased from Henry Kinney which he rented out.

On Sunday, Feb. 14, the weather was fine — "beginning to feel like spring" — when an English sailor named Peter Kershaw moved in with Noakes. Kershaw owned a boat which he kept moored on the river at the edge of Noakes' property. Noakes and Kershaw agreed to plant a field of corn and share the crop. They began to build a fence around the field.

Noakes borrowed a yoke of steers from George Reynolds to haul posts to make a fence and to plow the field. An old boatman friend of Kershaw came to visit and brought them a bucket of fine oysters. On Thursday, March 25, his dog Peter was bit in the head by a rattlesnake. Noakes killed the snake and used the fat to treat the snakebite. The dog survived. Soon afterwards, Noakes was bringing home a cart load of wood and came across six large rattlesnakes. He killed them and got nearly a full bottle of snake oil.

Noakes and Kershaw went to Corpus Christi in Kershaw's boat. On the way back, they got stuck on an oyster reef in Nueces Bay. They had guns, a net, fish spear, lines and oyster tongs so Noakes thought they were ready for anything. They pushed the boat over the bar, keeping their eyes on an alligator a few yards from the boat. They made it home by sundown.

As he worked on his fence, Noakes killed, on average, a rattlesnake a day. Each morning, his first task was to hunt down his horse and then hunt down his cattle.

The weather was warm and dry when Noakes went up the river in Kershaw's boat as part of a "grape party" to get dark muscadine grapes which grew along the river banks. They met another party from Nuecestown, young men and their sisters, who tied their horses to trees along the river.

*Thomas John Noakes, a self-drawn portrait. Noakes came to Corpus Christi sometime between 1846 and 1848 and settled by the Nueces River at the Motts, Nuecestown. He kept a detailed diary of his daily activities.*

Noakes and Thomas Wright went to Corpus Christi to get things for a Fourth of July dance — wine and sweet cakes, mostly, and Noakes bought himself some new clothes, "which I was badly in need of."

On July 2, Noakes and neighbors went hunting a panther (what we would call a cougar or mountain lion). They started by moonlight near the remains of a calf which the big cat had killed. When the hounds came across the scent, they started at full cry. They rode across a rough prairie to a jungle of thorny bushes where the dogs had the panther treed. One of the men fired a shot and wounded the panther. Noakes and another man fired and the panther came down. The big cat, hit by four shots, was torn up on the ground by the dogs. They drew straws for the skin, but Noakes was not the winner. He wrote an account of the panther hunt that was printed in the Corpus Christi newspaper, the Nueces Valley.

327

Noakes went to the July Fourth dance (for which they had bought the wine and sweet cakes) but he felt unwell and didn't stay.

In August, Noakes wrote that the weather was sultry with every indication of a storm. It turned out to be a small norther without rain or thunder. The grass was dying for lack of rain. Noakes made a deal with John Williams, a friend, to take a load of his watermelons to Corpus Christi to sell, but when Williams went to get them they had all been destroyed. Coons had cleaned out his watermelon patch.

*—July 8, 2015*

# Panther Hunt

Thomas John Noakes, an Englishman who came to Texas in 1848 and settled at Nuecestown, kept a diary that provides a graphic account of life in frontier Texas from 1858 to 1867.

On Sept. 2, 1858 Noakes hitched two steers to a cart and drove it to Nuecestown to be loaded with food and drink for a picnic. There was one wagon and two carts full of supplies. The site chosen for the picnic was a place of great beauty up the river. After the picnic, they held a dance at the Motts. Noakes wrote an account of the picnic for the Nueces Valley.

At the end of September Noakes noted that the river was rising "and we shall have fresh water again." When the river was down, saltwater from the bay advanced up the Nueces and river water became unfit for man and stock.

Noakes was sick for several months and when fever was on him he dreaded being alone. "Of all the miseries one can be exposed to in a wild country, the worst is being alone. Sick or unwell, I have to attend my stock, although hardly able to crawl." On Nov. 27 he felt better and took a walk with his gun. He killed a goose and partridge.

Kershaw, the English sailor, moved out of Noakes' house. Noakes and Kershaw were partners in planting a field of corn but they dissolved the partnership. Noakes said Kershaw turned out to be shabby in the end. Kershaw was living with some people on the other side of Nueces Bay who, Noakes reckoned, would soon get tired of him.

It was a hard life and Noakes was not contented with his lot. He was lonely, depressed and sad. He wrote — "Being out of grub, out of money, out of health, and my horse dead, I will now be off as I am no good at home." He left for Corpus Christi on Dec. 3 and stayed a month, boarding with the Joseph Almond family until Jan. 5, 1859.

The first week of January was bitterly cold. Noakes brought home a load of flour and things for housekeeping "for my lonely home." While he was away, his chickens had been killed, a heifer calf he had raised drowned in the river, and his dog Peter was shot to death by someone in the Motts. He got another puppy which he named Nipper.

Noakes rented his house in town to Robert Adams Sr. for $10 for three months. He joined a party of cattle-hunters in March. In June, Noakes took a sail down the river in Kershaw's boat, to fish, shoot alligators and hunt his hogs, which were foraging downriver. Noakes received a letter from his mother in England and a copy of the Sussex Express newspaper.

Because of an article Noakes wrote for the Nueces Valley, the account of their panther killing the year before had spread and in July Richard King at King Ranch invited the panther hunters to bring their dogs and go after the panthers that were killing his colts.

Noakes joined the party of hunters, which included his friend John Heward (the dogs were his), George Reynolds, and other men from the Motts. In a week of hunting they killed one panther and several bobcats or ocelots, which Noakes called tiger cats. King gave each man a mare in appreciation.

On Aug. 1, Noakes served as a clerk at an election in Corpus Christi. One of the judges told him he thought the place was improving because usually, before the voting was over, the clerks and judges would all be drunk but this time they were quite sober.

Noakes observed that he came down with the ague one year before, in September 1858. He was taking medicine that consisted of camomile leaves and red pepper steeped in whisky. "I believe it is doing me a lot of good."

On Aug. 4, 1859, Noakes went to look for his hogs. They had crossed the river and returned to the man he bought them from, an Irishman named William Cody. Cody shot some of them because they were rooting up his crops. Since he had no means of getting them home, Noakes wrote, "I suppose they are lost to me. This, like every other speculation I have made in this country, has turned out a failure."

In the second week of August, Noakes spent several days, in the hottest weather, with a large company of cattle hunters rounding up southwest of Corpus Christi. At Capt. Fullerton's ranch, they found a half-grown pig running about, which they killed, cooked and ate.

They sent word to Fullerton they had done so — "we did not want exactly to steal it."

In their cattle hunting around today's Flour Bluff, Noakes said they camped "in a barren waste of sand, with not a tree to be seen, and winding among the sand hills were salt lagoons whose waters in a dry time evaporate and leave a coating of salt. This cattle hunt rounded up several thousand head in the herd we had up, and we cut out more than 500 head belonging to our party."

On a Sunday in late August Noakes visited Mrs. William Gibbs who been bitten on the hand by a rattlesnake. The hand was horrid-looking, with nearly all the flesh withered away. Noakes said she would have died except they took the proper precautions. They tied a tourniquet about her wrist, cut the place where the fangs entered, and rubbed saltpeter in the wounds. To counteract the poison they gave her three pints of whisky.

On a trip to Corpus Christi on Nov. 9, Noakes found the town in a state of intense excitement with rumors that Juan Cortina was headed north with a thousand of his border raiders and several cannon. Martial law was declared and male inhabitants organized into the Corpus Christi Guards, with men on patrol every night. "I thought as everybody seemed so frightened there must be just cause for alarm, so I started for the Motts as soon as I could. After a good deal of joking, we decided there was no necessity for us to do anything but keep our guns in order."

*—July 15, 2015*

# Noakes Weds Mary Ludwig

Thomas John Noakes, an Englishman who settled at Nuecestown in the 1850s, wrote in his diary about the new teacher on May 17, 1860. His name was Ned Taylor and his wife was Hannah.

The school was attended by the youngsters at the Motts. Most of them had had no chance to get an education. Their parents were well-educated, Noakes wrote, and regretted that their children had been deprived of this advantage. Noakes contributed to the new school by making a blackboard for Taylor.

On a Sunday at the end of June Noakes engaged in soul-searching regret for the life he was living. "I felt so lonesome today. Feel as though I am all alone and no one to care for me although I get fine letters from home and can visualize the land of my birth with its culture and beauty of natural surroundings, but I have been ill so long that I miss someone to care for me. How I envy the birds. They have no regrets for the past, no cares for the present and no fears for the future."

Noakes rode to Corpus Christi on July 5 to visit the Robert Adams' family, fellow English immigrants. He was courting Adams' oldest daughter Elizabeth. Two weeks later Noakes repaired a guitar belonging to his new neighbors, a German family named Ludwig with two marriageable daughters.

Noakes noted on July 26 that cattle, already weak, would begin to die because of the drought. "Ruin stares us in the face. There is not a blade of grass and no water." In early August there were still no signs of rain. Under a pitiless sky, Noakes rode up the river with George Reynolds to rescue cattle bogged in the mud. They pulled out eight cows, a yoke of steers and a horse. They were too tired to pull out others and headed home.

Noakes started digging a well with the help of his neighbor John Orchard, a minister from England. Orchard hauled lumber from

Corpus Christi to curb the well and delighted Noakes with a copy of the Illustrated London News.

Well-digging took an infinity of labor. When Noakes worked alone, he got down into the well and filled the bucket and climbed up again and pulled it up and emptied it, then repeated the process. He was digging about four feet a day. On Wednesday, Aug. 8, he struck water at 18 feet and said he had not had a better streak of luck since coming to Texas. "The well will be worth a great deal to me."

There were heavy rains near the end of August and the river was in full flood, overflowing the river bottoms. Noakes dug a ditch from his yard to drain floodwaters. People celebrated their improved prospects by holding a dance at the Motts, which was almost broken up by hungry mosquitoes.

On Sept. 7, 1860, Noakes rode to Corpus Christi and rented his house in town to a widow woman with daughters. The rent was three dollars a month.

On Dec. 30, with the ground covered with snow, a young man named Cox, a stranger, attended a dance at the Motts. Afterwards he went to Corpus Christi and got into a gambling argument and was killed, shot four times. Cox had left a horse to graze at Noakes' place. It froze to death during the night.

On Jan. 2, 1861, Noakes visited the John Hinnant family. There was a quilting party for the women followed by a dance. Noakes said there were too many men for the number of girls so he went home. When he arrived at his bachelor home, he found it being serenaded by Mrs. Ludwig and her two daughters, but they were singing to an empty house, not knowing Noakes was gone.

The weather was frosty on Feb. 11, 1861 when Noakes wrote about his upcoming marriage. He rode to Corpus Christi, bought some seeds, a barrel of flour, and procured a marriage license at the county clerk's office. He left a notice of his marriage at the newspaper office.

That night, after supper, Noakes took the horses, riding one and leading the other, to Ned Taylor's in the Motts — he was the justice of the peace — and brought him to Ludwig's. "There Mary and I were married, unknown to anybody but the old folks and Mr. Taylor, as we did not wish to have any fuss. For my part, I could not have had a party if I had wished, as 30 cents was the most cash I possessed. I had not even the money to pay for a license, but Marie being willing to take me as I am, I thought it a waste of time to wait for better times." (Her name is given as Mary and Maria. Noakes called her Mary in early entries but later he referred to her as Marie.)

The newlyweds settled down to domesticity. That March, Noakes was sick and still working on a fence at his farm. There was a late frost on March 18, which damaged the vegetable gardens. He and Mary went fishing in the evenings and caught large catfish. Some they would cure and some they would give away.

Noakes noted that the country was greatly excited by "murderous depredations" supposedly committed by Indians. One of James Bryden's shepherds had been killed and others refused to work. Noakes doubted the culprits were Indians "but one thing is certain — there are some very mean people about." (Corpus Christi's newspaper, the Ranchero, reported on March 16 that 20 Indians passed Bryden's ranch and killed one of his shepherds.)

On March 27, with a gray and misty fog, Noakes joined a large party of cattle hunters. They rode around the Encinal (near Flour Bluff) and along the Oso Creek, where they killed a yearling for their supper. Noakes later wrote about the excessive cruelty practiced by the cattle hunters. "A man must leave his feelings at home when he starts cattle hunting and all those with anything like a sensitive stomach had better not start."

When he got home, Noakes was tired, hungry and disappointed that Mary was off visiting her parents. The house seemed unfriendly and inhospitable.

*—July 22, 2015*

# War and Drought

Thomas J. Noakes, an Englishman who left home for Texas when he was 18, settled in the Motts, Henry Kinney's second town, formally known as Nuecestown.

Noakes went on a five-day cattle hunt in April 1861. It was freezing cold when the hunters rode down the Oso, around Turkey Creek, and passed through the Juan Saenz community.

When the weather improved, Noakes joined a grape-gathering excursion up the Nueces River. He noted that there had been no rain and the river was as salty as the bay. The news was not encouraging, Noakes wrote on May 3, with war and a blockade threatened "and the deuce knows what by the North." On May 6, Noakes attended a meeting at Ned Taylor's on devising measures for protection.

Corpus Christi intended to raise three companies, one of which would consist of 100 mounted riflemen. Noakes and 10 others from the Motts joined this company. Frank Byler was captain and Noakes was first lieutenant. The muster roll was dated June 14, 1861.

On July 2, Noakes noted that the country was in a deplorable state — "nothing but war to be heard on all sides. Trade is stopped and there is no money. I am expecting every day to be called out on military duty."

At the end of July 1861 Noakes dismantled his house in Corpus Christi and moved the lumber to the farm and began rebuilding the house. In his diary, he wrote: "I have received my commission as first lieutenant and am ready to serve my country."

Noakes received a letter ordering him to put the reserve company on a war footing. The captain of the company, Frank Byler, told him to put up notices informing the men to assemble at the Motts on Jan. 27, 1862. They went to Beeville in March to attend for instruction.

Noakes said wives of men who went to war would receive $10 a month and "Marie is satisfied for me to go." Noakes joined a regular

337

company — Capt. John Ireland's infantry company, composed of 120 ranchers and ranch hands (Company K, 8$^{th}$ Texas Infantry). On May 9 they marched into Corpus Christi through nearly empty streets "to a place above the town where a couple of deserters were hanging from a tree."

There is a gap in Noakes diary, from May 1862 until late 1863. Lost in that period are Noakes' observations of the battle of Corpus Christi and his painting of that battle. Noakes, as a member of Capt. Ireland's company, would have participated in the battle. Another gap extends from late 1864 until the summer of 1865 which included the end of the war.

On Christmas Day 1863 Noakes, on medical leave, and Marie visited his in-laws — he calls them the old folks — and had eggnog. They heard that Yankees had raided King Ranch.

Noakes went hunting on Dec. 29 and found a buck sleeping under a tree. He shot him in the head not to mar the hide. He looked so clearly dead, with a hole in his head, that Noakes didn't slit his throat. But when he took hold of his horns and started dragging him to an open space, the buck leaped up and ran away, leaving a vivid red blood trail but Noakes was unable to get him.

On Dec. 31, the weather was bitterly cold and the wind howled around Noakes' ears. He wrote that it was the last day of a miserable year, with clouds of black dust blowing with a strong wind. "The whole atmosphere was thick with sand and dust. We could barely hear ourselves speak for the strong wind. Our faces were black with dust and the floor covered with dust and sand. I sat by the fire mending Marie's shoes. The company that passed me the other evening took a person named (John) Dix prisoner, who had been a traitor and communicating with the Yankees. So ends another year."

On New Year's Day 1864 Noakes noted that water inside the house froze. He stayed in and boiled soap, the first he had made. He drove his cart to Ned Taylor's and borrowed two bushels of corn. On Jan. 5: "Exceedingly cold, ice all day. Water froze close to the fire. I put my horse in the old house to keep him from perishing."

Noakes counted 42 cows bogged in the river, mired in mud, too weak to pull out, and slowly dying. Noakes would often skin a dead animal for its hide, which he used for making saddles.

On Jan. 10, he noted that there was a lull in the excitement of the war — "It may be because of the excessive cold. From the long drought and the cold, the cattle are suffering tremendously. The *page 3.*

*October 1860*

Fri 5. I and Ned Taylor rode out to Banquette
Creek and I skinned at cow that have
die during the night.

Sat 6. I rode to Corpus and stop at Adams.
sold my horse cart to Cannon.

Sun 7. I settle with Cannon about the cart
and dine at Almonds. and after seeing
Adam again, I returned home.

Mon 8. At home most of day.

Tues 9. Geese, and Sand Hill Cranes. flying too
this week. the up country people were
down to the motts and we help them
round up their cattle.

Wed 10. Jobbing at home.

Thurs 11. Started to Corpus when about half way
it began a pour down rain for three
hours I took shelter in a new house belong to Mr Biller. after the rain I rode to
Adam and staid all night.

Fri 12 - I then went in city and did by busi
ul took dinner at Adam and returned
home.

Sat 13 - I busy myself at home.

*A copy of a page from one of Thomas Noakes' journals, from Oct. 5 to Oct. 15, 1860. Some entries in the diaries, especially when Noakes was ill, are not so legible.*

country is in a deplorable state for want of rain. Cattle and sheep are dying all over. No rain worth mentioning since last July, over six months. Dead animals meet your gaze in every direction, look which way you will."

A black man with a wagon pulled by mules camped at Noakes' place. The man had a fever and was too sick to travel. He urged Noakes to find someone to drive the wagon to Corpus Christi. Noakes took on the chore. The wagon was carrying the baggage of Henry A. Gilpin, chief justice of Nueces County, whom Noakes had known since he came to Texas. In thanks for bringing his baggage, Noakes had dinner with Gilpin and Edward Ohler and his wife. Gilpin gave him two dollars — "not as pay but as a present, as I would only agree to take them on that understanding."

On Jan. 27 Noakes killed a cow and gave half the meat to the Ludwigs. At the Motts every man was his own butcher and since one family could not eat a whole cow, some of the meat would be salted to preserve and other cuts would be given to neighbors.

At the end of January 1864, Noakes, not having a barrel to hold water, put up four posts and strung a deer hide between them to use as a waterproof sack to make soap. Noakes was good at everything to which he turned his hand, except making money.

*—July 29, 2015*

# Searching for Corn and Flour

A drought during time of war made for harsh conditions for Thomas John Noakes, a Confederate soldier on medical leave. On the last day of January 1864, Noakes wrote that the appearance of the country was desolate, with not a green thing to be seen. Strong winds blew dust and sand and covered everything. Thousands of dead and dying cattle lined the river and a foul stench afflicted the nostrils.

"I rode to one watering place where it was entirely blocked with bogged cattle, there being 27 in one bunch." At another spot, he counted 120, some dead, some alive. "If privation of every description and a dreary life devoid of pleasure would help a man to heaven, we stand a good chance of getting there."

Noakes killed a pig that was getting too big for the milk they had to give him. Capt. James Ware, a Confederate officer, came to look at Noakes' horse to see if he was fit to be confiscated for his cavalry company. Noakes didn't say whether Ware took the horse. He later walked to Judge Josiah Doak's to borrow an encyclopedia to read. He skinned hides he had left in the river to soak and killed and skinned a rattlesnake "nine inches longer than my arm and two inches across the eyes."

On Feb. 14, the weather was warm, with a wind from the south. "We get no mail now," wrote Noakes, "no news of the war." They were cut off from the world. John McClane offered him a job herding sheep on shares but he declined. Noakes heard rumors that the Yankees on Mustang Island, who made raiding forays to Corpus Christi, would visit the Motts. He buried his valuables and slept 300 yards from the house.

Noakes traveled far looking for corn, flour and whatever food he could trade for. He got cartloads of salt from the Laguna Madre and Baffin Bay, with written permission from the Confederate provost

341

marshal at Corpus Christi, Col. Charles Lovenskiold. Salt was a valuable commodity in the South's barter economy. These were hard trips for Noakes, who had a bad lung and spit up blood.

On Saturday, March 12, he and Ned Taylor were driving two carts to Goliad to get corn. At a steep hill by the Aransas River, Noakes had trouble with his horse Joe, who began bucking and pitching. Noakes was jerked out of the cart and both horses took off running wildly at top speed with the cart lurching behind them. Noakes was afraid it would be smashed.

He found the cart on its side, one wheel in the air, and Joe fastened to the shaft. Neither Joe nor the cart was damaged, but his grey horse was gone. Noakes found the grey horse five miles away. "I galloped back till I came to Ned's camp, cooked something to eat, tied up the harness with rawhide, and in one hour we were on the road again, but I tied Joe behind Ned's wagon."

They got corn and sweet potatoes in Goliad and Noakes traded his troublesome horse Joe for a work horse. They started for home and Noakes found his new horse worked fine. Near Refugio Noakes caught a rabbit in a tree hollow and they cooked it for supper.

The sky was turning red at sunset when Noakes reached home, on Sunday March 20, after a trip of 10 days. He found the house empty, his wife and son away at her parents. "All was dark and cold and miserable and I had to get into the house by prying one of the windows. I tended to the horses and, feeling very tired, laid down for a nap before making a fire and cooking supper."

Since he had been away, Noakes wrote, there had been a fight between Confederates and Union raiders. Noakes was referring to a skirmish at Los Patricios between Confederate Major Mat Nolan's men and Cecilio Balerio's irregular cavalry. Balerio's son was captured and under threat of death led Nolan and his men to his father's hideout 50 miles below Banquete. Balerio's men were defeated in the battle on March 13, 1864.

On another trip to Goliad at the end of March, Noakes and Ned Taylor cut down trees so their horses could eat the moss. "As soon as we began cutting down the trees, crowds of cattle came running up and only with great difficulty could we get any moss for our horses, as the starved cattle fairly took it by storm. We could not drive them away. Very sad."

They bought corn, had it ground into meal, and bought sweet potatoes. As they went through Goliad, Noakes bought 30 pounds of course sugar for $120 Confederate dollars. "The money I obtained over a year ago in payment for a horse and a yoke of work steers."

They returned home on April 5. Noakes was always put out when Marie was not there to welcome him after one of his trips, but this time he found her there, and it was a pleasure to come home and have someone there to look after him. "Everything was nice and satisfactory. After dinner I unloaded and skinned a dead calf."

The weather was dry and windy. Noakes, in his diary on April 10, wrote: "The state of the country is worse than it has been and our prospects blacken. The cattle must now be about two-thirds dead and the balance going fast. There is nothing here that is fit for food, either beef, mutton, or anything else." Finally, on April 13, Noakes was working on some hides and making a saddle when it rained, the water running like a river in the hollows. It rained again the next day and was so cold Noakes wore his greatcoat as he worked on rawhides.

The rain changed the looks of everything, with a cover of green spreading over the land. "Our prospects seem brightening," Noakes wrote, "as regards the war and the country. We now have every reason to hope that the Yankees are withdrawing from this part of Texas. Anyway, we hear nothing of them and most of the excitement of a short time back seems to have subsided."

*—Aug. 5, 2015*

# Square Buckets

Thomas John Noakes noted in his journal on April 24, 1864 that the weather was cool and everything green and beautiful. "I should think there was no country in the world that revives quicker after a rain than this."

On May 5, Noakes and his wife Marie and the baby (Thomas John Jr.) rode to Corpus Christi in the cart on a shopping trip. Noakes went to get some corn which he had loaned a man named Mussett and Marie went to get a mirror and a mattress. Noakes said Corpus Christi, strangled by the blockade and the war, was gone to ruin. Houses were empty, stores closed, and hardly a living soul was seen.

Because manufactured goods were almost impossible to buy, Noakes made "square buckets" of skins and made his own lye soap. He made shot to kill small game by beating lead into sheets and cutting it into small squares which he found "answers very well." He made iron staples out of wire to fix his cart and made his own sacks out of rawhide.

On another trip east to barter salt for corn, Noakes found the slaves at Clinton "perfectly contented with their lot and their master and having no desire to change either."

It rained on June 1 and the river was running fresh. Late in June, with the weather hot, Noakes and two friends went to the Salt Lagoon (Baffin Bay) to get salt. At West Oso they found a place where women were living without their husbands, Noakes said, who had deserted them and gone over to the Yankees. A child had died the night before and Noakes made a coffin while his friends dug a grave. They buried the child and headed home with the last of the light.

Noakes went to Corpus Christi on June 26 to get some sacks. He got the sacks, a little bread and black pepper, which they had not

345

had for a long time. He found Corpus Christi more desolate than ever. "The Yankees are preying on Confederate property and the Confederates are making a pounce on Yankee property. Furniture can be bought for a song."

On another food bartering trip in late July and early August, Noakes had 15 bushels of salt to trade. He found Beeville a deserted-looking place and Helena "tumbled-down-looking" with the men gone to war and farms abandoned. He liked Seguin and thought it lovely. The streets at New Braunfels were lined with chinaberry trees and the houses were clean with shady gardens. He walked all over New Braunfels trying to trade salt for flour. He found the prices high. "We had to pay 15 cents for a small glass of beer and everything else in proportion."

There was a little rain while they camped near Seguin. A school boy of about 11 stopped at their camp to get a chew of tobacco. "I remarked that he had commenced chewing early. He said he had chewed tobacco for four years. At recess he came again for another chew. (Henry) Stephens handed him the plug. He bit out a large mouthful, enough to make me sick in five minutes."

Back at home in September Noakes went to Banquete to get paid for one of his beeves killed to feed Confederate troops. Noakes thought the beef was worth $15 but he was paid $2. "That is the first pay I have had for several they killed. Before we were in any danger, we had to feed the soldiers with our beeves. As soon as danger threatened, we were abandoned. Now that we are once more out of danger, the troops are being sent back to live on our beeves again."

Noakes was ordered to report for duty to his company (John Ireland's old company K) that had been moved to Galveston. Noakes had been on extended sick leave. He went to Banquete where Dr. Eli Merriman examined him, found his right lung "useless" and gave him a certificate of disability.

On Sept. 21, the sun was very hot, but every so often there would be a cooling wind from the northeast — "our usual fall weather." At the end of September Noakes drew a sketch of their pet javelina, since he planned to kill him. He had become so savage toward strangers that only Noakes, Marie and the boy could go near him. Noakes' painting showed his son with the javelina.

On Oct. 28, Noakes wrote in his journal: "I took a ride up the river, giving myself a Texas holiday, which consists in riding a

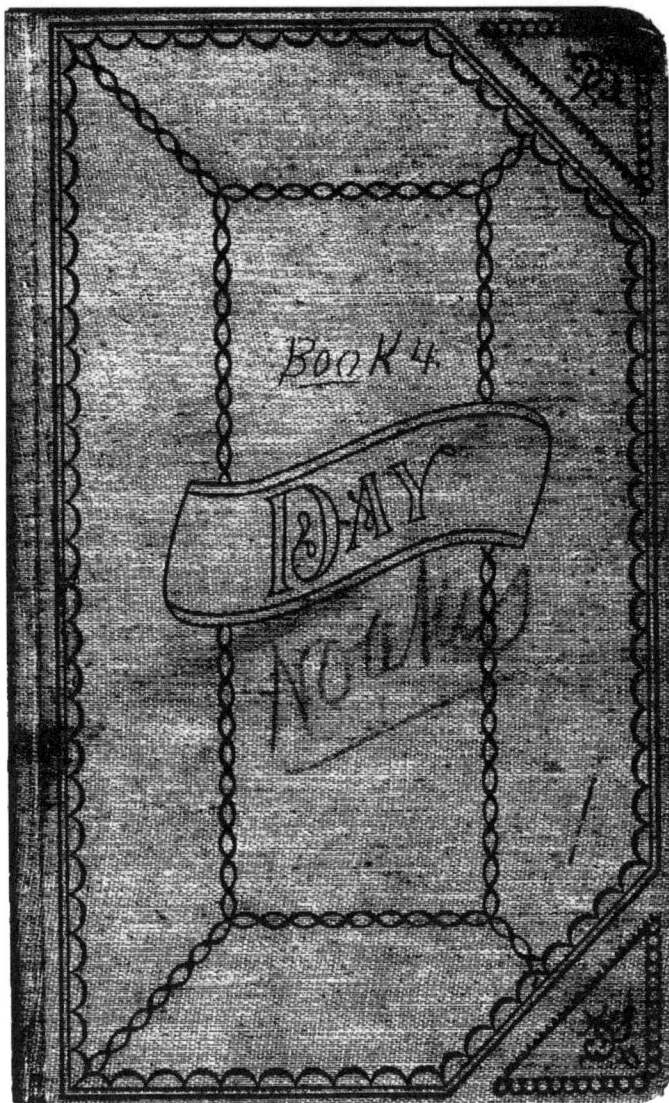

*The cover of one of Thomas Noakes' journals from the early 1860s. From the Corpus Christi Central Library.*

broken-down horse all day in search of game you never find and having nothing to eat." On Nov. 1, he was working on a saddle when he killed two large rattlesnakes. He took their fat, but having nothing to put it in, he skinned one of the snakes and turned it into a sack in which he brought home the fat.

That November, with winter in the air, Noakes worked on saddletrees he was covering with tanned leather. He thought that the prospects of the termination of the war were gloomy, that the war would go on and on. Were they never to know peace again? "It seems to be generally supposed that it will last another four years. If so, what will become of us?"

Noakes noted that an article in the paper said all men between the ages of 18 and 45 would have to report to the army, including those like Noakes with previous exemptions. Noakes' sentiments show how weary people were with Confederate conscription laws. "The war fiend," he wrote, "haunts every nook and cranny of the country and cannot rest when even the sick and broken-down are away from the horrid strife but must drag them from their ruined homes to perish from exposure and neglect."

On Dec. 2 Noakes, exhausted and weary of war, rode to the Confederate camp at Banquete to get his sick furlough extended. He moved his family from the Motts to a rented house in Corpus Christi before the end of the war. A gap in his journal extends from December 1864 to July 1865, which would have included the end of four years of war.

*—Aug. 12, 2015*

# Knuckling Under

In July 1865, with the weather fair and hot, Thomas Noakes and three others traveled to Padre Island to salvage a boat that was washed up on the beach. There was a man named Price, his brother-in-law named Hooper, and another man named Fields.

The weather was hot, with no breeze, when they reached the Curry settlement on the island. They shot a pig at Curry's deserted house and cooked it for breakfast. They saw 20 bales of cotton half buried in the sand.

They met William Murdock, whom Noakes described as a Yankee renegade, traveling in a light wagon pulled by steers. He told them the boat they were looking for was eight miles down the island. They found the boat and caulked it with cotton. They used driftwood to mend the hull and fashion a mast. Their food ran low and they were so tormented by mosquitoes they slept by the surf. Noakes and another man left on horseback while two others attempted to sail the repaired boat, which soon sank. "Like all my Texas trips," Noakes wrote, "the experience I gained was my only remuneration."

Back in Corpus Christi, Noakes heard the Yankees were in town and soon saw two regiments of black soldiers. "No one molested me and I rode straight to my yard."

On Thursday, July 20, Noakes stayed indoors writing in his journal. "The town is full of (black — Noakes used the "N" word) soldiers. I went into town, but there was nothing but (black) troops, turn which way I would." The next day Noakes was talking with W.N. Staples and other men about taking the oath required of former Confederates. "We came to the conclusion that, being whipped, we have to conform to their measure sooner or later and we considered it the best policy to do so at once. I went to the provost marshal's office and performed the ceremony." Humble acceptance, Noakes understood, was one of the requirements of defeat. They had to knuckle under.

Noakes, usually an active man, loafed around town, decorating street corners, and sometimes worked covering a saddle tree for Dr. Edward Britton, a former Confederate surgeon. Noakes noted that some black soldiers robbed Mrs. Swift's place and the Dunns' and that one of the Dunn boys caught one of the thieves and killed another.

The weather was hot and dry. Noakes bought a watermelon and took it home to eat. He was loafing away his time until he could figure out some way to use it. His ranch was deserted. "I would like to go to my place and see if I have anything in the shape of cattle left, but I have no horse and the cost of hiring one for that purpose will not pay."

Gen. Charles Russell, commander of the occupation forces at Corpus Christi, sent a request to see Noakes' painting of the battle of Corpus Christi. The painting was later returned with many thanks. Noakes went to see the black soldiers' dress parade and was surprised to see them drill so well.

On Aug. 9, Noakes prepared to move back to the farm. He engaged a team and wagon driven by a man called Uncle Ned to move their furniture and furnishings to the Motts. Noakes said they had the house and shed cleaned and everything in place by sundown.

Back at the farm Noakes took no pleasure in the resumption of his everyday chores. He confronted the same routine — "working, working, poor living, ragged clothes, no comfort, no pleasure, no security, no refinement, and no hope for anything better." He tried to get a clerk's job in Corpus Christi but it was already filled. He was then approached about teaching school.

George Reynolds asked him to teach school at the Motts. Noakes went to Corpus Christi to see William Carroll, a teacher at Hidalgo Seminary, and Carroll explained how he organized his lessons and Noakes spent a day observing Carroll's class. Noakes went to see Ned Taylor, the former teacher at Nuecestown, to borrow a blackboard, which Noakes made for him five years before.

Noakes began teaching on Oct. 1. He found his students eager to learn and had less trouble with them than expected. But the schoolhouse was a wreck, with the windows gone, sashes and all. After a day's teaching, Noakes had chores to do until dark, such as rounding up cows, butchering meat, digging a well, tanning a hide. He settled into his new pursuit and noted that teaching required more patience than education.

On Nov. 17 a freezing norther blew in. With the windows of the school out, it was very cold, even with a fire, and Noakes sent the students home. On Saturday he fixed the windows of the schoolhouse.

When Noakes' friend John Williams died, he expected to be named executor of the estate, which would entitle him to a percentage of the sale. But George Reynolds and James Bryden sought and got it. Bryden and Reynolds were close friends of long standing, but Noakes was furious, writing that "they hate to see me make a cent" and speculated that they wanted to keep him near starving to get their children educated. (In time, Noakes lost his resentment and again became friendly with Bryden and Reynolds.)

On Dec. 22, Noakes, in an unsettled temper, gave up his post as schoolteacher and said farewell to his students. "I did intend to say more, but so many sorrowful faces being turned on me at the same time quite unmanned me. I thanked them for their attention during the short time we had been together."

He rode into Corpus Christi to buy groceries, paying 60 cents for a pound for coffee, 50 cents for a pound for sugar, and $1 for a small tin of peaches — "those things being considered the height of luxury."

Noakes was in a despairing mood on Christmas Day, with no glad tidings of comfort and joy. He summed up his teaching experience. His income for the year did not exceed $4 and he noted that, "The only gain I made has been confined to experience and that may be good pay for future purposes, but it's a very poor article to live on."

*—Aug. 19, 2015*

# Bandit Raid

In January 1866, after giving up as a school teacher, Thomas John Noakes worked around the farm cutting firewood. They had been tearing down a fence to burn. On a trip to Corpus Christi he noted that most of the colored troops had been withdrawn and the town began to look like it did before the war.

On Feb. 5, with it too cold to work outside, Noakes showed Marie how to make a Sussex beef pudding, the first they had had since they were married.

He finished writing a song about the battle of Corpus Christi called the Two Twelve-Pounders and received a letter from his brother Edmund, who lived in Mobile, Ala., about his visit to England. Noakes, who had not set eyes on his native land for 20 years, intended to the save the letter until he got home but he stopped on the way and read it. He read it more times at home.

In early June, Noakes went on a cattle hunt and when he returned home he found that Marie, besides attending three horses, a mule, cows and pigs, made a pig pen and a hen house out of old fence pickets. They got a hog and three hens and Noakes noted that they were getting an extensive establishment.

He was in a gloomy mood on Christmas. Marie was staying with her mother and Noakes wrote that there was nothing he hated more than being alone. He bought some oysters and had an eggnog with Harry Coling and John Hinnant on Christmas Day.

It was a blowing a gale on New Year's Day 1867 and freezing cold inside, even with a blazing fire. About noon it began to sleet and from that to snow. At dusk everything was white. The river froze with ice nearly an inch thick.

Noakes mailed a letter to his mother, with power of attorney to sell land he owned. He made shoes for his sons out of his own dressed leather. On March 24, Noakes killed a calf whose mother had died in the river "to keep it and ourselves from starving" and divided it among the neighbors. During the night of June 2, mosquitoes stampeded Noakes' horses. Even his grey colt, tied to a log, ran off dragging the log behind him.

What we have left of Noakes' diary ends on June 18, 1867 with the notation that he was engaged in doing the same chores "as every other day." Noakes' first journal, which covered his early years in Corpus Christi from 1848 through 1867, was lost. So was his last journal or journals, which no doubt included entries from the summer of 1867 until his death. Several of his journals were believed burned in the the Nuecestown Raid on Easter weekend 1875.

How and when Noakes opened a store would have been detailed in that last diary. This is rank speculation, but perhaps when Noakes sold land he had inherited in England he used the proceeds to finance opening a store at the Motts. An ad in the Weekly Gazette in 1873 said, "Thomas J. Noakes, Dealer in General Merchandise, Nuecestown, Texas. Wool and Hides taken in Trade or for Cash."

It was a well-established store when it was burned in the bandit raid that began in the last week of March 1875. A bunch of 33 bandits from below the border stole horses at ranches near Tule Lake and took captives they encountered on the road. They robbed Frank's store at the Juan Saenz community and killed an old man who recognized one of them.

When Noakes saw the bandits ride up in front of his store, and saw some of his friends being held captive, he got his Winchester. As a bandit raised his pistol to shoot a man named Smith, a customer in the store, Noakes shot the bandit in the chest. Noakes' wife Mary ran from the store with their five children.

Noakes scuttled through a trap door and hid in a tunnel under the store. The bandits plundered the store then started a fire. Mary, who returned after seeing the children to safety, poured water on it. Several times a bandit started a fire only to have her put it out before the flames took hold.

With the store on fire, Noakes left his hiding place and had his rifle ready to fire when Mrs. Noakes yelled that the bandits were gone. She ran inside the burning store (they lived above) to save a prized featherbed, a sewing machine and several of Noakes' journals. Noakes thought it funny that she rescued the featherbed while leaving more valuable possessions behind.

*The burning of Noakes' store in the Nuecestown Raid as shown in John B. Dunn's book "Perilous Trails of Texas." Noakes rebuilt the store, but died not long afterwards.*

But the sight of his burning store was not so funny. "I had to stand and watch the huge tongues of flames shoot heavenward, knowing they were licking the fruits of ten years' toil and everything, except ourselves, that I valued in the world."

Noakes rebuilt his store, two miles from the original site. He died in 1878 and was buried on the family farm. (The details of his death are not known; Corpus Christi newspaper archives are missing for that year.) Sometime after the raid, he buried a large cache of money. He told no one where it was buried, not even Maria. For years, holes were dug and blisters earned but his money cache was never found. Mary (Marie) Ludwig Noakes remarried, to a man named Walter Hipp, and had two more children.

The Noakes Diaries provide a detailed look at life in South Texas before and after the Civil War. Thomas John Noakes and his neighbors at the Motts endured unrelenting hardship, coping with the miseries of drought, flood, pestilence and danger during times of war, occupation and reconstruction.

*—Aug. 26, 2015*

# To Dump Road

Anyone who drives down South Staples, say, from Kinney Avenue to Six Points, will pass run-down, boarded-up storefronts and the used car lots protected by chain-link fences. It's as attractive as a mouth full of rotten teeth. You wonder if any city plan of tax credits and incentives can ever reverse the decline of what used to be a vibrant commercial street.

The glory days of South Staples date from the time the city began to spread out from downtown and uptown, outward growth that started the decline of downtown and uptown. Businesses moved out and blight moved in.

In a brief review of the history of Staples Street, we can't list all the business places that lined this street but we can choose a few between Kinney Avenue, where South Staples begins, to Six Points.

The street was named for Wayman Staples, who came from Alabama and opened a store in Corpus Christi before the Civil War. He was elected mayor after the war. Parts of Staples had other names. North of Railroad Avenue (now Kinney) was Black Street, now North Staples. Beyond Six Points was Colorado Avenue and past that was Dump Road.

In the first block, past the Tex-Mex tracks, was a two-story brick building constructed in 1925. The old building is still there. It once housed Kardell's Pharmacy then McNabb's Liquor Store. At the end of the block, at Laredo, the Meuly Building was known as Carpenter's Hall and later occupied by Guess Lighting.

The first known business on S. Staples was a grocery store at the corner of Laredo owned by John and Elife Behmann. This was sometime after 1907. The Behmann's sons, Arno and Herman, took over the business. A story about the Behmanns in 1992 said they were known to provide credit to farmers in hard times. The store was closed in the late 1940s and the building occupied by Guarantee

Hardware. The Behmann Brothers Foundation was established in 1981 and, according to that 1992 story, quietly dispersed $2.2 million to worthy causes.

KC Barbecue and Eastern Seed Company was also in the 300 block. Vicente Lozano opened a general merchandise store on Mesquite before he relocated to the corner of Staples and Agnes in 1913. The 400 block of South Staples became the Lozano block.

The Lozano family moved to Corpus Christi after a hurricane hit Bagdad, Mexico in 1891. In Corpus Christi, Vicente Lozano worked as a fisherman and would sell his catch to the chef at the St. James Hotel. He opened his store on Mesquite in 1902, one story said, with $20 worth of borrowed stock. He built a new store on Staples in 1913. This was the second store on Staples, after Behmann's Grocery. One of Vicente's sons, Gabe, later became the city's first Hispanic mayor.

The Lozano building was built on the site of the old store. It opened in 1941 and housed Doctor's Pharmacy. Corpus Christi's first TV station, KVDO, began broadcasting in 1954 from the Lozano building. Down the street was Lozano's Café, run by Maria Lozano after her husband Manuel died.

Past the Marguerite intersection was the High Hat Drive-In. It opened in 1939 and lasted until the 1950s when it was torn down and Suniland Furniture built on the site. Across the street was Guy's Food Store, which became Peterson's Grocery in 1948. The Blue Bonnet Café was in this block.

In the 600 block was Mrs. Ira Holly's beauty salon. Down the street was the old William Petzel home. In the next block was Piggly Wiggly No. 2, operated by the H. E. Butt Grocery Company. That building, at 817 S. Staples, later became the City Bowling Parlor.

In the 900 block, at the intersection with Furman, stands the old Church of Christ, built in 1920. Forty years later, the congregation moved out to Weber Road and the old church was occupied by several businesses. It's in bad condition today. Across the street was Currie Seed & Nursery and in the next block was Emil Biel's Grocery No. 3.

Between Craig and Morgan on the east side was the Oriental Laundry, which moved from Third Street to the Staples-Morgan corner in the 1940s. The old building still stands, occupied today by a recording studio.

*Guy's Food Store was on the right in the 500 block of South Staples. Photo by Doc McGregor.*

*Road work was underway on South Staples, past the Six Points intersection, with Pat Limerick's grocery store on the right. Photo by Doc McGregor.*

Past the Booty intersection was the Orchard Building, which housed a cleaner's and Paul's Beauty Salon. Down the block was

Six Points Grocery, run by B. E. Cudd. This building later became Six Points Hardware.

At the intersection of Staples and Ayers was Limerick's Food Store, built in 1937. This marked the beginning of Six Points as a viable commercial center.

In a story in 1959, Pat Limerick recalled that he came to Corpus Christi in July 1937 on vacation. While here he made arrangements for a building to be erected at Six Points. He returned to Moline, Ill., and resigned his job with Shell Oil. "By the time I got back here in October, the building was nearly finished and we opened that month."

People told Limerick he was crazy to open a store so far out of town. "It's so far out in the country. Why put a grocery store out there?" When the store was closed in 1959, Limerick said, "It's breaking my heart to close it. It's the oldest store at Six Points."

Past Limerick's was open country where cows grazed and cotton grew. Limerick's was squeezed between Ayers and Colorado Avenue. In 1942, the City Council changed Colorado Avenue to South Staples. The road leading out of town, the old Chapman Ranch Road, was called Dump Road. It got that name from the Ropes boom, when E. H. Ropes planned to build a railroad to the south. Ties and rails were trucked out past Colorado Avenue and dumped, thus Dump Road. It's all Staples now.

From Kinney Avenue to Six Points, South Staples today is a sad street that has gone to ruin. It would not be on any tour guide's list of places to see. You think it could be revitalized if we got the right mix of enlightened decision-making at City Hall and intrepid businessmen willing to take a risk. The rejuvenation of Six Points, if it holds out, offers some frail hope for that stretch of Staples Street.

*—Sept. 2, 2015*

# Out By Pancho Grande's

A former slave named Hattie Littles once recalled that Leopard Street was a white shell road used by farmers and ranchers coming to town. Leopard was one of Corpus Christi's first streets, named by Henry Kinney, probably from cougars that people back then called leopards or panthers. All the area around Leopard was referred to as "the Hill." Much of Leopard was dirt or shell until 1930 when the city paved it to Palm Drive.

Leopard's great heyday began in 1927. Maston Nixon, a former Robstown cotton farmer, bought the old Meuly site at Leopard and Broadway, an empty lot where youngsters went to fly kites. On this site Nixon built the city's largest office building, the 12-story Nixon Building. The Nixon venture set off a building boom for that end of Leopard. Robert Driscoll built the Corpus Christi Bank & Trust at Leopard and Tancahua. Perkins Brothers built its store on the old Russell Savage homestead at Carancahua.

The Plaza Hotel was built in 1929 across from the Nixon building. Corpus Christi's first radio station, KGFI, broadcast from the hotel. It did not have a transmitting tower but used wires strung across Leopard from the Plaza to the Nixon building. Whenever the city scored some civic triumph a green flag was flown from between the two buildings. This was the center of town, where the green flag flew.

The Perkins Brothers department store was built in 1929 at the corner of Carancahua. Perkins was sold to Lichtenstein's in 1955 and became Lichtenstein's Uptown store. The Perkins' stockroom was said to be a veritable time capsule filled with old merchandise, like ladies button-up shoes.

In the 800 block, at Tancahua, was the Corpus Christi Bank & Trust. Clara Driscoll, ranch heiress and savior of the Alamo, managed the Driscoll estate from an office in this building. Nearby was the Little Mexican Inn run by Mrs. Reyes Ibarra. Across the street was Abraham Wolfson's Furniture Store.

In the early part of the century, Conrad Uehlinger's confectionary was at 902 Leopard. The Braslau brothers had two stores in the 900 block, a furniture store and a dry goods store. The Braslaus sold the dry goods store in 1942 and concentrated on their furniture business, which they moved to the Grande block. Stein's Dry Goods moved into the old Braslau furniture store and the Blanck brothers moved into the dry goods store. Across the street was San Jacinto Hardware.

Between Artesian and Waco, at 1002 Leopard, was Edward and Simon Grossman's department store. The Grossmans sold out in 1948 and moved out to Port. Next door was Sam Salem's Grocery, one of the first grocery stores on Leopard. Sugar and lard and other staples came in barrels and coffee was ground in the store. Across the street was Braslau's relocated furniture store.

The 1000 block featured two theaters, the Melba and the Grande. When the Melba opened in 1927 it was initially called the Leopard Street Theater and featured a tile mosaic of a crouching leopard in the entrance. Across the street, the Grande Theater was built in the mid-1930s.

Frank Grande's saloon was on the corner with Waco, a landmark on the street dating back to the 1880s. Hattie Littles said people would give directions by saying "out by Pancho Grande's." The Grande was Corpus Christi's most famous saloon, where a cowboy could ride up on his horse and get a drink while still sitting in the saddle and where cockfights were held in the courtyard behind the saloon.

When Frank Grande died in 1905 his son Ben took over and the saloon became known as the Ben Grande. During Prohibition it was a grocery store and other businesses located in the building. It was torn down in 1950. A new Braslau furniture store was later built on the site of the old Grande Saloon.

The Acebo home sat diagonally across the intersection from the Grande. This was later the site of Woolworths. Down the block was Joseph's Economy Store. Across the street was Juan Galvan's Pharmacy on the Johnny Blain corner, where the old Blain's store once stood.

Two blocks down was Dunn's Grocery, later Thomas Whelan's. The Chat N Chew, which opened in 1935, was down the block from

*Street scene of the 900 block of Leopard, looking east. On the right was San Jacinto Hardware and on the left was Braslau's Dry Goods, which later became Blanck Brothers Dry Goods. Photo by Doc McGregor.*

*Street scene of the 1000 block of Leopard, between Artesian and Waco. On the left was the Melba Theater, at 1016, and on the right was Braslau's Furniture, at 1001. The Melba was first the Leopard Street theater, built in 1927. Photo by Doc McGregor.*

Whelan's. A story in 1984 said the owners, Maudie and O. V. Jackson, got the name from a café they ate at in Alhambra, Calif. Past Chat N Chew, on the corner, was Bunk's Café, owned by Bunk Spence and known for its chicken-fried steak and five-cent hamburgers. Across the street from Bunk's were Cudd's Grocery and Sears, where City Hall is today.

City limits then extended to Palm Drive by Holy Cross and Rose Hill cemeteries. People going to Robstown turned left at Palm Drive, skirted Holy Cross and took Shell Road to the Old Robstown Road. Here, at the edge of town, Corpus Christi High School was built in 1929, on Palmer Street, later changed to Fisher and still later to Battlin' Buc Boulevard.

Where Shell Road (UpRiver now) crosses Leopard was the Fred Roberts Memorial Hospital, later renamed the Ghormley Hospital. By 1945, a dirt road connected the end of Leopard to Highway 9, where road-house bars and dance halls (Continental Tavern and Good Time Charlie's) were located, outside city limits.

In the 1960s, some businessmen lobbied to change the name of Leopard to Main Street, but the city chose not only to keep Kinney's historic old name but to extend Leopard Street all the way to Calallen, supplanting Highway 9 within the city.

Much of Leopard is in chronic decline, with boarded-up storefronts and closed businesses, like Staples between City Hall and Six Points. In its glory days, in the 1930s and 1940s, Leopard was a busy street, especially on a Saturday in cotton-picking season when it was always packed with families shopping in town. Back then, Leopard Street could have given Chaparral a good argument over which was the center of town. It was main street in all but name only.

*—Sept. 9, 2015*

# Downtown, A Special Place

People have fond memories of Shoop's Grill and the Pier Cafe but I am not one of them. I got here too late for that. When these restaurants were open the downtown must have been a very lively place, with a bustle and a busyness that hasn't been seen for many years. That busy period lasted from 1926, when the port opened, until around the end of the 1940s. The decline began, I suppose, sometime in the 1950s.

I spent several days looking over photos of downtown restaurants and cafes from the 1930s and 1940s, mostly. The most famous of that era — the Pier Café and Shoop's Grill — are fondly remembered by many. There were many others. For a short review of the popular eating establishments of that period, let's start with Water Street and proceed to Chaparral and Mesquite.

In the early 1940s the Purple Cow was on the south end of Water Street. A few years ago someone wrote me about this drive-in cafe. "I remember when we moved here we'd tell our friends to come visit Corpus Christi, the only town with a pink hotel (the Princess Louise) and a purple cow." On that site today is the U&I Restaurant. Another drive-in, the Playhouse, was at 509 S. Water. It was operated by George Zackie.

At 200 North Water was the new Shoop's Grill. The first Shoop's opened near the Princess Louise, then Bob Shoop moved to the new location, at Water and Laguna (now Sartain), around 1939 or 1940. At Shoop's Grill back then you could order a roast prime rib dinner for 75 cents or you could get a Shoop Steak dinner Ben Bennie for $1. It may seem cheap by comparison to today's prices but during the Depression it was a pricey meal. Shoop's old site is now a parking lot across the street from the Education Service Center.

Two blocks down was the Blackstone Café run by Elsie Black. Years before, this was the old Elite Café.

At 524 N. Water, at the foot of the Pleasure Pier and just across from the Nueces Hotel, was perhaps the city's most famous restaurant, John Govatos' Pier Café. Govatos came from the small Greek seacoast village of Metamorfosis with his brother Clem and his cousin John Nicols.

John Govatos bought the Pier Café in 1926. It was moved to the south side of the Pleasure Pier and remodeled several times. It provided a good view of the bay, fishermen on the pier and the famous three palms in the Nueces Hotel garden. At the Pier Café in 1939, a special seafood dinner, with shrimp, crab or oyster cocktail and broiled redfish, trout, or fried shrimp in butter sauce, cost 85 cents. And the quality, it was said, was always superb. When the Pleasure Pier was dismantled and the seawall was built, the Pier Café, away from the water's edge, lost its allure and John Govatos moved up to the Nixon Café on the bluff with John Nicols.

At Water Street and Taylor was Kyle Dowdy's A&W Root Beer and hamburger stand. Dowdy was credited with opening the town's first drive-in, next to the bascule bridge, in 1926.

The Ship Ahoy restaurant opened in 1942, as best as I can tell, in the old Shoop's Grill building at 1017 N. Water, at the intersection with Mann. The owner, M. J. Frangos, said it was named in honor of the new naval air station. A second Ship Ahoy was opened at 6102 Ocean Drive in 1965. In later years the downtown Ship Ahoy boasted on its menu "The Best Seafood Restaurant in the World." It closed in 1992.

A few blocks down on Water Street were the Lighthouse Restaurant, Roy's Drive-In, and Rose Baggett's Orange Café.

Chaparral Street had several well-known eating places. Douglass Eat-A-Bite and the Stag Buffet were in the 300 block, the Busy Bee Café was in St. James building, and the old Oil City Cafe was on the corner of Schatzel.

Down the street past the Nueces Hotel, on the west side of the block, was Ben Garza's Metropolitan Café. On Feb. 17, 1929, Garza hosted a sunrise breakfast meeting at this café for Mexican-American leaders from Corpus Christi, San Antonio and elsewhere in South Texas. They agreed at this meeting to form a new organization to pursue equality for Mexican-Americans. They met later at Obreros Hall to confirm the agreement. This was the beginning of the League of United Latin American Citizens. Garza later sold the restaurant after he came down with tuberculosis.

*The Oil City Café, in its short existence in the early 1930s, occupied the corner location in the Rankin Building. This was the site of the old Westervelt store at Chaparral and Schatzel. Photo by Doc Mcgregor.*

*Looking south down Chaparral. The Mayflower Café (on the left) was on the corner of Chaparral and Starr across from J. C. Penney's and south of the Rio Theater. It was on the site of the old Cooper's Clean Bakery. Photo by Doc McGregor.*

The Mayflower Café was on the site of the Cooper's Clean Bakery, at Chaparral and Starr, across from Penney's. The building was remodeled in 1941 to house K. Wolen's Department Store. In the next block was the White Kitchen Café, started by George Tahinakos, another Greek immigrant.

At the Mann intersection was Pete's Inn, later the L&G Café. It was a block west of the Princess Louise. In that same block was the Rainbow Café in the old Boyd's Drugstore building. Near the Bascule Bridge was a Pig Stand, one of several in the city.

In the 300 block of Mesquite Street was Angela Chapa's café, later named the Black Gold Café, and past Lichtenstein's Mesquite Street entrance was the Victory Café. William Radeker in his memoirs (Central Library) recalled that a patriotic waitress at the Victory had been a nurse in World War I and wore her sergeant's stripes on her waitress uniform.

The Alcove Coffee Shop, across Mesquite Street from City Hall, stood next to the McCampbell building. Agnes Kelley once recalled that when her husband ran the old Alcove "the firemen used to come over for coffee and they called my husband 'Alcove Kelley.' "

Past the Amusu Theater was the Southern Café and the Club Café was across the street. Other restaurants on Mesquite included Bennie's Café, the Rendezvous Grill, Mack's Café, and the lunch counter at the Boucher Pharmacy in the Furman Building.

On Peoples Street, across from the Nueces Hotel, was George Plomarity's Manhattan Café. Plomarity, another Greek immigrant, started the café in 1927.

There were other famous restaurants from that era outside the downtown, including Sheffield's Grill on North Beach and the Dragon Grill, where you could get a fancy meal, with lobster flown in from Maine, and lose your shirt. Looking at Doc McGregor photographs from the 1930s and 1940s one can see this was a special place back then. The downtown was the living, breathing, vibrant center of Corpus Christi.

—Sept. 15, 2015

# A Lone Survivor

If there was ever a center of Corpus Christi, it was on Upper Broadway at the corner of Blucher, what used to be Chatham Street. This was where Henry Kinney built his home in 1839.

J. Williamson Moses, an old Ranger, told of the time when an unruly mob of filibusters called "buffalo hunters" camped on Padre Island in 1848. They planned to invade Mexico to set up a republic. Their plans fell apart and they decided to rob Kinney.

As Moses tells it, they heard Kinney had $10,000 at his house on the bluff. When they marched to his place, they were met by Rangers commanded by Capt. John Sutton. The "buffalo hunters" were persuaded to leave quietly. About this time, Kinney brought in a well-digger from Alabama, J. M. Cooper, who lived in Kinney's house while digging wells on Kinney's ranches.

When Kinney hosted the Lone Star Fair in 1852, he brought in a band from New Orleans that played every night in front of his house, as guests sipped cocktails and listened to the music.

Kinney was shot to death in Matamoros in 1862 on a midnight visit to his former mistress. After his death, his home on the bluff sat vacant. On Jan. 9, 1874, the City Council discussed "the unsightly and dangerous old Kinney house." It was soon dismantled.

Hamilton Bee, a Confederate general known more for retreating than for fighting, built a home on that site. Anna Moore Schwien, a former slave, said Bee lived there until he moved the family to San Antonio. Behind the Bee home was Charles Lovenskiold's place on North Carancahua.

Alice Lovenskiold Rankin said, "East of us was where Kinney lived. The Bees built a house on that corner. It was brick in the lower part and lumber in the upper." She recalled a high brick wall between their house and the Bee's place. Some thought it had been built in Kinney's time, but she thought it was put up by Bee.

John S. Givens, an attorney (no relation to me), bought the place and added a second story. Givens came from Oakville. He was the prosecutor in the Chipita Rodriguez trial, in which she was found guilty of killing a horse trader and later hanged.

Givens sold the home to Atlee McCampbell. Coleman McCampbell, author of a history of Corpus Christi, was born here. It was turned into an apartment house then torn down to make way for the Southwestern Bell Telephone building.

Next to the Kinney site was Forbes Britton's house, built in 1848-1849. After Britton graduated from West Point in 1834 he was assigned to move Indians from their ancestral homes in Georgia and Alabama to Indian Territory on the "Trail of Tears."

Britton was at Corpus Christi with Zachary Taylor and fought in the Mexico War. One of his friends was war correspondent George Wilkins Kendall. They would drink warm champagne from a tin cup. Britton returned to Corpus Christi after the war and engaged in the wool, hide and commission business.

In an interview in 1939, Anna Moore Schwien said her mother told her that when she arrived as a slave on Jan. 1, 1849, Britton's house was being built. Britton, elected to the Texas Senate, went to Austin for a special session in February 1861. He died of pneumonia on Feb. 14, 1861.

The Britton home passed through several owners. It was owned by Judge Pat O'Docharty, Morris Levy, J. M. Howell, James Bryden and George Evans. Evans had it the longest, from 1882 to 1936, and it was known as the George Evans home. In 1949, they started calling it the Centennial House. It is still there, a lone survivor.

North of Britton's was a house owned by the Cook family. Anna Moore Schwien recalled that "Mrs. Cook died there and soon after Mr. Cook died, leaving two children, Cora and Jack. These two children were taken in by Mr. and Mrs. Richard Power, who lived across the street and had no children of their own. Cora Cook taught school here after the Civil War."

The old Cook property was bought by Daniel Dowd who sold it to Mifflin Kenedy. It was said that Kenedy wanted to build his home at the corner of Leopard and Broadway, but the owners wouldn't sell for what Kenedy wanted to pay. So he bought the old Cook/Dowd property at Lipan and Broadway.

Kenedy built his home in 1885. It was described as an Italianate villa painted in three shades of olive green. It had a 65-foot tower

370

*Forbes Britton's home, known as Centennial House, shown in 1935, was built in 1849. Photo by Doc McGregor.*

*Mifflin Kenedy's Italianate mansion was built in 1885 and dismantled in 1937.*

above the roof line. It was designed by an English architect, Alfred Giles. The house, as described, had alternating projections and recesses of porches and bay windows to reflect patterns of light and shadow at different times of the day.

The interior was finished with walnut, oak, mahogany, cherry and cypress. The trim on the grand stairway was polished mesquite that came from the Kenedy ranch. Acetylene gas was produced in a small building in the back for the 200 gas lights in the mansion. The Caller in an article on March 8, 1885 said, "The residence is one of most complete in the state, and is furnished with all the modern improvements that can make a home comfortable."

The house was completed three weeks before Mifflin's wife Petra died in 1885. After her death, his adopted daughter, Carmen Morell Kenedy moved into the mansion and kept house for him.

Kenedy died in the mansion in 1895, following a heart attack. After Carmen Morell Kenedy died in 1899, Mifflin Kenedy's daughter, Sarah Josephine, and her husband, Dr. Arthur Spohn, moved into the house.

There must have been a few stray cattle roaming around. Dr. Spohn, it was said, had the trees wrapped in barbed wire to keep cattle from rubbing up against them. I guess that's true. Another resident once recalled that a young man, dressed up for a dance, bumped into a cow on a dark downtown street. Several families kept milk cows pastured near the old Fullerton house, where the First Presbyterian Church is now.

The Mifflin Kenedy mansion was torn down in 1938 and the salvaged materials taken to the Kenedy ranch at Sarita.

*—Sept. 22, 2015*

# The Cattle Queen's Mansion

When the cattle barons built their homes on the bluff, North Broadway became Corpus Christi's most stylish address, before there was an Ocean Drive.

Across Lipan Street on North Broadway were two cottages owned by Judge Dickie Power. The judge lived in the corner cottage. Eli Merriman said Dickie Power wrote poems and that many of them "were just splendid." His home on the bluff, Merriman said, "had little bitty windows on account of the Indians."

On the site of the second cottage was where Martha Rabb built her home. John Rabb, a former Confederate cavalry officer, died on April 15, 1872 and his widow Martha took over the ranch, which consisted of 10,000 cattle on the open range. She began to buy land and soon had 30,000 acres of enclosed pasture in Nueces County. She smoked little black cigars called cheroots and was called the Cattle Queen of Texas.

Martha Rabb built her home, which she called the Magnolia Mansion, in 1875. She clearly had it built as a display of grandeur. When she married the Rev. C. M. Rogers, they moved to Austin and she sold the home to David Hirsch. He in turn sold it to Mifflin Kenedy who bought it for his son, John G. Kenedy. The house was used as a temporary hospital in the wake of the 1919 storm. In 1925 it was given to the Catholic Church and used as a parochial school.

When Mifflin Kenedy's home was torn down in 1937, the old Magnolia Mansion was moved across Lipan to that site. It was torn down in 1952. On the old site of the Magnolia Mansion the new cathedral was built.

Richard King, Texas' most famous cattleman, died at the Menger Hotel in San Antonio on April 14, 1885. Eight years after King's death, Henrietta King built a mansion on the bluff, just north of Martha Rabb's old Magnolia Mansion, with a good view of the whole sweep of the bay. The turreted and gingerbread-trimmed home was built on the site where, long ago, William Mann's home stood.

Living with Henrietta King in the mansion were her daughter and her husband, Robert J. Kleberg Sr., and their five children. As related in "King Ranch," Mrs. King would get the newspaper first in the morning, read all the news, and sit on the paper in her rocking chair. She would play a guessing game with members of the family about who was getting married or whatever news was in the paper.

The bluff before the balustrade was built was a slippery slope. In front of the King mansion were wooden steps with a hand railing that led down the hill. In an interview in 1961, Miss Amelia Daimwood recalled "having to climb the old wooden steps in front of the King-Kleberg home to get to the original wooden church (Presbyterian) on the bluff."

When President William Howard Taft visited Corpus Christi on Nov. 22, 1909, Henrietta King hosted a lunch for him. Knowing his reputation for enjoying a good meal, she had a 60-pound turkey sent from Cuero for the main course.

The old King/Kleberg mansion was dismantled in 1945 after the Corpus Christi diocese acquired the site.

North of the King/Kleberg mansion and past the Mestina intersection was Charles and Sarah Weil's home, where they raised 11 children. The illustrious Weil family owned a general mercantile store and later a grocery store and ranch in Starr County. They first lived on Chaparral then moved to the bluff. An old interview said the Weil children went to school by crossing through their back yard to the school buildings on Carancahua. The boys played baseball and flew kites on the empty lot where the Meuly house once stood.

Sometime after the turn of the century the Weils moved into a new home on South Broadway. I think the old Weil place was later the home of L. M. Thomas, who owned Thomas' Model Pharmacy. The Weil home was next to where the Show Room of Finer Furniture was built. There's a parking lot there now.

At Leopard and Broadway was the Fitzgerald home, which was later owned by the Meuly family. Their original home, called the house with the iron front, was on Chaparral. The house on the bluff was vacant at the end of the Civil War. When Corpus Christi was occupied by Union regiments designated as United States Colored Troops, the Meuly house was ransacked by these troops. A news-

*The John G. Kenedy home, which was Martha Rabb's old mansion, after it was moved across Lipan to the site formerly occupied by Mifflin Kenedy's home. Photo by Doc McGregor.*

*Henrietta King's home was built in 1893 and used as the winter home of the Kleberg family. It was taken down in 1945.*

paper report at the time said they pulled out furniture and fixtures, including a rosewood piano, to use as firewood. Margaret Meuly filed a claim for damages.

One of the more sensational murders of the 1860s occurred in this house. Anna Moore Schwien in her memoirs, Mary Sutherland in "The Story of Corpus Christi," and John Dunn in "Perilous Trails of

Texas," wrote about this crime. Two drifters (we would call them homeless today) were living in the Meuly place. One, an ex-soldier, found odd job on the docks. The other, described as "an old Mexican," cooked for the ex-soldier for part of his wages. They had a falling out and the ex-soldier was brutally stabbed to death, his body left in a closet. The killer was a little crazy and died in jail before he could be hanged.

The old Fitzgerald/Meuly house was torn down as a public nuisance in 1871. This was the site Mifflin Kenedy tried to buy to build his mansion and it was the site chosen by Maston Nixon for a high-rise office building.

When the port opened in 1926, Maston Nixon could see the need for additional office space. Nixon organized the "Blackland" train trip in 1924 to promote farming in the Coastal Bend. Nixon bought the site at Leopard and Broadway and constructed a 12-story office building. It opened on April 2, 1927. In 1946, the Nixon Building was sold to oilman Sam Wilson. It has been the Wilson Building ever since.

*—Sept. 30, 2015*

# Broadway's Makeover

The transformation of Upper Broadway from a street of fine old mansions and elegant homes to one of modern office buildings and hotels began with the Nixon Building. It was the end of one era and the beginning of another. This transformation took another step with the building of the Plaza Hotel.

Across Leopard from the Nixon building was the Redmond home. Anna Moore Schwein said Henry Redmond and his first wife, Louisa Baskin, lived there. It was built in the 1850s when Redmond was engaged in the Mexican trade with William Mann. He moved to Zapata County.

The house was purchased by railroad promoter Uriah Lott. Mifflin Kenedy bought the house and gave it to his daughter, Mrs. Arthur Spohn. It was then sold to Dr. Henry Redmond, son of the original owner.

Maston Nixon thought the Redmond site would be a good location for a new hotel. He organized two companies, one in Corpus Christi to finance building the hotel and one in San Antonio to run it. The result was the Plaza Hotel, which opened in 1929. It was demolished in 1962 to make way for the 600 Building.

Next to the Plaza, when it was first built, was the First Presbyterian Church. The original church on this site was built in 1867, during the yellow fever epidemic. Dressed lumber on the site was diverted to make coffins, according to church history, "On This Bluff," a new church was completed in 1902. Three decades later, they were feeling hemmed-in by the Plaza Hotel and Nixon building. Beginning in 1929, the current church was built on South Broadway.

Principal investors behind the Plaza Hotel were Robert and Clara Driscoll, who inherited the oil-rich Driscoll Ranch. After Robert's death, Jack White, who was operating the hotel, bought out the other investors. They were eager to sell during the Depression. But Clara Driscoll refused to sell. A court suit resulted, which White won, and he changed the hotel's name to the White Plaza.

Clara Driscoll built a competing hotel next door. It was built on property north of the Plaza Hotel, the lot the Presbyterian Church had occupied and the old Seaton place, which, in 1936, was converted into the Cage-Mills Funeral Home. This was the old Rube Holbein house. The Robert Driscoll Hotel was built here.

The Driscoll opened on May 25, 1942. Clara Driscoll occupied a 20th floor penthouse from where she could look down on the White Plaza. The Driscoll Hotel building is still there, but known today as the Wells Fargo Building.

Across Antelope, on the corner of the block, was Mrs. Sinclair's home. William Adams, who arrived as a boy with his family in 1852, once recalled that this was the old Ohler place, built sometime in the 1850s. "The Ohler family — Mr. Edward Ohler, wife and two sons — had a house where the new post office is now being built." William's brother, Robert Adams, also recalled the Ohler place. "The Ohlers lived on the hill. One day I went up there and they were making soap. I saw him making it. He was cooking it in a large cast iron pot. It was yellow and was sold there in the town."

Mrs. Delmas Givens (no relation to me) in an interview said the nicest looking place in the city, when she arrived in 1876, was the A.M. Davis home, just past the old Ohler home. This house was later known as Mrs. Thomas Hickey's place.

The house next to this on the north was the home of Gov. E. J. Davis, which was sold to Norwick Gussett. In 1924, according to Marie Blucher, the Hennesseys of San Antonio bought the property. In 1937 it was sold to the government as a site for a new post office. The old Davis/Gussett house was moved to Carancahua and used as the Hennessey Apartments.

The post office on the bluff was built on the site of the old Ohler, A.M. Davis and E. J. Davis homes. Four decades later, the post office was torn down to make way for the Texas Commerce Plaza, fronting on Carancahua with a courtyard on Broadway.

When the post office was first built in 1938 it sat next to Mrs. Delmas Givens' home. Her late husband had been a longtime city attorney. In an interview in 1939, Mrs. Givens told Dee Woods of her early life during the Civil War. When she was eight, one of Sherman's soldiers demanded of her mother, "Where is your

*The Henry Redmond home, the First Presbyterian Church, and the old Seaton home were replaced by two of the three tall buildings on the bluff: the Plaza Hotel and the Driscoll Hotel.*

*The Nixon Building, White Plaza Hotel and Driscoll Hotel transformed the bluff from a scene of stately homes and a church to one of commercial high rises.*

pocketbook?" Her mother said, "In my apron pocket. And you don't dare take it because your general ordered that no woman in North Carolina was to be molested." She remembered her mother scolding her, saying that she was "an insolently self-sufficient child."

Mrs. Delmas Givens' home was torn down for the Vaughn Petroleum Building, built in 1959. Next to Mrs. Givens' place, on the corner of Buffalo and Broadway, was the home of Horatio Gussett, son of Norwick Gussett. He had the house built when he married Mary Henrietta Barnard in 1898.

The Gussetts' new home had nine large rooms with galleries on both floors. The bluff then was clay and treacherously slippery when it rained. In front of their home, Horatio had a boardwalk laid down the side of the bluff. Mrs. Gussett in an interview said their home overlooked a mesquite thicket (where the Caller-Times stands today) and at the edge of the thicket was a blacksmith shop. Mrs. Gussett said they kept fine horses and drove a smart buggy, but when motorcars replaced horses and buggies they walked.

"Nettie" Gussett sold the house in 1953 to make way for the Oil Industries Building. She wanted them to hurry and tear it down. She hated to pass by and see it in its decrepit state. The Oil Industries Building is still there, but boarded-up.

Upper North Broadway, Corpus Christi's most stylist street, was transformed in the years between 1926 and the 1950s, with old homes giving way to the Cathedral, hotels and office buildings. The Kenedy, Rabb and King mansions — gone. The E. J. Davis home — gone. The Delmas Givens and Horatio Gussett homes — gone. The people who lived in them died. Then the houses died.

*—Oct. 7, 2015*

# Louis P. Cooke, Fugitive

One of the most unusual characters to come through Corpus Christi was a West Point dropout who became the secretary of the Texas Navy. He was a soldier, legislator, and author (no doubt) of the most important law passed by the Texas Congress, the homestead exemption act. He was also a murder suspect on the run.

He was known as Louis P. Cooke, but his real name was John Lane Cooke, sometimes spelled as Cook. He was born in 1811 in Tennessee, the oldest son of a Kentucky couple.

He entered West Point in 1833 but did not graduate. He left the military academy in 1836 to join 110 New York volunteers bound for Texas, under the command of Maj. Edwin Morehouse. Somewhere between West Point and Texas he began to call himself Louis P. Cooke.

The New York volunteers arrived too late to take part in the battle of San Jacinto, but Cooke was elected lieutenant colonel in the Texas Army and, as an ally of Mirabeau Lamar, was elected to the Third Congress of the Republic from Brazoria.

In December 1838, he introduced a bill to exempt certain property from taxation. It was passed by the House and Senate and signed into law in January 1839. It became known as the homestead exemption law, one of the most important laws ever passed by a Texas legislature. Some question whether Cooke wrote the bill, but no evidence has been found that he did not.

Cooke was appointed secretary of the Texas Navy and he held that post from 1839 to 1841. He was also one of five commissioners who chose Austin as the site of the state capitol.

In those early years, Austin was a dangerous place on the frontier. One night, Cooke's gardener, Dutch John, was returning home with a bag of meal on his shoulder. He was attacked by Indians. He ran to Cooke's home with three arrows stuck in his meal sack and one in his arm. Cooke met him at the front door and returned fire, driving off the Indians. As the story was told, when Dutch John came to, he looked around and said, "Where is my meal sack?" When it was pointed out, under his head, he got up, took his meal sack and made his way to his own place behind Cooke's house.

Cooke got into trouble with the law in late July 1843. An account in a newspaper at the time (the Northern Standard) reported that when John Nolan was walking down the street he met Capt. Mark Lewis who asked him whether he had said that he (Lewis) was a liar. Nolan said he had. Lewis drew a pistol and shot at Nolan but missed. Nolan shot and also missed. Lewis drew a second pistol and shot Nolan, who died two days later.

The sheriff arrested Lewis and was taking him to appear before a justice of the peace. On the way, Cooke and a young man named George Barrett ran out with their guns to kill Lewis. Alexander Peyton, walking with Lewis, shot at Barrett and missed him. Barrett shot Peyton down. Cooke shot Lewis, who died that night. Peyton died a few days later. The newspaper reported that Nolan and Lewis were old enemies, as were Cooke and Lewis, and that the affray "cast a gloom over the town."

Cooke was indicted in Travis County for murder. He conveyed a tract of land on the Colorado to a lawyer, James Mayfield, to defend him. On a change of venue the trial was moved to Bastrop. In December 1843, Cooke took the first opportunity to take his leave and escaped. He made his way to Corpus Christi, taking with him his wife, Mary Ann, and their young children.

At Corpus Christi, Cooke, the former secretary of the Texas Navy, worked as a bricklayer. On a Comanche raid in 1844, he joined Henry Kinney and 10 other men who chased and overtook a Comanche war party west of the town. In what became a general man-to-man fight, three of the Corpus Christi men were killed and many others wounded. Cooke was wounded, hit by an Indian arrow that disfigured his face and cost him an eye. It left a ghastly scar.

A year later, when Zachary Taylor's army was camped at Corpus Christi, Cooke was the primary suspect in an attack on a friendly Lipan-Apache, Chief Castro, who was ambushed one dark night. The chief suffered grievous wounds to the head and chest, but somehow survived. Suspicion fell on Cooke and he was questioned about the shooting. He denied he shot the Indian chief and there was no evidence to charge him.

*An illustration in S. Compton Smith's book on the Mexican War, "Chili Con Carne," depicts Smith and Louis P. Cooke riding pell-mell, with guns blazing, through the nighttime camp of startled Mexican guerrillas.*

When Taylor's army marched to the Rio Grande, Cooke went with it. He became a trader on the border, according to several accounts, and had some position as sutler with the army. In "Mexico Under Fire," Joseph Chance wrote that Cooke led retaliatory attacks on three Mexican ranches after U.S. wagon trains were attacked and burned by Mexican guerrillas.

S. Compton Smith, an Army surgeon, in "Chili Con Carne" told of accompanying a wagon train in Northern Mexico which included Cooke. This was during the Mexican War. He and Cooke and couple of other men rode ahead of the train and in the dark inadvertently came upon a camp of Mexican guerrillas. As they were vastly outnumbered, Cooke proposed they charge the camp, shooting in the air and yelling like banshees. In this fashion they rode through it, with guns blazing, and came out on the other side unscathed.

After the war, in March 1849, Louis and his wife Mary died in cholera epidemic that swept Brownsville. They left four children, a boy and three girls, who were raised by Louis' brother, Dr. Wilds K. Cooke. Another brother, Hiram W., was a Texas Ranger in Coryell County during the Civil War.

383

Louis P. Cooke was a man of major achievements and major failures. He was a soldier, Indian-fighter, secretary of the Texas Navy, legislator, author of the Texas homestead exemption law, as well as being a murder suspect and fugitive from justice. Along with his wife, he was buried in some unknown cemetery in Brownsville where he has rested in obscurity ever since.

*—Oct. 7, 2015*

# Forbes Britton, Big Chief

The Corpus Christi Ranchero on Feb. 23, 1861 reported the death of Forbes Britton in Austin. The paper noted that the coffin, a box of red cedar, was sealed with zinc and on the silver name plate was engraved: "Hon. Forbes Britton. Died February 14, 1861."

Who was Forbes Britton? The short answer is he was an Army officer for 16 years. He fought in the Seminole War and the Mexican War. He settled in Corpus Christi, became a prominent businessman and was elected state senator.

But we know more than the dry facts about Forbes Britton because he was a friend of Daniel P. Whiting who kept a diary. (A book on Whiting's memoirs, "A Soldier's Life," was published in 2011.) Britton and Whiting were in the 7th Infantry, stationed at Fort Gibson in Indian Territory, in Florida during the Seminole War, and in Corpus Christi in the buildup before the Mexican War.

When Britton graduated from West Point in 1834 he was assigned to the 7th Regiment and stationed at Fort Gibson. He married Rebecca Millard, from a prominent family. They were at Fort Coffee when she had twins, a boy and a girl, in 1838. Britton wrote his friend Whiting at Fort Gibson.

As Whiting related, the news came "in a letter enclosed in a double envelope, stamped with two seals, addressed and written throughout with a pen that made double marks and was signed twice with his name in full. He proclaimed the twins, said he could do nothing except in doublets, took two bites to one before at his lunch and two drinks of his toddy when one had sufficed in previous conviviality. He could not account for the twins except that, as quartermaster, his vouchers had to be submitted in duplicate."

Whiting said when Britton visited Fort Gibson some months later "he entered the garrison from the steamboat landing, with a baby on each arm and a parasol in each hand."

As a young lieutenant, Britton was assigned duty escorting Indians from their ancestral homes in Georgia, Alabama and Florida to Indian Territory (now Oklahoma). As Whiting tells it, Britton was ordered to take charge of some Indians arriving at Fort Meade in Florida and to escort them to Fort Arbuckle in Indian Territory. After a number of Indian families came in, Whiting wrote, Britton moved into a tent in their midst. "He told us that it was best for him to 'turn Indian' while he was engaged as their 'big chief.' "

Whiting said Britton later took charge of a large body of Seminoles being moved from Florida to Fort Gibson. "One of their great regrets in leaving Florida was the loss of their pine knots, so ready for fuel and ignitable. They understood there would be no pine knots at their new home. When the boat landed at Fort Gibson, and the Indians were leaving for the shore, Forbes opened some boxes he had filled with pine knots that he distributed among them, one to each man, woman and child, to their delight and satisfaction." (What a sad image that presents: such small recompense for what was taken from them.)

Whiting tells another story about Britton. When he was ordered to take charge as quartermaster at Fort Fanning in Florida, he was given overly belabored instructions by his superior, a Capt. Dusenbury, which seemed to overlook the fact that Britton was an experienced officer of proven judgment.

"One day at Fort Fanning, Britton entered the room of an officer and joined in the conversation," wrote Whiting. "Thrusting his hand abstractedly into his pocket I was surprised to see him pull out a half-dozen horse flies of the largest size. 'What on earth,' I said, 'are you doing with such articles in your pocket?' Britton said, 'I caught them from the backs of the government oxen, and I intend to send them to Capt. Dusenbury to show my zeal in the public service."

Britton and Whiting were in the 7th Infantry with Zachary Taylor's army at Corpus Christi, in 1845 and early 1846. Whiting left us the famous drawing of the army encampment. After Taylor's army moved on to the border at the start of the Mexican War, Britton was with the quartermaster corps of the 7th Infantry. At Camargo, he was a frequent drinking buddy of George Wilkins Kendall, the war correspondent, and Edward Burleson, former vice president of the Republic of Texas. They drank warm champagne from an army canteen.

386

*Forbes Britton, a young second lieutenant in the 7th Regiment of Infantry, settled in Corpus Christi and became a wealthy merchant and state senator.*

After another tour of duty escorting Seminoles from Florida to Indian Territory, Britton resigned from the army in 1850 and moved to Corpus Christi. He was one of several Mexican War veterans who settled here after the war.

He engaged in the Mexican trade with John Baskin and William Mann. Britton also entered the grocery, dry goods and commission business with an old army friend, Cornelius Cahill. Their business was located in the Cahill building on Water Street. Britton loaned Henry Kinney $45,000 to put on the Lone Star Fair.

Britton built "Centennial House" on the bluff in 1849 and another house at his ranch at Britton Motts, eight miles west of town. His daughter Elizabeth (Lizzie), one of the twins, married Judge Edmund J. Davis, who became a brigadier general in the Union Army and Reconstruction governor of Texas.

When Britton, William Mann and John Baskin ended their partnership, in the division of property Britton received a young slave woman named Malvina. When she became pregnant in 1855, Britton sent her to live on a sheep ranch he and George Wilkins Kendall owned near New Braunfels. Malvina gave birth to a daughter. I speculated in a column two years ago that Forbes Britton was the father of Malvina's daughter. She became well-known to Corpus Christi as a former slave and teacher, Anna Moore Schwein.

Britton was elected to the Texas Senate in 1857 and again in 1859. He was one of Sam Houston's supporters who tried to keep Texas in the Union. Britton was sick when he went to Austin for a special session. He died of pneumonia on Feb. 14, 1861. He was the third person buried in the State Cemetery; the second man buried there was Ed Burleson, Britton's old drinking buddy in Camargo in the Mexican War.

*—Oct. 21, 2015*

# Duke of Padre Island

Patrick Francis Dunn's domain was an empire of sand, cattle and 112 miles of Gulf beaches. For five decades, from 1879 until 1929, he developed the island into Texas' most unusual cattle ranch.

Dunn gave himself the title, duke of Padre Island. He received a letter from someone in England whose name was decorated with a list of initials for various titles. Dunn, in his reply, added "D.P.I." to his name. His lawyer, Edward Kleberg, asked what the letters meant. Dunn said, "Duke of Padre Island."

When he was growing up, Dunn lived with his family five miles from Corpus Christi on the road to Nuecestown. His parents, Thomas and Catherine Dunn, had married in Dublin and left the next day for Texas. They arrived in December 1849. Pat Dunn was born in 1858.

"Us kids used to go over to Uncle John's and play," Dunn once said in an interview with a reporter. "He was building a well. He had some ox chains and things he did not want to get pressed (confiscated) by Confederate authorities. He took the best chains and oxbows and wheels off the wagon and hid them in the well. Some soldiers came to confiscate Uncle John's things. They looked at the wagons and harness and there was nothing but junk. One said, 'Why, Dunn, you're a teaming contractor. You've got better stuff than this. This is junk. We can't use it.'

"I said, 'There's a good harness down there in the well.' Uncle John slapped me and I ran into the house crying. I told my aunt that Uncle John slapped me for telling about the harness in the well. She said no wonder I got slapped."

In 1865, when Dunn was seven, his father died. "We had just loaded our wagon with cotton when my father passed on. My mother decided to haul the cotton to Brownsville herself. She took me along. We got no further than Santa Rosa when the war ended."

In July 1879, when Dunn was 21, he and his brother Lawrence moved their cattle to the island. "I made arrangements with the McCampbells and Welch (a law firm) whom I afterwards bought out," Dunn said. He also bought out his brother and called his ranch "El Rancho de Don Patricio."

Dunn didn't just build a ranch, but a way of life. "Padre Island was the best cow ranch in the world when I came to it. That's a broad assertion, but a fact."

Dunn built four cattle stations on the island, with corrals and holding pens, a day's ride apart. Number one was at the head of the island, called Owl's Mott; number two was Novillo Station; number three was Black Hill, so-called because of its dark green grass; and number four was Green Hill, the highest elevation on the island. Between these stations were Campo Bueno and Campo Borrego.

There was plenty of freshwater. "You can find good water in most places within a few feet of the surface," Dunn said. He had 75 water tanks dug in the sand. These were long trenches shored up with ship hatch covers and salvage material to keep out the sand. They had to be constantly cleaned out.

With the Laguna Madre on one side and the Gulf on the other, there was no need for fences. Dunn built traps and cutting chutes to eliminate roping, which he thought cruel, following the lead of Robert Driscoll, founder of the Driscoll Ranch. "He was a fine man and a great cattleman. He would have torn the house down if he caught a man roping one of his cows."

Dunn's cattle grew fat from sedge grass, sand crabs and dead fish. They waded in the surf and their hides showed tar spots from lying on the beach. Dunn said they were the most religious cattle in Texas since they had to kneel to drink.

In 1884, Dunn married a widow, Mrs. Clara Jones, and adopted her daughter Lalla. They moved 17 miles down the island to the Curry settlement. In 1890, after Dunn's younger daughter May got scarlet fever, he moved the family to Corpus Christi and built a home on South Broadway.

Dunn spent most of his time on the island except when he served in the Legislature and stayed in Austin. He was a political ally of Democratic powerbrokers Jim Wells of Brownsville and Archie Parr of Duval County. When visiting in Corpus Christi, Dunn liked to sit on the porch of the St. James Hotel and gossip with other citizens in the long purple evenings.

*Patrick Francis Dunn as a young man, date unknown, perhaps not long before he moved his cattle onto Padre Island, in 1879, when he was 21 years old. Dunn in later years represented the district in the Texas Legislature and was a political ally of Jim Wells of Brownsville and Archie Parr of Duval County. He sold the island ten years before he died in 1937.*

*Patrick F. Dunn's vacant ranch house and corral on Padre Island in 1950. Dunn ran cattle on Padre Island for 50 years before he sold the island in 1926. During Dunn's lifetime, about 4,000 head of cattle were pastured on the island. After Padre Island was dedicated as a National Seashore in 1967, cattle continued grazing on the island for three more years, until Dec. 31, 1970.*

Dunn was a diligent beachcomber. He built corrals and bunkhouses from pine and mahogany logs that washed ashore during storms. His two-story house, built in 1907 on Packery Channel, was made of driftwood and furnished with door hinges from ship refrigerators and chairs from the wrecked steamer Nicaragua. A wooden cask with Japanese letters served as a washbasin. Whisky barrels caught and stored rainwater. On the south porch by the kitchen was a long table made of driftwood where hands were served their meals by Dunn's cook, a man named Aurelio. "The cook is the key to the situation," Dunn explained in 1927. "In olden times, people didn't use to eat, but they do now."

The 1916 hurricane destroyed the two-story ranch house — "not a piece of furniture was found after the storm." Dunn built a one-story house a mile away. He didn't live there long. In 1926, he sold the island to Sam Robertson, who planned to develop Padre Island and built the Don Patricio Causeway in 1927. Dunn kept grazing rights for his cattle and moved into town.

Dunn regretted selling the island. In his lamentation he said, "When all is said and done, if the good Lord would give me back the island, wash out a channel in Corpus Christi Pass 30 feet deep, and put devilfish and other monsters in it to keep out the tourists, I would be satisfied." He died on March 25, 1937 at the Nueces Hotel. Dr. Harry Heaney, his physician, said he died of a heart attack. He was 79. No one ever possessed the island more completely nor loved it more than Patrick Francis Dunn who for five decades was the Duke of Padre Island.

*—Oct. 28, 2015*

# Orders for Texas

Ethan Allen Hitchcock, grandson of Revolutionary War hero Ethan Allen, was with Zachary Taylor's command at Fort Jesup, La., in July 1845. He was the commander of the 3$^{rd}$ Infantry and considered Taylor's most capable senior officer.

The West Point-trained Hitchcock was a serious scholar who studied mystical philosophy and, generally, while other officers went out carousing he was reading Spinoza's Ethics and writing letters to Ralph Waldo Emerson.

On June 29, 1845 as tattoo sounded, Taylor's adjutant, Capt. W. W. S. Bliss, read to Hitchcock the orders to move the army to Texas. Hitchcock could hardly sleep for worrying about what he needed to do to get the 3$^{rd}$ Infantry ready to leave Fort Jesup. Hitchcock opposed the move to Texas and wrote in his diary that he thought the movement would lead to war.

Hitchcock's regiment marched to Natchitoches and boarded two steamboats. The soldiers arrived at New Orleans on July 10 and moved into an empty warehouse that cost the government $100 a day, which Hitchcock thought too expensive.

In the night of July 22, 1845, elements of Hitchcock's 3$^{rd}$ Infantry boarded the steamboat Alabama. Taylor was also on board. The steamboat arrived off St. Joseph's Island on Friday July 25. Hitchcock noted that the men were quiet as they watched two or three small sailboats beyond the island.

Early Saturday morning, Hitchcock sent Lt. D. T. Chandler ashore to look for water. Chandler planted a small American flag on a sand dune, the first to fly over Texas soil. He reported that it was next to impossible to obtain water. They saw cattle and noticed that people were living higher up the island.

All eight companies of the 3$^{rd}$ were on the island by July 28. Hitchcock went ashore where he found the encampments of his regiment scattered for three miles. They found water by digging down about the depth of a barrel, but it was brackish.

Gen. Taylor was anxious to get the troops on the mainland. Hitchcock urged him to wait until a southwest wind increased the depth of water over the shoals blocking the bay. Taylor ignored Hitchcock's advice and ordered companies K and G of Hitchcock's 3$^{rd}$ to board the lighter Undine, sail across the bay, and set up camp at Corpus Christi.

The Undine ran aground in the mudflats between Aransas and Corpus Christi bays. After two days of efforts, they decided the mudflats could not be crossed by the Undine. Fishing boats were hired to transport the companies. They landed on North Beach on July 31, 1845.

Hitchcock wrote in his diary that he was on shore, at Corpus Christi, with companies K and G. Next morning, some citizens of Corpus Christi visited Hitchcock, offering offered assistance and information. Other companies of the 3$^{rd}$ continued to arrive through the first week of August.

One of Hitchcock's officers, Capt. H. Bainbridge, was slow in landing his company; he sent a note that he would land the next day since he wanted to sleep. Hitchcock sent him a direct order that brought him and his company ashore without delay. Hitchcock thought Bainbridge was too fond of his comforts.

Taylor arrived on Aug. 15 and issued his first order from Corpus Christi. Hitchcock had embankments thrown up as a line of defense and, since no artillery had arrived, he borrowed two old cannons from Henry Kinney, the founder of Corpus Christi.

Traders came over from Camargo on the Rio Grande. Hitchcock said they brought silver bars and coins to buy tobacco and American goods. He liked their sarapes — he called them "traveling blankets" — with a hole for the head and offering protection against rain. As he watched the traders pack the goods they had purchased, he thought the whole thing a business, a science.

When they heard that the 2$^{nd}$ Dragoons, which marched overland from Fort Jesup, would arrive the next day at San Patricio, Taylor rode out to meet them. Hitchcock and Henry Kinney rode part of the way and returned to Corpus Christi. On the way back, Hitchcock heard about Kinney's history.

Kinney told Hitchcock he established his trading place in 1839, that when he first arrived he shot at a spotted tiger on the hill above

*Ethan Allen Hitchcock in uniform in 1851, six years after he commanded Zachary Taylor's Third Infantry at Corpus Christi, in late 1845 and early 1846, before the war with Mexico. Hitchcock's diary recounts episodes during the Corpus Christi encampment.*

the beach. Kinney told Hitchcock that the Mexican government imposed such heavy duties on tobacco and other American products that an illicit trade resulted. Kinney, Hitchcock said, was employed as a secret agent for Sam Houston in Mexico in 1842; he was arrested, sentenced to be shot, and led out blindfolded. He escaped by a bribe tendered by a friend at Matamoros. Hitchcock said Kinney had an eventful life for a young man of 31, that he had had enough incidents in his life for a dozen men.

A violent thunderstorm with a heavy rain hit on Sunday, Aug. 24. Hitchcock covered his bed with an overcoat. Tents were blown down and a tarpaulin covering commissary stores was blown off.

They heard a deafening crack of thunder and saw a vivid flash of light.

"In a moment I saw Lt. (W. H.) Henry running past my tent calling for a doctor." The lightning struck Lt. Braxton Bragg's tent pole, killing a slave and injuring another. As the storm passed on, they repaired the damaged camp.

During the thunderstorm, the 2nd Dragoons were north of San Patricio and supposed the thunder to be an artillery bombardment. They decided, Hitchcock wrote, "to leave their baggage on the other side of the Nueces and push on with all speed to the support or relief of this place which they supposed under attack. The regiment moved up to the river, hastily constructed a raft, passed the river and commenced their march. This was when they were met by Gen. Taylor." He was on his way to visit them.

Hitchcock received his mail on Aug. 29, which included a map of Texas from the War Department. An earlier map had been modified to add a line marking the Rio Grande as the boundary. This shocked Hitchcock. "Our people ought to be damned for their impudent arrogance and domineering presumption. It is enough to make atheists of us all to see such wickedness in the world."

*—Nov. 4, 2015*

# Dead March in Saul

Lt. Col. Ethan Allen Hitchcock was the commander of the 3rd Infantry in Zachary Taylor's army encamped at Corpus Christi. Hitchcock called the annexation of Texas "monstrous and infamous" but he was a soldier who followed orders.

On Sept. 7, 1845 Hitchcock visited Corpus Christi's Henry Kinney, who was in bed sick. He found Taylor and William Mann, a prominent trader, visiting Kinney. He met Kinney's spy, Chipito Sandoval, who came from the Rio Grande with reports of army movements in Mexico.

On Sept. 12, boilers on the Dayton, an old steamer hired to ferry troops across the bay, exploded off McGloin's Bluff. Ten men were killed and 17 wounded. Hitchcock picked a burial site on a slope with a view of Nueces and Corpus Christi bays, "a very beautiful spot." At sundown, as a regimental band played "Dead March in Saul," the soldiers were buried and left to their long sleep.

The weather turned cool at the end of September. Taylor visited Hitchcock in his tent on Sept. 30 and broached the topic of moving the army to the Rio Grande. Hitchcock told him that if he suggested such a movement President Polk would seize upon it.

"The general is instigated by ambition, or so it seems to me," Hitchcock wrote in his diary. "He seems to have lost all respect for Mexican rights and is willing to be an instrument of Mr. Polk for pushing our boundary as far west as possible . . . I think the general wants an additional brevet and would strain a point to get it."

In the past two weeks, a number of vessels had arrived bringing more troops. Hitchcock noted that the 3rd, 4th and 7th regiments were at Corpus Christi, along with the 2nd Dragoons, a company of regular artillery and two companies of volunteer artillery.

The settlement of Corpus Christi, Hitchcock wrote, began along the shore to the south. The first house was a store owned by Kinney, which was rented by the government for use as a hospital. Next was William Mann's store and residence followed by a lagoon and then an eating house "for loafers," a bakery, Owens' store. There was a two-story house, also rented by the government for use as a hospital, then a cluster of drinking houses, some of them wooden frames covered with cloth.

After the stores and saloons came the volunteer camp, which consisted of two artillery companies from New Orleans, then the 4th and 3rd regiments, Braxton Bragg's artillery company, followed by a fieldwork thrown up by the 3rd when it first arrived. Behind the fieldwork was a supply depot, a cluster of large tents. Next in line came the 5th and 7th regiments, then a small lagoon, followed by the camp of the 2nd Dragoons. Beyond an inlet from Nueces Bay (Hall's Bayou) was the 8th Infantry, followed by three or four companies of artillery serving as infantry. Hitchcock said the distance between the south and north end of the camp was about a mile and a quarter.

Since the Second Dragoons had arrived, Hitchcock noted, there had been several "disgraceful brawls" in which the dragoons were the instigators. One scrape involved "a low vulgar slut of a strumpet." The commander of the Dragoons, Col. David Twiggs, said Hitchcock, was well known for "licentiousness with women in open defiance of public opinion." Hitchcock heard that at some orgy Twiggs got drunk and had liquor poured over his naked body. (Twigg Street was named for David Twiggs, though the city misspelled the name.)

The last of the troops ordered to Corpus Christi arrived on board the steamer Alabama on Oct. 13. Paymasters arrived on Nov. 2 with $60,000 to pay the troops.

Hitchcock continued to fret over the assertion that the border was the Rio Grande rather than the Nueces. He wrote that Texas' original limit was the Nueces and that Texas "has never conquered, possessed, or exercised dominion west of the Nueces, except for that of a small smuggling company at this place, living here by Mexican sufferance if not under Mexican protection." But "the government is bent on taking advantage (of Mexico) to insist upon 'our claim' as far as the Rio Grande. I hold this to be monstrous and abominable."

Much of October and November was cold and wet and many days it rained with a steady drizzle. A fierce norther hit on Nov. 30 and men made barriers of chaparral limbs as a windbreak. Hitchcock

*Gen. Zachary Taylor (left) and one of his senior officers, David E. Twiggs, who commanded the Dragoons at Corpus Christi. Hitchcock considered Taylor "utterly ignorant" and said of Twiggs that he was well known for "licentiousness with women in open defiance of public opinion."*

spent most of that time in his tent, suffering recurrent bouts of diarrhea. He read the works of radical free-thinkers and studied the works of Christian mystic Emanuel Swedenborg, who wrote about heaven, hell and the afterlife. Hitchcock kept up a correspondence with Ralph Waldo Emerson, a follower of Swedenborg. (Hitchcock's first book, "The Doctrines of Spinoza and Swedenborg," was published in 1846.)

Before Christmas, an old dispute resurfaced over the subject of brevet rank vs. field rank. Brevet rank rewarded officers for actions in battle and became a way to promote officers who were blocked by a lack of retirements of senior officers. The higher ranks were limited and younger officers could not move up until older officers retired or died. The question was whether a brevet, or honorary promotion, enabled a man to outrank someone who was senior in the line.

The issue resurfaced in a feud between Brevet Brig. Gen. William Worth and Col. David Twiggs of the Dragoons. The two men disliked each other and both had fiery tempers. The question of seniority became more than academic when rumors circulated that

Taylor might retire. Next in line would be Worth or Twiggs. Both were colonels in field rank, with Twiggs the senior, but Worth was a brigadier general in brevet rank.

In Washington, General of the Army Winfield Scott stood strongly for brevet rank. Officers at Corpus Christi who did not hold brevet rank opposed Scott's position. A letter of protest was drawn up by Hitchcock and signed by 158 officers, including Twiggs. The letter argued that giving preference to brevet rank would violate law and reason. Hitchcock's letter appealed to the Senate to override Scott and set the matter right.

*—Nov. 11, 2015*

# Rumors of War

Ethan Allen Hitchcock, commander of the 3rd Infantry stationed at Corpus Christi in 1845 and early 1846, was one of Zachary Taylor's senior commanders. He was a severe critic of Taylor and opposed the coming war with Mexico.

New Year's Day 1846 at Corpus Christi was mild and balmy. Hitchcock remembered that it was New Year's and noted that the day would go as other days with drinking, horse-racing, gambling, and theatrical amusements. A ball was advertised for the evening.

"Colonel Kinney thinks there are 2,000 people here besides the army," he wrote in his diary. "They are nearly all adventurers, brought here to speculate on events growing out of the presence of the troops. There are no ladies here, and very few women. I take no part in the amusements, but remain quiet in my tent." Content with the excitement of intellectual speculation, Hitchcock was reading Spinoza's Ethics "and let the news go by unheeded, though rumors and reports of war are rife."

On Jan. 8 he noted that the resolution for the admission of Texas to the Union passed the Senate; it passed the House a few days before. Hitchcock noted that the camp had another duel, this one between an officer, Lt. E. Deas of the Dragoons and a sutler (army storekeeper) named Irwin.

"The quarrel grew out of a gambling affair between others," Hitchcock wrote. The two men exchanged sharp words then blows and later met "on the field of honor." They fired at each other without effect. "Some mutual friend standing near said it must be ended and after a powwow the opponents advanced towards each other and shaking hands on the ground the difficulty was declared to be honorably terminated."

On Jan. 11, 1846, a Sunday, Hitchcock took a walk with Capt. T.J. Crain of the Topographical Engineers. The day was "exceedingly beautiful" as they walked on the bluff above the camp and discussed the chances of war with England "for a few acres in Oregon." Later that day, Hitchcock rode south of town where he came upon a brickyard and two "Negro huts."

From inside of one of the houses he heard the silence broken by a simple Methodist hymn. "I sat on my horse overlooking the calm bay, with the sun shining brightly, and thought what a happiness it would be to live in this world if it were not a place for sin and misery and all sorts of wretchedness. I rode home in a pensive mood — a little saddened."

Hitchcock spent much of his time making himself a legible copy of Spinoza's Ethics. On Feb. 4, he noted that he had copied 560 pages in two weeks, "no small job." Two days later he finished his copying of Spinoza and noted that Gen. Taylor had received orders to move the army to the Rio Grande and that the general proposed to move to the north bank of the river opposite Matamoros. "This will make a considerable stir," wrote Hitchcock.

On Feb. 11, Hitchcock wrote that reports from beyond the Rio Grande varied by the hour. "All these reports go for little or nothing and they show only how utterly ignorant our general is of everything one inch beyond his nose. When he came here with only 800 men he was perfectly blindfolded and only stumbled into success."

Hitchcock wrote that when he came through New Orleans in July 1845, on his way to Corpus Christi, he ordered a covered wagon from Philadelphia "supposing I might possibly go into the interior for a permanent station and would need it. But for the expedition now contemplated to the Rio Grande, I will not require it – it would be in my way. I have therefore sold it, harness and all, for $150." He also sold his horse.

On Feb. 14, he noted that another freezing norther passed over the camp. "I have had a headache most of the morning and having completed my copy of Spinoza I am out of employment and restless."

The brevet rank vs. field rank quarrel rose again. As Hitchcock noted, Gen. Taylor commanded the army. Next in line was Col. Twiggs. After him was Col Worth. But Worth held the brevet rank of brigadier general. Taylor, said Hitchcock, had avoided calling out the whole army in a body to avoid bringing Twiggs and Worth together. However, on Feb. 24 the general ordered a review and

Ethan Allen Hitchcock as a civilian in the 1850s. His diary and memoirs "Fifty Years in Camp and Field" provide a unique perspective of Zachary Taylor's encampment at Corpus Christi in preparation for the war with Mexico.

designated Twiggs for the command. Worth immediately protested. Taylor cancelled the review. Hitchcock said the entire camp was in a state of excitement, with some blaming Taylor for not acting decisively one way or the other. Hitchcock drilled his 3rd regiment for an inspection by the inspector general.

On March 8, 1846, the 2nd Dragoons and a company of artillery marched out of Corpus Christi at 10 in the morning. Hitchcock's 3rd Infantry, which had been the first to arrive at Corpus Christi on Aug. 1, 1845, was the last to leave. Hitchcock himself was sick and in bed for three days before his regiment departed. His doctor advised him not to travel with the regiment but Hitchcock insisted. On the way to the Rio Grande he rested on a makeshift bed on boxes of ammunition in a wagon pulled by oxen. At the end of the

Hitchcock as a major general during the Civil War. He was a military adviser to Abraham Lincoln and was offered command of the Union Army in 1862.

trip he began to recover enough to ride a horse, though he was "excessively fatigued and weak to the last degree."

Later, in the war, Hitchcock served as an adviser to Gen. Winfield Scott and was put in charge of covert operations; he formed an organization of operatives called the Mexican Spy Agency. He resigned from the army in 1855 but returned to active duty in the Civil War. He acted as a military adviser to Abraham Lincoln and was offered command of the Union Army in 1862 but turned it down, citing age, ill health and lack of command experience. He died in Sparta, Ga., on Aug. 4, 1870.

*—Nov. 18, 2015*

# Cabin Boy

Richard King, the man who would establish the King Ranch, was born in the summer of 1824 — July 10, to be specific — in New York City. We know nothing of his parents beyond the fact they were Irish immigrants. Where did they come from and when did they arrive? What were their names? These are missing chapters in the life of Texas' greatest cattle rancher.

Some accounts of King's life say he was born in Orange County, N. Y., but King in a sworn deposition in 1870 said he was born in New York City. Tom Lea, in his two-volume history, "The King Ranch," said King's family may have moved to Orange County after Richard's birth.

Did King ever recall his childhood? Did he recall happy and carefree days? There is no record. We know a few bare facts, but not the detail. The color is not there. The bare facts have been repeated over the years until they have become clichés, polished like old silver.

King's parents died in 1829, which must have been a tragedy for the five-year-old boy. But of this we know nothing. And nothing of King's parents survived, except for King. In later years, there would be no family portraits to hang on the walls. Nothing is ever lost so long as there is someone to remember, but there was no one to remember, except for a five-year-old boy. And he remembered very little.

There was at least one relative, for King was sent to live with aunt, though her name is unknown. If he had other kinsmen, he didn't know them.

The aunt kept the boy for four years, until he was nine, before she apprenticed him to a jeweler. That was in 1833. As an apprentice, part of his responsibilities was to babysit the children of the jeweler. King did not like minding the kids. That, he always remembered.

In 1835, when he was 11, he ran away. He hid on board a ship that he later remembered was called the Desdemona. Like the missing names of his parents, there is a question about this.

A ship named Desdemona sailed out of the harbor of New York in June 1835. This fits the facts of King's story. But it was a whaling ship under the command of Capt. Smith bound for the south Atlantic. There are reasons to doubt that King stowed away on a whaler. He never said so, for one, and the ship docked at Mobile, Ala., an unlikely port of call for a whaling ship. But no freighter or tramp steamer named Desdemona operating in 1835 has been found.

Whether whaler or freighter, King was hidden on board the ship Desdemona when he was found and marched before the captain. He said he ran away because he didn't like babysitting the kids of the New York jeweler. He earned his passage working as a cabin boy.

At the port of Mobile, the captain found King a place on an Alabama steamboat. The steamboat captain was Hugh Monroe. King spent two years working for Monroe and then got a job with Capt. Joe Holland whose boat operated on the Alabama River, from Montgomery to Mobile. This was the golden age of steamboats. They carried bales of cotton — the lifeblood of the South — to Southern ports and from there to the markets of the world.

Tom Lea in "The King Ranch" wrote that Capt. Joe Holland "sent this exceptional cub all the way to Connecticut to live with members of his family to go to school." King was in Connecticut for about eight months and always remembered Capt. Holland's two elderly sisters with affection.

He did not remember school as affectionately. He liked the classroom about as much as he liked minding the jeweler's kids. He returned from his exile in Connecticut to the only family he knew, the roistering, tobacco-chewing, blaspheming deckhands and crew of the steamboat.

He could read and write but the intricacies of grammar always troubled him. His real education was gained on the Alabama River. He became a pilot in 1840 when he was 16. This was a time when ability, however it showed itself, counted for more than education or parental lineage. What he learned — or must have learned — on Alabama steamboats was an important lesson that would serve him well. That was the art of getting on in the world.

King moved to Florida and in 1841 he was on the steamboat Ocochohee under the command of Capt. Henry Penny. This was

Richard King, an orphan from New York, remembered little of his
early life. His parents, Irish immigrants, died when he was five.

during one of the Seminole wars. Little is known of his time in
Florida except that he was on board the Ocochohee when a
Seminole chief named Hospertarke was lured on board, under a flag
of truce, and captured. The same thing happened to Chief Osceola
four years before.

In Florida he met Mifflin Kenedy, the captain of the Champion
operating on the Apalachicola and Chattahoochee rivers. Kenedy,
the son of Pennsylvania Quakers, had once taught school and sailed
before the mast, to ports in India and back. The King and Kenedy
friendship lasted a lifetime. Early in their friendship, the older

407

Kenedy, with more experience, was the dominant personality but eventually King would overtake him. However, the bond between them was never broken, apparently never even strained.

After the Seminole war wound down, the war with Mexico was looming. Kenedy was commissioned to take the Champion to New Orleans and up the Mississippi and Ohio Rivers to Pittsburgh. His task was to find and purchase steamboats for use on the Rio Grande to supply Gen. Zachary Taylor's army.

Mifflin Kenedy purchased three steamboats — the Colonel Cross, Whiteville, and the Corvette, which had been a luxury passenger boat on the Ohio. Kenedy became captain of the Corvette and wrote his friend in Florida, urging him to join him on the Rio Grande.

The journey of Richard King, Irish orphan, was a remarkable procession — from a jeweler's apprentice in New York to steamboat cub on the Alabama River and steamboat pilot during the Seminole wars in Florida. His exceptional story became even more exceptional after he landed in Texas, where he found his life's destiny.

*—Dec. 9, 2015*

# Grass and Cattle

Richard King arrived on the Rio Grande in the spring of 1847. It was almost a year after the battles of Palo Alto and Resaca de La Palma had been fought.

King was second pilot on the Colonel Cross. His friend Mifflin Kenedy was captain of the Corvette. They ferried troops and supplies for Zachary Taylor's army from the mouth of the Rio Grande to Camargo, a trip of six days over the shallow twisty river.

King was promoted to first pilot of the Corvette and near the end of the war named captain of the Colonel Cross. Tom Lea in "The King Ranch" said he may have been at the helm when Zachary Taylor traveled on the steamboat on his way home.

After the war King used his savings to buy a waterfront dive — a combination flophouse and saloon — at Boca del Rio, on the north side of the river from Bagdad. When the Colonel Cross was put up for auction, King bought it for $750; it cost the government $14,000 three years earlier. King, Kenedy and Charles Stillman formed a partnership and bought the Grampus and Comanche and other boats specially built for the Rio Grande. The firm was named M. Kenedy and Company.

From carrying supplies for the army, they went to carrying merchant's goods bound for markets in northern Mexico. This was quite the place to make money. Charles Stillman, King's business partner, would become one of the richest men in the world.

In late April or early May 1852, King and several companions rode north to attend Henry Kinney's Lone Star Fair at Corpus Christi. On the way King visited the Bobedo Ranch near Baffin Bay and asked the ranchero, Manuel Ramirez, about land for sale. Ramirez told him about the Santa Gertrudis tract to the north.

In Tom Lea's account, King and party camped by a small stream, the Santa Gertrudis. What King saw (we can guess by his later actions) was grazing ground of enormous potential. We don't know what his plans were, but he must have been struck by the idea that this boundless range was ideal for raising cattle. The literary cliché is "sea of grass." The expanse was oceanic. There were waves of grass. The vast prairie was like a great green sea of grass, grass and more grass.

They rode on to attend Kinney's fair at Corpus Christi, 45 miles away.

When King returned to Brownsville he bought 15,500 acres of the Santa Gertrudis grant, the land where they camped. He paid two cents an acre. The deed was filed on Nov. 14, 1853 in Corpus Christi. This marked the beginning of one of the great cattle empires of Texas.

King enlisted a partner, Gideon K. "Legs" Lewis, who was at the fair. Like King, Lewis was an orphan. He had been a printer's devil in New Orleans, a reporter in Galveston, and joined the Mier Expedition when he was 19. Lewis was captured with other Texans and in the notorious bean lottery he drew a white bean and lived. He moved to Corpus Christi, where he helped Kinney organize the Lone Star Fair.

Lewis gave King $2,000 for a half interest in the ranch. He also brought protection for the enterprise, as captain of a company of Rangers.

King was no cattleman. He was a steamboat captain who was more accustomed to walking a deck than riding a horse. But he knew enough to hire men who had expertise that he himself did not have. He hired vaqueros in Mexico who had worked cattle and horses all their lives and from them he learned the fundamentals of handling stock.

In Brownsville, the Rev. Hiram Chamberlain could find no suitable house to rent so he moved his family onto a surplus riverboat on the Rio Grande. It was docked where King usually docked his boat, the Colonel Cross, and King exchanged words with the reverend's oldest daughter, Henrietta.

King was enchanted with the young woman, though they were an unlikely pair. She was the preacher's daughter who would rather sing hymns than party. He was as rough as the deckhands he employed. But they were married on Sunday, Dec. 10, 1854. She wore a peach-colored dress and sang in the choir. King was rigged out in his Sunday clothes. After the sermon, Rev. Chamberlain

*Levee Street sloped down an embankment to the ferry landing on Brownsville's riverfront with two steamboats docked upriver at the steamboat landing. This Louis de Planque photo dates from 1864 or 1865.*

conducted the wedding rites and gave the couple a Bible. Henrietta was 22; King was 29. He called her Etta. She called him Captain.

King bought a carriage for the trip to Santa Gertrudis Creek. The couple stayed in a crude jacal at the camp. They made their first home in Brownsville in a house on Elizabeth Street, a cottage set back from the street with orange trees in the yard.

The following year, Legs Lewis was accused of having an affair with the wife of Dr. Jacob Yarrington of Corpus Christi. Yarrington found love letters between Lewis and his wife. Lewis went to Yarrington and demanded the letters be returned. Yarrington refused and warned him not to come back. Lewis returned on April 14, 1855 and Yarrington shot him to death with a shotgun.

Lewis left no heirs. His half-interest in the ranch was put up in auction. King had Maj. W. W. Chapman bid for the property by proxy. Chapman bought Lewis' share and left word for King that he had to bid more than expected because of the bidding by Capt. S.W. Fullerton. He signed a promissory note which King paid.

The first child of Richard and Henrietta was named Henrietta Marie (called Nettie). She was born in 1856. Their second child, Ella Morse King, was born in 1858, Richard King II was born in 1860, Alice Gertrudis King in 1862, and Robert E. Lee King in 1864. The captain and Henrietta lived in Brownsville, next door to Kenedy, until they moved to the ranch in 1857. King built a low

411

rambling house on a hill between the Santa Gertrudis and San Fernando creeks.

Rip Ford in his memoirs wrote that for King to take his wife into the wild brush country, an unpeopled land menaced by hostile Indians and roving bandits, was an act of extreme audacity.

*—Dec. 16, 2015*

# The Fortunes of War

Richard King's friend Mifflin Kenedy joined him in the ranching operation in 1860. They were already partners, with Charles Stillman, in the steamboat business on the Rio Grande.

When the Civil War broke out, King and Kenedy had 20,000 cattle and their longhorns were trailed to New Orleans to help feed the Confederacy. As the U.S. Navy tightened its blockade of Southern ports, cotton traveled down the Cotton Road to Mexico. It was not a "road" but a line of transit marked by tufts of cotton snagged on bushes.

The Cotton Road ran from the railroad terminus at Alleyton, west of Houston, to the Santa Margarita ferry crossing on the Nueces. From there it wound down to King Ranch on the Santa Gertrudis and from there traveled across the desert-like country known as the Big Sands.

It was a matter of luck, of serendipity, but Richard King and his two partners were uniquely situated — with their steamboats on the Rio Grande and King's ranch headquarters on the Cotton Road — to gain wealth from the war.

King, Kenedy and Stillman, with their freight-carrying monopoly, signed a contract to supply Confederate troops on the border. In return, they were promised 3,000 bales of cotton over a six-month period. That was worth, as Tom Lea figured, $900,000 in gold. Of course, that was only a portion of the money the three men made hustling cotton during the war.

In the division of labor, King was in charge of keeping the flow of cotton moving south from Santa Gertrudis. Kenedy ran the boats on the river. Stillman oversaw the counting house and business deals in Matamoros.

As the Cotton Road passed through King Ranch, the ranch supplied the caravans with horses, mules and provisions. There they

413

could rest and replenish their water before heading for the Big Sands. As Tom Lea wrote, King could stand on the watchtower and watch cotton wagons crawling south into the hazy distance. Hundreds of wagons and cumbrous ox-carts, top-heavy with cotton, pulled by horses, mules and oxen, stirred up a long ribbon of dust as they moved toward the river. Day after day it went on, an unending stream.

At Brownsville, the King, Kenedy and Stillman steamboats operating under Mexican registry ferried the valuable cotton to ships riding anchor off the mouth of the Rio Grande. The western Gulf became the most frequented waters in the world, crowded with ships. Cotton went out to European markets and a stream of gold went into the pockets of King, Kenedy and Stillman. Back came military essentials like lead from Mexico, so they wouldn't run out of bullets. This was the back door of the Confederacy.

A British military observer, Lt. Col. Arthur James Lyon Fremantle, traveled up the Cotton Road in April 1863. At Brownsville, he visited Confederate soldiers huddled around a campfire contemplating a pan of boiled potatoes. Fremantle's party reached King Ranch — "which I had heard of as a sort of Elysium, marking as it does the termination of the sands and the commencement of comparative civilization." The Kings were in Brownsville, but Mrs. Hamilton Bee, wife of the Confederate general in Brownsville, was at the ranch. Fremantle described her as "a nice, lively little woman, a red-hot Southerner."

Union Gen. Nathaniel Banks led an invasion of Texas to close the back door and stop the commerce in Confederate cotton. In Virginia, Confederate soldiers had stolen his supplies so often they called him Commissary Banks.

Gen. Banks' invasion force landed in November 1863. The Confederate commander on the border, Gen. Hamilton P. "Fall Back" Bee, was in such a lather to escape that he set Brownsville on fire trying to destroy cotton bales before the Yankees arrived. Part of Brownsville was burning, with a cloud of smoke hanging over the city, as Bee and staff skedaddled, sowing panic as they fled. Bee's jumpiness did more damage to Brownsville than the Union invaders.

With Banks' soldiers making themselves at home in Brownsville, there was an inconvenient interruption in cotton traffic. But soon the Cotton Road shifted west to Laredo and Eagle Pass and crossed the

*Richard King's original ranch house was built between the Santa Gertrudis and San Fernando creeks in 1857. A raid on this house by Union cavalry brought the reality of war home to Henrietta King. The house, enlarged over the years, burned in 1911.*

river — "el otro lado del rio" — and traveled safely down to waiting ships off Bagdad. Mexican territory was a sanctuary for both sides.

The war reached King Ranch at Christmastime 1863. A lone rider warned King that Yankee cavalry was on the way to capture him. King had his horse saddled and told a ranch hand, Francisco Alvarado, to look after his family. Henrietta and children were at the ranch.

Shots were fired at the house before dawn. Alvarado ran out, yelling, "Don't fire on this house! There is family here!" He was shot in the doorway, where he died. When the raiders — 80 men in blue uniforms under Capt. James Speed — didn't find King they vandalized the house and took ranch hands captive. After the raid on the ranch, on the way to San Antonio, Henrietta had her fifth baby at the home of friends in San Patricio. She named the boy Robert E. Lee King.

King stayed busy moving cotton to the waiting ships. Despite the profits, it was war work all the same.

The long-awaited news arrived: Lee had surrendered and the Confederacy had fallen. The war was over and the cotton times on the border came to an abrupt end. King retired to Matamoros to wait and see what peace would bring. Former Confederates who owned taxable property valued at more than $20,000 had to apply to the president for amnesty. In his request for a pardon, King valued his holdings at $300,000.

Throughout the war King worked hard and did well. The amassed wealth that made King Ranch the greatest cattle ranch in the country came not from the sale of longhorns but from the sale of cotton and the fortunes of war.

How much did King make? Tom Lea wrote that no one would ever know, but that however much it was "he did it buying and selling cotton, supplying Confederate troops, running wagon trains and steamboats. He rode a tide of good fortune during a tragedy of war. He rode it in plain view, unlike many of the border operators around him."

*—Dec. 23, 2015*

# A Rough Man, But a Good Man

After the end of the Civil War, Richard King and Mifflin Kenedy took action to reorganize their steamboat operations on the Rio Grande and their ranching enterprise on the Santa Gertrudis.

On the Rio Grande, they ordered four new steamboats. The third partner, Charles Stillman, withdrew and moved to New York, where he would became one of the world's richest men. King showed less interest in the steamboat business and more interest in converting grass into meat. "His heart was in ranching," Tom Lea wrote, "not in steamboating."

Two years after the war, King and Kenedy agreed to divide their ranch holdings, taking share and share alike, and part ways in the cattle business. An inventory was made and agreement signed on May 31, 1868 on the division. Kenedy purchased the Laureles tract from Charles Stillman's brother, Cornelius, while King became the sole proprietor of the Santa Gertrudis. But the two men remained close friends and allies.

Troubled times followed the war. Rustlers, hide thieves, and bandits worked the ranges, traveled the roads, and terrorized remote ranch houses. It was a lawless time. King Ranch kept lookouts atop a 75-foot watchtower on alert day and night. But away from the ranch house, on the vast ranch, there was no protection. Between 1866 and 1869, King reported the loss of 34,000 head of cattle.

South Texas ranchers, in the troubled times, appealed to Washington for protection. What they got in response was a congressional commission, the Robb Commission, to investigate and report on conditions on the border.

Richard King appeared before the commission, meeting in Brownsville, on Aug. 26, 1872. He testified about an incident three weeks before when he was leaving his ranch in a coach to appear before the commission. His coach was ambushed at San Fernando

Creek, some 25 to 30 shots were fired, and a traveling companion, Franz Specht, was killed. King told the commissioners he believed the dozen or so attackers were bandits from Mexico.

The Robb Commission issued a long report about the violent conditions, but Washington did nothing else to solve the problem. Not until Texas turned loose Leander McNelly and his company of Texas Rangers to clean up the border country were peace and order restored.

While cattlemen were trying to cope with bandit alarms, they were sending huge herds of cattle up the trail to Kansas and from there by railroad to the beef markets of St. Louis and Chicago. A clipping from a Corpus Christi paper reported that, "James Bryden starts off with the first drove of cattle for the Kansas market, his herd consisting of 4,120 head from Nueces County." Bryden was a trail boss for King Ranch.

Tom Lea in "The King Ranch" described one trail drive in 1875. John Fitch, a ranch foreman, was in overall charge. In February and early March, the hands gathered 4,737 head, which were divided into four herds and road-branded for the trail. In July, the cattle were sold at Denison, thereby avoiding the necessity of trailing them another 400 miles to Abilene, Kansas. King's proceeds from this one sale, Lea wrote, amounted to $61,886. And this was only one of many such drives.

King had other interests. He donated land in Corpus Christi for the city's first public school. He built the city's first ice plant in a warehouse off Water Street. And he was one of the main financial backers of Uriah Lott's railroad-building endeavors that opened up South Texas to settlement.

One story revealed King's fierce temper. On a stay at the Menger Hotel Mrs. King complained that there was no water in the pitcher in their room. King, who had come up from the bar, picked up the glass pitcher, went to the balcony overlooking the lobby, and threw it to the floor below, smashing it into a thousand pieces. He yelled down, "If we can't get any water up here, we don't need this pitcher." But this may be apocryphal.

After King's youngest son, Robert E. Lee King, died in St. Louis of pneumonia, when he was 19, the rancher started drinking heavily. He developed stomach pains that were diagnosed as cancer. Tom Lea wrote that he died at sunset in his room in the Menger Hotel in San Antonio overlooking Alamo Plaza. Most of his family was by

*After the Civil War, Richard King turned his attention from the steamboat operation on the Rio Grande to his ranch at Santa Gertrudis. He suffered losses from rustlers and hide thieves but sent huge herds up the trail to Kansas.*

his bedside, with Mifflin Kenedy, who had recently buried his wife Petra. It was April 14, 1885. King was 59.

Rip Ford, the legendary Ranger and King's longtime friend, said, "As a pioneer he came and labored." Tom Lea used that as his closing line at the end of volume one of "The King Ranch." A better epitaph came from a longtime ranch hand, who praised his late boss in simple terms. "He was a rough man, but he was a good man. I never knew a rougher man or a better man."

Richard King prospered and left a great ranch. It was a long journey that began in New York City in 1824 and ended in San Antonio in 1885. Like other journeys, it ended at the cemetery. Forty years later, after Henrietta died, Richard King's body was moved from San Antonio to a family cemetery at Kingsville.

King began his ranch with 15,500 acres. He left "Etta" 618,000 acres. He always followed the advice of his friend Robert E. Lee, who told him, "Buy land and never sell." However much he bought, it was not enough. It was never enough. Before Henrietta died in 1925, she doubled the size of the ranch, to 1.2 million acres. But it all started when Richard King came up from the Rio Grande and bought that first tract on the Santa Gertrudis, at the great expense of two cents an acre.

*—Dec. 30, 2015*

# NOTES ON SOURCES

(In the Notes on Sources Murphy Givens is denoted as "M. G.")

## Column 1, Fandango Riot, 1854

Galveston Weekly News, Jan. 10, 1854. New York Daily Tribune, Jan. 24, 1854. Galveston Weekly News, Jan. 31, 1854. U.S. Census, 1850. Maria von Blucher's Corpus Christi, edited by Bruce Cheeseman. City by the Sea, Eugenia Reynolds Briscoe. Opening Routes Across West Texas, 1848-1850, Southwestern Historical Quarterly. The Texas Frontier, 1848-1861, Southwestern Historical Quarterly. W.G. Freeman's Report on the Eighth Military District, Southwestern Historical Quarterly. Personal Memoirs of P. H. Sheridan. Corpus Christi: A History, M. G. and Jim Moloney. Columns, M. G., Aug. 16, 2006; Sept. 15 and Sept. 22, 2006; Aug. 29, 2008. Nueces Valley, newspaper, as cited.

## Column 2, Gutzon Borglum's Plan

Caller, Jan. 7, 1928. Brochure, Borglum's plan for colossal art from Corpus Christi to Brownsville, Corpus Christi Central Library. Bill Walraven columns, Feb. 20, 1977 and Nov. 6, 1987. Caller, July, 1911; April 1, 1935; April 27, 1952, May 18, 1982. Caller-Times, Aug. 6, 1960; Sept. 22, 1969. Nueces County History. Early Aviators, Lionel DeRemer. The Cliff Maus Airport, by Harry B. Adams, American Aviation Historical Society Journal. M. G. columns, Feb. 13, Feb. 20, 2002. Corpus Christi: A History, M. G. and Jim Moloney.

## Column 3, Mr. Giles and Mr. McCaughan

Corpus Christi Caller, Centennial Issue, 1883-1983. Corpus Christi: A History, M.G. and Jim Moloney. Caller, Jan. 29, 1935; Jan. 7, March 24, and April 16, 1939; May 19, 1950. Caller-Times, Feb. 21, 1935; Oct. 29, 1936; March 28, 1937; April 4 and April 6, 1937; March 23, 1956; Feb. 10 and Feb. 11, 1964. Caller-Times Biographical Form, July 28, 1955. Daily Voice, March 8 and April 7, 1937. Nueces County News, March 15, March 20 and July 14, 1939. Times, April 2, 1940; Oct. 17, 1941; March 22, 1956; April 3, 1956; Feb. 10, 1964; Nov. 25, 1965. Bill Walraven column, July 31, 1985. M. G. columns, Jan. 17 and Feb. 28, 2001; Aug. 14 and Aug. 21, 2013.

## Column 4, Caller's First Edition, 1883

Caller, Jan. 21, 1883, reprinted Jan. 18, 1959; M. G. columns on same subject: Aug. 2, 9, 16, 2000; Oct. 1, 8, 15, 22, 29, 2003; Nov. 5, 12, 19, 26, 2003; Dec. 3, 10, 2003.

## Column 5, When the Century Was Young

When the Century and I Were Young, Theodore Fuller, Corpus Christi Central Library. Bill Walraven columns, Jan. 3 and Jan. 4, Jan. 9, 1985. M. G. column, June 7, 2000.

## Column 6, Remember Pick's?

Caller, Sept. 24, 1969; Dec. 31, 1992. Times, March 13, 1965; Jan. 11, 1971; June 15, 1984. Caller-Times, May 28 and Aug. 23, 1939; undated, 1941; Dec. 21, 1961;

March 23, 1971; May 3, 1987; June 4, 1990. Oct. 20, 1996. Bill Walraven columns, 1978, and undated; vertical files, Corpus Christi Central Library. M. G. column, Jan. 12, 2000.

## Column 7, Donigan's Castle
The Armenian Pioneers of Texas, David Zenian. Caller, April 23, 1922; July 7, 1961; July 30 and Aug. 12, 1965; Jan. 4, 1983. Times, Sept. 11, 1926; Sept. 22, 1929; Jan. 21, 1965; Sept. 22, 1975; Nov. 12, 1979. Caller-Times, Sept. 14, 1926; Feb. 9, 1936; April 14, 1940; June 6 and June 7, 1943; Jan. 12, 1946; May 27 and June 26, 1979; Dec. 8, 1985.

## Column 8, Three Courthouses
Caller, July 4, 1976. Times, June 10, 1985. Caller-Times, Nov. 12, 1939; Sept. 29, 1940; Jan. 1, 1950; Sept. 26, 1954; July 15, 1956; Sept. 30, 1956; March 15, 1964; June 21, 1987; March 23, 1989. Bill Walraven columns, July 4 and July 7, 1980; March 19, 1982. Corpus Christi: A History, M. G. and Jim Moloney. M. G. columns: April 4, 2001; April 9 and April 16, 2003; Dec. 27, 2006; July 30, 2008; Jan. 18, 2012; Feb. 17, 2012; May 29, 2013.

## Column 9, The Devil's Hat Band
Caller, Oct. 11, 1885; Sept. 23, 1939. Times, Aug. 20, 1946. Caller-Times, Jan. 18, 1959; Oct. 18, 1959. The Fence Cutters, Southwestern Historical Quarterly. Fence-Cutting Days in Texas, Ira Aten, Frontier Times. Nueces County History. Western Words, Ramon Adams. Sixty Years in the Nueces Valley, Mrs. S. G. Miller. Lone Star, T. R. Fehrenbach. Great Plains, Walter Prescott Webb. A Vaquero of the Brush Country, J. Frank Dobie and John Young. M. G. columns, April 18, 2007; July 8 and July 15, 2009. Great Tales from the History of South Texas, M. G.

## Column 10, The Boys of '98
Corpus Christi Caller, Dec. 9, Dec. 16, 1898; Feb. 16, 1898; March 4, March 10, March 17, 1898; April 22, 1898; Caller, undated, 1898; May 2, May 3, May 4, May 6, May 13, May 19, May 29, 1898; June 7, June 14, June 17, 1898; July, 1898; Oct. 14, Oct. 21, 1898; Nov. 4, 1898; Dec. 9, 1898; Dec. 25, 1898; Jan. 1, Jan. 5, Jan. 6, Jan. 8, Jan. 13, 1899; Feb. 3, Feb. 24, 1899; March 17, March 31, 1899; April 10, April 14, April 17, 1899. Southwestern Historical Quarterly, Roosevelt's Rough Riders. Lone Star, T. R. Fehrenbach. Story of Corpus Christi, Mary Sutherland. Texas, James L. Haley. Previous M. G. columns: Feb. 18, 1998; April 5 and April 12, 2006; March 5, 2014.

## Column 11, The Cotton Road
Matamoros: Cotton Trading Capital of World, Holland McCombs, Caller, Times, Jan. 18, 1959. Heel-Fly Time in Texas, John Warren Hunter. City by the Sea, Eugenia Reynolds Briscoe. Matamoros, Port for Texas During Civil War, Robert W. Delaney, Southwestern Historical Quarterly. Rip Ford's Texas, Stephen B. Oates. The Fremantle Diary, Lt. Col. James Arthur Lyon Fremantle, Coldstream Guards. Two Sixshooters and a Sunbonnet, Dan Kilgore. King Ranch, Tom Lea. Los Algodones, the Cotton Times, Judi Hopkins McMordie. Cotton on the Border, 1861-1865, Ronnie C. Tyler, Southwestern Historical Quarterly. Kings of Texas,

Don Graham. Boom to Bust, Milo Kearney and Anthony Knopp. Sam Houston, John Hoyt Williams. Previous M. G. columns: Aug. 19, 1998; June 26, 2002; April 7, 2004; July 25, Aug. 3, Aug. 10, 2005; Aug. 1, 2007; Dec. 30, 2009; Jan., 13, 2010; March 31, 2010.

## Column 12, Salt of the Confederacy
History of a Texas Seaport, Coleman McCampbell. El Sal de Rey, Wallace Hawkins. Refugio, Hobart Huson. Dee Woods, Caller, July 24, 1939. Caller-Times, April 27, 1952. City by the Sea, Eugenia Reynolds Briscoe. The Story of Salt in Texas, Frontier Times. Military Events in Texas During Civil War, 1861-1865, Vol. 64. Padre Island, Writers' Roundtable. Learning by Hard Licks, Robert Adams. Salt Wars, New York Times, Dec. 26, 2013. Rip Ford's Texas, Stephen B. Oates. Historic Rio Grande Valley, Marjorie Johnson. Texas' Forgotten Ports, Keith Guthrie. Raw Frontier, Keith Guthrie. Pictorial History of Texas, Homer Thrall. Rancho Perdido, Ruth Dodson, thesis. Refugio County History. Previous M.G. column, Sept. 27, 2000.

## Column 13, Roosevelt's Big Fish
Fishing Yesterday's Gulf Coast, Barney Farley. Roosevelt's itinerary, Pare Lorentz Center of the FDR Presidential Library. Potomac's Log, Port Aransas Preservation and Historical Association. Caller-Times, April 20 and April 21, 1985; Jan. 18, 1959; Caller and Times, May 1-9, 1937. Times, Dec. 9, 1965. Corpus Christi: A History, M. G. and Jim Moloney.

## Column 14, La Quinta and Watsonia
Caller, Nov. 21, 1926; June 22, 1966. Caller-Times, Nov. 23, 1941, Jan. 15, 1956. Times, Dec. 22, 1947; April 12, 1966; Feb. 3, 1967. Vertical Files, Corpus Christi Central Library: May Mathis Green Watson. Watsonia, Dee Woods, Frontier Times. San Patricio County History, Keith Guthrie. Taft Ranch, A. Ray Stephens. Taft Ranch, May M. Green Watson and Alex Lillico. Washington State Department of Archaeology & Historic Preservation: William Doty Van Siclen. Previous M. G. column, Sept. 6, 2008.

## Column 15, Camp Scurry
Caller and Daily Herald, Feb. 27, 1916; July 4 and July 8, 1916; Aug. 31, Sept. 1, 2, 3, 4, 6, 7, 8, 9, 12, 13, 14, 1916; March 18, 1917; June 27, 29, 1917. Nov. 10, 11, 12, 13 and 26, 1918. Daily Voice, March 12, 1938; Caller, Sept. 29, 1940. Caller, Dec. 28, 1956 and Nov. 20, 1957; Caller-Times, March 12, 1941; Jan. 18, 1959; Times, Nov. 15, 1963. Vertical Files, Corpus Christi Central Library: Camp Scurry. Historic Rio Grande Valley, Marjorie Johnson. Rincon, Maude T. Gillilaland. Storm Over the Bay, Mary Jo O'Rear. When the Century and I Were Young, Theodore Fuller. I Shook the Hand, Harold Ratliff. Houston Chronicle, Sept. 14, 15, 16, 1957 on John A. Hulen. Corpus Christi: A History, M. G. and Jim Moloney. Previous M.G. columns: Nov. 11, 1998; Feb. 4, 2004; Oct. 26, 2005. Diary, Anita Lovenskiold, Corpus Christi Central Library.

## Column 16, The Great Western

Monterrey Is Ours, Napoleon Jackson Tecumseh Dana. My Confessions, Samuel Chamberlain. Mexico Under Fire, Joseph E. Chance. Captain Sam Grant, Lloyd Lewis. A Soldier's Life, Daniel P. Whiting. Anecdotes of General Taylor and the Mexican War, Thomas Bangs Thorpe. Rip Ford's Texas, Stephen B. Oates. Shady Ladies of the West, Ronald Miller. Legendary Ladies of Texas, Francis Edward Abernethy. George Washington Trahern: Texan Cowboy Soldier from Mier to Buena Vista, Southwestern Historical Quarterly. Taylor's Trail in Texas, Robert H. Thonhoff, Southwestern Historical Quarterly. The Great Western: Sarah Bowman, J. F. Elliott, Journal of Arizona History. Sarah Bowman, the Great Western, A.J. Flick. The Great Western, Leah Alden Jaswall, the Tombstone Times. Sketches from the Five States of Texas, A. C. Greene. The Handbook of Texas. Bill Walraven column, Nov. 26, 1975. Previous M. G. column, Dec. 30, 1998.

## Column 17, Cutting the Herd

Western Words, Ramon Adams. Cowboy Language: The Original Lingo of the Cow Town Frontier, Laurence Gesell. The Cowboy, Philip Ashton Rollins. Cowboy Culture, David Dary. Cowboy Lore, Jules Verne Allen. Warpath and Cattle Trail, Hubert Collins. North From Texas, James Shaw. North to Yesterday, Robert Flynn. The Trail to Ogallala, Benjamin Capps. The Day of the Cattleman, Ernest Staples Osgood. Previous M. G. column, June 1, 2005.

## Columns 18, 19, 20, 21, Nueces Valley Towns

San Patricio County History, Keith Guthrie. Raw Frontier, Keith Guthrie. Texas Forgotten Ports, Keith Guthrie. The San Patricio County Means-Garner Feud, Keith Guthrie, Journal of South Texas. Sixty Years in the Nueces Valley, Mrs. S. G. Miller. Lagarto: A Collection of Rememberances, Hattie Mae Hinnant New. Taft Ranch, A. Ray Stephens. The Rachals of White Point, Rachel B. Hebert. Nueces County History. Vaquero of the Brush Country, J. Frank Dobie and John Young. Hood's Texas Brigade, Harold B. Simpson. Trail Drivers of Texas, J. Marvin Hunter. Handbook of Texas. Caller-Times, Dec. 12, 1954; Oct. 13, 1957; Jan. 18, 1959; Sept. 20, 1960; Oct. 14, 1960; July 4, 1976; Oct. 6, 1983. Caller, July 9, 1939; Aug. 10, 1939; Dec. 1, 1940. Previous M. G. columns: April 22, 1998; April 26, 2000; Jan. 22, 2001; Feb. 14, 2001; Nov. 7, 2007. Corpus Christi: A History, M. G. and Jim Moloney.

## Columns 22, 23, Lost Waterfront and Seawall

Caller, Jan. 14, 1922; Aug. 15, 1922; Sept. 29, 1922; Dec. 9, 1922; Feb. 23, 1924; April 10, 1925; April 17, 1926. Jan. 13, 1939; Jan. 15, 1939; Nov. 15, 1939; Nov. 11, 1941; Aug. 4, 1961; Sept. 11, 1964. Times, Jan. 21, 1939; April 26, 1939; May 23, 1939; Feb. 22, 1956; April 8, 1965. Caller-Times, Oct. 29, 1936; Jan. 1, 1939; Feb. 5, 1939; March 16, 1939; Nov. 5, 1939; Jan. 1, 1950; April 27, 1952; Sept. 26, 1954; Jan. 18, 1959; July 4, 1976; Oct. 13, 1979; April 10, 1988. Caller-Times Centennial Journal. Corpus Christi Port Book, 1940. Bill Walraven columns, Dec. 2, 1980 and Sept. 10, 1984. M. G. columns, Oct. 27, 1999; Sept. 4, 2009. Corpus Christi: A History, M. G. and Jim Moloney.

## Column 24, Cattle Queen of Texas
Caller-Times, March 10, 1946; Jan. 23, 1983. Perilous Trails of Texas, John Dunn. Frank Wagner's Research Notes. Indian Wars and Pioneers of Texas, John Henry Brown. An American-Mexican Frontier, Paul Shuster Taylor. Mrs. Rabb's Pasture, Dan Kilgore. Previous M. G. columns: May 10, 2000; April 9, 2008.

## Column 25, Big Fire in 1892
Caller, July 14, July 15, 1892; Aug., 1904; Jan. 31, 1908; Jan. 20, Feb. 10, March 9, May 5, May 25, June 2, July 7, Aug. 25, 1905; July 13, 1939; March 16, 1978; . Caller-Times, Nov. 20, 1955; Jan. 18, 1959; Nov. 8, 1964; Times, Nov. 27, 1957; Nov. 17, 1965; Sept. 26, 1968. Caller-Times Centennial Journey. Corpus Christi: A Quarter Century of Development, 1900-1925, Dan Kilgore, Southwestern Historical Quarterly. A History of Corpus Christi's Municipal Water Supply, John S. McCampbell. Czech Pioneers of the Southwest, Estelle Hudson, Henry Rudolph Maresh. Previous M.G. column, Feb. 23, 2005. Corpus Christi: A History, M. G. and Jim Moloney.

## Column 26, Garner's Our Man
Corpus Christi Crony, March 8, March 22, April 5, April 19, May 10, May 17, June 14, June 28, July 19, July 26, Aug. 2, Sept. 13, Sept. 20, Sept. 27, Oct. 25, Nov. 8, Nov. 15, 1902; Jan. 31, 1903. Caller, Nov. 7, 1902; Jan. 26, 1903; July 23, 1904; Oct., 1936; Nov. 8, 1967. Associated Press Biographical Service, Jan. 1, 1955. Boss Rule, Evan Anders. Garner of Texas, Bascom N. Timmons. The Emergence of the New South, George B. Tindall. King Ranch Papers, Nov. 8, 1957. Saga of a Frontier Seaport, Coleman McCampbell. U.S. News & World Report, Aug. 27, 1959. Caller, Nov. 8, 1957. Previous M. G. column, Sept. 9, 1998; Sept. 4, 1999; Nov. 24, 1999; Sept. 4, 2012; Feb. 17, 2013.

## Column 27, Webster on Cattle
Shanghai Pierce: A Fair Likeness, Chris Emmett. Trail Drivers of Texas, J. Marvin Hunter. A Vaquero of the Brush Country, John D. Young and J. Frank Dobie. The Longhorn, J. Frank Dobie. Cowboy Culture, David Dary. The Sutton-Taylor Feud, Chuck Parsons. The Handbook of Texas. Shanghai Pierce, Cattleman, Margaret Pierce, Frontier Times. Shanghai Pierce, Colorful Cowman of Texas, A. C. Payne.

## Column 28, The Tarpon Club
Captain Sam Grant, Lloyd Lewis. Caller, Nov. 25, 1898; May 28, 1908; July 3, July 4, 1916; Jan. 18, 1959. New York Times, Oct. 11, 1902. The Numismatist, July 1936. A Hundred Years of Texas Waterfowl Hunting, R. K. Sawyer. Aransas, William Allen and Sue Hastings Taylor. Previous M. G. column, Dec. 3, 2008.

## Columns 29, 30, Spanish Place Names
The Journey of Alvar Nunez Cabeza de Vaca, translated by Fanny Bandelier; also by Buckingham Smith. The Route of Cabeza de Vaca, Bethel Coopwood, Southwestern Historical Quarterly. Spanish Exploration in the Southwest, Herbert Bolton. Wilderness Manhunt: The Spanish Search for La Salle, Robert S. Weddle. La Salle's Survivors, Weddle, Southwestern Historical Quarterly. San Juan Bautista, Gateway to Spanish Texas, Weddle. The Karankawa Indians of Texas,

Robert Ricklis. Old Texas Trails, J. W. Williams. Refugio, Hobart Huson. Spanish Expeditions in Texas, William C. Foster. Handbook of Texas. De Leon's Expedition of 1689, Elizabeth Howard West, Southwestern Historical Quarterly. Doomed Road of Empire, Hodding Carter. Southwestern Historical Quarterly: April 1899, April 1938, October 1993. Caller-Times, Jan. 18, 1959; March 4, 1962; Nov. 2, 1990; Nov. 14, 1990. Times, Oct. 9, 1962; April 20, 1978. Caller, March 22, 1961. M. G. columns: Dec. 4, 11, 18, 2002. Great Tales From the History of South Texas, M.G.

## Column 31, Ada Wilson

Caller: Feb. 18, 1957; May 2, 1959; Jan. 2, 1977; Feb. 17, 1977; Feb. 18, 1977; March 5, 1977. Times: April 15, 1966; June 16, 1966; Feb. 16, 1977; March 4, 1977; Dec. 1, 1977. Caller-Times: Feb. 17, 1963; Oct. 25, 1970; March 18, 1973. April 5, 1987; July 22, 1987. Mary Alice Davis, Caller-Times, Feb. 8, 1976; Caller, Feb. 9, 1976. Edward H. Harte, Caller, Feb. 22, 1976. Corpus Christi: Lyric and Music, Ada Wilson, 1951.

## Column 32, Shootout at Bessie Miller's

Times, July 6 and July 7, 1925. Caller, July 6, July 7, July 8, July 9, July 10, July 13, July 16, July 26, 1925. 50 Years Ago: Shootout at Bessie Miller's, Dan Kilgore, Caller, June 29, 1975. Caller-Times, Oct. 28, 1962. Tempers Were Hot As Summer in 1925, Tomme Call, Corpus Christi Caller, undated. Caller-Times Centennial Journey. Corpus Christi: A History, M. G. and Jim Moloney.

## Column 33, The Skeleton That Testified

Bill Walraven columns, Oct. 12 and Oct. 23, 1978. The Talking Skeleton, Ike Elliff, detailed first-person account in the author's possession; it was included in the "Pathfinders of Texas" by Mrs. Frank DeGarmo. Previous columns by M. G.: June 9 and June 16, 1999.

## Column 34, The St. James Site

American Flag, June 14, 1848. New York Herald, Feb. 11, 1850. Nueces Valley, July 27 and Aug. 1, 1874. Caller, Nov. 3, Dec. 8, and Dec. 15, 1905; May 29, 1908; April 27, 1922; Jan. 4, 1937; Aug. 6, 1939; June 5, 1952; Times, July 18, 1966. Caller-Times, Nov. 8, 1969. Caller-Times Centennial Journey. Frank Wagner's Research Papers. Bill Walraven columns, Sept. 15, 1978 and April 8, 1981. Indian Wars and Pioneers of Texas, John Henry Brown. Texas Indian Papers, 1846-1859. Texas Rangers, Walter Prescott Webb. City by the Sea, Eugenia Reynolds Briscoe. Story of Corpus Christi, Mary Sutherland. The Flight of the Grand Eagle, James H. Mundy and Earle G. Shettleworth Jr. That's Billy's Mark, Dan Kilgore. Previous M. G. columns: Feb. 3, 1999; Aug. 29, 2001; Aug. 2, 2006; Aug. 5, 2009; Oct. 31, 2012; Nov. 13, 2013. Great Tales From the History of South Texas, M.G.

## Column 35, J. W. Moses, Mustanger

Reminiscences of J. Williamson Moses were published in a series of columns in the San Antonio Express between 1887 and 1890. These were re-edited and printed in a volume, "Texas in Other Days," edited by M.G.

## Column 36, The Red Rovers

Alabama in the Texas Revolution, Claude Elliott, Southwestern Historical Quarterly. Alabama Settlement in Jackson County, the Cavalcade of Jackson County. History of Texas, John Henry Brown. Texas and Texans, Henry S. Foote. Handbook of Texas. Red Rovers at Coleto: A Comprehensive History of Texas, Dudley Wooten. The Red Rovers, letter, Jack Shackelford, Southwestern Historical Quarterly. Refugio, Hobart Huson. Presidio La Bahia, Kathryn Stoner O'Connor. Slaughter at Goliad, Jay A. Stout. Texian Iliad, Stephen L. Hardin. Muster Rolls: Capt. P.S. Wyatt's Company; Capt. Shackelford's Red Rovers. We Cousins: Families Comprising the Alabama Settlement of Austin's Colony, Florence Sutherland Hudson. Reminiscences of Fifty Years in Texas, John J. Linn. The Papers of the Texas Revolution. Sam Houston, John Hoyt Williams. A Critical Study of the Siege of the Alamo, Southwestern Historical Quarterly. Savage Frontier, Stephen L. Moore.

## Columns 37, 38, 39, Water, Chaparral and Mesquite

Caller: Jan. 21, 1883; Dec. 2, 1892; May 3, 1907; Feb. 28, 1908; May 28, 1939; July 4, 1939. Times, June 3, 1965; Aug. 10 and Aug. 25, 1965; Nov. 17, 1966; Feb. 6, 1974. Caller-Times, Jan. 30, 1921; Dec. 10, 1939; Jan. 1, 1950; April 27, 1952; Sept. 21, 1954; May 18, 1969. Caller-Times Centennial Journey. Saga of a Frontier Seaport, Coleman McCampbell. Story of Corpus Christi, Mary Sutherland. The Poenisch Family History, Harriett Tillman. Bill Walraven column, Jan. 24, 1979, Caller. Vertical Files, Corpus Christi Central Library: Water, Chaparral and Mequite; Reminiscences of Anna Moore Schwien. Previous columns by M. G.: March 18 and July 8, 1998; June 23 and June 30, 1999; May 24, May 3, May 31, June 7, Aug. 2, 9, 16, 2000; Nov. 21, 2001; April 3, 10, 17, 2002; Oct. 1, 8, 18, 22, 29, 2003; Nov. 5, 12, 19, 26, 2003; Dec. 3, 10, 2003; Aug. 2, 2006; Jan. 2, 2008; Feb. 20, 2008; May 7, 2008; March 17, 2010; Oct. 31, 2012; Jan. 22, 2014.

## Column 40, Boom and Bust, 1840s

Morning Star, Houston, Jan. 11, 1842. Corpus Christi Gazette, Feb. 5, 1846. The Telegraph, Houston, March 25 and April 1, 1846. Republic of the Rio Grande, June 6 and June 16, 1846. The American Flag: June 6, July 7, 16, 17, 19, 24, 1846; Aug. 3, 1846; March 4 and 13, 1847. Corpus Christi Star, assorted editions from September 1848 through June 1849. Caller-Times, Jan. 18, 1959. Times, Jan. 5, 1960. Bill Walraven column, Feb. 22, 1988. Saga of a Frontier Seaport, Coleman McCampbell. Story of Corpus Christi, Mary Sutherland. City by the Sea, Eugenia Reynolds Briscoe. Indian Depredations in Texas, J. W. Wilbarger. Memoirs, U.S. Grant. Reminiscences of Fifty Years in Texas, John J. Linn. Zachary Taylor in Corpus Christi, M. G. Lamar Papers. Col. Henry L. Kinney, Founder of Corpus Christi, Charles G. Norton. Previous columns by M. G. Feb. 25, May 6, 1998; Feb. 17, 1999; Aug. 18, 1999; Aug. 25, 1999; Oct. 13, 1999; Dec. 28, 2005; Jan. 4, 2006; April 4, 2007; June 10, 2009; Sept 6. And Dec. 2, 2009; May 12, 2012; Aug. 21, 2013.

## Column 41, Army Returns in 1850s

Galveston Weekly News, Jan. 10, 1854. New York Daily Tribune, Jan. 24, 1854. Galveston Weekly News, Jan. 31, 1854. New York Daily Tribune, Jan. 24, 1854.

Indianola Bulletin: March 11, 18, 25, April 8, 15, 22, 29, 30, May 6, 13, 20, 1852. Nueces Valley, March 1852. Texas State Gazette: March 6, May 8, 22, 29, 1852. First State Fair of Texas, Hortense Warner Ward, Southwestern Historical Quarterly. Ranchero, October-December, 1859. City by the Sea, Eugenia Reynolds Briscoe. Opening Routes Across West Texas, 1848-1850, Southwestern Historical Quarterly. The Texas Frontier, 1848-1861, Southwestern Historical Quarterly. W.G. Freeman's Report on the Eighth Military District, Southwestern Historical Quarterly. Personal Memoirs of P. H. Sheridan. Old Days in the Army, Lydia Spencer Lane. History of Texas, Louis J. Wortham. Corpus Christi: A History, M.G. and Jim Moloney. Columns, M. G.: Dec. 22, 1999; Jan. 1, 2003; April 2, 2003; Oct. 29, 2003; Aug. 16, Sept. 15, Sept. 22, 2006; Aug. 29, 2008.

## Column 42, War Brings Blockade, Misery

The Bombardment of Corpus Christi, William Adams, vertical files, Corpus Christi Central Library. Do You Know the Story of Corpus Christi? Andrew Anderson, biographical files, Corpus Christi Central Library. City by the Sea, Eugenie Reynolds Briscoe. Maria von Blucher's Corpus Christi, Bruce Cheeseman. The Vicksburg of Texas, Norman C. Delaney, Times, Aug. 14, 15, 16, 17, 1977. Ernest Morgan articles: Feb. 5, Feb. 19, March 5, March 12, 1961. The Capture of Corpus Christi, Texas, New York Herald, Nov. 16, 1862. War of the Rebellion, Official Records of the Union and Confederate Armies. William C. Thompson Letters, Corpus Christi Central Library. Rip Ford's Texas, Stephen B. Oates. Frank Wagner's Research Reports. The Almond Diary. The Story of Corpus Christi, Mary Sutherland. History of Nueces County. San Patricio County History, Keith Guthrie. The Corpus Christi Advertiser, Aug. 14, 1867. Caller, July 7, 1939. Caller, June 26, 1946; May 9, 1952; Jan. 18, 1959; Oct. 2, 1957; March 12, 1958. Centennial Journey. Previous M.G. columns: July 15, 1998; Oct. 28 and Nov. 4, 1998; Feb. 24, May 21, May 26, 1999; Jan. 19 and Sept. 6, 2000; May 9, 2001; Dec. 31, 2003; Jan. 7, 14, 21, 28, 2004; March 16, 17, 2005; July 25, 2007; Aug. 4, 2010; April 6, 2011; Oct. 24, 2012; Nov. 6, 2013. Corpus Christi: A History, M. G. and Jim Moloney.

## Column 43, Bandits Burn Noakes' Store

Corpus Christi Weekly Gazette, March 27, 1875. Caller, Nov. 28, 1902; April, 1920. Aug. 18, Aug. 24, 1939; Aug. 27, 1939; July 4, 1976. Times, March 28, 1950; Feb. 20, 1956; Feb. 20, 1958. Caller-Times, Nov. 22, 1936; April 15, 1956; Jan. 18, 1959. Beef Packing Houses, Hortense Warner Ward, Caller-Times, Jan. 18, 1959. E. J. Davis, Frontier Times, August 1930. Andrew Anderson, biographical files, Corpus Christi Central Library. E. H. Caldwell Memoirs. The Noakes Raid, Ruth Dodson, Frontier Times. Perilous Trails of Texas, John Dunn. Handbook of Texas. Refugio, Hobart Huson. King Ranch, Tom Lea. The Mexican Raid of 1875, Leopold Morris, Texas Historical Quarterly. Noakes Diary. A Vaquero of the Brush Country, John Young and J. Frank Dobie. Previous M.G. columns: March 11, 1998; July 29, 1998; Aug. 5, 1998; Sept. 9, 1998; Feb. 3, 1999; Feb. 16, 23, March 1, 2000; May 10, 2000; April 4, 2001; Aug. 29, 2001; Nov. 21, 2001; Feb. 27, March 6, 13, 2002; July 9, 16, 23, 2003; Aug. 18, 25, Sept. 1, 8, 2004; June 21, 2006. Great Tales From the History of South Texas, M. G. Corpus Christi: A History, M. G. and Jim Moloney.

## Column 44, Making Tracks in 1880s

Caller, Jan. 21, 1883; Oct. 26, Nov. 2, Nov. 14, Dec, 21, 1889; June 19, 1939; Aug. 5, 1984. Times, March 30, 1979. Caller-Times, March 9, 1924; April 27, 1952; Jan. 18, 1959. Corpus Christi Crony, March 8, 1902. Bill Walraven column, June 8, 1981. Random Recollections of Nearly Ninety Years, Eli Merriman. Gringo Builder, J. L. Allhands. Perfectly Exhausted With Pleasure, Bruce Cheeseman. The Story of Corpus Christi, Mary Sutherland. Saga of a Frontier Seaport, Coleman McCampbell. City by the Sea, Eugenie Reynolds Briscoe. Previous M.G. columns: March 28, 2007; Sept. 2, 2009; Feb. 24, March 17, May 26, Oct. 20, 2010; Nov. 22, 2011; Feb. 8, 2012; Jan. 22, 2014. Great Tales From the History of South Texas, M. G. Corpus Christi: A History, M. G. and Jim Moloney.

## Column 45, Century Ends With Crash

Andrew Anderson, biographical files, Corpus Christi Central Library. Frank Wagner's Research Papers. When the Century and I Were Young, Theodore Fuller, Corpus Christi Central Library. Caller, Aug. 18, 1893; Feb. 17, 1899. Dec. 21, 1900, Dec. 30, 1901; Nov. 25, 1904; June 2, 1905; May 18, 1906; Jan. 22, 1922; Sept. 23, 1939; March 12, 1941; Feb. 12, 1960; March 21, 1971; March 30, 1979. Corpus Christi Herald, April 13, 1910. Caller-Times, April 27, 1952; Aug. 12, 1956; Jan. 18, 1959; Aug. 5, 1964; Nov. 23, 1986. San Antonio Express, Feb. 17, 1899. Laredo Times, Feb. 17, 1899. Centennial History. War and the Weather, Edward Powers. Previous columns by M.G.: Feb. 18, 1998; June 10, 1998; Jan. 27, 1999; July 26, 2000; March 27, 2002; Oct. 26, 2004; March 1, March 22, April 5 and 12, Dec. 3, 2006; Dec. 26, 2007; April 16, 2008; Dec. 23, 2009; Feb. 10, Oct. 27, Nov. 24, Dec. 1, Dec. 7, 2010; Aug. 24, 2011; Nov. 14, 2012.

## Column 46, First Sheriff Left Mystery

Ranchero, Nov. 12, 1859; March 23, April 27, 1861. Caller, May 19, 1888; Aug. 4, 1920; June 15, 1924; April 6, 1930; June 4, 1936. Reminiscences of Anna Moore Schwien. Census, 1850 and 1860. Pathfinders, Mrs. Frank DeGarmo. Frank Wagner's Research Papers. City by the Sea, Eugenie Reynolds Briscoe. Research notes from Rev. Michael Howell. Previous columns by M. G.: Aug. 25, Sept. 1, 1999; Aug. 23, 30, Sept. 6, 2000; Jan. 28, 2004; Jan. 11, 18, 2006; May 31, June 7, 2006; Aug. 4, 2010; Oct. 5, 2011.

## Column 47, Peeling and Tanking

Corpus Christi Advertiser, undated, 1869. Corpus Christi Advertiser, July 26, 1872. Corpus Christi Gazette, March 29, 1873. Caller, Nov. 28, 1902. Times, Oct. 9, 1957. Caller-Times, Nov. 22, 1936. Centennial Journey. The Longhorns, J. Frank Dobie. Perilous Trails of Texas, John Dunn. Great Slaughter Made Coast a Boneyard, Hortense Warner Ward, Caller-Times, Jan. 18, 1959. Andrew Anderson, biographical files, Corpus Christi Central Library. Robert Adams, biographical files, Corpus Christi Central Library. History of Corpus Christi, Eli Merriman. Memoirs, E. H. Caldwell. The Great Plains, Walter Prescott Webb. Texas Coastal Bend, Alpha Kennedy Wood. A Vaquero of the Brush Country, John Young and J. Frank Dobie. Refugio, Hobart Huson. Aransas, William Allen and Sue Hastings Taylor. City by the Sea, Eugenie Briscoe. Previous M. G. columns: March 11, 1998; Dec. 15, 1999; Feb. 27, March 6, 13, 2002; Nov. 26, 29, 2006; Dec. 18, 2007; Nov. 14, 2012.

## Column 48, Roy Miller, Go-Getter

Caller, Caller and Daily Herald, Jan. 10, 1912; Feb. 27, 1916; July 4 and July 8, 1916; Aug. 31, Sept. 1, 2, 3, 4, 6, 7, 8, 9, 12, 13, 14, 1916; Oct. 18, 1918; Oct. 10, 1919; May 24, 1922; Sept. 15, 1926; Sept. 28, 1958; April 9, 1959; Sept. 12, 1976; Oct. 26, 1978. Times, June 13, 1950; June 26, 1958. Caller-Times, Aug. 27, 1950; July 22, 1955; Caller-Times Centennial Edition, Jan. 23, 1983. Roy Miller, biographical files, Corpus Christi Central Library. History of Nueces County. The Hurricane Almanac, Michael J. Ellis. A Brief History of the Port of Corpus Christi, M. Harvey Weil, manuscript, Corpus Christi Central Library. The Seaport of the South, Carl Helmecke, manuscript, Corpus Christi Central Library. Bill Walraven column, Jan. 11, 1984. 1919: The Storm, by Jim Moloney and M. G. Corpus Christi, A History, M.G. and Jim Moloney. Previous M. G. columns: May 30, June 6, 2001; Feb. 4, 2004; May 6, 2009; Jan. 4, 2012; Jan. 2, 2013.

## Column 49, Louis de Planque, Photographer

Corpus Christi Advertiser, April 8, 1870. Nueces Valley, October, 1872. Weekly Caller, Aug. 8, 1891. Caller, May 6, 1898; May 28, 1939. Caller-Times, April 27, 1952. Old Bayview website, research by Msgr. Michael Howell. Texas Handbook. Indianola, Brownson Malsch. Civil War and Revolution on the Rio Grande Frontier, Jerry Thompson and Lawrence T. Jones III. Previous columns by M. G.: Nov. 21, Dec. 12, 2001; Feb. 27, March 6, March 13, 2002; Nov. 19, 2003; May 7, 2008.

## Column 50, The First Decade of the 20th Century

Caller, Sept. 12, 1902; Aug. 11, 1904; Jan. 13, 20, 27, Feb. 17, March 9, April 14, April 28, June 2, Dec. 15, 1905; Sept. 14, 1927; Sept. 21, 1939. Caller-Times, Oct. 22, 1939; Aug. 21, 1955; July 15, 1956. Corpus Christi Crony, August, 1904. Corpus Christi Herald, March 17, 1905. The Story of Corpus Christi, Mary Sutherland. Saga of a Frontier Seaport, Coleman McCampbell. Frank Wagner's Research Papers. Taft Ranch, A. Ray Stephens. Taft Ranch, May M. Green Watson and Alex Lillico. Corpus Christi, A History, M.G. and Jim Moloney. Previous columns by M. G.: Feb. 3, 1999; Oct. 20, 1999; Jan. 2, 2002; March 20, 2002; Feb. 23, 2005; Oct. 21, 2009; Oct. 27, 2010; Feb. 22, 2012; Nov. 13, 2013.

## Column 51, A Stormy Decade

Caller, Feb. 3, 1911; June 30, July 3, July 4, 1911; May 23, 25, 26, 30, 1915; June 6, 9, 1915; Sept. 1, 3, 4, 7, 18, 1915; June 24, 1939. Caller and Daily Herald, Jan. 10, 1912; Feb. 27, 1916; July 4 and July 8, 1916; Aug. 31, Sept. 1, 2, 3, 4, 6, 7, 8, 9, 12, 13, 14, 1916. Nov. 10, 11, 12, 13 and 26, 1918. Caller-Times, Aug. 3, 1952; Aug. 1, 1965. Vertical Files, Corpus Christi Central Library: Camp Scurry. Storm Over the Bay, Mary Jo O'Rear. When the Century and I Were Young, Theodore Fuller. Diary, Anita Lovenskiold, Corpus Christi Central Library. Frank Wagner's research papers. Bill Walraven column, Sept. 23, 1975. 1919: The Storm, by Jim Moloney and M. G. Corpus Christi, A History, M.G. and Jim Moloney. Previous M. G. columns: April 15, Nov. 11, 1998; Feb. 4, 13, 20, July 17, 2002; June 1-5, June 9, 16, 2004; July 13, Oct. 26, 2005; May 6, 2009; Sept. 22, Nov. 3, Dec. 29, 2010; Feb. 16, 2011; July 25, Nov. 21, 2012.

## Column 52, The 1920s Came Roaring Back

Caller, March 29, Sept. 30, 1890; Nov. 20, 21, 1921; Caller, July 6, July 7, July 8, July 9, July 10, July 13, July 16, July 26, 1925. Anniversary Edition, 1933; Caller Jan. 1, 1950; April 2, 1952. Times, July 6 and July 7, 1925. 50 Years Ago: Shootout at Bessie Miller's, Dan Kilgore, Caller, June 29, 1975. Caller-Times, Oct. 28, 1962. Tempers Were Hot As Summer in 1925, Tomme Call, Corpus Christi Caller, undated. Caller-Times Centennial Journey. Caller-Times: Sept. 22, 1929; April 27, 1952; Oct. 11, 1961; Jan. 20, Nov. 10, 1963; June 13, 1965; Aug. 19, 1973. Rockport Record, Nov. 18, 1982. Seaport of the South, Carl Helmecke. Maston Nixon, vertical files, Corpus Christi Central Library. Corpus Christi: A History, M. G. and Jim Moloney. Previous columns by M. G.: Sept. 9, 1998; Nov. 24, 1999; May 30, June 6, Nov. 28, Dec. 5, 2001; April 14, 2004; Aug. 29, 2005; Dec. 5, 2007; March 5, Nov. 19, 2008; March 11, 2009; July 4, 2012; Feb. 13, 2013.

## Column 53, Hard Times in the 1930s

Caller: Jan. 12, Feb. 21, 1930; July 29, Aug. 30, 1930; Feb. 15, Feb. 23, 1932; Caller, May 1-9, 1937. July 4, 1976. Times: Sept. 27, 1929; Sept. 5, 1933; Jan. 4, 1937; Feb. 10, 1964; Times, Dec. 9, 1965. Caller-Times, June 22, 23, 1935; Nov. 19, 1955; Nov. 1, 1957; Jan. 18, 1959; March 2, 1973; April 20 and April 21, 1985; June 2, 1988. Corpus Christi Water Supply History, Atlee Cunningham. A History of Corpus Christi's Municipal Water Supply, John S. McCampbell. Bill Walraven columns, Oct. 12 and Oct. 23, 1978, and June 2, 1983. The Talking Skeleton, Ike Elliff. Corpus Christi on Parade, June 1936. Fishing Yesterday's Gulf Coast, Barney Farley. Roosevelt's itinerary, Pare Lorentz Center of the FDR Presidential Library. Potomac's Log, Port Aransas Preservation and Historical Association. Corpus Christi: A History, M. G. and Jim Moloney. Previous columns by M. G.: June 9, 16, 1999; Feb. 28, Oct. 28, 2001; Oct. 28, 2009.

## Column 54, City Was Booming in 1940s

Caller, Sept. 6, 1939; Aug. 1, Dec. 9, 1941; April 14, 1945; May 18, 1953; Dec. 7, 1961; Dec. 7, 1976; Feb. 16, 1983. Times, Dec. 16, 1940; April 13, 1945; Oct. 9, 1978. Caller-Times, May 21, 1939; Oct. 6, 1940; Jan. 16, 20, March 15, May 24, Sept. 24, Nov. 20, 1942; April 22, 1943; Feb. 11, 1944; Sept. 2, Dec. 20, 1945; Feb. 1, April 30, 1946; Sept. 9, 1951; Jan. 18, 1959; Jan. 25, March 16, 1966. Vertical files, Corpus Christi Central Library. History of Nueces County. Centennial History. Bill Walraven column, Feb. 16, 1983. News to Me, Juliet K. Wenger. Previous columns by M. G.: Feb. 3, Sept. 29, Oct. 6, Oct. 27, 1999; Jan. 17, 2001; Aug. 29, Dec. 7, 14, 21, 2005; Sept. 13, 2006; July 11, 2007; Sept. 30, 2009; July 28, Aug. 26, 2010; June 1, July 13, 2011; March 14, 21, Dec. 19, 26, 2012; Feb. 6, Nov. 13, 2013. Corpus Christi: A History, M. G. and Jim Moloney.

## Column 55, Building Harbor Bridge

Caller, July 3, 1950; Jan. 30, Feb. 1, 1951; Jan. 8, June 10, 19, 20, 1954; Aug. 25, 1955; March 27, 1957; July 3, 1958; Feb. 26, 1959; Nov. 8, Dec. 7, 1963; Jan. 9, 15, 1964; July 4, 1976; June 9, 1988. Times, June 17, 1950; Feb. 1, 1954; Jan. 7, 1964; Feb. 15, 1966. Caller-Times, Sept. 9, 1951; May 28, June 19, 20, Sept. 26, 1954; Jan. 18, Oct. 23, 1959; Jan. 1, 1960; Feb. 24, 1963; Jan. 12, Sept. 10, 1964;

Nov. 10, 1988. News to Me, Juliet K. Wenger. Vertical files, Corpus Christi Central Library. History of Nueces County. Centennial History. Bill Walraven columns: April 16, 1975; Sept. 29, 1978; Oct. 20, 1987. Previous M. G. columns: Jan. 12, April 12, July 19, 2000; Feb. 20, 2002; Nov. 22, 2006; March 28, April 4, Nov. 28, 2012. Corpus Christi: A History, M. G. and Jim Moloney.

## Column 56, The Dobie Ranch
I'll Tell You a Tale, The Longhorns, Out of the Old Rock, Tales of Old-Time Texas, The Mustangs, Coronado's Children, J. Frank Dobie. Biographical Sketch, Dec. 29, 1958, J. Frank Dobie. Afield With J. Frank Dobie, edited by Neil Carmony. Lagarto: A Collection of Rememberances, Hattie Mae Hinnant New. The Handbook of Texas. Caller, June 8, 1953; June 5, 1955. Caller-Times, Jan. 18, 1959; Oct. 27, 1963. Austin American-Statesman, Dec. 24, 1961. Recollections of Other Days, edited by M. G. and Jim Moloney. Previous M. G. column: Oct. 10, 2012.

## Column 57, Up the Trail
Corpus Christi Advertiser, April 8, 1870. Corpus Christi Gazette, Feb. 15, April 24, 1873. Caller, Sept. 15, 1939; Oct. 2, 1952; Caller-Times, Feb. 15, 1948; Jan. 18, 1959; undated article, 1968. San Antonio Express-News, Oct. 3, 1965. Hutchinson (Kansas) Herald, Feb. 2, 1952; The Newton Kansan, Aug. 21, 1997. The Longhorns, A Vaquero of the Brush Country, J. Frank Dobie and John Young. Texas After the Civil War, Carl Moneyhon. King Ranch, Tom Lea. Raw Frontier, Keith Guthrie. Changing Tides, Robert Weddle. Storms Brewed In Other Men's Worlds, Elizabeth A.H. John. History of the Cattle Industry in the Southwest, Clara M. Love, Southwestern Historical Quarterly. The Chisholm Trail and Other Routes, T.V. Taylor. Cowboy Culture, David Dary. Shanghai Pierce: A Fair Likeness, Chris Emmett. Days When Corpus Christi Was Young, W.G. Sutherland. Miracle on the Chisholm Trail, Henry B. Jameson. Refugio, Hobart Huson. Nueces County History. Reminiscences of C.C. Cox, Southwest Historical Quarterly. Cowboy Lore, Jesse James Benton. Trail Drivers of Texas, J. Marvin Hunter. Previous columns by M.G.: Feb. 16, 23, March 1, 2000; Feb. 27, 2002; Feb. 13, 2008; May 26, 2010; Jan. 19, 2011; July 18, 2012; Dec. 4, 2013. Great Tales From the History of South Texas, M. G.

## Column 58, Steamer Mary Wrecked in 1876
Sixty Years in the Nueces Valley, Mrs. S.G. Miller. Corpus Christi Gazette, Dec. 3, 1876. Andrew Anderson, vertical files, Corpus Christi Central Library. Corpus Christi Caller, July 18, 1939. Previous columns by M.G.: Oct. 18, 2000; Feb. 5, 2008; July 6, 2011; April 11, 2012.

## Column 59, Trade Route to Chihuahua
Year of Decision: 1846, Bernard DeVoto. Reminiscences of Fifty Years in Texas, John J. Linn. Sam Houston, John Hoyt Williams. Indianola, Brownson Malsch. Great River, Paul Horgan. Texas' Forgotten Ports, Keith Guthrie. Old Texas Trails, J. W. Williams. Texas Rangers, Walter Prescott Webb. Road of Empire, Hodding Carter. City by the Sea, Eugenia Reynolds Briscoe. Nueces County History. Through the Years, Anna Marietta Kelsey. The Kingdom of Zapata, Virgil Lott,

Mercurio Martinez. Notes on Early Steamboating on the Rio Grande, Harbert Davenport, Southwestern Historical Quarterly. Pedro Vial and the Roads to Santa Fe, Southwestern Historical Quarterly. Indian Wars and Pioneers of Texas, John Henry Brown. History of Nueces County to 1850, Marvin Lee Deviney. Memoirs, E. H. Caldwell. Random Recollections of Nearly Ninety Years, Eli Merriman. Robert Adams, biographical files, Corpus Christi Central Library. Tragedy at Taos, James A. Crutchfield. Life of Henry Lawrence Kinney, W. R. Gore. Corpus Christi Star: Jan. 1, 1846; Oct. 10, 17, 24, Nov. 1, 21, Dec. 16, 23, 1848; Feb. 10, March 10, 25, April 21, 1849. Ranchero March 31, 1860; March 16, 23, 1861. Previous column by M.G.: May 23, 2012.

## Column 60, The Skinning War

Refugio, Hobart Huson. City by the Sea, Eugenia Reynolds Briscoe. Raw Frontier, Keith Guthrie. Vaquero of the Brush Country, J. Frank Dobie and John Young. The Longhorns, J. Frank Dobie. Perilous Trails of Texas, John Dunn. E. H. Caldwell Memoirs. Cowboy Culture, David Dary. Taming the Nueces Strip, George Durham and Clyde Wantland. Handbook of Texas. King Ranch, Tom Lea. Nueces Valley, March 1870. San Antonio Express, Feb. 11, 1934. Trail Drivers of Texas, J. Marvin Hunter. Shanghai Pierce: A Fair Likeness, Chris Emmett. Untold Story of Reconstruction in South Texas, Kenneth Howell, South Texas Studies, Victoria College. Raids and Counter-Raids on the Rio Grande, W.G. Sutherland, Caller, Sept. 2, 1923. Caller, Aug. 4, 1939. Caller-Times, Jan. 18, 1959. Nueces Valley: July 9, Oct. 29, 1870; March 8, 15, 1872; Aug. 10, 1872; Aug. 8, 1874. Corpus Christi Gazette: Jan. 6, 1872; June 13, July 4, 1874. Previous M. G. columns: March 31, 1999; Feb. 27, 2002; March 6, 2002; Sept. 7, 14, 2005; April 26, 2006; July 30, Aug. 20, Sept. 10, 2008; March 16, 2011; July 10, 17, 2013.

## Column 61, Vigilantes in the Saddle

Refugio, Hobart Huson. Vaquero of the Brush Country, J. Frank Dobie and John D. Young. Corpus Christi Gazette, June 13, July 4, 1874. Refugio County History. History of Goliad County. John Young in Frontier Times. Saint Mary's of Aransas, Hobart Huson. San Antonio Express, Nov. 13, 1889. Weekly Caller, Feb. 28, 1891. Perilous Trails of Texas, John Dunn. Stolen Heritage, Abel C. Rubio. Tejano Legacy, Armando G. Alonzo. Trail Drivers of Texas, J. Marvin Hunter. Personnel of the Texas State Government, L. E. Daniell. Law and Lawlessness on the Texas Frontier, W. C. Holden, Southwestern Historical Quarterly. Great Tales From the History of South Texas, M. G. Previous M. G. columns: Sept. 7, 14, 2005; March 16, 2011.

## Column 62, Hanging Chipita

Refugio, Hobart Huson. District Judges of Refugio County, Huson. History of San Patricio, Keith Guthrie. Raw Frontier, Guthrie. City by the Sea, Eugenia Reynolds Briscoe. A Noose for Chipita, Vernon Smylie. History of a Texas Seaport, Bill Walraven. Empresarios' Children, Bill and Marjorie Walraven. Reminiscences, Eli Merriman. Vertical files, Corpus Christi Central Library. Ranchero, Oct. 29, 1863. Nueces Valley: June 11, 1870; July 16, 1873. Weekly Gazette, July 19, 1873. Caller, Dec. 21, 1900. Caller-Times, Jan. 18, Nov. 13, 1959; May 14, 28, 1961. Great Tales From the History of South Texas, M. G. Previous M. G. columns: April 22, 1998; April 21, 1999; April 26, 2006; Nov. 7, 2007.

## Column 63, Summer of Yellow Fever

Story of Corpus Christi, Mary Sutherland. City by the Sea, Eugenia Reynolds Briscoe. History of a Texas Seaport, Coleman McCampbell. Maria von Blucher's Corpus Christi, edited by Bruce Cheeseman. Indianola, Brownson Malsch. History of San Patricio, Keith Guthrie. Perilous Trails, John Dunn. Joseph Almond Diary. Helen Chapman Diary. Memoirs, Anna Moore Schwien. On This Bluff, History of First Presbyterian Church. Saddlebag Priest of the Nueces, Sister Mary Xavier. Memoirs, Andrew Anderson. Recollections, Eli Merriman. History of a Texas Seaport, Bill Walraven. Bill Walraven column, Feb. 5, 1987. Handbook of Texas. Frank Wagner's Research Papers. History of Nueces County. Nueces County Commissioners' Minutes, Book C. Recollections of Other Days, edited by M. G. and Jim Moloney. Corpus Christi: A History, M. G. and Jim Moloney. Advertiser, Aug. 14, 1867. Caller, July 7, 1939; May 9, 1952. Times, June 20, 1946. Caller-Times, April 27, 1952; Jan. 18, 1959. Centennial Journey. Previous M. G. columns: July 15, 1998; May 21, 1999; May 3, May 10, Nov. 26, 2006; Nov. 20, 2013.

## Column 64, Replacing the Reef Road

The Reef, Corpus Christi Star, 1848. Caller and Daily Herald, Dec. 10, 1915. Caller, May 2, 1920; Jan. 23, Oct. 5, 8, 9, 1921; Sept. 9, 14, 17, 20, 21, 1933; July 18, Aug. 11, 1963; Aug. 13, 1971; Oct. 16, 1976. Times, Oct. 1, 1946; Nov. 28, 1950; Oct. 19, 1951; Sept. 20, 1965; March 24, Aug. 4, 1966; May 12, 1967; March 17, 1971; Jan. 12, July 8, 1977. Caller-Times, Jan. 19, 1959; April 30, 1967. Corpus Christi Press, June 23, 1949. History of San Patricio, Keith Guthrie. Story of Corpus Christi, Mary Sutherland. City by the Sea, Eugenia Reynolds Briscoe. History of a Texas Seaport, Coleman McCampbell. Corpus Christi: A History, M.G. and Jim Moloney. Texas In Other Days, reminiscences of J. Williamson Moses. 1919: The Storm, by Jim Moloney and M. G. Corpus Christi Causeway Contains 2300 Feet of Reinforced-Concrete Girder Spans, Engineering Record, March 18, 1916. First Nueces Bay Causeway, Cathy Nix, vertical files, Corpus Christi Central Library. Memoirs, E. H. Caldwell. Previous M. G. columns: Oct. 13, 1999; March 21, 2001; June 15, 2005; Nov. 14, 2007.

## Column 65, Norwick Gussett, Wool Merchant

Ranchero, March 9, 1861. Corpus Christi Advertiser, Dec. 21, 1872. Caller, Feb. 21, 1889; Oct. 2, 1908; Dec. 12, 1933; July 13, 14, Aug. 12, 1939; Oct. 12, 1940; Oct. 13, 1948. Corpus Christi Crony, Oct. 3, 1908. Times, Feb. 14, 1951; undated interview, 1953. Corpus Christi Public Library, Box 10, DeGarmo Collection. Memoirs, E. H. Caldwell. Recollections, Eli Merriman. Frank Wagner's Research Papers. Pathfinders of Texas, Mrs. Frank DeGarmo. Letter to Mrs. DeGarmo, Sept. 17, 1935. Statement of Military Service of Norwick Gussett, War Department, July 28, 1938. Peter Benson papers, Corpus Christi Central Library. Corpus Christi: A History, M. G. and Jim Moloney. Centennial Journey. Previous M. G. columns: March 3, Dec. 22, 1999; Feb. 27, July 10, 2002; Sept. 3, 2003; June 21, 2006; Sept. 2, 2009; July 23, 2010.

## Column 66, The Greatest Ranger

Great Comanche Raid, Donaly Brice. Texas Border, Robert Casey. Border Wars of Texas, James DeShields. Lone Star, T.R. Fehrenbach. Texas Ranger: Jack Hays in the Frontier Southwest, James Kimmins Greer. Journal of Lewis Birdsall Harris, Southwestern Historical Quarterly. Recollections of Early Texas, John Holland Jenkins. Papers of Mirabeau Lamar. Memoirs of Mary Maverick. Savage Frontier, Stephen Moore. Flowers and Fruits in the Wildness, Z. N. Morrell. The Indians of Texas, W. W. Newcomb. Telegraph and Texas Register, July 3, 1844. Men Who Wear the Star, Charles Robinson III. Texas Indian Fighters, A.J. Sowell. The Life of Bigfoot Wallace, Sowell. Evolution of a State, Noah Smithwick. Texas Indian Papers, 1844-1845. Texas Rangers, Walter Prescott Webb. The Handbook of Texas. Indian Depredations in Texas, Josiah Wilbarger. The Writings of Sam Houston, Amelia Williams and Eugene Barker. Sam Houston, John Hoyt Williams. Great Tales From the History of South Texas, M. G. Previous M. G. columns: Sept. 21, 28, 2011; June 6, 13, 2012.

## Column 67, E. H. Caldwell
Memoirs, E. H. Caldwell, edited by Robert J. Caldwell. Recollections of Other Days, edited by M. G. and Jim Moloney. Falfurrias, Dale Lasater. Dee Woods in the Caller: June 19, 29, July 4, Aug. 24, 25, 1939. Obituary, Caller, March 15, 1940. Great Tales From the History of South Texas, M. G. Corpus Christi: A History, M. G. and Jim Moloney. Previous M. G. columns: Aug. 4, 11, 2004.

## Column 68, Seaside Hotel
Daily Ranchero, Brownsville, Jan. 29, 1870. Nueces Valley, undated, 1874. Caller: June 19, 1904; July 21, 1905; Aug. 25, 1905; Oct. 20, 1905; Aug. 8, 1906; Jan. 10, 1908; March 21, 1921; March 5, 1941; Oct. 3, 1983. Times, March 6, 1926. Caller-Times: Jan. 18, 1959. Crony Special, March 13, 1909. City Directory, 1907-1908. Old Bayview research notes, Rev. Michael Howell. Reminiscences of Anna Moore Schwien. The Building of Corpus Christi, Evans Wyatt. The Gringo Builders, J. L. Allhands. Memoirs, Andrew Anderson. Seaside Hotel Menu, Jan. 1, 1908. Pathfinders, Mrs. Frank DeGarmo. Memoirs, E. H. Caldwell. Corpus Christi: A History, M. G. and Jim Moloney. Centennial Journey. Old South Texas, M.G. 1919: The Storm, by Jim Moloney and M. G. Previous M. G. columns: Oct. 3, 2001; Oct. 15, 2003; Jan. 18, 2006; Feb. 20, 2008; Aug. 26, 2009; Sept. 15, 2010; July 11, 2012.

## Column 69, Laguna Madre Murders
Caller, Jan. 25, 1916; April 23, 1952; May 15, 1954; Oct. 27, 1958; April 15, 1965; May 12, 1966. Times, April 1, 1959; Aug. 9, 1969. Caller-Times, April 27, 1952; Jan. 2, 1966. San Patricio County History, Keith Guthrie. Taft Ranch, A. Ray Stephens. Wooden Rigs-Iron Men, Bill and Marjorie Walraven. Oil! Titan of the Southwest, Carl Coke Rister. Corpus Christi: A History, M. G. and Jim Moloney. Centennial Journey. Previous M. G. columns: April 26, 2000; Sept. 21, 2005; Aug. 22, 2012.

## Columns 70, 71, 72, 73, 74, Corpus Christi's Newspapers
Centennial Journal, Caller-Times, Jan. 23, 1983. History of Press Here Begins With Republic, Bill Walraven, Caller-Times, Jan. 18, 1959. Walraven columns, Jan. 19, 1977; July 29, 1977; June 17, 1983, Caller. Corpus Christi Gazette, Jan. 1, Jan. 8, March 8, 1846. Corpus Christi Star, Sept. 5, 19, Oct. 17, 1848; Jan. 20, 27, March

24, 1849. Ranchero, various editions from Oct. 22, 1859 to Jan. 21, 1864. Ranchero War Extra, July 20, 1861; Aug. 19, 1862. Gazette, Jan. 4, July 19, 1873. Caller, Jan. 21, 1883; Sept. 16, 1919; April 22, 1952; July 23, 1958; Jan. 14, Aug. 3, 1960; Dec. 7, 1975. Times, July 31, Sept. 3, 1958, March 11, 1959; Jan. 20, 1960; May 17, 1961. Caller-Times, Golden Anniversary Edition, 1933; Sept. 26, 1952. Corpus Christi Crony, Feb. 14, 1903. Pioneer Printing in Texas, Southwestern Historical Quarterly. Random Recollections of Nearly 90 Years, Eli Merriman. Pioneer Printing, Merriman. Eli Merriman's Scrapbook. Pathfinders, Mrs. Frank DeGarmo. History of the Caller-Times, newspaper morgue. Lone Stars and State Gazettes, Marilyn McAdams Sibley. Pioneer Printer, Lota M. Spell. The Maltby Brothers Civil War, Norman C. Delaney. Supreme Court of the U.S., October Term, Craig v. Harney. A Salute to Ed Harte, Sept. 26, 1987, M. G. Corpus Christi: A History, M. G. and Jim Moloney. Previous M. G. columns: Feb. 25, 1998; Oct. 29, 2003; Oct. 22, 2004; March 16, 17, 2005; Sept. 13, 2006; April 11, Dec. 7, 2007.

## Columns 75, 76, 77, NAS in World War II

Caller, July 2, Sept. 8, Sept. 29, Oct. 13, 17, 1940; Dec. 8, 1941. Times, Sept. 12, 1940; March 12, Oct. 31, 1941; Sept. 24, 1942; Oct. 11, 1961; April 7, 1965; Jan. 24, March 16, 1966; Jan. 18, 1968. Caller-Times, March 12, April 20, 1941; March 12, April 7, Nov. 2, 1941; March 15, Aug. 29, 1942; April 21, May 31, 1943; Aug. 6, 1945; March 11, 1956; Jan. 18, 1959; Dec. 7, 1961; Dec. 1, 1963. Women Work by Day and Study by Night ... undated article, Caller-Times. Corpus Christi Press, April 23, Oct. 29, 1943; June 9, 1944. Naval Air Station photographs, Library of Congress. A&R News, Dec. 1, 1944. Chamber of Commerce magazine, December 1939; February, June, October 1940; March, July, 1941. Wings of Gold, May 9, 1991.Naval Air Station Corpus Christi Yearbook. History of the Corpus Christi NAS, Naval Aviation News, March 1956. Collier's, June 7, 1941. The Battle of Midway Roundtable, Ens. Gerald F. Child. Tyrone Power, notes from Naval Aviation Museum. Corpus Christi's 'University of the Air', Norman Delaney, Naval History, June 2013. Old Corpus Christi, M. G. Corpus Christi: A History, M.G. and Jim Moloney. No Ordinary Time, Doris Kearns Goodwin. Previous M. G. columns: Jan. 17, 2001; Dec. 7, 14, 21, 2005; July 28, 2010; March 14, 21, 2012.

## Column 78, Independence Day

Caller, Nov. 16, 1906; Jan. 17, April 3, 1908. Times, April 28, 1976. Caller-Times, July 4, 1976. July Fourth Celebration Here In 1876 Was A Grand and Glorious Event, Eli Merriman, Caller, July, 1926. Frank Wagner's research papers. Boss Rule in South Texas, Evan Anders. Nueces County History. Handbook of Texas. Falfurrias, Dale Lasater. Maria von Blucher's Corpus Christi, edited by Bruce Cheeseman. Texas Rangers, Walter Prescott Webb. Nueces County History. Corpus Christi: A History, M. G. and Jim Moloney. Previous M. G. column: March 13, 2002.

## Columns 79-86, The Noakes' Diary

Thomas John Noakes' Diary: January 1858-March 1862; December 1863-November 1864; July 1865-October 1866; October 1866-April 1867. Raid by Mexicans in 1875, Thomas J. Noakes, Caller, Dec. 22, 1912; reprinted in Frontier

Times. Pathfinders, Mrs. Frank DeGarmo. Dee Woods in the Caller, June 29, July 3, Aug. 24, 25, 26, 31, 1939. Caller, Jan. 18, 1957; Feb. 15, 1958. Caller-Times, Jan. 18, 1959. Nueces County News, July 14, 1939. Corpus Christi Times, March 28, 1950. Mexican Raid on Corpus Christi, Southwestern Historical Quarterly. Corpus Christi on Parade, September 1936. Columns by Bill Walraven: Dec. 3, 1980; Jan. 9, 12, 1981; April 7, 1982; Feb. 26, 1988. Perilous Trails of Texas, John Dunn. Corpus Christi: A History, M. G. and Jim Moloney. Great Tales From the History of South Texas, M. G. Previous M. G. columns: Aug. 5, Nov. 4, 1998; May 5, 12, 1999; Sept. 1, 2004; Oct. 19, 2005; Oct. 14, 2009; May 5, 2010; April 25, 2012; Jan. 23, 2013.

## Column 87, To Dump Road

Caller, April 9, 1939; Nov. 8, 1941; March 26, 1947; Aug. 24, 1949; June 15, 1950; Sept. 20, Oct. 14, 1954; April 23, 25, July 9, 1959; Nov. 24, 1974; July 4, 1976; Sept. 20, 1979; March 28, April 4, May 30, 1983; Aug. 9, 1984. Times, May 30, 1925; March 26, 1947; Aug. 24, 1949; April 20, 1948; May 25, 1964; March 2, 1976. Caller-Times, April 9, 1939; Sept. 26, 1954; Feb. 16, 1992. Centennial Journey. Chamber of Commerce magazine, July 1941. City directories from 1930s and 1940s. Previous M. G. columns: Dec. 27, 2000; Feb. 25, 2009.

## Column 88, Out by Pancho Grande's

Caller, May 16, 1930; Aug. 21, 1937; May 6, 1957; Dec. 4, 6, 1962; Feb. 7, March 6, 7, 1963; Feb. 28, 1964; Oct. 6, 1965; Oct. 29, 1968; Aug. 28, 29, Sept. 19, 1972; April 20, 1976; Sept. 21, 1978; May 3, 1979; Feb. 23, 1984; Sept. 24, 1986. Times, Sept. 22, 1929; Jan. 24, 1950; March 30, July 8, 9, 1965; April 7, 26, 1966; Sept. 24, 25, 1986. Caller-Times, May 18, 1958; Feb. 25, 1971; April 8, 1989; Sept. 18, 1999. Centennial Journey. City directories from 1930s and 1940s. Previous M. G. columns: Feb. 28, 2001; Oct. 2, 2002; April 14, 2004; Jan. 5, July 20, 2005; March 28, Dec. 5, 2007; Nov. 19, 2008; Feb. 9, 2011.

## Column 89, Downtown, A Special Place

Caller, Feb. 28, 1942; Feb. 9, 1984. Times, July 24, 1959; Aug. 9, 1966. Caller-Times, May 24, 1942; Oct. 19, 1947; June 8, 1949; Sept. 22, 1954; May 6, 1972; Feb. 4, 1973. Corpus Christi on Parade, April 1936. City directories, 1920s to 1950s. Pier Café Menu, 1939, Corpus Christi Central Library. Shoop's Grill Menu, 1939, Corpus Christi Central Library. Bill Walraven columns: Dec. 2, 1981; Jan. 11, 1982. William Radeker's Memoirs. Previous M. G. columns: Jan. 12, 2000; July 20, 2005; July 11, 2007; March 2, 2011; Aug. 14, 21, 2013.

## Columns 90, 91, 92, Upper Broadway

Caller, March 8, 1885; March 14, 1895; Jan. 18, Feb. 2, 1922; March 29, Oct. 11, 1961; June 18, 1965; Jan. 7, 1969; April 1, 1971; Sept. 17, 1981; Feb. 21, June 30, Dec. 5, 1983; April 14, 1988. Times, Sept. 22, 1929; April 3, 1951; Feb. 5, 1953; Jan. 26, 1955; Sept. 11, 1957; Oct. 6, 1965; Oct. 26, 1983. Caller-Times, Dec. 10, 1937; March 26, Nov. 5, 1939; Oct. 12, 1952; Oct. 13, 1953; Dec. 9, 1956; Jan. 20, 1962; April 3, 1968; March 21, 1970; Oct. 30, 1992. Reminiscences of Anna Moore Schwien. Memoirs, Andrew Anderson. Random Recollections of Nearly Ninety Years, Eli Merriman. Memoirs, E. H. Caldwell. Bill Rankin, Recollections of Other Days. Mrs. Delmas Givens, Recollections of Other Days. J. Williamson Moses, Texas in Other Days. On This Bluff, History of First Presbyterian Church. Perilous Trails, John Dunn. The Story of Corpus Christi, Mary Sutherland. Alice Lovenskiold Rankin, biographical files, Corpus Christi Central Library. Clara Driscoll, Time magazine, July 30, 1945. Corpus Christi: A History, M. G. and Jim Moloney. Previous M. G. columns: May 10, 2000; May 17, June 27, 2001; April 9, 14, 2004; April 9, 2008; Sept. 23, 2009; June 10, 16, 2010; Feb. 9, March 9, May 11, 2011.

## Column 93, Louis P. Cooke, Fugitive

Frank Wagner's research papers. Handbook of Texas. Biographical Directory of the Texian Conventions and Congresses, 1832-1845. Pictorial History of Texas, Homer Thrall. Encyclopedia of the New West. Author of Texas Homestead Exemption Law, A. E. Wilkinson, Southwestern Historical Quarterly. The Initial Homestead Exemption in Texas, Lena London, Southwestern Historical Quarterly. History of Bastrop County, Kenneth Kesselus. After San Jacinto, John Milton Nance. Indian Depredations of Texas, J. W. Wilbarger. Rangers and Pioneers of Texas, A.J. Sowell. History of Travis County and Austin, Mary Starr Barkley. An Editor's View of Early Texas, Lorna Geer Sheppard. Monterrey Is Ours, Napoleon Jackson Tecumseh Dana. Chili Con Carne, S. Compton Smith. News From Brownsville, Caleb Coker. City by the Sea, Eugenia Reynolds Briscoe. Great Tales From the History of South Texas, M. G. Corpus Christi: A History, M. G. and Jim Moloney. Zachary Taylor in Corpus Christi, M.G. Previous M. G. columns: Aug. 25, 1999; Dec. 8, 2004.

## Column 94, Forbes Britton, Big Chief

A Soldier's Life, Daniel P. Whiting, edited by M.G. Reminiscences of Anna Moore Schwien. Cullum's West Point Register. The Seminoles of Florida, James Covington. Kendall of the Picayune, Fayette Copeland. The Mexican War Journal of Captain Frank Smith, Joseph Chance. King Ranch, Tom Lea. City by the Sea, Eugenia Reynolds Briscoe. News From Brownsville, Caleb Coker. Raw Frontier, Keith Guthrie. First State Fair of Texas, Hortense Warner Ward, Southwestern Historical Quarterly. Rip Ford's Texas, Stephen B. Oates. Through the Years, Anna Marietta Kelsey. Texas in Other Days, J. Williamson Moses. Frank Wagner's research papers. Nueces Valley, Oct. 3, Nov. 28, 1957. Ranchero, Feb. 23, 1861. Previous M. G. columns: Jan. 22, 2003; Aug. 22, 2007; April 10, 2013.

## Column 95, The Duke of Padre Island

Caller, July 24, 31, Aug. 7, 14, 21, 1927; March 26, 1937; July 4, 1939. Times, Sept. 20, 1977. Caller-Times, June 11, 1950; Aug. 27, 1965; April 24, 1966. Oct. 19, 1978. Houston Chronicle, Feb. 22, 1938; March 25, 1977. Robstown Record, June 17, 1965. History of Padre Island, Pauline Reese, thesis. Padre Island, Writers' Round Table. Padre Island Ranch House, Grace Dunn Vetters, vertical files, Corpus Christi Central Library. Great Tales From the History of South Texas, M. G. Corpus Christi: A History, M. G. and Jim Moloney. Zachary Taylor in Corpus Christi, M.G. Previous M. G. columns: Sept. 30, 1998; Sept. 28, Oct. 5, 12, 2005.

## Columns 96, 97, 98, Ethan Allen Hitchcock

Fifty Years in Camp and Field, edited by W. A. Croffut. Ethan Allen Hitchcock's handwritten diaries from the Gilcrease Museum in Tulsa, copied and transcribed for Corpus Christi's Friends of the Library. Year of Decision: 1846, Bernard DeVoto. Captain Sam Grant, Lloyd Lewis. Zachary Taylor, K. Jack Bauer. Campaign Sketches of the War with Mexico, W. S. Henry. Dictionary of American Biography, Ethan Allen Hitchcock. Encyclopedia of the Mexican War, Mark Crawford. Zachary Taylor in Corpus Christi, M.G.

## Columns 99-102, Richard King and the King Ranch

Caller, undated article from 1925, reprinted from the Kingsville Record: Captain King's Body Interred at Kingsville. Caller-Times, July 12, 1953. Corpus Christi` Gazette, 1874. The King Ranch, Tom Lea. Kings of Texas, Don Graham. Rip Ford's Texas, Stephen B. Oates. The Fremantle Diary, Lt. Col. James Arthur Lyon Fremantle, Coldstream Guards. Indian Wars and Pioneers of Texas, John Henry Brown. Cattle Kings of Texas, C. L. Douglas. The King Ranch Papers, Dick Frost. Reports of the 1872 Robb Commission. Bill Walraven column, April 15, 1985. Bill Walraven column, April 15, 1985. Previous M.G. columns: Aug. 12, 19, 1998; Aug. 22, 2001; April 2, 2003; April 13, Aug. 10, 2005; Dec. 20, 2006; Jan. 30, Sept. 3, 10, 2008; May 4, 11, July 20, 2011; July 10, 17, 2013.

# INDEX

440

443

444

445

446

448

449

47, 81, 85, 95, 109, 147, 150, 170,
171, 182, 236, 273, 274, 291, 418,
419
San Antonio & Aransas Pass
Railroad 42, 43, 87, 183, 186,
264, 265
San Antonio Express 145, 232
San Antonio Light 288
San Antonio, Uvalde & Gulf
Railroad 88
San Diego 134, 147, 148, 174, 278
Sandoval, Chipito 397
San Felipe de Austin 149
San Fernando Creek 412, 415, 417,
418
San Jacinto 273
San Jacinto Hardware 362
San Patricio 75, 81, 82, 83, 84, 88,
145, 176, 255, 256-258, 263, 282,
394
San Patricio Battalion 119-120
San Patricio County 175, 254, 256,
259, 264, 265, 288
Santa Fe Trail 243, 246
Santa Gertrudis Creek 170, 172,
409, 412, 413, 415, 417
Santa Gertrudis tract 409, 420
Santa Margarita 33, 81, 82, 83, 88,
294, 413
Santa Petronila Ranch 123
Saunders, George 113, 114
Saunders, W.D.H. 235
Saus Creek 251, 253
Savage, John 75, 255, 258
Sawyer, R.K. 118
Saxet Well, Field 215, 219, 288
Schenk, Clarence 219
Schwein, Anna Moore 143, 260,
369, 370, 375, 388
Scott, Henry 251, 253 (Photo), 254
Scott, James F. 248
Scott, John 109, 110, 119
Scott, Mrs. G.R. 89
Scott, Winfield 269, 400, 404
Scurry, Thomas 62, 214
Seaside Electric Theater 282
Seaside Hotel 155 (Photo), 156,
281-284, 283 (Photos)
Seaside Pavilion 156, 212, 281,

282, 284 (Photo)
Seaton, Margaret 378
Seawall 13, 14, 91, 92, 95-99, 98
(Photos), 309
Second Dragoons 394, 396, 398,
399, 401
Second Infantry, Camp Scurry 61,
62, 63
Segrest, Dave 12
Seguin 109, 276, 346
Seventh Infantry 398
Sevier, Henry 130
Shackelford, Jack 150-151
Shaffer, William 11
Sharpsburg 78-80, 88, 278
Shaw, J.B. 135
Shaw, Jim 137, 138
Sheffield's Grill 368
Shellbank Island 256
Sheridan, Phil 2, 170
Sherrill, Warren 223
Ship Ahoy 366
Shoop, Bob 365
Shoop's Grill 365, 366
Shudde, L.J. 312
Sidbury, Edward 142
Sierra Madre Hotel 158, 190
Silvera, Juan 255, 256, 257
Simon, Joe 12
Simon, Sam 362
Sinclair, Fred 137
Sinton 58, 84
Sinton, David 57
Six Points 221, 317, 357, 359
(Photo), 360, 364
Six Points Grocery 360
Sixth Brigade, Camp Scurry 61
Skinning War 247-250
Skull, Sally 101, 298
Smith, Persifor 1, 170
Smith, S. Compton 383
Snapka, Method and Rudolph 25
Snyder, ----------, yellow fever
victim 175, 259
Sonora, Mexico 290, 291
South Bluff Park 221
South Texas Exposition 220
Southern Academy of Aeronautics 7
Southern Alkali 221

455

OTHER BOOKS AVAILABLE FROM NUECES PRESS

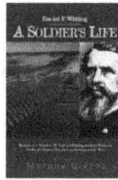

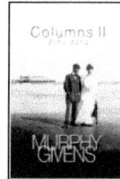

Corpus Christi – A History

A Soldier's Life

Great Tales from the History of South Texas

Recollections of Other Days

Columns   2009 – 2011

Perilous Trails of Texas

Columns   2012 – 2013

www.nuecespress.com

www.ingramcontent.com/pod-product-compliance
Lightning Source LLC
Chambersburg PA
CBHW060419100426
42812CB00030B/3234/J